Theft of an Idol

E D I T O R S

Sherry B. Ortner, Nicholas B. Dirks, Geoff Eley

A LIST OF TITLES

IN THIS SERIES APPEARS

AT THE BACK OF

THE BOOK

PRINCETON STUDIES IN
CULTURE / POWER / HISTORY

Theft of an Idol

TEXT AND CONTEXT IN THE
REPRESENTATION OF COLLECTIVE VIOLENCE

Paul R. Brass

PRINCETON UNIVERSITY PRESS
PRINCETON, NEW JERSEY

Library of Congress Cataloging-in-Publication Data

Brass, Paul R.
  Theft of an idol : text and context in the representation of
collective violence / Paul R. Brass.
    p.   cm. — (Princeton studies in culture/power/history)
  Includes bibliographical references and index.
  ISBN 0-691-02651-3 (alk. paper). — ISBN 0-691-02650-5 (pbk. : alk. paper)
    1. Violence—India—Case studies.   2. Violence—Political aspects—India—Case
studies. 3. Riots—India—Case studies. 4. Ethnicity—India—Case studies. 5. India—
Ethnic relations—Case studies. 6. India—Politics and government—Case studies.
I. Title. II. Series.
HN690.Z9V5   1997
303.6'0954—dc20   96-9315
                                                                              CIP

This book has been composed in Times Roman

Cover Illustration: An object of unknown date and provenance
found in north India by Anand Singh of Mankapur.
Photo by Susan L. Halon.

Printed in the United States of America by Princeton Academic Press

1 3 5 7 9 10 8 6 4 2

1 3 5 7 9 10 8 6 4 2
(Pbk.)

For my sister,
Frances Ruth Yoeli
and
in memory of my brother-in-law
Abram (Avi) Yoeli
1935–1984

———————————————

CONTENTS

FIGURES AND TABLES

PREFACE

I BEGAN the research for this book in 1982–83 as part of a larger project on structures of local power in north Indian politics, during which I carried out six months of field research in the five districts of Uttar Pradesh that I had first visited twenty years before. The purpose of that larger project was to assess the political and economic changes that had taken place in the previous two decades in those districts, whose politics I had first discussed in my *Factional Politics in an Indian State: The Congress Party in Uttar Pradesh* (1965). Among the changes to which I paid close attention was the apparent increase in violence in those districts, as in the province as a whole, associated with increased Hindu–Muslim tensions, intensified inter-caste hostilities, and the development of closer links among politicians, police, and criminals.

My method in 1982–83, as in 1961–63, was to collect information primarily through personal in-depth interviews with local politicians, administrators, police, and villagers. In each district, I sought to interview all the known persons of rank, authority, and power, but I also made tours in the countryside, stopping at numerous villages to talk for an hour or two at a time with the headmen and other villagers. Also, wherever it was relevant to a particular line of inquiry concerning incidents of local violence discussed in this book, I interviewed all persons whom I could find, whether of high or low rank, authority, and power who were said to have been centrally involved.

Some of my research material concerning changes in the political economy of these districts was published in articles, but this book is the first longer study based on that earlier research and since augmented by several additional visits between 1983 and 1994. I have for this study selected out of the many hundreds of interviews I have conducted in these five districts over the past thirteen years only those materials pertaining to incidents of violence that came to my attention. This material is, therefore, drawn from a relatively small selection of my notes, which contain further materials on politics, economic changes, and other incidents of Hindu–Muslim violence not covered herein.

Although the bulk of my research was carried out within the districts through local-level interviews, I have also pursued linkages upward to the state and national levels whenever they have been relevant, which is normally the case. So, the range of my interviews has been from the village and country town to district headquarters to provincial capital to the central government. In some cases, where relevant material has been available, I have also made use of newspapers and other documentary material, such as court cases and affidavits submitted to commissions of inquiry.

Although I was trained as a political scientist and continue to practice the craft, I have never been fully satisfied with its predominant methods: survey research, ecological analyses, and comparative studies of political institutions. I have always found ethnographic research at the local level more challenging and rewarding, but I have also avoided the traditional anthropological method of staying in one spot or one relatively small local area. I have preferred instead to move about, to ask a few simple questions over and over again, following lines of inquiry as they develop spatially, hierarchically, and temporally.

In my movements, I have been often accompanied by assistants, students, or colleagues who have made it possible for me to carry out my interviews with my imperfect knowledge of Hindi. I also carry a tape recorder, which I use whenever there is no objection to it, which enables me to check later the translations of my interviews done on the spot. Though I carry a tape recorder, I have always followed a rule of confidentiality: I will use whatever information is given to me, but I will not normally identify by name the person interviewed. This rule has been extremely difficult for me to continue to follow with the material presented in this volume since so much of it depends upon the analysis of the statements of my interview respondents. I have, however, gone as far as I can without distorting the facts to continue to follow the rule. This has required in some cases the adoption of pseudonyms for persons and places, in others the attribution of particular statements to a generalized category of person without naming his or her precise political or institutional position. I have, however, retained in all cases the names of the districts in which the incidents of violence occurred and have identified the names of persons and places whenever there is a public record in newspapers, legislative proceedings, and other public documents. Thus, I have adopted pseudonyms for most persons and places in the first two case studies, for which there is no public record, but not in the last three, for each of which there is. I regret that, in a few cases, some striking linkages between persons and places and some dramatic information have had to be concealed.

It is not possible for me to name and thank all the persons who have accompanied me on my travels in north India during the past thirteen years, but there are several who were especially fine assistants or companions. They include Sunil Singh, Pallav Kumar, and most recently Professors Gyan and Jayati Chaturvedi. During my visits to the five districts of Uttar Pradesh over the past thirty-four years, I have also established life-long friendships with two persons, two families really: that of Anand Singh of Mankapur in Gonda district, whose name has appeared countless times in my books and articles over the years, and that of S. P. Mehra of Kanpur. I look forward always to renewing my friendship with them both and to their never-failing hospitality during my frequent visits.

The research for this project was begun under a fellowship provided by the American Institute of Indian Studies for the academic year 1982–83. It was concluded during my sabbatical leave from the University of Washington in 1994–95 at the Woodrow Wilson International Center for Scholars in Washington, D.C., where its director, Charles Blitzer; the then head of the Asia Program, Mary Bullock; the staff of the fellowships office, Ann Sheffield, Arlyn Charles, and Denise Liebowitz, all contributed in their separate ways to providing a most congenial and relaxing environment to complete the writing of this book. So, too, did all the other members of the staff with whom I came in contact.

Over the years, beginning in 1987, I have presented summaries of the introduction or of one or another of the case studies at numerous institutions and professional meetings: at the Conference on Indian Parties and Elections, UCLA, in June 1987; the Centre d'Etude de l'Inde et de l'Asie du Sud in Paris, in November 1987; the Centre of South Asian Studies Seminar, School of Oriental and African Studies, London, in November 1987; the South Asia Inter-University Colloquium, University of British Columbia, in October 1988 and again in October 1995; the meetings of the International Society for the Comparative Study of Civilizations, held at the University of California, Berkeley, in June 1989; the South Asia Seminar, Massachusetts Institute of Technology (MIT), in November 1989; the Conference on Religion, Identity and Politics: India in Comparative Perspective, Centre for Indian Studies, Hull University, England, in October 1991; the Center for South and Southeast Asian Studies, University of Michigan, in October 1992; the conference on Nationalizing the Past, sponsored by the American Council of Learned Societies-Social Science Research Council, Goa (India), in May 1993; the Center for the Study of Developing Societies, Delhi, in September 1993; the Center for South Asian Studies, University of Virginia, in January 1995; the annual meetings of the Association for Asian Studies in Washington, D. C., in April 1995; the Wilson Center in Washington, D. C., in May 1995, and the SSRC-sponsored conference on Political Violence in India held at Amherst, Massachusetts, in September 1995. The responses that I received to my presentations from colleagues and students at all these meetings have sustained me over the many years it has taken me to finally complete the book. I want to thank for their comments on my presentations or on all or parts of the manuscript they have read over the years especially Benedict Anderson, Daniel Chirot, E. Valentine Daniel, Nicholas Dirks, Clea Finkle, Stanley Tambiah, Ashutosh Varshney, and Myron Weiner.

Of course, none of the institutions or persons named above have any responsibility for the opinions expressed or the conclusions reached in this book.

Seattle, Washington
December 26, 1995

ABBREVIATIONS

BJP	Bharatiya Janata Party
BJS	Bharatiya Jan Sangh
BLD	Bharatiya Lok Dal
BSF	Border Security Force
BSP	Bahujan Samaj Party
CB	Central Bureau of Investigation
CID	Criminal Investigation Department
CO	Commanding Officer
CPI	Communist Party of India
CPM	Communist Party of India (Marxist)
CRPF	Central Reserve Police Force
DIG	Deputy Inspector General of Police
DM	District Magistrate
DySP	Deputy Superintendent of Police
FIR	First Information Report
IAS	Indian Administrative Service
IG	Inspector General of Police
INC	Indian National Congress
IPS	Indian Police Service
ISI	Inter-Services Intelligence (Pakistan)
JP	Janata Party
ML	Muslim League
MLA	Member, Legislative Assembly
MP	Member of Parliament
PAC	Provincial Armed Constabulary
RAC	Rajasthan Armed Constabulary
RAF	Rapid Action Force
RSS	Rashtriya Swayamsevak Sangh
SDM	Subdivisional Magistrate
SO	Station Officer
SP	Samajwadi Party or Superintendent of Police (depending on context)
SSP	Senior Superintendent of Police
UP	Uttar Pradesh
VHP	Vishwa Hindu Parishad

Theft of an Idol

Chapter 1

TEXT AND CONTEXT

IN *I, Pierre Rivière*, Foucault presents the text—the memoir of a parricide and the dossier associated with it—as "a case, an affair, an event that provided the intersection of discourses that differed in origin, form, organization, and function." The discourses of judges, prosecutor, country doctor, the great psychiatrist Esquirol, the villagers, including "their mayor and parish priest," and "the murderer himself" all appear[ed] to be speaking of one and the same thing, of the murders that occurred on June 3, 1835, but the multiplicity of discourses "form[ed] neither a composite work nor an exemplary text, but rather a strange contest, a confrontation, a power relation, a battle among discourses and through discourses," "used as weapons of attack and defense in the relations of power and knowledge."[1] This contest was one for the definition of the "truth" of the parricide's act, the truth not of its commission, for which the murderer's own confession provided sufficient evidence, but the truth of its explanation and meaning, for the context in which it should be placed, and for its broader implications concerning the workings of the human mind in an age of reason from which madness could not be banished.

This struggle for the appropriate explanation of the parricide's act and for the choice of the appropriate punishment as well involved a contest for domination within domains of legal, medical, criminological, and psychiatric truth and within the institutions in which those domains of truth and knowledge were generated: courts, prisons, hospitals, asylums. It also brought clearly into view the gap in local and national systems of knowledge and explanation. The local doctor, unable to find scientific categories in which to place and define the parricide and his act, saw no reason for the intervention of medico-psychiatric knowledge into this case, which he thought should be left to the judicial system. The Parisian psychiatrists, of course, ultimately succeeded in establishing *their* claim and the consequent spread of psychiatric "knowledge" not only into the judicial and penal system but throughout modern Western society.

Another consequence of their ultimate victory was the removal from local societies of the power to define and interpret local incidents of violence, to

[1] Michel Foucault, ed., *I, Pierre Rivière, having slaughtered my mother, my sister, and my brother . . . A Case of Parricide in the 19th Century*, trans. Frank Jellinek (Lincoln: University of Nebraska Press, 1975), pp. x and xi.

place them in a specific context based on local knowledge. Knowledge of human behavior in nineteenth-century France and in the rest of Western society became nationalized and universalized. Events that occur in isolated villages and hamlets or on the city streets have become subject to placement in categories and contexts previously not known to or incidental to the lives of those who experience them. People with personal knowledge at the sites of occurrences of violence, lacking knowledge of the appropriate scientific categories in which to place them or refusing to accept the contextualizations of them imposed by outsiders, continue to generate their own interpretations. The more perfectly integrated contemporary societies become, however, the more local and national interpretations merge and the more persons in the localities find themselves also readily placing local events into ready-made categories and contexts.

In the twentieth century, local acts of violence are often also commonly placed in other, more direct kinds of political contexts depending upon the ethnic identities of the persons involved in them. Interethnic relations have become such a pervasive concern in contemporary societies that the interpretation of virtually any act of violence between persons identified as belonging to different ethnic groups itself becomes a political act. But the interpretive process is not only political; it also generates competing systems of knowledge concerning interethnic relations, the sources of tension between members of ethnic groups, the causes of discrimination and prejudice, their social and economic bases, and the like. The developers of these systems of knowledge generally claim to stand apart from and above the ethnic interactions they seek to explain and to describe "objectively," whereas in fact they themselves play a role in their perpetuation by the very process of placing interethnic incidents of violence in broader political contexts.

Interethnic incidents of violence in modern states invariably involve other parties in addition to those who contextualize them in journalistic or social scientific accounts, notably the authorities and especially the police. The police often prefer to define local incidents of violence, whether between members of different ethnic groups or not, simply as crimes and to treat them as such, that is, to localize and confine them. Such localization, however, becomes more difficult when isolated incidents of interethnic violence become transformed into something broader, a "riot" involving large numbers of massed persons from opposing ethnic groups engaged in assaults on persons, lives, and property. In such situations, the police may themselves take sides; even when they do not, they are often accused of doing so, particularly by the side that emerges with the greater losses. Some ethnic "riots" do not even involve two ethnic groups, but often only one community and the police, with the latter perceived or described by spokesmen for the rioting community as responsible for the precipitating incidents leading to the "riot." When it can be proved that the police and the state authorities more broadly are directly implicated in a "riot" in which one community provides the principal or sole victims, then, of course, one is confronted with a pogrom.

The definition of occurrences of violence involving members of one or more ethnic groups as being merely isolated incidents having no broader significance or as being "riots" or pogroms is frequently itself a part of the political struggle. The boundaries between isolated incidents and proven pogroms are clear enough. However, those between local incidents of violence and "riots," on the one hand, and between "riots" and pogroms, on the other hand, are not. Some so-called riots are no different in origin from everyday incidents of violence. Others, however, may be pogroms in disguise.

Interethnic or police–people confrontations involving violence in contemporary states almost always lead to the construction of interpretations of them by authorities, media, politicians, and political activists. The struggles to gain acceptance for particular constructions of violent and riotous behavior are inherently political, with important consequences for state policies and resource distribution.[2] The constructions that become officially or broadly accepted are usually far removed from the actual precipitating incidents and from local interpretations of them. The scholar who inserts himself into the description of such incidents in a search for objective truth can do no better than to place himself on one side or another in the political struggle. When the search for categories, constructs, and contexts is central to the political struggle, the scholar's own concepts and the scholar himself cannot stand apart from and outside of them.

Where, then, can a scholar interested in questions of violence place himself in relation to these constructions? One possible posture is to seek to expose the falsifications contained in all of them. However, if one starts with the premise that violence in which innocent persons are harmed and killed is an evil, such a rhetorical strategy provides a poor vantage point. One must, therefore, take a stand rather in relation to the whole process of construction and contextualization. It is my purpose in this volume to find a place to stand in relation to the contextualization of incidents of violence in contemporary Indian society and to ask whether some kinds of constructions contribute more and others less to their perpetuation.

THEORY AND METHOD

The focus of this book is on issues of ethnicity and violence and their relationship to state-building and national unity in India. It is based on field

[2] A point well made by Allen D. Grimshaw, "Three Views of Urban Violence: Civil Disturbance, Racial Revolt, Class Assault," in Allen D. Grimshaw, ed., *Racial Violence in the United States* (Chicago: Aldine, 1969), p. 387.

research carried out between 1982–83 and 1994 and on incidents that occurred between 1980 and 1994 at sites of police–public and interethnic violence in north India, which in recent years has given all appearances of
undergoing the most extreme paroxysms of caste, communal, and other
forms of violence that appear to threaten the unity of the country and the
stability of the Indian state. The original research for this project in 1982–83
was carried out with no other intent at the time than to engage in the social
scientist's conventional search for the truth of contemporary public violence
through the use of comparative case studies, one of the accepted methods of
the social science disciplines. A change in my design came afterward as I
looked over my interviews in new ways, treating them as "texts" subject to
multiple interpretations rather than as sources of valid or confirmed information or data about events.

I raise three questions concerning the increased incidence and intensity of
violence in India in recent years. The first concerns the relationship between
issues of ethnicity, communalism, and violence, on the one hand, and national unity, on the other hand. To what extent does this upsurge in violence
and the specific forms it has taken indicate a serious threat to the continued
unity and integrity of the country and the relations among its major peoples?
Since questions of intercaste relations and even more of Hindu–Muslim relations are at the heart of much of this upsurge in violence, the second question is why caste and communal riots persist in India. Third, why especially
have Hindu–Muslim riots become endemic? These three questions, I will
show, are interrelated.

The argument I develop is that the publicized versions of many so-called
caste and communal riots in India, like many aspects of ethnic identity itself, are constructions upon events that are usually open to a multiplicity of
interpretations. When examined at the actual originating sites of ethnic and
communal violence, it is often the case that the precipitating incidents arise
out of situations that are either not inherently ethnic/communal in nature or
are ambiguous in character, that their transformation into caste or communal
incidents depends upon the attitudes toward them taken by local politicians
and local representatives of state authority, and that their ultimate elevation
into grand communal confrontations depends upon their further reinterpreta-
tion by the press and extralocal politicians and authorities. The "official"
interpretation that finally becomes universally accepted is often, if not usually, very far removed, often unrecognizable, from the original precipitating
events. This is particularly the case with those riots that are labeled as "communal" or "Hindu–Muslim" riots. Indeed, I intend to demonstrate that the
persistence of riots so labeled is in large part a consequence of their functional utility for all dominant political ideologies, both secular and communal, in contemporary India. Their persistence helps local, state, and national

leaders of different ideological persuasions in capturing or maintaining institutional and state power by providing convenient scapegoats, the alleged perpetrators of the events, and by providing as well dangers and tensions useful in justifying the exercise of state authority.

The approach adopted here is quite different from the conventional social science accounts of riots and their explanations, which are broadly of two types. The first seeks to develop from descriptions of riots at different times and places an abstract, "objective" model of their sequential character. The classic sequence in the literature on collective violence describes a progression from the juxtaposition of opposed ethnic groups or one ethnic group and the police to the creation of an atmosphere of tension arising out of grievances, conflicts, and frustrations followed by a triggering incident, which then produces a conflagration as does a spark upon some combustible material.[3] This sequence is common also in popular and official accounts of the development of riots in India.

The second general approach to the explanation of riots, particularly in societies in which they are endemic or occur in "waves," discards description and dynamic analysis for ecological comparison, seeking to identify the demographic, economic, and/or political conditions that distinguish cities and towns in which riots have occurred from those in which they have not. Such analyses usually produce tables and charts and ultimately regression equations that account for a percentage of the variance ranging most often from 25 percent to 50 percent, which is considered quite good in social science statistics. Thus, for example, a conclusion may be reached that 40 percent of the riots in America or in India have occurred in cities and towns where blacks and whites or Hindus and Muslims, respectively, live side by side in a 40–60 ratio or some other proportion. Other characteristics are then added to the regression equation that may increase the variance explained to 50 percent or sometimes even more. However far one goes, a substantial amount of the variance always remains unexplained.[4] When one keeps in mind that large numbers of people are being killed in those cities and towns

---

[3] See esp. Neil J. Smelser, *Theory of Collective Behavior* (New York: The Free Press, 1962), chap. 7; and the critique of the classical approach in Doug McAdam, *Political Process and the Development of Black Insurgency, 1930–1970* (Chicago: University of Chicago Press, 1982), chap. 1.

[4] A classic study of this type for seventy-six American race riots between 1913 and 1963, using the method of "paired comparisons" of riot and non-riot cities, is Stanley Lieberson and Arnold R. Silverman, "The Precipitants and Underlying Conditions of Race Riots," in Grimshaw, *Racial Violence in the United States*, pp. 354–70. One finding, for example, concerned the hypothesis that a "rapid influx of Negroes" into cities was an underlying factor in race riots, concerning which the authors reported that "in 56 percent of the comparisons the control cities experienced greater percentage increases in Negro population than the riot cities did" (p. 363).

where the variance is unexplained, such forms of analysis provide cold comfort even if there were some hope that the explanations of social scientists could be translated into corrective public policies.

I have three objections to these alternative approaches. The first is that the claim of objectivity is unsustainable. No academic accounts of riots I have read are free of subjectivity. Second, these accounts, particularly the statistical, but also the classical sequential model, eliminate agency and responsibility from their explanations. They objectify a sequence or a demographic situation and fail to identify specific persons, groups, organizations, and state agents, who actually inaugurate and sustain riotous events and commit the arson, property destruction, and murder. Third, they fail to identify clearly the linkages between individual and social responsibilities and those of the state and society. Insofar as they do so, they tend to refer vaguely to the existence in the minds and hearts of the people of prejudices and antipathies from which in turn state actors are not free. Such statements have a pious ring to them, but they constitute smokescreens that mask persistent forms of speech, social practice, and organizational activities and the ways in which they form a net of complicity that may spread widely in societies.

In the research on the case studies for this volume, I found it impossible to present an "objective" account that explained each case or all of them fully, that is, which accounted for the event as a whole. Instead, I found more or less persuasive and unpersuasive, more or less scrupulous or self-serving, more or less dispassionate or prejudiced accounts, some of which contained elements of a whole "truth" of the event, but none that could explain the whole. Nor could I free myself completely from my own Western rationalist skepticism, social science training, and personal biases in seeking to construct a holistic account. At the same time, it was also evident that the riotous events I have here documented were not primarily "spontaneous" occurrences or chance happenings and that there were identifiable culprits who had conspired to produce or who had committed acts either designed to produce or whose effects were to produce riotous and murderous results.

Social scientists are trained to be skeptical of conspiracy theories and to leave the attachment of blame to journalists and the judicial system, but this has too often led to the objectification of social processes and the reification of categories such as class, ethnicity, or even "human nature" in a fruitless search for ultimate causes that ignores the dynamics of events, the significance of the interpretations—more or less tendentious—which are presented to "explain" them, and the uses to which the events and their explanations are put. I have in my accounts of riotous events in northern India, therefore, chosen to focus on neither the remote nor the precipitating "causes" of them, but on the action that occurs in the intermediate space and time, the interpretations that follow after the events, and, in the case of Hindu–Muslim "riots," the existence of a grand interpretive framework, which provides for many an automatic explanation for any riot that can be traced to a triggering incident involving one or more Hindus and Muslims.

In some areas of India, such as the western districts of Uttar Pradesh, it is accepted journalistic and scholarly wisdom that virtually any incident between, say, a Hindu and a Muslim can easily lead to a "flare-up" and a "communal riot." Does this, therefore, not reflect the latent hostility between the opposing communities, which requires only a spark to ignite it? How can such group antagonisms be considered social constructions? While it would be foolish to deny the existence of such hostilities in these areas, it is equally foolish to talk about latent hostilities as if all members of the opposing groups are poised to commit acts of violence.

Although most people everywhere are capable of committing acts of violence under a variety of circumstances, the kinds of violence that are committed in "communal riots" are, I believe, undertaken mostly by "specialists," who are ready to be called out on such occasions, who profit from it, and whose activities profit others who may or may not be actually paying for the violence carried out. Such regions have developed what I call "institutionalized riot systems," in which known actors specialize in the conversion of incidents between members of different communities into "communal riots." Even here, however, not every such incident is allowed to develop into a "riot." When full-fledged riots develop, the local politicians and authorities are often either incompetent or they themselves desire the riots to take place, and are willing to place a communal interpretation on the precipitating incidents.

The phrase "institutionalized riot systems" requires some elaboration and needs to be related to contemporary social science theories concerning the origins and development of movements of collective action and violence. Riots occupy a marginal and ambiguous place in contemporary theories of collective action, despite the work of historians such as E. P. Thompson, Natalie Zemon Davis, George Rudé, and Eric J. Hobsbawm,[5] and the outpouring of social science analyses of the Black ghetto riots of the late 1960s in the United States.[6] They fall out of the definition of social movements as defined by Charles Tilly and used by him, Sidney Tarrow, and others,

---

[5] See esp. Natalie Zemon Davis, "The Rites of Violence: Religious Riot in Sixteenth-Century France," *Past & Present* 59 (May 1973): 51–91; Eric J. Hobsbawm and George Rudé, *Captain Swing* (New York: Norton, 1975); George Rudé, *Paris and London in the Eighteenth Century: Studies in Popular Protest* (New York: Viking, 1971); and E. P. Thompson, "The Moral Economy of the English Crowd in the Eighteenth Century," *Past & Present* 50 (February 1971): 76–136.

[6] Excerpts from much of this early literature are found in Grimshaw, *Racial Violence in the United States*, but many more books and articles followed the publication of this compendium over the next decade.

namely, as "sustained" and "contentious" forms of collective action.[7] Clearly, riots are "contentious" forms of collective action, but they are not sustained. Their very episodic character, their apparent unpredictability, and the relative brevity of the time period in which they commonly occur have made them far more difficult to study than social movements involving large numbers of people concerting together for long periods of time. By the time the social scientist arrives on the scene, the riot exists only in memory and interpretation and its principal actors, some of whose activities, if revealed, would entitle them to a death sentence or life imprisonment, are either not to be found or are born liars.

The great outpouring of literature on the Black riots of the 1960s has led to some integration of riot theory into the general body of theory on collective action, but at some cost in the understanding of riots in their particularity. Most of the early literature on these riots fell into the categories already discussed above, namely, the sequential and ecological. The most imaginative writing on the subject, however, that by Doug McAdam, made a major contribution to collective action and collective movement theory in general by relating the Black riots to the history of Black protest and interpreting the riots as extensions of a historic insurgent movement.[8] McAdam's contribution in this regard was to develop a political process model to replace the older sociological sequential and ecological approaches. However, this model does not help us interpret particular riots either in the United States in the 1960s or elsewhere because it eliminates the question altogether of why a riot occurred in one city and not another, why it was more severe here than there, what interests were served in particular incidents, and how they relate to the broader goals of Black insurgency.

A further problem in the literature on riots and its relationship to the theoretical literature on collective action is the shift in the historical meaning of riots. After all, the term "riot" has historically meant a disorderly action that constitutes a direct assault upon or represents a danger to established authority. Even where riots were directed against groups other than the state, they were often considered assaults upon the state's order or upon groups entitled to state protection. Thompson and Davis have separately argued that food riots in eighteenth-century England and religious riots in sixteenth-century France in effect constituted encroachments on state authority by groups who saw themselves as acting in place of the state.[9]

In some cases, such as nineteenth-and early-twentieth-century Russia, a

---

[7] Sidney Tarrow, *Power in Movement: Social Movements, Collective Action and Politics* (Cambridge: Cambridge University Press, 1994), p. 37.

[8] McAdam, *Political Process and the Development of Black Insurgency*.

[9] Thompson, "The Moral Economy of the English Crowd in the Eighteenth Century"; and Davis, "The Rites of Violence," p. 61.

specialized term, "pogroms," was used to describe riots in which Jews were the main victims. This term, however, has now entered the theoretical literature on the subject to mean state-instigated and -supported riots against a minority ethnic group. In the twentieth century, the term "riots" continues to refer to challenges to the authority of the state, but those that draw the most journalistic and scholarly attention are ethnic or interethnic in form. In either case, riots do conform in part to the Tilly–Tarrow definition of social movements as involving collective action against the state or other groups, though, as already mentioned, they fail on the grounds that they are not sustained.

From the point of view of the questions raised in this volume, however, it is less important to find a definitional place for riots in theories of collective action than to consider the question of the changing meaning of riots and the scope the historical change has offered to the state authorities for dealing with riots. Why does the modern state, particularly the developing state such as India, see some kinds of riots as assaults on its authority and others not? Why are interethnic riots usually not so considered? How is it that state leaders may even find riots useful in justifying their authority?

For, indeed, some riots in India, notably "communal riots," as I have already suggested, have larger political uses. They are used by state and national Muslim politicians to mobilize the Muslim minority, on the one hand, and by militant Hindu nationalists to consolidate Hindu communal sentiment, on the other hand. They also have political uses for secular nationalists. They provide a justification for their argument concerning the need to create a composite nationalism and a strong, united state. Secular nationalists also use riots for their own purposes of mobilizing the minorities. Riots also provide a useful smokescreen to divert attention from the demographic and economic context in which riots take place—in filthy slums unfit for human habitation whose habilitation does not fit into their economic development plans and designs for the transformation of India into a great and powerful industrial-military state.

Riots, Movements, and Theories of Collective Action

Riots, however much they differ from social movements, are nevertheless forms of collective action. Moreover, as just noted, some theorists, notably McAdam, but others also who wrote of the Black ghetto riots of the 1960s in the United States, even went to the extent of integrating those riots into the broader, historical social movement of what they described as Black insurgency or else treated them in the manner of Davis, Hobsbawm, Rudé, and Thompson "as basically structured, purposeful, rational, and politically meaningful."[10] This theoretical move was made possible largely because the riots of the 1960s, like some of the other movements that preceded them, such as the lunch counter sit-ins, occurred in "waves." Such waves or chains of riots have also occurred in other places at other times—the pogroms against the Jews in fourteenth-century Spain[11] and nineteenth-century Russia[12] being notable examples, as well as the post–World War I and –World War II racial riots in the United States, and Hindu–Muslim riots in India in the 1920s at the time of partition and in the aftermath of the destruction of the mosque at Ayodhya in 1992, among many other examples.

Riots, therefore, may occur in isolation or may follow upon one another in rapid succession. Riot analysts differ, however, on the significance of such waves. Those who see riots as spontaneous expressions of mass anger and resentment against the state or another group tend to see such waves or chains as feeding upon the news or rumors from the initial riot or riots, leading to acts of "retaliation" by the victims in one city or town upon the members of the other ethnic group alleged to have been the attackers in the preceding riots. Those who see riots as planned and orchestrated events, in contrast, are likely to see such waves or chains as part of an overall plan being implemented by a political party, the state, or, in the view of the state authorities, "outside agitators."

There is yet a third possibility (which is the principal subject of this volume), namely, the fitting of the isolated riot into a broader framework. In this case, even a single riot may be transformed into something bigger and more "meaningful" through interpretation after the event. However, my argument goes beyond this point to encompass in the same process waves of riots as well. That is, I do not accept the easy integration of those riots that occur in waves or chains as either instances of insurgency or coordinated party or state action. In some cases, the argument is not only plausible, but obvious, as in Nazi Germany during *Krystallnacht*. In other cases, however, waves of riots may provide opportunities for a multiplicity of interests and purposes to be satisfied and expressed under the cover of the claim or interpretation of insurgency or communalism. Waves of riots may also occur as by-products of mass mobilizations in which incidents of violence break out in a number of places in the aftermath of provocative actions taken by participants in a broad social movement.

Such incidents, however, may or may not actually have something to do with the mass mobilization in question, that is, they may be part of the

[10] James W. Button, *Black Violence: Political Impact of the 1960s Riots* (Princeton, N.J.: Princeton University Press, 1978), p. 7.

[11] Michel Mollat and Philippe Wolff, *The Popular Revolutions of the Late Middle Ages*, trans. A. L. Lytton-Sells (London: George Allen and Unwin, 1973), pp. 212–25.

[12] See the collection of articles in John D. Klier and Shlomo Lambroza, eds., *Pogroms: Anti-Jewish Violence in Modern Russian History* (Cambridge: Cambridge University Press, 1992).

design of the movement or at least partly anticipated consequences of its leaders or they may take place under the cover of a movement to vent personal grievances or gain economic advantage. In the former case, it is important to consider the strategy of riots just as one considers the strategy of those who plan collective movements such as strikes, marches on a nation's capital, or other forms of mass demonstration or civil disobedience. Even where riots are merely anticipated consequences of a mass movement rather than part of an overall design, the effects may be analyzed as if they constituted a strategy. The strategy or effects of a wave of riots and even of some that occur in isolation include intimidation of another group; protection of one's own; the promotion of a myth concerning the violent intentions of another group by provoking its members into violent actions; the interpretation of the events afterwards to cast blame upon and discredit rivals, another group, or another group's or party's support base.

Further difficulties in incorporating riots into general theories of collective action arise when one considers that riots also stand in an ambiguous relationship to both routine and movement politics. In most civil societies, riots are considered both by the authorities and by elite public opinion as outside the boundaries of everyday politics. Yet, in Weimar Germany before its collapse and in contemporary South Asian societies, they have been associated with the routine politics of public rallies, demonstrations, and elections. In Weimar Germany, they were associated with a movement that ultimately brought down the regime and replaced it with another. In Sri Lanka in 1983 they proved to be the prelude to a prolonged civil war. However, in India, riots and other forms of localized violence appear to have been integrated into routine politics. They are anticipated by-products of election campaigns and mass mobilizations that precede them. They are associated with movements by caste and communal groups to assert their rights or maintain their privileges against challengers.

Perhaps, then, we should consider riots themselves as part of the "traditional repertoire" of political action, of both routine politics and movement politics. Or should we consider riots as older forms of collective action that have been infused with new meanings?[13] While there is ample evidence that contemporary riots in India and elsewhere have different meanings from those ascribed to them by Hobsbawm, Rudé, and Davis, many traditional practices seem common between riots in sixteenth-century France and twentieth-century India. Riots, it would seem, are among the most versatile forms of collective action, capable of carrying many meanings in different times and places, occurring as part of routine as well as movement politics, and displaying a multiplicity of ritualized practices.

For example, much of what Tarrow describes as the "old repertoire" of

---

[13] Cf. Tarrow, *Power in Movement*, p. 40.

collective action appears in riots in India today. Just as Catholics burned Protestant churches with the parishioners inside them,[14] so Hindu rioters attack Muslims seeking refuge in their mosques, burn the houses of Muslims with their occupants inside, and vandalize or destroy their mosques. Similarly, funerals and funeral processions today in India, as in nineteenth-century Europe,[15] provide occasions for riots and massacres. More than two thousand Sikhs were massacred in Delhi in 1984 in the anti-Sikh riots that followed Mrs. Gandhi's assassination, beginning during her cremation and continuing for some days afterwards.

However, unlike other forms of collective action in which the action itself is designed to convey precisely the demand, riots involve what Stanley J. Tambiah calls "focalization and transvaluation" of meaning.[16] Riots are supposed to appear spontaneous, rather than planned, even when, as in the case of Nazi Germany, they are precisely organized, directed, and limited to specific targets. Moreover, there is in fact much that occurs during most riots that is not preplanned and precisely organized. Riots, therefore, are either designed to convey or their meaning must be captured to convey a diffuse message about alleged popular feelings and how they may be used against the authorities or one's opponents or scapegoats. They are a warning to one's ethnic and political rivals. It is here that the struggle for representation and meaning comes in, which most distinguishes riots from other forms of collective action. Riots, therefore, are partly organized, partly spontaneous forms of collective action designed to appear or made to appear afterwards as spontaneous expressions of popular feeling. In the hands of social scientists, they may even be transformed after the fact into rebellions, insurgencies, insurrections, and revolutions.

Riots, it is argued here, like other forms of collective action, have characteristic "forms of organization and leadership,"[17] sometimes occur in waves that appear similar to "sustained campaigns" or "movement cycles," and also display a characteristic "repertoire of collective violence."[18] Riots, too, like other forms of collective action, have become "modernized." They must have a broader meaning that goes beyond the particular acts of violence associated with them. They must be interpreted and represented. Their meaning must be made clear, though in divided societies—and societies in

[14] Ibid., p. 35.

[15] Ibid., pp. 38–39.

[16] Stanley J. Tambiah, "Presidential Address: Reflections on Communal Violence in South Asia," *Journal of Asian Studies* 49, no. 4 (November 1990): 750. By focalization, Tambiah means the stripping of local riotous events of all their complexities, focusing on a particular aspect of them. Transvaluation then involves the further step of integrating the events into broader "loyalties and cleavages" by altering their meaning to fit them.

[17] Tarrow, *Power in Movement*, p. 46.

[18] Tambiah, "Presidential Address," pp. 755–57.

which riots are endemic are virtually by definition divided—their meaning will certainly be contested.

In some societies, such as India, riots are transformed into routine and ordinary events even while they are deplored and condemned as extraordinary threats to public order. Moreover, just as the press in revolutionary America made rebellion ordinary,[19] so does the press in India make riots ordinary. Just as Philadelphians could read about rebellion in the North in New York papers, so riot news is conveyed in India through both the sedate English-language presses and the less sedate and sometimes scurrilous vernacular presses. But India now has the more modern media as well, including both radio and the spreading availability of TV, so that the news of riots and news precipitating riots may be spread rapidly by the mightiest and most prestigious of all news transmitters, the BBC, and lately by CNN as well.

In some cities and towns, riots are endemic. I have argued above that sociological and ecological analyses do not provide an adequate basis for distinguishing those that are riot-prone from those that are not. What does invariably distinguish such cities and towns from others is the presence of what I have called above an institutionalized riot system. However, the "forms of organization and leadership" that characterize riots are different from those described by Tarrow for other forms of collective action.[20] They are not open and formalized. Regular meetings are not held. Leaderships are not elected. Memberships are fluid. There are, nevertheless, known persons who perform leadership roles, pools of persons from whom riot actors are drawn, and established links of communication.

Some of the leadership and communication roles are evident, for example, in descriptions of the Delhi Riots of 1984. Local members of the ruling party, including among them persons who had occupied and have since occupied high positions in the party organization and even in ministerial positions in the central government, provided direction, "mobilized their local clients and thugs, provided them with liquor, and directed sellers of kerosene oil, whose sale was restricted to permit holders, to distribute the fuel for arson. They also provided information about the targets—Sikh houses, business establishments, schools, and *gurudwaras*."[21] Such information in turn was provided by "informers and collaborators" within the residential colonies selected for attack. The riot squads themselves were recruited from nearby castes, communities, and villages, from groups whose members have in the past done, or who are known to be available for, such work. Transportation for the riot squads also had to be provided, which meant recruiting bus drivers and vehicles from the Delhi Transportation Corporation, a public

[19] Tarrow, *Power in Movement*, p. 54.
[20] Ibid., p. 46.
[21] Tambiah, "Presidential Address," p. 746.

corporation. To start the riot and spread it, to provide noise, cover, and additional "spontaneous" recruits, further riot specialists also came into play: specially designated forces from the riot squads to act as "mobile gangs," persons designated to spread rumors, "shouters of slogans" and "instigators of violence among the public."[22] There are, then, a whole series of specialized roles that are occupied in larger riots, including provocateurs, monitors, informers, "riot captains and thugs,"[23] provisioners of transport and liquor, criminals, bomb manufacturers, journalists and pamphleteers, graffiti writers, and distributors and plasterers of scurrilous posters.

It is evident from most accounts that formal organizations such as the ruling party and its party offices and public employees and public organizations were involved in the Delhi Riots of 1984, but not as such. That is to say, there exist in effect in Delhi lists of persons who form a loosely organized network that can be called up quickly when the need arises, when it is desired to produce a riot. Such networks exist elsewhere in India and, I believe, have existed in Russia in the nineteenth century and in many other places, including cities in the United States today.

Although it would be a mistake to imagine that all riots are like those in Delhi in 1984 and that they all involve such deliberate planning, I believe that all riot-prone cities and towns do have to a greater or lesser degree such informal organizational networks. They also have something else, which is central to the notion of institutionalized riot systems, namely, a network of persons who maintain communal, racial, and other ethnic relations in a state of tension, of readiness for riots. Here I part company definitively with the "sequence" theorists of collective action, who imagine a state of tension arising out of grievances, frustrations, and discriminations in the relations between two communities, which requires only the proverbial spark to ignite it. On the contrary, there are regular fire-tenders who maintain the fuel at a combustible level, sometimes stoking it, sometimes letting it smolder. They are the conversion specialists, who know how to convert a moment of tension into a grander, riotous event.

These fire-tenders occupy formal and informal roles in existing organizations and outside them. In the most riot-prone cities, one is certain to find community organizations, cultural organizations, and/or political parties devoted to the advancement of their community, who also depict members of another, designated community as either an enemy, an oppressor, or a threat to their own community. Such organizations in India include especially the RSS and the BJP,[24] the former a Hindu cultural organization and the latter a

---

[22] Ibid., p. 747.

[23] Ibid., p. 753.

[24] These organizations are virtually always referred to by their acronyms, for the titles to which they refer are quite meaningless. RSS stands for Rashtriya Swayamsewak Sangh, which translates to National Volunteer [or Social Service] Organization [or Society]. BJP stands for Bharatiya Janata Party, Indian People's Party.

party of militant Hindu nationalism, whose leading positions are occupied by RSS-persons. Other organizations in the RSS "family"[25] include the Vishwa Hindu Parishad (VHP)[26] and the Bajrang Dal.[27] The former organization is devoted to mobilizing the Hindu community in India to "rectify" alleged past wrongs committed against Hindus by Muslims, notably the construction of mosques upon temples allegedly destroyed for the purpose. The Bajrang Dal is a fighting "protection" squad for the other organizations, a somewhat pathetic, but nevertheless dangerous, version of the Nazi SA.

In other towns in some parts of India there are Muslim organizations of this type, but they are far less widespread and less well organized, disciplined, and directed. There are other organizations as well, most of whose members are honestly devoted primarily to cultural activities and/or religious reform within their communities, whose members also may nevertheless play roles, deliberate or inadvertent, in riot systems. Such organizations include the Arya Samaj among Hindus in north India. Some towns known to be riot-prone do not necessarily have a full panoply of organized groups or the groups may be in an early stage of organization. But they all have individuals, formally affiliated or informally associated with such organizations or the ideas for which they stand, who play the roles of fire-tenders.

The role of fire-tender, moreover, is not always one of ignition. Most often, in fact, it is one of merely tending the flame and preventing its ignition when the circumstances are not "right" for a riot. Indeed, some of these fire-tenders masquerade as promoters of communal peace and harmony. They may even be members of local "peace committees." In whatever role they are playing at the moment, there is nevertheless a constant purpose, namely, to maintain an awareness at all levels of society of the potential for a riot. In India, such persons are, for example, immediately informed whenever a Hindu girl elopes with a Muslim boy, a cow dies under circumstances that appear suspicious and when Muslims are involved, a Hindu idol miraculously appears in some public place or on some site occupied by Muslims, a Hindu is injured or rumored to have been injured or killed in a brawl with a Muslim, a well-off Muslim buys property in a predominantly Hindu area, and so on and on.

When, then, are the circumstances "right" for a riot? These circumstances differ in different countries at different times, but there is one that is common in party-electoral polities, namely, before and during elections and during movements of mass mobilization, especially when the political balance between contending forces appears to be changing, that is, when political

---

[25] For a description of the RSS "family" of organizations and the interrelationships among them, see Walter K. Andersen and Shridhar D. Damle, *The Brotherhood in Saffron: The Rashtriya Swayamsevak Sangh and Hindu Revivalism* (New Delhi: Vistaar, 1987).

[26] World Hindu Society.

[27] Bajrang Dal is not translatable. The term suggests a society of the followers of the god, Hanuman.

opportunities are such that a riot may increase public sympathy for one's own party or movement and weaken one's rivals. The same kinds of circumstances also may determine the selection of otherwise everyday, trivial, and isolated incidents or small riots for magnification and "transvaluation."

The roles of fire-tenders are crucial to the maintenance of riot systems, but to revert to analysis of the system as a whole and change the metaphor, the view presented here is that riots are best seen as dramatic productions with large casts of extras. They are productions, in other words, which are partly organized and in which the extras are cleverly used or, so to say, in which extensive ad-libbing occurs in order to convey the impression of spontaneity.[28] When a riot "goes off,"[29] then very large numbers of "extras" may indeed become involved. Even some of these, however, may be eagerly waiting for the signal to play their part, to come on stage. That signal may come in the form of provocative shouts and slogans to incite a crowd to attack or from the hurling of brickbats or the sound of breaking glass. Everyone knows his part or makes his own part as the scenes develop.

It is widely believed in India, and it is also one of the most common beliefs about riots in most places, that they are nearly always urban phenomena. Indeed, in India this demographic observation is commonly followed by a sigh of relief, suggesting many assuaging beliefs and feelings about them, to wit: The villagers, at least, have not been corrupted by the tensions and turmoils of urban life; bad relations between our peoples of different religions are not endemic, not built into the prejudices of the people, but are manufactured in the cities; the country is safe since these riots are contained in what is, after all, only a small part of it. Sometimes this demographic observation is accompanied by popular sociological explanations, which repeat much of the academic sociology of riots: They are consequences of urbanization; of uprooting and migration of rural people into the cities, juxtaposing peoples of different castes and communities in unfamiliar surroundings in a dog-eat-dog, competitive economic environment; of political mobilizations made possible by the existence of large masses of common people.

In fact, however, here as elsewhere in both popular and academic accounts of riots, this belief, if not simply false, is a function of definition, labeling, and the construction of meaning. If a riot is defined as requiring a minimum number of persons, as in most official riot acts, then most village brawls fall short of official requirements. But so do most urban brawls. In the cities, however, even a small brawl between a black and a white in America or a Hindu and a Muslim in India easily turns into a potential or an actual riot.

---

[28] See also Tambiah, "Presidential Address," p. 755.

[29] This is the term used by Bill Buford's "football hooligans," for which see his *Among the Thugs* (New York: Norton, 1992), e.g., pp. 87, 177.

The differences between the two situations relate to the diffusion of information and to the relative importance of local knowledge. News of a barroom or teashop or street-corner brawl in the United States or India is transmitted rapidly in the cities by rumor, association of people in common organizations, print, and electronic media. The persons involved in the incident are known through such forms of transmission only as categories, not as real persons. In an Indian village, in contrast, the persons are known, the cause of their conflict is often also obvious, their group affiliations and the numbers of supporters each is likely to be able to produce in a broader conflict are also known, as are the consequences for village life if the brawl is allowed to expand. These are factors that make for containment rather than expansion, but they do not prevent the frequent outbreak of violent brawls and killings.

Large-scale riotous events are also easier to produce where faceless crowds are available, that is, where anonymity is possible, though often the culprits are known and identifiable even in the cities. Indeed, in the United States, the widespread availability of individually owned video cameras makes such anonymity increasingly doubtful. It nevertheless remains a difference between village and city in India that when a large-scale violent confrontation occurs between villagers or between persons from adjacent villages, virtually every person as well as his caste and religious identity is known to everyone else. When large crowds do mass, as they indeed do in villages,[30] and a fight ensues, it is not labeled as a riot. In cases where forces are equally matched, it appears in accounts of them as a kind of local warfare. Where forces are not equally matched in numbers of arms and the victims are mostly poor people of low caste, they are characterized as massacres.

But sometimes it is also said that, though most villages remain pure while riots rage in the cities, villages near urban areas may be affected. When reports do occur of such alleged spreading of riots to nearby villages, they refer to them in the same way as do accounts of their spread in the cities, as of infection or contagion, with rumor providing the mechanism leading to, as usual, "retaliation" against the members of a group in the village whose presumed compatriots in the nearby city were the aggressors against *their* compatriots. However, when one goes to the scene of such a village in the aftermath of an urban riot, different stories emerge from those presented in the press and in the town about the events in the village and multiple accounts may also be heard within the village itself. It is more likely to appear, then, not that the village riot occurred as a consequence of sponta-

---

[30] For a well-documented example, see Government of Gujarat, Home Department, *Report on the Police Firing at Village Parthampura, District Baroda, on 14th August, 1972*, by Shri K. M. Satwani, District and Sessions Judge Ahmedabad (Rural), Narol, Commission of Inquiry (Gandhinagar, 1975).

neous anger against a categorized, stereotyped foe, but as a deliberate assault by one group upon another to take vengeance for a previous insult or to steal their land. In this respect, the village "riot" is no different from the city riot. Riots in both cases provide opportunities for persons and groups in such villages as for urban people to take violent action that would otherwise be prevented by the village leaders or, in some cases, by the police as well, though the intervention of the latter often has contrary effects from those desired by village actors.

What distinguishes rural and urban brawls and their transformation into larger riotous events, therefore, is principally the ability to mass large numbers of people, to spread rapidly the news of an event that has occurred some distance away, and the opportunity for crowds to move from place to place with a degree of anonymity. Most riots that occur in rural areas, therefore, tend to be isolated within a village or between persons in two villages or between villagers and the police. But they do indeed occur with great frequency. Moreover, there have been occasions in India even in the nineteenth century when riotous behavior spread throughout the countryside from village to village.[31] In such cases, as in the cities, movement-like organizations have existed and have been clearly implicated in them.

FIVE CASES

During my field research in north India in 1982–83 and in subsequent visits during the past dozen years, I gathered considerable material on a number of incidents involving both police–village confrontations and so-called Hindu–Muslim riots in villages, small towns, and large cities. Five of those incidents have been selected for presentation in this volume. They include the following: (1) an incident involving the theft of an idol from a Jain temple in Aligarh district, later "found" by Hindu villagers from an important local caste; (2) an incident in a small town in Meerut district involving the alleged rape, allegedly by Muslims of the alleged daughter of an old Hindu man who had been traveling with the woman on a bus (the repeated use of the term "alleged" here is deliberate, reflecting the ambiguities that riddle this case rather than bad grammar); (3–4) two incidents of police–village confrontations involving alleged police brutalities committed against villagers of backward caste and minority status, one of which became transformed into an example of police brutality against backward castes, untouchables, Muslims, and women and was used by Mrs. Gandhi and her son, Sanjay, to precipitate national elections in 1980, and the other of which attracted vir-

---

[31] As in the case of the cow protection riots of 1893, on which see Sandria B. Freitag, *Collective Action and Community: Public Arenas and the Emergence of Communalism in North India* (Berkeley: University of California Press, 1989), chap. 5.

tually no national attention; (5) the post-Ayodhya destruction and killings in Kanpur city in December 1992.

The procedure I have followed with regard to these events has been, first, to construct "texts" from my field notes of the accounts given to me by respondents concerning their origins and interpretations. Second, I then proceed to analyze the texts to reveal the multiplicity of interpretations, explanations, and contexts that are provided by participants and observers of them to describe the happenings and to show the internal contradictions in each account. Third, I then try to reconstruct the incidents into coherent accounts of two types: a "who dunnit?" account that attempts to figure out who the actual culprits were in transforming the incidents into police–village or communal confrontations and a social science account that attempts to provide a coherent contextual "explanation" of the happenings. The final step, however, is to show how the reconstructions themselves can lay no claim to a special truth status.

In playing this game, as it were, I am aiming at something serious. In the manner of Foucault in *I, Pierre, Riviere*, I treat each text as "a case, an affair, an event that provided the intersection of discourses that differed in origin, form, organization, and function" and which "form neither a composite work nor an exemplary text, but rather a strange contest, a confrontation, a power relation, a battle among discourses and through discourses," used "as weapons of attack and defense in the relations of power and knowledge."[32] In treating each incident this way, I am also arguing that contemporary Indian society as a whole is a battlefield of competing beliefs, ideologies, faiths, and worldviews, behind each one of which lies a set of power relations.

The first incident I call "Theft of an Idol." The text I have created about it is not based upon the methodology of contemporary social science, which involves the systematic creation of a coherent text. Rather, it is a text created out of my own interactions with myself, with my disciplines of political science and South Asian studies, and with India and Indians. The text emerged because I was looking for pitched battles between villagers and police in all my districts. I was also engaged in a "search for truth," to perhaps naively figure out what happened, why, and who was responsible. I appointed myself a one-man commission of inquiry into the disturbances in village Pachpera.

The "text" for "Theft of an Idol" was created from ten interviews in which I originally sought the truth and the local context surrounding an incident that developed into a serious, but *local* melee. That is, the incident was not taken out of the local context and placed within the dominant framework of communalism. Beyond a few basic facts, absolutely everything else is in

---

[32] Foucault, *I, Pierre Rivière*, pp. x–xi.

doubt and subject to differing interpretations, which I have identified and characterized as being embedded in different contexts or narrative frameworks that constitute forms of explanation based upon different perceptions of human motivations and relationships.

At the local level, one can see not merely contested facts, but a multiplicity of voices confronting each other. Some of these voices appear to arise out of and articulate deeply held beliefs, centering on faith and religious sentiment or their presumed opposites, interest and profit, the predominant elements in the creed of Western, rational man. Others are state-centered and politics-centered, revolving around concepts and constructions of caste and community, criminality, law and order, police brutality, and the like. There is also interpenetration and masquerading, as well as confrontation of beliefs and faiths. The question I am asking now is different from the one I originally asked. I am now not asking what the truth about this incident is—though my ideas about that form part of my interaction with the text—but what types of narratives are predominant in presenting the "truth," with what consequences.

Although this incident appears far removed in its local contextualization and in the absence of questions of Hindu–Muslim relations surrounding it from the grand confrontations over caste and communal issues that have been at the center of Indian political struggles in the past fifteen years, it is the principal purpose of this book to demonstrate linkages between this incident and those issues in Indian society. Although the argument will be developed throughout the book, I want to note two connections here. The first is with one of the explanatory frameworks prominent in the efforts to place this incident in an appropriate context, that of faith and sentiment. The second is a linkage between this event in 1983 and the vast communal rioting that took place in numerous cities and towns in India in December and January 1992–93 in the aftermath of the demolition of the mosque at Ayodhya.

The linkage is in the virtually identical arguments used by representatives of a particular political party, the BJP, in relation to both incidents. In the incident at village Pachpera, Nihal Singh, then an ex-MLA (member of the legislative assembly) and a person of only local political importance, was the principal defender of the villagers who found the Jain idol and the principal accuser of the police who descended on the village to remove the idol forcibly from their possession. In December 1992 the chief minister of the entire state of Uttar Pradesh (UP), who allowed the mosque to be destroyed, indeed deliberately saw to it that the numerous police, paramilitary, and military forces stationed in the vicinity took no action to prevent its destruction, was a man of the BJP, the then ruling party. His argument was identical to that used in 1983 in the local incident in village Pachpera, namely, that the faith and sentiment of the people had to be respected. In the first case, the argument was used in justifying the claim to a "found" idol, in the second in justifying the reclaiming of a site believed to be the location of Ram's birthplace and of a temple formerly dedicated to him.[33]

The second case presented in this volume, "Rape at Daphnala," also occurred in 1983. It brings us closer to the issues of Hindu–Muslim relations, communal conflict, and violence. Indeed, the incident that occurred in this town is precisely of the type that has led repeatedly in the past century to communal violence in numerous cities and towns throughout the subcontinent. Moreover, some of the other elements that have elsewhere been present, required to convert such incidents into communal riots, were also present here at the time, particularly the presence and active involvement of local militant Hindu political activists. Yet this incident, like the one at village Pachpera, developed instead into a police–public confrontation. What were the factors that turned this incident in the latter direction rather than into a Hindu–Muslim riot?

My account emphasizes especially the role and actions of the district administration which, in the aftermath of the great Hindu–Muslim riot of 1982 in the district headquarters town of Meerut, was extremely sensitive at this time and alert to any kind of provocative actions that might lead to a similar result anywhere in the district. This incident is noteworthy also for the existence in the midst of the competing contextualizations of it, of yet a different form of explanation from those discussed elsewhere in this volume, which took it out of the context of Hindu–Muslim relations and placed it instead in a civic one. The existence of this alternative contextualization is noteworthy, on the one hand, because it suggests the possibilities for placing such issues in an entirely different moral framework. On the other hand, it is equally noteworthy for its feebleness, presented most earnestly, though not exclusively, by one old man, devoted to Gandhian ideals that seemed remote in north India in the 1980s.

The third case, little different from countless incidents of its type that occur commonly in the north Indian countryside, nevertheless achieved great notoriety and was placed within the context of the major issues in political struggles at the time: police brutality, the victimization of the lower castes, minorities, and women. Indeed, although the incident was a minor one in comparison with many others of its type, especially in relation to most communal riots, it is among the best-known incidents of police–public confrontation that have occurred in post-Independence India. The purpose of presenting the account of the Narayanpur incident as well as the one after it in this volume is to consider the circumstances under which such incidents do

---

[33] Moreover, the linkage in this book is entirely coincidental. My research for Theft of an Idol was done in 1983, several years before the beginnings of the Ram Janmabhumi/Babari Masjid mobilization and countermobilization.

or do not achieve notoriety, do or do not come to stand for the general ills of society and to reflect its major internal struggles. The argument, presented by means of a contrast between the Narayanpur incident and a second one of a similar type that achieved no public notice outside the district in which it occurred, is that both the achievement of such notoriety and the framing of the issues involved in such incidents are largely independent of their circumstances. They are dependent rather on the opportunities that they do or do not make available to outside actors to use them for their own purposes, in the course of which only the most tenuous relationship is maintained between the facts of the incident and the meanings with which outsiders seek to invest it.

The final case presented is taken from a major Hindu–Muslim riot that occurred in the city of Kanpur between December 6 and 11, 1992. I have chosen to focus in my materials on this riot on the figure of a single person, who was said to have played a prominent role in it, for a presentation of a more complete study of these riots would take up the better part of another volume. Moreover, I have added to it materials derived from the aftermath of the 1992 rioting, from a murder that took place in February 1994, which itself led to a smaller riot that many feared would become a repetition of the December 1992 riots.

The pattern of rioting in Kanpur after the destruction of the mosque at Ayodhya was similar to that in the more famous case of Bombay in the sense that the initial actions were begun by Muslims coming into the streets in protest against the demolition of the Babari Masjid. However, in contrast to Bombay, where a second riot occurred a month later in which mostly Muslims were killed, a second stage of killings followed in Kanpur within days, during which large crowds of Hindus massed and moved against Muslims. The bulk of the murders in Kanpur occurred during the second stage.

In the midst of the terror, murder, and destruction, a man known as Kala Bachcha (Black Boy) emerged as the central figure, alternately portrayed as the principal leader of murder squads directed against Muslims in the second stage of the riots and as a hero and protector of both Muslims and Hindus. For the Muslims, he was a killer; for the BJP, a hero. The stories told by and about Kala Bachcha, who was killed in a bomb attack in February 1994, traverse the boundaries of truth and falsehood, lies and myth, in the ongoing struggle in contemporary Indian politics and society to capture and control the meaning of those recurring murderous events defined as "Hindu–Muslim riots."

CONTEXTS, IDEOLOGIES, DISCOURSES

In general, there are two favored public frameworks of explanation in India for interpreting the types of events described in this volume. One, very often preferred in discussions of rural police–public confrontations, that of criminality and law and order, places them in the context of police brutality against disadvantaged groups. One problem with this perspective, however, is that the villagers are not innocents harassed by a police force looking for victims. The police are, it is true, often looking for victims, for money, for profit and will take it where they can find it, but their victims are not always mere innocents.

The second, the framework of caste and community, interprets such events as part of the ongoing struggle among caste groups for supremacy or among competing religions claiming priority for their worship, their sacred site, their idol. The Theft of an Idol incident, for example, has most of the aspects of similar situations that have led to violence between Hindus and Muslims, which in origin are usually no more or less communal than this one.

Among many difficulties with the explanations of such incidents in terms of caste and community are, first, that they are weapons of critique, in a polity that claims to be secular, which are used to attack the alleged groups that are said to be "behind" the incident. Second, accounts based on caste and community provide categorical explanations for particular events that may disguise and certainly always simplify, covering a variety of personal and political behaviors. The most dramatic recent instance of the latter use of this discourse was the creation before our eyes of Sikh–Hindu communalism, which hardly existed in India before the 1980s and probably hardly exists now, but has had its uses in the contemporary struggles for state power in Indian politics.[34]

A third framework has become more prominent with the decline in the past decade or more of the ideology of secularism, and the critique of it by both Westernized intellectuals and militant Hindu nationalists, that of faith and sentiment, which was used here and at Ayodhya by representatives of the same party using the same words. What about this discourse of faith and sentiment? It exists, it is real, most Indians live in it. They believe in the differences between castes, in the sanctity and effectiveness of religious rituals, perhaps even in the boundless merit to be obtained and spread by a woman's act of *sati*, which does not necessarily mean at the same time that they are not ready to make a bundle out of it.[35] These things, however, were not part of the dominant post-Independence ideologies of the contemporary state and politics, of secularism, Marxism-Leninism, and feminism, at least until recently with the rise—or better the exposure to fuller view of the reality—of Hindu communal sentiments.

[34] The Punjab crisis is not one of the "incidents" on which I am focusing in this volume, but I have written on the subject and have it in mind as a reference point, like Hindu–Muslim communalism, of one of the grand constructions that have been created in the battle of ideologies, faiths, and discourses in modern Indian history and politics.

[35] See Ashish Nandy, "Sati as Profit Versus Sati as a Spectacle: The Public Debate on Roop Kanwar's Death," in John Stratton Hawley, ed., *Sati, the Blessing and the Curse: The Burning of Wives in India* (New York: Oxford University Press, 1994), esp. p. 144.

None of these interpretive frameworks, however, including the latter, respect the beliefs of the people: They dismiss them or they exploit them or they distort them. Most of all, they blame the people for these "incidents," try to implicate their values in them, when in fact they are almost all creations out of the material of everyday existence or politically manipulated and directed movements of crowds, who have been paid or persuaded to believe that their problems are due to "the other" and will be solved by the other's humiliation, repression, or elimination.

All these frameworks in turn exist within a broader political context provided by the functioning of India's competitive polity, in which a multiplicity of parties, some with distinctive ideologies, compete with each other for primacy and access to resources, including wealth and safety, at all levels from the local to the national. They are especially brought into play at the time of elections and preparation for elections.[36] They may also be brought into play when there appears to be a prospect or the actuality of a changing political balance of power and competition between contending political forces.[37] Such frameworks also become more prominent when mass movements arise seeking to mobilize around simple slogans large numbers of people in a particular community or from among a group of people designated as disadvantaged. Or they may arise as a consequence of efforts pursued through the media or through "print and association . . . to construct a controversy."[38]

It is at such times that police–public confrontations and so-called communal riots also tend to occur. What most distinguishes the noticed from the unnoticed riotous events, what brings the larger interpretive frameworks into play are the political opportunities that exist to transform a local incident

[36] Tambiah, "Presidential Address," pp. 753–55.

[37] I have argued elsewhere that the rise and fall of ethnic and nationality movements and changes in their intensity tend to occur in three types of situations of changed political context: when there appear to be "possibilities for realignment of political and social forces and organizations," when there is a change in "the willingness of elites from dominant ethnic groups to share power with aspirant ethnic group leaders," and when there appears to be a "potential availability of alternative political arenas." Such changes in political context occur especially at dramatic moments such as leadership successions, declines in the power of central authorities, or dramatic changes in the relative balance of power between contending political forces. See Paul R. Brass, "Ethnic Groups and Nationalities: The Formation, Persistence, and Transformation of Ethnic Identities," in Peter F. Sugar, ed., *Ethnic Diversity and Conflict in Eastern Europe* (Santa Barbara: ABC-Clio, 1980), pp. 53–61; and idem, *Ethnicity and Nationalism: Theory and Comparison* (New Delhi: Sage, 1991), pp. 55–62. A similar argument in recent political science literature is that protest movements tend to arise when the "structure of political opportunities" changes; McAdam, *Political Process and the Development of Black Insurgency*, p. 40, citing Peter K. Eisinger, "The Conditions of Protest Behavior in American Cities," *American Political Science Review*, 67 (1973): 11–28. I believe both these arguments apply also to the incidence of riots.

[38] Tarrow, *Power in Movement*, p. 51.

into a categorical event, into something larger, reflecting a presumed broader contestation in society in which leaders and parties wish for political advantage to portray their opponents as either the instigators of the riot or as incompetent governors who cannot control them or as the enemies and oppressors of a group whose votes they seek.

Four of the five case studies in this volume fit into the several types of "opportunity structures" just described. The incident at village Pachpera occurred at the time of a local rural election. In the incident at Daphnala, the sitting member of the legislative assembly (MLA) and his rival were central actors. In Narayanpur, the incident occurred at a time of preparation for state legislative assembly elections. The latter incident also occurred and was enlarged into one of national importance when there was a grand struggle in progress between Mrs. Indira Gandhi, who had just returned to power in parliamentary elections and now wished to hold state elections throughout most of India to consolidate her power in the country, and her rivals, who continued to hold power in many state governments, including Uttar Pradesh (UP).

The riots in Kanpur occurred in the wake of a vast movement of militant Hindu political mobilization whose ultimate aims were to gain power at the Center for its proponents. In the late 1980s and 1990s, the Ayodhya movement to dismantle the mosque there and replace it with a temple expanded and precipitated riots initially, in 1989–90, to protect the support base of the BJP. Once in power in UP, the BJP leaders had to consider whether that power should be used to actually gain control of the disputed site and remove the mosque. While it is a matter of considerable dispute how it happened that the mosque finally was destroyed while the BJP government was in power, it is evident that the wave of riots that followed in its wake were not merely precipitated by that event, but were an extension of the struggle for power in process in Indian politics between militant Hindu and secular forces—or forces claiming to be secular. Moreover, these riots, as will be shown in the Kanpur chapter, were not necessarily, or even commonly, "spontaneous" reactions, but involved the organization and participation of individuals and groups associated with the RSS and the BJP.

It is, therefore, notable that riots are associated with "democratic," that is, competitive politics. Moreover, it is generally true that they occur mostly under such regimes, not under authoritarian regimes, except when the latter appear to be vulnerable or are actually crumbling. Indeed, riots may be used not only as a means for achieving power within a competitive political system, but also as a means of destroying democracy and bringing to power murderous regimes that then maintain peace on the streets. Such was the case with Nazi Germany. It is also notable that the BJP claims that riots do not occur when they are in power, only when the Congress or other secular parties are in power. In fact, no party in India can sustain such a claim. On the contrary, large-scale riots and waves of riots tend to occur whenever it is convenient in the competitive struggle for power.

In any case, riots may be part of the "normal" democratic process at certain times and in certain places or they may be preludes to the rise of a fascist regime. This association of riots and waves of riots with both democratic and antidemocratic forces obviously raises fundamental questions concerning the nature and future of "democracy." Riots, I have said, have functional utility in competitive political systems, including in the latter category those in both Western and non-Western societies. In some polities, such as those in South Asia, they are part of routine politics, precipitated deliberately to gain political advantage. Even if they are not always deliberately precipitated, it is part of the competitive political game to create and magnify incidents, promote movements, and incite one's rivals and their supporters to a point where a riot may be anticipated as a likely consequence. Moreover, in both East and West, even where riots are neither planned nor incited, their occurrence is invariably useful in the political struggle to capture their meaning that follows thereafter. Finally, riots are commonly used, especially in developing countries, to justify centralization of state power on the plea that, without such power, not only riots but internal warfare among the diverse peoples encompassed within the state's boundaries are likely to occur. It is here that riots may also be used to justify the displacement of a competitive political system by an authoritarian regime, which then imposes its "peace" upon the populace, a peace that may be the proverbial peace of the dead or the intimidated in a polity dominated by a particular ethnic or religious or militant nationalist group.

Of the five case studies of violence described in this volume, only one, the rural incident at Kurman Purwa, did not occur at a time of election or in anticipation of one. Politicians, nevertheless, became very much involved in it and sought to make use of it for their own purposes. It thus supports both positively and negatively the general arguments of this book. On the one hand, it demonstrates how even the most trivial brawl in the Indian countryside can hardly escape integration into a broader framework of both meaning and political interest. Such is the state of politicization in a country still lacking modern means of communication in most rural areas. On the other hand, the absence of a structure of political opportunity in the district in which the incident occurred and at the time it occurred made it possible to confine the incident, to localize it, and to cut short attempts to magnify its significance and bring it into an external political framework of meaning and political contestation.

While I find the procedure of creating, interpreting, and reinterpreting texts for each incident a useful analytical device, the weight of my analysis and conclusions is upon the uses of different types of contextualizations in structuring interethnic relations and in extending networks of power relations in Indian politics. Although I will argue that the choice of the level and type of explanation for incidents of violence is inevitably a partisan matter, it is not a matter of indifference. In contemporary Hindu–Muslim "riots," some of which have become in fact pogroms in which the dominant political party, the Congress, or its leading rival in recent years, the BJP, and the state authorities and police are directly or indirectly implicated, we are faced with the question of evil and cannot, therefore, remain neutral or treat all forms of explanations as of equal merit. Rather, it is necessary to identify those that most promote and foster violence.

However, since I argue that all the general, extralocal narratives of violence are implicated in its perpetuation in India, a choice among existing narrative frameworks amounts to choosing the lesser evil which, for some, is good enough. Ideologies such as secularism, which claim to ignore religious and other caste-communal differences, cannot do so in practice. Whether one opts for the lesser evil or seeks an entirely new ground, it is essential to recognize that selection of a level of explanation, a context in which to place major incidents of violence, is a serious political act.

The last point leads to the question whether there are broader unities among the several types of explanations that appear in my texts, notably an encompassing discourse of the modern state and national identity that contributes to the placement of peoples into distinct categories, ethnic groups prone to communal violence. The antagonisms among such groups must, it is often argued, be transcended by building loyalties to the state or be accommodated through pluralist compromises. In either case, they are recognized as fundamental.

It is within the broad discourse of the modern state and national unity that one must look for an explanation for the persistence of that most pernicious and violence-producing subdiscourse of Hindu–Muslim confrontation in South Asia. The latter, though subordinate to or embedded within the former, is a discourse in the full Foucauldian sense of that term.[39] It is grounded within a set of institutions that promote its persistence: communal organizations, political parties, peace committees, and the like. It includes a set of practices and behaviors as well: communal postures, secular counterpostures, appointments of commissions of inquiry to analyze riots, appointments of minority commissions to report on incidents of communal tension of all sorts, funding of social science research institutes to examine the causes of Hindu–Muslim communalism and riots. The latter in turn are en-

[39] Gyanendra Pandey prefers the term "master narrative" for this construction in his *The Construction of Communalism in Colonial North India* (Delhi: Oxford University Press, 1990), which I find useful and refer to again below. But it does not convey as effectively as Foucault's term ("discourse") the interrelationship of institutions and systems of knowlege that sustain Hindu–Muslim communalism and its social practices, including the practice of violence, in India. On the creation of communal consciousness in north India before Independence and its consequences after, see also Paul R. Brass, *Language, Religion, and Politics in North India* (London: Cambridge University Press, 1974).

gaged in a so-called search for the "truth" of communalism and violence, which is often found—in the best liberal tradition of the search for truth—within the innermost beings of Indian selves. While this search for the truth of communalism goes on decade after decade, the roll of the dead which, if one counts the violence of partition in 1947, now numbers in the hundreds of thousands, increases year by year. But it is not only Indians who are involved in this search for the "truth" of Hindu–Muslim communalism, but those of us who have produced and continue to produce volume after volume on the subject, who have made our livings, as it were, and our reputations on the dead bodies of the hundreds of thousands of victims of the systems of violence that have stalked the Indian subcontinent for the past century.

METHODOLOGICAL NOTE

The use of case studies in the social sciences occupies an accepted but still somewhat dubious methodological status. Questions are invariably raised by those who use universalistic methods of survey research and ecological analysis concerning the representative character of the cases selected. If they are not "representative" of the broader society demographically, economically, and politically, it is usually argued that no sustainable generalizations can be drawn from them.

The districts in which these incidents of violence occurred were selected some thirty years ago in my first field research in India. The criteria that I then used in selecting them were designed to provide a cross-section of the most important demographic, economic, and political features of the state. They thus included four mostly rural districts and one large city; two western, two eastern, and one central district; districts with distinct forms of pre-Independence land tenure arrangements; prosperous and poor agricultural districts; and districts where Hindu–Muslim relations had historically been tense and others where there had not been significant communal conflicts.

It would nevertheless be misleading to suggest that the cases presented in this volume, drawn from the same districts that I have visited repeatedly over the past three decades, constitute a valid random sample of incidents of violence in the state of Uttar Pradesh. I have noted in each case the particular demographic, economic, and communal characteristics of the districts in which the incidents occurred and indicated the relevance of those aspects that struck me as important. I have not, however, attempted to construct from these characteristics a sociological theory to explain the "causes" of these incidents of violence.

At the same time, I do attempt an overall understanding of the dynamics of riots and their relationship to competitive politics and more broadly to power relations in Indian society and politics. What I have found through my method of textual analysis is not a theory based on controlled comparisons, of difference and differentiation, but the links that bind all the cases. They are first of all bound or not bound by the presence or absence of institutionalized riot systems. But, further, they are bound by the presence in Indian society of a discrete set of interrelated narrative frameworks for the interpretation of the meaning of violence. The cases, therefore, are most interesting not because they are *representative*, but because, though each is virtually unique, totally unrelated to the others in most significant demographic, economic, and communal aspects, they are linked by discourse.

Chapter 2

BACKGROUND

WHEN I BEGAN this research, as part of a broader project concerning political and economic changes in local politics in north India during the previous two decades, Indian politics in general and north Indian politics in particular were on the point of major transformations, whose dimensions were not clear at the time. The authoritarian regime known as the Emergency, imposed on the country by Mrs. Gandhi between 1975 and 1977, had come and gone. In its aftermath, the Congress was defeated for the first time in its history and replaced by a political formation known as the Janata Party, which restored the essential features of the pre-Emergency constitutional order. The Janata government, having completed this major task, disintegrated in July 1979, paving the way for the return of the Congress to power at the Center and the installation of Mrs. Gandhi once again as prime minister in 1980.

At that time, there was a general sense that over the course of the twenty years between the early 1960s and 1980s, there had been an increase in violence at the local level,[1] including police–public confrontations, Hindu–Muslim riots, atrocities committed against lower castes, and interpersonal violence arising out of the criminalization of politics and the development of local linkages among criminals, politicians, and the police. The actions of the police and paramilitary forces, particularly the Provincial Armed Constabulary (PAC) in the state of Uttar Pradesh, had also been subjected to increased scrutiny as numerous instances of police victimization of allegedly innocent persons in the villages and small towns received attention in the press and as charges became more and more common that the PAC in this state had become an anti-Muslim force engaged in the massacre of Muslims instead of the control of Hindu–Muslim riots.

Many of the changes that had already occurred in Indian politics by the early 1980s were attributed by various observers to an increased intensity of competitive struggle for power at the national level in which Mrs. Gandhi's attempts to centralize power in New Delhi and control the politics of the states from the Center were considered of particular importance. Mrs. Gandhi virtually dismantled the old Congress organization by doing away with the practices of inner party elections and debate, appointing state and local

[1] David Bayley, "The Police and Political Order in India," *Asian Survey* 23, no. 4 (April 1983): 492.

party officers herself or through her spokesmen, and concentrating the selection of party candidates for state and national elections in her own hands and those of her principal advisers. A further degradation of the party organization was brought about through the actions of her youngest son, Sanjay Gandhi, who recruited into the party large numbers of youth, who in turn introduced hooliganism and thuggery into the party and into its struggles with local rivals in the districts. Supporters of Mrs. Gandhi, on the other hand, argue that the measures adopted by her, including the imposition of the Emergency regime from 1975 to 1977, were a reaction to the increase in violent movements led by students and opposition forces in the 1970s, such as those against the duly elected state governments of Gujarat and Bihar in 1974.[2]

Side by side with the increased violence of all sorts and the organizational decline of the country's leading political party, the Indian National Congress, changes also occurred in the role of political leadership, in the terms of political debate, in the sense of danger to the unity of the country, and in the decline of secular ideologies and practices. Insofar as political leadership was concerned, Mrs. Gandhi had quite simply become the center of the Indian political order, whether in power or out, a centrality that was transferred to her son, Rajiv Gandhi, immediately after her assassination in 1984. The Congress had become dependent upon her whereas the opposition, especially after her imposition of the Emergency, thought principally of how to keep her from power after her displacement in 1977 and how to cope with her return to power after 1980. The stunning landslide victory of the Congress under Rajiv Gandhi's leadership in the 1984 parliamentary elections focused similar attention upon him. Indeed, within three years after his elevation to the prime ministership, an epic struggle developed between him and a challenger from within the party, V. P. Singh, who was ultimately expelled from the party, formed the Janata Dal, and mounted an effective challenge in the 1989 elections, which led to the defeat of the Congress and the installation of the second non-Congress government in the history of post-Independence India at the Center.

This struggle between Rajiv Gandhi and V. P. Singh had further consequences: the final destruction of the Congress as a viable organization in north India, in its two most populous states, Uttar Pradesh and Bihar, and the replacement of the old rivalry between the Congress and non-Congress parties for power in Uttar Pradesh by a rivalry between two different forces.

---

[2] For an objective account of these two famous movements, see John R. Wood, "Extra-Parliamentary Opposition in India: An Analysis of Populist Agitations in Gujarat and Bihar," *Pacific Affairs* 47, no. 3 (Fall 1975): 75. Wood's account, however, also gives grounds for believing that police misbehavior and overreaction were as much or more responsible for the violence that occurred during these movements as the actions of the students, many of whom were killed in police firings in both states.

One consists of a coalition of backward castes, lower castes, and Muslims originally formed partly by V. P. Singh and consolidated by a breakaway party known initially as the Samajwadi Janata Party, later as simply the Samajwadi Party (SP), led by Mulayam Singh Yadav. The second force is that of militant Hindu nationalism, led by the Bharatiya Janata Party (BJP), in which upper castes are predominant, but which also has had some success in appealing to backward castes.

However, when this research began in the winter of 1983, Mrs. Gandhi was still in power at the Center, the Janata Dal and the SP did not exist, and the BJP was at a low ebb. The case studies in this volume, however, include one that occurred in 1980, shortly after Mrs. Gandhi's return to power. Moreover, this 1980 incident at Narayanpur became the pretext used by Mrs. Gandhi to dismiss most of the then existing state governments, including that in UP, in order to call new state legislative assembly elections, which brought the Congress back to power in most of them, including UP. At that time, the principal opposition to the Congress in the state was the Lok Dal of Charan Singh, who was, for a very brief time, prime minister of India before the 1980 elections.

By the time the field research for the last case study was completed, in 1994, both Mrs. Gandhi and her son, Rajiv, had been assassinated, Charan Singh had died, the Congress was a spent force in north India, and the rivalry between the SP and the BJP had become central. Between 1983 and 1994, three general elections were held: in 1984, producing the landslide Congress victory under Rajiv Gandhi; in 1989, generating the victory of the Janata Dal/National Front coalition led by V. P. Singh; and in 1991—in the midst of which the assassination of Rajiv Gandhi occurred—bringing forth a minority Congress government under Narasimha Rao.

Insofar as UP is concerned, the Congress government that had been in power after the 1984 elections was replaced in 1989 by a Janata Dal government. However, the elections of 1991 brought the BJP to power for the first time in this state. It was when this government was in power, with Kalyan Singh as chief minister, that the conditions were created for the destruction of the mosque at Ayodhya. The dismissal of the BJP government by the Center and the imposition of President's Rule thereafter was followed by another election in November 1993, from which the SP, the BJP's principal rival, emerged victorious in alliance with the Bahujan Samaj Party (BSP),[3] a party representing Scheduled Castes.

[3] McGregor translates Bahujan as "a large group of people" or "the community." Since the aim of the BSP is to unite the lower castes and other disadvantaged groups into a majority party, the term "Bahujan" carries a double meaning , referring to those groups constituting the largest number of people in the country and to the Bahujan Samaj Party as the Socialist Party of the Majority. See R. S. McGregor, ed., *The Oxford Hindi-English Dictionary* (Oxford: Oxford University Press, 1993).

The terms of political debate had also changed considerably between the 1960s and the 1980s. In the earlier period, public dialogue on domestic issues focused on planning for development, the respective roles of the public and private sectors in the economy, the relative weight to be given to industry and agriculture, and the like. At the local level, the language of debate was rather different, of course, and emphasized issues of prices and resource availability for irrigation, seeds, fertilizer, and link roads, among other matters, while the private language of political coalition building revolved around caste and community. During Mrs. Gandhi's long and only briefly interrupted tenure in power between 1966 and her death in 1984, greater emphasis was placed upon issues concerning resources for the poorest in the country, the Scheduled Castes and agricultural laborers, on the status of minorities, particularly Muslims, and on the mobilization in several parts of the country of the middle-status castes (generally referred to as "backward castes").

However, in north India Mrs. Gandhi's basic political coalition consisted of upper-caste Hindus, Scheduled Castes, and Muslims whereas the opposition, led principally by Charan Singh, maintained a firm hold on the bulk of the backward-caste/middle peasant vote. Since Mrs. Gandhi's political coalition in north India was barely sufficient to produce a one-third vote and a bare majority in the UP legislature and her defeat in 1977 after the Emergency was principally caused by the mobilization of the backward castes behind the Janata Party and the defection of Muslims and Scheduled Castes from her coalition, the rivalry between the Congress and the opposition was intense in this state thereafter. Not only was it intense, but the public dialogue became debased. Mrs. Gandhi used demagogic tactics to appeal to the lower castes and the minorities, deliberately seeking out from newspaper reports and reports from political workers in the districts incidents of atrocities against lower castes and minorities for which her political rivals could somehow be blamed.

Where an incident was particularly atrocious *and* the political circumstances for its manipulation were right, Mrs. Gandhi would personally proceed to the scene. The more remote the location and the more difficult the access, the more dramatic would be her entrance upon the spot, the most spectacular being her arrival by elephant at the notorious site of Belchi.[4] The opposition responded by pointing out similar incidents for which the Congress could be condemned. There was little public debate on the issues of providing resources for the poor and the minorities, on the adequacy of

---

[4] In July 1977, six months after Mrs. Gandhi's defeat in the 1977 General Elections, in a remote village in Bihar by this name, a number of low-caste, landless agricultural laborers and their families were massacred by landowners angry over their demands for increased wages. For a stirring account of Mrs. Gandhi's journey to this village, see Pupul Jayakar, *Indira Gandhi: An Intimate Biography* (New York: Pantheon, 1992), pp. 263–65.

political and police protection for the disadvantaged classes, and on the provision of educational and other facilities for them. Rather, the focus was on assigning blame for the alleged failures to improve their conditions and to protect them by pinpointing particular incidents. This process of pinpointing incidents of violence for public attention, however, was based more upon their political utility than upon the merits of the cases, as will be shown in the discussion of the incidents at Narayanpur and Kurman Purwa described in chapters 4 and 5.

Another difference between the political atmosphere of the early 1980s and the 1960s was an enhanced sense of threat to the unity and integrity of the country, produced in part by objective circumstances, but even more by the political uses of a paranoid style of politics articulated incessantly by Mrs. Gandhi in which blame for many of the country's problems was placed upon the machinations of outside forces, with the implication that those forces were the United States and/or Pakistan. Objectively, the Punjab insurrection had already begun by 1983 and was to intensify for a full decade thereafter until it was finally terminated in 1993. Problems in Assam and the northeastern part of the country also intensified at this time, notably around the issues of illegal migration from Bangladesh into this region of the country, precipitating violence and mass mobilizations that proved difficult to contain for many years. Although the secessionist movement in Kashmir had not yet begun, changes in political alliances were taking place in which Mrs. Gandhi was directly involved after the death of the most important political leader of Kashmir, Sheikh Abdullah. Within a few years, however, the government was faced, simultaneously, with explicit, violent insurrectionary and secessionist movements in the northeast, Punjab, and Kashmir and with a number of other "violent social conflicts" in other parts of the country as well.[5]

Finally—and closely connected with two of the other differences already mentioned—the former consensus on the ideology of the secular state and political practices associated with it began to break apart. The increased intensity of political competition and the fragility of political coalitions tempted Mrs. Gandhi and later her son, Rajiv, to seek a broader base of support for the Congress through direct appeals to the religious sentiments of Hindus and to the widespread feeling that India was a Hindu country in which the minorities were making excessive demands. This shift was also related to the fact that the insurrectionary movement in Punjab and the developing problems in Kashmir were associated with the demands of minorities, Sikhs in Punjab and Muslims in Kashmir, and that Pakistan was perceived to be behind the problems in both places. The most dramatic instance

[5] Myron Weiner, "Rajiv Gandhi: A Mid-Term Assessment," in Marshall M. Bouton, ed., *India Briefing, 1987* (Boulder, Colo.: Westview, 1987), p. 9.

of this shift took place in 1986 when, in response to a local court decision in the district of Faizabad and to militant Hindu demands, the central government led by Rajiv Gandhi allowed the opening for Hindu worship of the disputed site at Ayodhya occupied for centuries by a Muslim mosque. This shift in Congress attitudes amounted in some respects to a virtual stealing of militant Hindu slogans and appeals previously used exclusively by the BJP. The reponse of the BJP was to associate itself increasingly with the developing mass movement launched by its sister organization, the Vishwa Hindu Parishad (VHP), to remove the Babari Masjid and replace it with a grand new temple to Ram, a movement that culminated in the destruction of the mosque on December 6, 1992, precipitating the riots in Kanpur that are the subject of the final case study in this volume.

Uttar Pradesh and Indian Politics

The critical importance of UP—the state from which all the case studies in this volume have been drawn—should be evident from this brief summary of major changes in Indian politics during the past two decades. The centrality of this state for the issues raised goes even beyond what has already been noted, though politics in some other parts of the country, notably in Bengal and the southern states, diverge considerably from the patterns set in the north.

The origins of contemporary Hindu–Muslim communalism, tension, and violence in India as a whole lie largely within this state and go back to the last quarter of the nineteenth century. Their source lies in the historic dominance of Muslim administrative elites within the province, which was challenged by the rise of new elites from among educated, upper-caste Hindus at that time. Urdu, a language not much different from Hindi except in the script but associated with Muslim dominance, was the official and court language and the language of primary education in the province during British rule. The rising Hindu elites demanded that Hindi replace Urdu as the official language of the province, but succeeded only in 1900 in attaining equal status for Hindi with Urdu;[6] the displacement of Urdu occurred only after Independence.

The language issue became a surrogate for elite competition between the older, privileged Muslim classes and the rising Hindu middle classes. The former, fearing political displacement by the overwhelming Hindu majority in the political life of the province, demanded protection of their privileges, though they framed their demands in specious terms, claiming that they

---

[6] For the history of Hindu–Muslim competition and the Hindi–Urdu language controversy, see Paul R. Brass, *Language, Religion, and Politics in North India* (London: Cambridge University Press, 1974), pt. III.

were "backward" in relation to the rising Hindu educated classes. The leading articulator of Muslim fears and demands was Syed Ahmad Khan, a representative of the Muslim administrative-aristocratic elite, whose ideas and institutions he founded, inspired, and often led from 1875 through the first decade of the twentieth century became the foundation for Muslim political separatism. These institutions included the Aligarh Muslim University founded initially as the Mohammedan Anglo-Oriental College in 1875 and located in Aligarh district in western UP, the Muslim League founded in 1906 in Dacca in Bengal, and several associations for the advancement of Muslim education and the preservation of the status of the Urdu language.

Though the Pakistan Movement was led ultimately by Mohammad Ali Jinnah from Bombay and though Pakistan itself was formed from provinces of British India other than UP, the center of the movement in the 1930s, from which it took off and gained support in the rest of the country, was in UP. Between 1875 and 1947, though there were brief periods of Hindu–Muslim cooperation and though the Indian National Congress always had significant support from both elite and nonelite—and under the restricted franchise of those days nonvoting—Muslim groups, the predominant trend was toward increased political competition and political differentiation between Muslim and Hindu elites. Moreover, these differences sometimes precipitated Hindu–Muslim riots, which now and then also occurred in waves as well as in isolated incidents.[7] Major waves of such riots occurred in the early 1920s and at Independence. One of the most spectacular Hindu–Muslim riots in pre-Independence India was precipitated in part by demands made by Hindu Congress activists for Muslim traders to close their shops as part of the Civil Disobedience Movement in the city of Kanpur in 1931.

This history of elite competition and Hindu–Muslim violence infected the politics of post-Independence India, taking the form especially of resentment among Hindus over the partition of the country, and again it was in the state of UP that the resentment was greatest despite the fact that the partitioned provinces were Punjab and Bengal, not UP. That resentment took concrete form in UP through the adoption of discriminatory policies against Muslims, notably their virtual elimination through restrictive recruitment procedures and other methods from the state police forces in which they had occupied nearly half the posts and the failure to provide in the public schools adequate opportunities for Muslims to be educated through the medium of Urdu. It was also in UP that the leading political organization of militant Hindu na-

---

[7] The numbers of riots in the pre-Independence and early post-Independence years in UP were usually in the hundreds and sometimes in four digits, as indicated by the figures for the following years: 1939, 1,127; 1946, 374; 1947, 467; 1950, 468. The figures cited come from N. S. Saksena, *Communal Riots in India* (Delhi: Trishul, 1990), p. 107; the official source for these figures and the definition of "communal riots" used are not given.

tionalism, the Jan Sangh, had its greatest strength in the 1950s and 1960s, and then again in its reincarnated form as the BJP in the 1980s and 1990s. Although there was considerable resentment within indigenous Hindu opinion in UP after Independence both as a consequence of the history of Hindu –Muslim political relations and the partition of the country, it was reinforced by the migration of Hindu Punjabi and Sindhi refugees from Pakistan into many of the larger cities and towns of the state. These refugees have provided the strongest support for militant Hindu nationalist sentiment and political organization in such towns even though their proportions in them are for the most part less than 5 percent of the total.

When Muslim leaders and organizations arose again in the 1960s in protest against actual and perceived discriminatory policies toward them—once again centered in UP—their demands failed to make significant headway among the contending political parties and a new sequence of vicious communal rioting took place. Though the turning point in the rise of Hindu–Muslim violence in north India occurred in the adjacent state of Madhya Pradesh in the town of Jubbulpore in 1962 and though major riots also occurred in another adjacent state, Bihar, in the 1960s, several western districts of UP also became notorious for riots, including Aligarh in the 1960s and Meerut district somewhat later. It was also in UP that the VHP, formed initially in 1964, launched its Ayodhya movement in the mid-1980s, which bore its final fruit of destruction and violence in the demolition of the mosque known as the Babari Masjid on December 6, 1992.

From what has been said already, it is evident that, despite the centrality of UP in the rise of Hindu–Muslim competition and violence, neither of these circumstances has been confined to this state. Violence was even greater at partition in the provinces of Punjab and Bengal. In the post-Independence period, it extended as well to the adjacent provinces of Bihar and Madhya Pradesh. In recent years, the western state of Gujarat, the metropolis of Bombay, and the southern city of Hyderabad have also experienced extensive Hindu–Muslim rioting. Such competition and violence between Hindus and Muslims did not, however, continue in the Punjab or Bengal and never extended substantially to the southern states. In the case of Punjab, the entire Muslim population was either assigned to or left for Pakistan at the time of partition. In Bengal, the rise and ultimately the dominance of leftist forces, particularly the Communist Party of India (Marxist) (CPM), deflected Hindu–Muslim tensions and focused political competition on economic issues. The southern states, however, have almost never experienced either the elite competition or the Hindu–Muslim violence associated with the north, partly for demographic reasons, partly because of the less privileged position of Muslims in the south in the pre-Independence period, and partly because the organizations of militant Hindu nationalism have never taken hold here, where caste and linguistic issues have been more important than issues pertaining to politicized religious identity. Even in the south, however, communal riots do sometimes take place.[8]

If Hindu–Muslim issues have tended to move outward from their center in north India to other parts of the country, caste issues were more salient earlier in the south and west than in the north. Although conflict between elite castes and those below them in status from among both the lowest and the economically better-off middle castes began earlier in the south and the west, they have gradually become prominent in most of the country with the notable exception again of Bengal and the adjacent state of Orissa. In north India, elite castes retained virtually complete political dominance until the late 1960s. Moreover, it was not until the 1980s that the political dominance of the upper castes was overthrown and the balance turned in favor of the majority of middle and lower castes, especially in the states of UP and Bihar. Indeed, in UP in the late 1980s issues of caste conflict, centering on the question of reservations for the backward castes, acquired an importance as great as that of Hindu–Muslim conflict and spawned considerable violence, though less dramatic in the size and viciousness of the confrontations than that associated with Hindu–Muslim riots.

With regard to caste conflicts, however, UP cannot claim originality. The types of conflicts that have occurred there have had their counterparts all over the country. Some of the most notorious incidents of intercaste violence occurred elsewhere: in Kilvenmani in Tamil Nadu in 1968; in Ahmedabad, the most important city of Gujarat, in 1981 and 1985; in widespread upper-caste protest agitations against reservations policies in Bihar in 1978; in statewide rioting in Andhra Pradesh among backward castes in 1986, also in connection with the issue of reservations; and in countless other incidents recorded in statistics and case materials in the annual reports of the Commissioner for Scheduled Castes and Tribes.[9]

Whether the most important social cleavages originate in UP or come to this state after originating in other parts of the country, there can be no doubt about the pivotal role of this province and its politicians in the political history of post-Independence India and in the construction and framing of controversy on these and other issues. Most of the prime ministers of India since Independence have come from this state, including its first, Ja-

---

[8] Nor are such riots always Hindu–Muslim. A major Christian–Muslim riot occurred among rival fisherfolk in Kerala on May 14, 1995. See K. M. Seethi, "Vizhinjam Riots: Fishing for High Stakes," *Secular India* 1, no. 3 (July–September 1995): 1–6.

[9] There are actually two annual reports with similar titles and terms of reference, concerning which see chap. 5, n. 79 below. They are: *Report of the Commissioner for Scheduled Castes and Scheduled Tribes* and *Report of the Commission for Scheduled Castes and Scheduled Tribes*. The former is published under the office of the commissioner, a constitutionally designated officer. The latter is a publication of a permanent commission established under the Home Ministry of the Government of India.

waharlal Nehru (1947–64); his successor Lal Bahadur Shastri (1964–66); Indira Gandhi (1966–77, 1980–84); Charan Singh for a few weeks in 1979; Rajiv Gandhi (1984–89); and V. P. Singh (1989–91). Only two prime ministers, Morarji Desai (1977–79) and P. V. Narasimha Rao (1991 to the present), have not come from UP.

Among the factors that have contributed to this decisive importance of UP, aside from those already mentioned above, has been the partly circumstantial one that the Nehru family has provided three of the prime ministers. In addition, UP is the largest state in India with a population in 1995 of approximately 130 million people, providing thereby the largest number of members of the Indian Parliament (85 out of 543). The state's proximity to Delhi also must be considered of some significance.

The importance of UP and the other adjacent Hindi-speaking states increased dramatically after the Fourth General Elections in 1967, when the balance of political forces between the ruling Congress and opposition parties first began to change. At that time the Congress, while retaining a tenuous hold on power at the Center, lost its position of political dominance in half the Indian states, including all the northern states, introducing a period of unstable coalition politics in them. In all the subsequent transfers of power since then, the struggle for power in UP in particular and in the rest of the Hindi-speaking states has been critical.

It was principally by means of a grand sweep in the northern states that Indira Gandhi regained Congress dominance in the national Parliament in 1971, winning a two-thirds majority therein, made possible only by capturing 85.6 percent of the seats in the northern states. And it was through a virtually total sweep of 97.6 percent of the seats in the north by the Janata Party that the Congress lost power for the first time at the Center in the post-Emergency election of 1977. Although the 1980 elections produced a somewhat more even distribution of wins and losses in different parts of the country, the centrality of the north became apparent again in Rajiv Gandhi's massive electoral victory in 1984, when the Congress won more than 90 percent of the seats in the north (though even more, above 94 percent, in the smaller western region). Again, in 1989 the victory of the Janata/National Front coalition against the Congress under the leadership of V. P. Singh was made possible principally by victories in the north, where the non-Congress parties won two-thirds of the seats.[10]

Further, the dramatic struggle between Rajiv Gandhi and V. P. Singh, which dominated Indian politics from 1987 until the former's assassination in 1991,[11] was largely centered in UP between these two men, both from this

---

[10] The seat percentages in this paragraph were taken from David Butler et al., *India Decides: Elections 1952–1991*, 2nd ed. (New Delhi: LM Books, 1991), pp. 82–91.

[11] Rajiv Gandhi's assassination had nothing to do with this struggle and has been generally

state. The controversy centered upon charges made by V. P. Singh that the highest leaders in the Congress, including by implication Rajiv Gandhi himself, had taken kickbacks amounting to approximately $50 million in defense contracts awarded to the Swedish Bofors company. In this contest, Rajiv Gandhi sacrificed the Congress organization itself, allying against the party's best interests with the leader of a breakaway faction from the Janata Dal led by Mulayam Singh Yadav, in order to protect himself from the onslaught led by V. P. Singh. The Congress in UP has as a result been decimated, reduced to third position among the major parties in UP politics, behind the two leading contenders for power in that state, the SP of Mulayam Singh Yadav and the BJP.

The destruction of the Congress organization in UP has by no means lessened the centrality of the issues and controversies generated therein for the future of Indian politics. If anything, it has increased them, for it has been here since 1989 especially that issues of caste and communal conflict affecting much of the rest of the country have been generated. It was here that the controversial decision made by Prime Minister V. P. Singh in August 1989 to reserve 27 percent of places in central sector jobs for backward classes generated the most intense opposition and it was here also that the Ayodhya movement was launched by the BJP and the VHP in an effort to counteract the political advantage expected to accrue to their political rivals by this move.

COMPETITIVE POLITICS IN UP

A multiplicity of parties have contended for political power in the state's politics since Independence. For purposes of placing the case studies in this volume, it is not necessary to present a detailed analysis of party/electoral competition during the past forty-five years, but several broad trends in those patterns need to be kept in mind. In order to present this history in a coherent manner, a great deal of simplification is required. For that purpose, it will be convenient to divide patterns of political competition in the state into a few periods and the strongest contending forces into three groups.

The first period in the state's history was one of Congress dominance, which lasted from 1952 until 1967. In this period, the Congress governed the state alone. The principal opposition forces consisted of several parties of the Left, whose combined vote percentages ranged from 14 percent to 22 percent, on the one side, and the militant Hindu parties, whose vote shares ranged from 8 percent to 22 percent, on the other side of the Congress. By 1967 the Jan Sangh was the only remaining party of this type and had be-

---

attributed, though there has not yet been a court ruling, to militants acting on behalf of the Liberation Tigers of Tamil Eelam, the Tamil secessionist movement in Sri Lanka.

come by far the largest opposition party in the state, holding 98 seats in a legislative assembly containing 425 members.

The second period in the state's political history begins with the downfall of the Congress in the aftermath of the 1967 General Elections with the defection of Chaudhuri Charan Singh—a man from the backward Jat caste and a spokesman for the interests of the middle peasants—from the Congress with a small group of followers, his selection as the first non-Congress chief minister in the state, and the formation of a strong new force of opposition to the Congress under his leadership. From 1967 until 1971, the state's politics was marked by the alternation in power of unstable government coalitions led by either Charan Singh's party or the Congress. Although the Congress restored its dominant position in the state in 1971 and maintained it until 1977, this period is marked by a more intense competition for power between the Congress and its principal rival, an agrarian party under Charan Singh's leadership, which went through several changes of name, of which the best known is the Lok Dal. By 1974 the Lok Dal had absorbed all the principal parties of the Left. In this period, the rise of the Lok Dal took place largely at the expense of independents and the Jan Sangh. The Lok Dal displaced the Jan Sangh as the principal party of opposition in the elections of 1969 and 1974. Between 1971 and 1974, however, divisions among the opposition prevented the formation of any coalition that could displace the Congress from power in the state.

The Emergency regime between 1975 and 1977 had a profound effect on the state's politics in the succeeding years, but it did not change the basic form of political competition. In the elections of 1977, all the important opposition forces in the state disbanded their separate organizations and joined together in a new party called the Janata Party, which defeated the Congress at the Center and in the province as well. The principal source of support for the Janata Party in UP, however, as for the Lok Dal, continued to come from the middle peasant castes, middle both in the size of their economic holdings and in their ritual status. Divisions within the Janata Party, nevertheless, especially between the former Lok Dal and the former Jan Sangh elements, made it impossible to prevent the return of the Congress to power at both the Center and in the state in the 1980 elections. The Congress remained in power in New Delhi and in Lucknow, the state capital, until 1989.

The third phase in the pattern of competitive politics in UP begins with the defection of V. P. Singh from the Congress in 1987 on the Bofors issue and his formation of a new Janata coalition similar to the one formed in 1977, with the notable exception that the party of militant Hindu nationalism, now re-formed as the BJP, chose to maintain its separate identity and freedom of action. Charan Singh in the meantime had died and the forces that had owed loyalty to him now joined with V. P. Singh. The Janata Dal came to power at the Center in the 1989 elections with V. P. Singh as prime minister and in UP in the same year under Chief Minister Mulayam Singh Yadav, a man from the Yadav caste, the largest backward caste in the state.

During the two-year period in which V. P. Singh was prime minister, the foundations were laid for a new pattern of competitive politics at both the Center and in the province. The struggle between V. P. Singh and Rajiv Gandhi, noted above, ended with the latter's assassination in the midst of the Tenth General Elections in May 1991, but not before the destruction in the process of the primacy of the Congress in the state's politics. Since 1991, therefore, the pattern of political competition in UP has been completely transformed into a struggle for power between relatively evenly balanced political forces, the SP led by Mulayam Singh Yadav and the BJP, with the Congress reduced to third place. The BJP succeeded in capturing power in UP in the 1991 state legislative assembly elections, after which Kalyan Singh became chief minister. He remained chief minister long enough to preside over the destruction of the mosque at Ayodhya, after which the central government dismissed the BJP from power, imposed central rule upon the state, and called for new state elections in 1993. In those elections, the SP and the BJP each won nearly the same number of seats in the Legislative Assembly, 176 for the SP and 177 for the BJP. The SP, however, had an alliance with a party representing the Scheduled Castes, known as the BSP, and was able to form the government.

Two issues formed the focus of controversy and competition in the state's politics as well as at the Center in these years after 1989: the rise of the backward castes and the Scheduled Castes to power with their demands for increased representation in public sector positions, including the police, and the polarization of Hindu–Muslim relations over the issue of the status of the mosque at Ayodhya. Insofar as the latter is concerned, Mulayam Singh Yadav and Kalyan Singh, representing their opposed formations, stood symbolically at opposite sides of the ramparts of the mosque. Mulayam Singh Yadav, chief minister at the time, ordered a police firing on the Hindu mobs that gathered in October 1989 in the first attempted assault on the mosque. Kalyan Singh, in complete contrast, ordered the withdrawal of police forces from the scene of the assault on December 6, 1992, which made possible the mosque's destruction. Mulayam Singh's advocacy of the interests of the backward castes and his defense of the mosque made it possible for him and his party, in alliance with the BSP, to establish a voting coalition comprising backward castes, low castes, and Muslims. The BJP, for its part, has drawn the bulk of its support from the elite castes of Brahmans and Thakurs, who formerly supported the Congress, and from some segments of the backward castes. Since there was little prospect for a shift in Muslim support while BJP strength among the upper castes also remained strong, the principal electoral struggle in this period was for advantage among the backward castes and Scheduled Castes, who form the majority of the population of the state.

ON THE INCIDENCE OF VIOLENCE IN INDIAN POLITICS

The changes described in Indian and UP politics during the past decades have been associated with marked increases in public and political violence, including the increasing use of a multiplicity of armed forces in addition to the civilian and armed constabulary to control them. These changes have occurred in most of the Indian states, not only in those like Assam, Punjab, and Kashmir, which have undergone sustained insurrectionary movements for a decade or more in which tens of thousands of persons have been killed in each. Moreover, there appears to be an association between the rising incidence of violence and the state of political competition in the country and in its several states. In India as a whole, the incidence of political violence, defined as the number of riots per million persons in the population, remained low and relatively stable during the long period of Congress political dominance after Independence until the Fourth General Elections of 1967. Thereafter, there was a sharp rise, continuing upward with little fluctuation until the imposition of an authoritarian regime during the Emergency between 1975 and 1977. Even in this period, however, although there was a steep drop in the incidence of riots, their numbers did not go down to the relatively low level of the earlier post-Independence years. After the relaxation of the Emergency, on the other hand, the incidence of riots showed a steep upward trend until 1985, the last year for which figures are available.[12]

Although the levels of violence in particular periods vary from state to state, the general trend has been both upward and clearly associated with the intensity of political competition in each state.[13] One notable exception to the former tendency, but clearly consistent with the latter, has been the sharp decline in violence in West Bengal, after reaching a peak in 1970. This decline occurred initially as a consequence of a campaign of "state terror" against "revolutionary groups," whose members were largely eliminated between 1971 and 1977, but was associated thereafter with the consolidation of power in the state under the CPM.[14]

Insofar as UP is concerned, the overall crime rate as well as the incidence of riots has often been higher than one would expect from its population proportion in the country. For example, in 1970, UP, with a population proportion of 16 percent, accounted for 24.5 percent of all cognizable crime

[12] See the figure in Atul Kohli, *Democracy and Discontent: India's Growing Crisis of Governability* (Cambridge: Cambridge University Press, 1990), p. 7.

[13] See the figures for Bihar and Gujarat in Kohli, *Democracy and Discontent,* pp. 215 and 245.

[14] Kohli, *Democracy and Discontent,* pp. 274–75.

in the country.[15] Its largest city, Kanpur, had the second largest "volume of crime" per 100,000 population after the much larger city of Delhi in the same year and was unrivalled among India's largest cities in the high volume of registered "offences under the Arms Act."[16] Insofar as riots are concerned, defined officially as "an unlawful assembly" of 5 or more persons,[17] their percentage growth moved steadily upward in the decade of intensified political/electoral competition between 1960 and 1970, increasing by 154.1 percent over the decade compared to a population increase of only 27.4 percent.[18] Furthermore, the volume of riot crimes in UP in 1970, at 15.4 per 100,000 population, was higher than the average, 12.5, for the country as a whole in 1970.[19]

Table 2.1 and figure 2.1 show the trend in the absolute numbers of riots for years for which figures have been available to me from 1948 to 1991.[20] These figures suggest a general upward trend, actually rather moderate on the whole, but marked by clear breaks in the decades of the 1960s and 1980s and by a very sharp increase in the year 1970. The increase in the 1960s is associated with both a rise in Muslim political assertiveness and Hindu–Muslim riots, on the one hand, and with intensified political competition, on the other hand, in the period of unstable coalition politics in the late 1960s and early 1970s. Further peaks in riotous activities occur in the years between the relaxation of the Emergency in 1977 and the return of the Congress and Mrs. Gandhi to power in 1980. The latter peak is followed by a substantial leveling off from 1981 on, the highest peak of riot violence being reached in this decade in 1990, the year of the *rath yatra* of L. K. Advani and the riots associated with that bloody journey. Insofar as the figures can be trusted—and there are many good reasons not to[21]—it would appear on the face of it that, despite the publicity given to the waves of riots that occurred in the late 1980s as the intensity of the Ayohdya movement in-

[15] Government of India, Bureau of Police Research and Development, Ministry of Home Affairs, *Crime in India, 1970* (New Delhi: Government of India Press, 1972), p. 5.

[16] Ibid., 1970, p. 34.

[17] Saksena, *Communal Riots in India*, p. 110.

[18] *Crime in India, 1970*, p. 32.

[19] Ibid., p. 89.

[20] The gap in the data between between 1970 and 1979 should be especially noted when examining figures 2.1 and 2.2.

[21] Among the more important reasons are that enforcement of the riot act varies and underreporting of riot activity is probably common. For example, when Charan Singh was either home minister or chief minister (the latter in 1967–68 and 1970) in the state in the 1960s, district officers were instructed to report all "cognizable offences by any processions, political or otherwise," as a consequence of which the reporting of riots went up drastically from 1969 to 1970. However, this more strict accounting was then followed by more rigid enforcement, leading to a great drop in the number of riots. On these points, see Saksena, *Communal Riots in India*, p. 110.

TABLE 2.1

Absolute Numbers of Riots and Numbers per 100,000
Population for Uttar Pradesh, for Available Years, 1948–1991

Year	Number	Number per 100,000 Population
1948	3,514	5.7
1949	3,722	6.0
1950	3,770	6.0
1951	3,408	5.5
1952	3,281	5.1
1953	2,975	4.6
1954	3,110	4.7
1955	2,795	4.2
1956	3,087	4.5
1957	3,002	4.3
1958	3,045	4.3
1959	2,900	4.1
1960	2,743	3.6
1961	4,856	6.5
1962	6,057	8.0
1963	5,997	7.8
1964	6,094	7.8
1965	6,057	7.6
1966	6,540	8.0
1967	7,116	8.6
1968	7,114	8.4
1969	7,337	8.6
1970	14,015	16.1
1979	12,663	12.3
1980	14,611	26.5
1981	10,136	9.1
1982	10,027	8.8
1983	9,016	7.7
1986	10,135	8.3
1988	9,411	7.3
1989	9,818	7.4
1990	11,696	8.7
1991	10,317	7.4

Sources: 1948–65: Uttar Pradesh, *Report of the Uttar Pradesh Police Commission, 1970–71* (Allahabad: Superintendent, Printing and Stationery, UP, 1972), p. 12; 1966–70: Uttar Pradesh, Pulis Mukhyalay, *Varshik Pulis Prashasan Riport, varsh 1970* (Allabahad: Government Press, 1980), p. 188; 1979–91: Government of India, Ministry of Home Affairs, Bureau of Police Research and Development, *Crime in India, 1979 . . . 1991* (Nasik: Government of India Press, 1983–92); after 1983, the issuing authority changes to Government of India, Ministry of Home Affairs, National Crime Records Bureau.

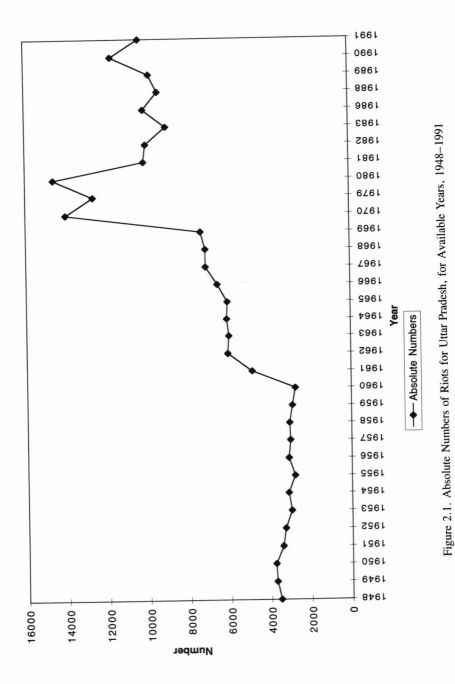

Figure 2.1. Absolute Numbers of Riots for Uttar Pradesh, for Available Years, 1948–1991

creased and strife occurred on the issue of backward-caste reservations, rioting in this period did not reach the highs attained in 1970, 1979, and 1980.
Moreover, when the data are transformed to a proportion related to the population of the state, the level of riot activity appears stable throughout the
entire decade, 1981–91 and roughly comparable to the level of the 1960s
(table 2.1 and figure 2.2).

Using the same compilation of riot data, but for the period 1979–91 only,
table 2.2 and figure 2.3 show riot activity for the five districts from which
the case studies for this volume have been drawn. For the most part, the
figures for these districts show a similar trend line from 1979 to 1991 to that
for the state as a whole, namely a downward trend after the peak of riotous
activity recorded in 1980. They also show a similar rise in 1990, most spectacular in Kanpur city. These figures also allow for some discrimination
among districts, showing—in conformity with expectations based upon the
known incidence of large-scale Hindu–Muslim riots—Aligarh, Meerut and
Kanpur with much higher recorded numbers of riots compared to Gonda and
Deoria, which lack large urban centers.

It needs to be kept in mind that these figures for the state as a whole and
for the districts encompass minor noncommunal fracases as well as large-
scale communal riots so that that they cannot tell us much about the latter,
for which a different series of figures are required. Figures are available for
communal riots in UP for its largest cities and towns.[22] According to one
compilation, there were 115 such riots between 1950 and 1990. In rank
order, the largest number have occurred in Meerut (21), Aligarh (18), Allahabad (10), Moradabad (9), Varanasi (9), and Kanpur (6). These towns
range in population from 272,000 in the case of Ghaziabad to 2.1 million in
Kanpur, the state's largest city. The proportion of Muslims in the population
of these cities ranges from 9 percent in Ghaziabad to 49 percent in Moradabad. The districts in which the largest number of riots have occurred,
some 77 out of the total of 115, are heavily concentrated in the western part
of the state, with the greatest concentration in the westernmost Upper Doab
districts of Meerut (21), Aligarh (18), Moradabad (10), and Ghaziabad (8).
Although analysis of variance for riot-prone and non-riot-prone cities in UP
"explains" much of it in terms of the proportion of the Muslim population,
the proportion of Hindu refugees from Pakistan, and the proportion of artisa-
nal occupations, there remain as always in such attempts to provide ecological explanations a substantial proportion of the variance unexplained as well
as notable individual exceptions. Most important in relation to my argument
concerning institutionalized riot systems, analysis of variance cannot explain

---

[22] These figures come from an unpublished paper by Steven I. Wilkinson, "What Large
Datasets Can Tell Us about the General Explanations for Communal Riots," delivered at the
annual meetings of the Association for Asian Studies, Washington, D.C., April 1995.

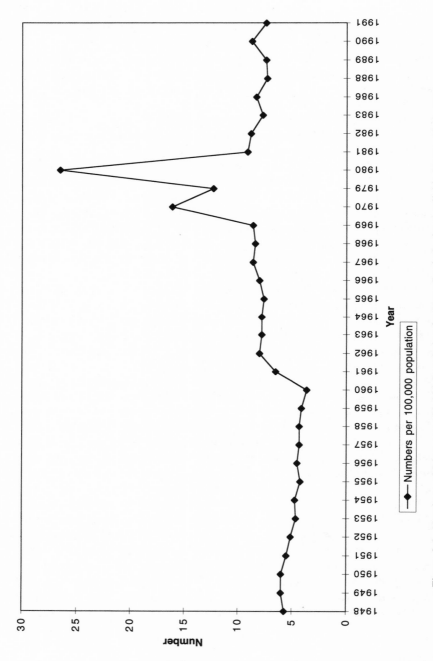

Figure 2.2. Numbers of Riots per 100,000 Population for Uttar Pradesh, for Available Years, 1948–1991

TABLE 2.2
Absolute Numbers of Riots for Five Districts of Uttar Pradesh, 1979–1991

Year	Aligarh	Meerut	Deoria	Gonda	Kanpur City
1979	325	405	363	354	NA
1980	559	386	349	301	581
1981	301	345	160	197	NA
1982	293	345	84	187	249
1983	289	249	119	156	228
1986	270	380	142	257	279
1988	293	425	124	202	189
1989	321	390	131	234	174
1990	430	345	227	632	332
1991	418	456	220	203	233

Sources: As for table 2.1.

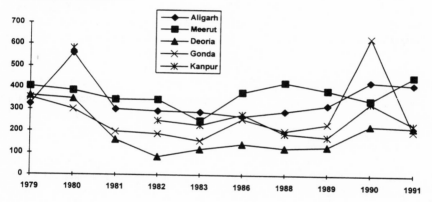

Figure 2.3. Absolute Numbers of Riots for Five Districts of Uttar Pradesh, 1979–1991

why riots have become endemic in cities such as Meerut and Aligarh, among others, while other cities and towns with ecological characteristics even more favorable for riots have experienced far fewer such riots or none at all.

A NOTE ON THE POLICE AND THE ARMED FORCES

The police figure prominently in all the case studies in this volume and paramilitary and military forces also come into the picture in two of them. A few words are necessary, therefore, to describe the organization, personnel, and roles of the various police and other armed forces in India.

There are two principal police forces in the Indian states, under the jurisdiction and command of the state and district governments. The first, the civilian police, are normally unarmed except for a baton or the Indian bamboo stick known as a *lathi*.[23] In times of civil disturbance, they will be provided with arms which, however, they may not use to control crowds except in self-defense or under the orders of higher police or civilian authority. In most large-scale disturbances or riots, another force is available, stationed at several locations in different parts of the state and increasingly in recent years stationed permanently in the cantonment areas of cities that are considered to be riot-prone. This force is known in UP as the Provincial Armed Constabulary (PAC). The two forces are separate, organized into distinct hierarchies, and "recruited and trained separately."[24]

In Uttar Pradesh, the strength of the police force in 1960 was 64,874, of whom 25,050 were armed (that is, mostly the PAC) and 39,824 civil or unarmed police.[25] By 1983 the force had doubled to 137,259 persons, of which 54,807 were armed police and 82,452 were civil police.[26] By 1987, the last year for which figures are available, the total strength of the combined armed and civil police had reached 156,000.[27] The state's population increased from 74 million in 1960 to nearly 111 million in 1985, that is, by 50 percent compared to an increase of 140 percent in police strength in the same period. Although the police force has, therefore, increased much more rapidly than the population of this state, its size is not disproportionate to the forces maintained in other states and in the country as a whole. In fact, UP maintains only 15 percent of the country's police force compared to its population proportion of 17 percent.

In India's federal system, control, recruitment, and supervision of the police are state functions. The hierarchy runs down from the inspector-general of police for the state as a whole, to a number of deputy-inspector generals (DIGs) responsible for different police departments, to DIGs responsible for a division of the state comprising a number of districts,[28] to the police officers within each of the fifty-six districts of the state. Within the district, the chief police officer is the senior superintendent of police (SSP), under whom there will be several deputy SPs (DySPs) in charge of subdivisions of each district. Each district is also divided into a number of police circles in each of which there are several *thana*s or police stations. The head

---

[23] David H. Bayley, *The Police and Political Development in India* (Princeton, N.J.: Princeton University Press, 1969), p. 59.

[24] Ibid.

[25] Ibid., p. 64.

[26] Government of India, Ministry of Planning, Department of Statistics, Central Statistical Organization, *Statistical Abstract India* (New Delhi: Government of India Press, 1988), p. 518.

[27] R. K. Raghavan, *Indian Police: Problems, Planning and Perspectives* (Delhi: Manohar, 1989), app. I.

[28] Bayley, *Police*, pp. 76–77.

of a police circle holds the rank of inspector. The *thana* head is known as the station officer or station house officer (SO or SHO) and has the rank of subinspector.[29] At the bottom of the hierarchy, comprising the bulk of the force, are the constables. There is a further level of village police known as *chowkidar*s, who reside in the villages in which they serve and have little responsibility or control, acting for the most part as watchmen.[30]

Recruitment and posting of district police are done at the district level under the authority of the SSP. Although there is considerable local political interest in and influence over this process, the police are not, as in the United States, directly accountable to the community and its elected officials. The senior police officers are drawn from an all-India service, the Indian Police Service (IPS), recruited like the Indian Administrative Service (IAS) through national competitive examination. The great majority of these senior officers, like their IAS counterparts, are highly educated persons from upper-class and upper-caste urban families, who give the appearance of considerable urbanity, intellect, and broad-ranging interests. There is a substantial decline in the level of education, class background, and to some extent also caste in the lower ranks. There is also a corresponding decline, very dramatic, in the level of pay and perquisites. The senior officers in the state capital and in the districts are part of the uppermost elite of society, while the constables in the *thana*s, though not usually from the lowest castes, come from much more diverse caste backgrounds, from low-income to very poor families, and are inadequately paid and provided with few decent facilities at the stations where they not only serve, but eat, sleep, and bathe, separated from their families, who are likely to remain in the villages from which they come.[31]

Recruitment procedures for each rank are different. Officers and constables are recruited into specific ranks. Below the senior IPS ranks, deputy superintendents are appointed by the public service commissions within their home state, whereas inspectors and constables are appointed by the district authorities. There is very little movement between ranks. A constable generally remains in his rank throughout his career and can aspire only to the position of head constable.[32]

The Indian police have a popular reputation for bribery, corruption, incrimination of innocent persons in false cases, failure to pursue charges against known criminals, commission of acts of violence and rape in the police stations, routine torture of persons suspected of crimes, gratuitous or undisciplined attacks upon crowds gathered for public demonstrations, com-

[29] Ibid., pp 77–78.
[30] Ibid., p. 73.
[31] Ibid., pp. 92–93.
[32] Ibid., pp. 81, 88, 95–96.

plicity with criminals, and partiality on the side of Hindus in Hindu–Muslim communal riots.[33] There is ample evidence from newspaper reports, scholarly accounts, reports of international human rights agencies,[34] and this author's personal knowledge and observations to support all these charges, though there is no way of providing statistical evidence for them. It is certain, however, that most of these acts are widespread and many of them are routine. This does not, however, mean that, in all circumstances, it can be assumed that the charges made against particular police personnel or the force as a whole in a particular disturbance are likely to be correct.[35] The police often does its duty creditably, particularly when senior police and administrative officers and higher political authorities demand it. The case studies presented in this volume provide evidence for police misbehavior, but also present cases in which the police behaved in a more commendable fashion than their critics among the press and the politicians.

The relationship between politicians and the police in this environment is purposefully ambiguous. That is to say, little is done to correct the objective circumstances under which policemen serve or to professionalize the force in such a way as to provide incentives for good—that is to say, professional—conduct rather than bad or unprofessional conduct. Politicians, particularly at the local level, prefer rather to bring the police under their control and to use them for their own purposes.[36] Those purposes are both material and rhetorical.

It is necessary—increasingly so in recent years—for local politicians in the countryside and even in the cities and towns to be able to protect themselves and their supporters from police depredations and to direct police power against their enemies when necessary. Such use of the police ranges from providing evidence to local politicians of alleged criminal activities of one's rivals to be used against them in electoral campaigns to allowing harassment and intimidation of one's opponents and their supporters during elections and at other times as well. It includes also failing "to protect one side from criminal attacks of the other" or failing "to take action against known criminals sheltering under the wing of a powerful individual."[37] There is, therefore, a direct and deliberate policy on the part of politicians to

---

[33] Ibid., pp. 367–68; and Barnett R. Rubin, "The Civil Liberties Movement in India: New Approaches to the State and Social Change," *Asian Survey* 27, no. 3 (March 1987): 387–88.

[34] See, for example, Rubin, "The Civil Liberties Movement in India," pp. 376–82, citing reports of the Peoples Union for Civil Liberties (PUCL), based in New Delhi, and also numerous publications in recent years on police misbehavior in India published by Human Rights Watch in its Asia Watch Reports.

[35] Bayley, *Police*, p. 376.

[36] Paul R. Brass, "National Power and Local Politics in India: A Twenty-Year Perspective," in Paul R. Brass, *Caste, Faction and Party in Indian Politics*, vol. 1: *Faction and Party* (Delhi: Chanakya, 1984), pp. 191–226.

[37] Bayley, *Police*, pp. 382–83.

use the forces in these ways rather than to even consider a drastic change in their working conditions and emoluments.[38]

A corrupt and dangerous police force also provides indirect benefits to politicians, who find it convenient to use charges of police brutality, "injustice, exactions, and stupidities"[39] as a rhetorical device to condemn their rivals in power at the state and national levels. Although one would think that the politicians would find it in their mutual interest to bring the police to account to civilian authority in general rather than to risk the dangers associated with their becoming partial to one's rivals, the dynamics of contemporary Indian politics do not allow it. That struggle has become so barren of debate or concern on matters of public policy, so oriented to the collection of corrupt income and to the distribution of patronage, favors, appointments, contracts, and the like, that most politicians cannot imagine an alternative. In this struggle, control over the police is one of the most important prizes.

The police and the politicians both know the rules of the game. Although some police are demoralized by them, most accept and most as well probably willingly abide by them. In this way, the politicians benefit materially when they are in power and find it useful to be able to condemn their rivals for failing to control the police when they are out of power, while the police themselves are permitted to make a living through their exactions from the public they are supposed to serve.[40] These practices were common enough even in the 1960s, but they became even more pronounced and more vicious during and since the Emergency,[41] in association with the general intensification of political competition and its debasement, which has been noted above.

In the countryside, within each district, there are likely to be one or several powerful politicians with wide political influence throughout a district or a large part of it. These persons are apt to play important roles in the ap-

---

[38] Bayley considers that the politicians are "captives" of the changed circumstances of the past decades, that is, "the decline in the capacity and discipline of the Indian police force," "the insecurity of the people in a climate of perceived lawlessness," and "grass-roots manipulation of criminal justice." In these circumstances, he argues, the politicians "do what they can to use the police and courts to provide constituents with a modicum of safety and advantage" (Bayley, *Police*, p. 495). Although I agree with his excellent description and analysis of the objective conditions pertaining to the police, the status of law and order, and the nature of political manipulation, I believe that all are complicit in the circumstances, creators of them, rather than their captives.

[39] Bayley, *Police*, p. 367.

[40] Robert Wade reports that, as in other departments of government in India, postings to police stations "are auctioned" and that bids are made by "officers of relevant rank" according to the amount of corrupt income that each station is likely to generate ("The Market for Public Office: Why the Indian State Is Not Better at Development," *World Development* 13, no. 4 [April 1985]: 477).

[41] Bayley, "The Police and Political Order," p. 485.

pointment and posting of constables, subinspectors, and station officers and may also have considerable influence with the senior police personnel. Individual members of the state legislative assembly (MLAs) also are likely to have such influence within their constituencies.[42] In urban areas also, there are powerful persons with influence in an entire town or city and local politicians, members of the municipal and town councils, who seek to maintain good relations with and control over the actions of the police in their areas.

Although there is a high degree of local control over the police, the state government, too, has a strong interest in district affairs and considerable powers over the district police through its senior officers. That control comes directly from the highest level of the state government, that is to say, from the home minister, a portfolio so important that it is almost always nowadays taken by the chief minister of the state.[43] The principal sanction available to the home minister is transfer of the senior officers to less lucrative or otherwise less attractive postings.

Transfers of station officers are likely to be made through the actions of locally powerful persons. The politicization of the police administration in a context of increased political competition has become so intense that such transfers are frequent. It is rare for a senior district police officer to serve more than a year in a district and for a station officer to serve more than six months in a *thana*.[44] Disciplining of senior officers almost never occurs, though very mild forms of disciplinary actions are sometimes taken against constables and inspectors, usually involving no more than temporary suspension or removal of the officer to the police lines, that is, removal from any posting temporarily.

Although Bayley reports that "IPS officers speak passionately about the corrupting effects of politics"[45] and I have heard similar reports in my own research, all know the rules of the game and make their choices accordingly. Indeed, the complicity of the police in the nexus of relations between them and the politicians is made possible by two operative conditions: the opportunity for corrupt income and the knowledge that, though they will be subject to abuse and condemnation by those politicians against whom they run afoul, the sanctions that can be exercised against them are minimal and their chance will come again quite soon.[46] The police in turn use the politicians

---

[42] Bayley, *Police*, p. 371.

[43] Bayley, "The Police and Political Order," p. 487.

[44] Ibid.

[45] Ibid., p. 488.

[46] Bayley has noted the existence of strains in the state police forces between the officers recruited through the state services and those recruited into the IPS. As a consequence of these strains, in 1980 eight of the Indian states "had formally asked that no more IPS officers be sent to them." Bayley's interpretation of this request is consistent with my own observations concerning the mututal dependence of state and local politicians and the police, for he views these

"to obtain choice postings"—that is to say, ones that provide the potential for significant corrupt income—to avoid unfavorable postings, to protect them when they are charged with violations of their duties, and to obtain promotions.[47]

The increased intensity, frequency, and scale of much of the group violence that has been occurring in north India in recent years, at the same time that the police have become undisciplined and untrustworthy, has contributed to the diversification and expansion of the police and paramilitary forces available for use in quelling domestic disorders. The first resort after the police have failed or after a disturbance has proved too massive or dangerous to be left in the hands of even a disciplined police force is the Provincial Armed Constabulary. This force, however, though it does not have the opportunities available to the regular police for corruption, has developed a reputation for even greater viciousness, brutality, and partiality, especially in confrontation with students and during Hindu–Muslim riots. Increasingly, therefore, in large-scale disturbances, the PAC's presence tends to increase rather than reduce the scale of violence, to be associated with its spread rather than its containment. The next step, therefore, is often the calling in of military forces. When such forces are called up in north India, the public generally refers to them as the army or, in Hindi, as the *fauj*. Often, the army is in fact brought in from the nearest command post, but sometimes the paramilitary or semimilitary forces, such as the Border Security Force (BSF) or the Central Reserve Police Force (CRPF), are sent. These and numerous other such forces have both proliferated and increased in size and in their use by the central and state governments during the past two or three decades.[48]

---

efforts, which did not succeed, as a further move toward "the politicization of the rule of law, representing a putative alliance between state-level politicians and police officials that would cement rather than weaken their mutual dependence" (Bayley, "The Police and Political Order," p. 493).

[47] Bayley, *Police*, p. 377.

[48] Stephen P. Cohen, "The Military," in Henry C. Hart, ed., *Indira Gandhi's India: A Political System Reappraised* (Boulder, Colo.: Westview, 1976), pp. 223–24; see also Stephen P. Cohen, "The Military and Indian Democracy," in Atul Kohli, ed., *India's Democracy: An Analysis of Changing State–Society Relations* (Princeton, N.J.: Princeton University Press, 1987); and Henry C. Hart, "Introduction," in Hart, *Indira Gandhi's India*, p. 18.

Chapter 3

THEFT OF AN IDOL

I BEGIN with an incident that took place in village Pachpera[1] in the district of Aligarh in western Uttar Pradesh (UP), an incident involving many ambiguities and a multiplicity of conflicting interpretations. However, I begin with this incident not because of its labyrinthine complexity, in which it may not be different from many others of its type, but because it did not undergo the process of acquiring an official, accepted public interpretation. It was not integrated as a major symbol into any of the larger narrative frameworks that clutter the battlefield of contemporary Indian society, though interpretations were offered locally that did fit several of them.

The incident was certainly big enough in terms of the numbers of persons involved, its character as a confrontation between police and people, the backward-caste status of the villagers involved, and the violence inflicted to warrant national attention. Yet it did not receive such attention. I ask why it did not and what we can learn from the fact that it did not about the nature of local violence in contemporary north India, the process of contextualization, power relations in the countryside, and the battle of discourses that rages in a country whose local, "traditional" societies, communities, castes, and religions have been perceived for two centuries as undergoing processes of "modernization," Westernization, nationalism, and the penetration of universalistic legal, judicial, and administrative norms to the rural areas under the aegis of the modern bureaucratic state.

THE TEXT

In July 1983, in connection with my fieldwork in Aligarh district in western UP, I learned from conversation with the local authorities that a violent incident involving the police and the inhabitants of village Pachpera had taken place a few months before. I decided to include this incident in my field research and proceeded to visit the village and other places in the surrounding area in search of persons who could provide me with an account of it. I succeeded in locating and interviewing ten persons who had some personal knowledge of or involvement in the incident and/or the events preced-

---

[1] To preserve confidentiality, the names of the sites and persons involved in this case and of my respondents have been changed. However, in the interests of authenticity, I have not altered the name of the district.

ing it. Those interviews constitute the text for this incident and comprise everything I was able to discover about it.

After constructing the text from my interviews and in the course of going through them to "make sense" of them, my natural social science instinct to turn the interviews into a coherent account of power relations and political conflict in the north Indian countryside were deflected by the discordance of the voices that interpreted the event for me. It was not merely what one might ordinarily expect from any incident involving criminal actions and violence, namely, that people would seek to defend themselves and blame others, but that the very idioms used by different persons to describe the events surrounding the incident and the contexts in which they were placed differed. It appeared to me, in fact, that some of the voices came from entirely different systems of thought, involving different interpretations of human motivation.

At the same time, none of the voices spoke in isolation from the others. Each was aware of the existence of entirely different voices, anticipated the reactions of others, and responded to them. Moreover, people were able to switch voices as well, perhaps even to use one voice to justify actions that they knew would not stand the scrutiny of a different interpretation. In effect, therefore, the different interpretations interpenetrated each other and masqueraded as well, sometimes using one for a mask of defense or attack against another. It was at this point that I recalled Foucault's introduction to *I, Pierre Rivière* and began to think that, rather than seek only to provide my own coherent account and interpretation of the incident at Pachpera, it might provide more insight into conflict and power relations in the north Indian countryside and into the interpretation of acts of violence in India generally to follow out the several conflicting interpretations and to underscore the extent to which Indian society and politics remain after two centuries of British rule and four decades of "modernization" and economic development a battlefield of competing discourses, systems of thought, and relations of domination.

Although I think I figured out who the culprits were in this incident, my broader conclusions concern what the incident and the events surrounding it suggest about rural power relations in north India as well as the various uses of rhetoric and competing frameworks of meaning to "explain," cast blame for, avoid blame for, and so on, an event that was, after all—even if there was a conspiracy in the climax—merely an occurrence arising out of a series of individual and group actions by many people operating from diverse motives and with a multiplicity of goals in a context of ongoing struggle for power, wealth, and safety in the north Indian countryside.[2] I have tried both

---

[2] This statement itself suggests the origins of my own thinking about events such as these. I have become accustomed by disciplinary training and personal beliefs to view politics in this

to interpret the text and to step back from it. In the interpretation, I suspect I do little more than fall into a trap of one or another of the power relations in the countryside and become a party on one side or another. Only by stepping back—and I doubt I have stepped back far enough—can one hope to discern the map of discourses that litter the battlefield of contemporary Indian society.

In the text concerning the incident at Pachpera, there appear to be five discrete narrative frameworks, though they all interpenetrate each other and masquerade in various forms. The police and the local administration confront the *faith* of the villagers, who claim they found an idol and proceeded to worship it, with an account that assumes they were motivated by the desire for *profit*. In the perspective of profit or *interest*, faith is a cover behind which the villagers hid their theft of the idol for the sake of money. The villagers and their advocates defend them with a rhetoric of simplicity and faith. The politicians involved in this incident used a standpoint of *justice* to justify their own intervention in the case, whereas others said they were merely pursuing power and profit. The police used the discourse of *caste and community* to attack the politicians, seeing behind their interventions ostensibly for the sake of justice prejudiced involvement on behalf of their own caste or community or the castes or communities to which they were tied. They also used the concepts of *law and order* and *criminality* to attack the people who, they claimed, were far from innocent victims but were rather members of a group with a long history of criminal activity.

We have, therefore, a constructed text concerning an incident of violence in a village in Aligarh district. The method to be followed below involves three stages of analysis. In the first, I scrutinize the text, showing that embedded in it are a multiplicity of voices, contextualizations, and explanations, none of which serve adequately by themselves to illuminate the events, but instead serve as foils for each other.

In the second stage, I reexamine the text, the event described, at two levels. At one level, I reconstruct it as if I were a detective investigating the case and treat the competing explanations as smokescreens to hide the secret motives and devious behavior of all the participants and to identify those responsible for the violent finale. On the second level, I put on my social science hat and treat these events as just one set among many others within the ongoing struggle for power and influence in the countryside among identifiable social and political groups. In this mode, I delineate the interrelationships among the cooperating and competing individuals and groups, arguing that the events themselves have no special significance outside their local

---

Laswellian vein as a struggle for "who gets what, when, and how." The text and my interpretation of it, therefore, have to be seen also in the light of these kinds of assumptions that I bring to it.

context. That is, they are not unique, merely a violent sample of patterns of behavior and interaction that are part of everyday life in north India.

Finally, I conclude by questioning my own reconstructions. I argue that no explanation, including that of the outside "objective" observer or the impartial judge, can capture fully the "causes" and mixed motivations of those involved in such an incident. Rather, every construction or reconstruction is an artifact that has its own life and its own uses. The most useful function the social scientist can perform in this situation is to identify the uses to which a construction is put and the power relations that are expressed through it. In other words, the point here is that the explanation that prevails is no more or less valid than other equally coherent explanations. Rather, it reveals only the dominant discourse, the prevailing context or framework into which local events are made meaningful in the broader society, the filter—constructed by those with control over the flow of information— which selectively reveals and hides local power relations from view.

THE SETTING

Village Pachpera lies within the Madrauna tahsil in the northeastern corner of Aligarh district. It is not a remote, inaccessible, backward village. It abuts the main road between the district capital of Aligarh and the small bazaar town of Madrauna.

Aligarh district is best known in the rest of India and in Pakistan for the location in it of the Aligarh Muslim University, famed for its contribution not merely to education but to the building of Muslim communal solidarity in prepartition India and for providing much of the leadership of the separatist movement that led to the creation of Pakistan. After Independence, the university and the town also became foci of Hindu–Muslim conflict and of numerous incidents of communal riots.

The vast majority of the population of the district lives in the rural areas, where Hindu–Muslim relations are less prominent and less bitter, though they do remain a factor in political party and electoral contests. Most of the population of the rural areas are Hindu, among whom there are a half dozen major castes. Traditionally, the three main proprietary castes in the rural areas of this district have been the elite castes of Brahmans and Rajputs, on the one hand, and Jats, a dominant landowning caste group of intermediate or so-called backward-caste status. These three castes comprise approximately a third of the Hindu population of the district and probably still control more than half the cultivable land. The other important landowning castes in the Aligarh countryside are from other "backward castes" of middle status, usually having somewhat smaller landholdings on the average than members of the major proprietary castes. These backward castes include the Lodhas (the largest in this category), Yadavs, and Gadarias. The largest caste grouping in the district and the least powerful are the Chamars, who are Scheduled Castes ("untouchables"), comprising more than 20 percent of the district population but owning altogether probably less than 10 percent of the land. Muslims comprise around 14 percent of the total population of the district and have in the past controlled about the same proportion of the cultivable land, approximately 15 percent.[3]

Within Madrauna tahsil, the caste and communal composition of the population differs from that of the district as a whole. During British rule, the bulk of the land was controlled by great Muslim landlords and tax farmers. Muslims still comprise around 16 percent of the population of the tahsil. Among Hindus, Chamars are the largest caste (est. 18%), followed by Lodhas (est. 11%), Brahmans, Ahirs, and Jats (est. 6–7% each), and Rajputs of several clans (est. 4%).

Aligarh district lies in the Upper Doab region of western UP and is, therefore, among the principal Green Revolution districts. In fact, it was selected as one of the most promising agricultural districts for intensive development in 1961, even before the beginning of the Green Revolution. It is not, however, the best agricultural district in this region, ranking below several other Upper Doab districts, particularly Meerut, Muzaffarnagar, Bulandshahr, and Saharanpur by most measures of agricultural progress. In Madrauna tahsil, Lodhas and Brahmans are the leading cultivating castes.

Aside from the Aligarh University in the city, the district is not known for any major educational institutions or religious shrines. Movements of religious and social change have penetrated this district, including especially several that have been in progress for a century among persons from the Chamar caste to raise their status and economic position. Aligarh has also been influenced by the Arya Samaj movement among Hindus, which has always been strong in the neighboring states of Punjab and Haryana. However, there are no famous religious shrines or *dargah*s in this district to give to it any extraordinary flavor of religiosity.

Politically, Aligarh, like the other districts of western UP in the early 1980s, was notable for the rise of the BKD/Lok Dal of Chaudhury Charan Singh as a major force challenging the Congress and often displacing it by mobilizing the backward castes, particularly the Jats, against the dominant political and economic position of Brahmans and Rajputs in the district and their control of most available sources of agricultural, educational, and other

---

[3] These figures are estimates based upon the *District Gazetteers of the United Provinces of Agra and Oudh*, vol. 6: *Aligarh*, by H. R. Nevill, and the *Final Settlement Report of the Aligarh District*, by S. Ahmad Ali (Allahabad: Superintendent, Printing and Stationery, 1943). See also the tables constructed from these sources in Paul R. Brass, *Caste, Faction and Party in Indian Politics*, vol. 2: *Election Studies* (Delhi: Chanakya, 1985), p. 217; and Zoya Hasan, *Dominance and Mobilisation: Rural Politics in Western Uttar Pradesh, 1930–1980* (New Delhi: Sage, 1989), p. 46.

forms of local patronage. The third important party in the district at that time was the Jan Sangh/BJP, which generally contested in Aligarh city, in the Scheduled Caste constituency of Loki, and in the constituency of Madrauna in which village Pachpera lies. In the latter constituency, the most prominent Jan Sangh/BJP person is Nihal Singh, a Lodha, who has been in all recent elections up to 1993 either the strongest candidate against the Congress or the winning candidate in this constituency. Politically, the other important castes and communities in the constituency are Muslims, Brahmans, and Chamars.

INCIDENT AT PACHPERA: DRAMATIS PERSONAE

AN IDOL OF LORD MAHAVIRA, composition and value not determined, that is, whether it is *ashtadhatu* or not

RESIDENTS OF VILLAGE PACHPERA, mostly Lodha (Lodhi Rajput) by caste

JAINS OF MADRAUNA TOWN from whose temple this and other idols were stolen in 1975

NAWAL KISHORE GAURI, station officer, Madrauna *thana*

OTHER POLICE PERSONNEL, members of the Provincial Armed Constabulary (PAC), and members of the Rajasthan Armed Constabulary (RAC) stationed at or near Madrauna *thana*

NIHAL SINGH, then ex-MLA (BJP), Madrauna constituency, Lodha by caste

SHAH AHMAD, then sitting MLA (Cong-I), Madrauna constituency, having defeated Nihal Singh in the 1980 elections

PRADHAN, Jatav by caste, of Manauli village, also in Madrauna constituency

K. B. MANI, the district magistrate, Aligarh district

H. K. MISRA, senior superintendent of police (SSP), Aligarh district

BASIC FACTS

The basic facts surrounding the violent events at village Pachpera, on which all informed persons agree, are as follows. An idol of Lord Mahavira (the founder of the Jain *dharma* or religion), originally installed in a Jain temple in Madrauna town and stolen from it in 1975, was found in village Pachpera in February 1983. Jains of Madrauna, having learned of the discovery of their idol, visited the village and requested its return. Failing to retrieve it from the villagers, they initiated proceedings to recover the idol, including reporting the matter to the police, requesting the help of the ex-MLA and the sitting MLA, and initiating litigation. The court declared the idol to be the property of the Jains.

In the meantime, the villagers constructed a *mandir* (temple) for the *murti* (idol), on the roadside opposite the village, a brick structure. Orders were issued to the police for the recovery of the idol from the village. At 1:00 A.M. (referred to in the text as the night of May 28, but actually the early morning of May 29), a mixed force of local police from the Madrauna *thana*, Provincial Armed Constabulary (PAC), and Rajasthan Armed Constabulary (RAC), consisting of ninety men armed and with more than three thousand charges, descended upon the village and recovered the idol. In the ensuing melee, one *subedar* (police captain) and an ox were killed and others were injured.

During the time between the issuance of orders to the police to recover the idol and the incident at village Pachpera, *pramukh* elections (for president of the Madrauna Block Development Committee) were in progress and were scheduled for May 29. In connection with these elections, it is known that:

1. Nihal Singh was supporting the candidacy of Nirmal Singh, Lodha by caste.
2. Shah Ahmad was supporting the candidacy of a Brahman.
3. Nihal Singh went on a fast-unto-death on May 20, demanding the transfer of N. K. Gauri, who was allegedly working on behalf of the candidate of Shah Ahmad.
4. Nihal Singh terminated his fast on May 25, after the intervention of the District Magistrate, who promised that Gauri would be transferred.
5. Gauri himself thereupon went on leave for three days, apparently to his home district of Meerut, and was, therefore, not present or in the vicinity on the night of the incident, which was carried out under the direction of Subinspector K. K. Singh.

The subinspector was suspended after the incident.

THE ACCOUNTS

The Perspective of Faith and Sentiment

Nihal Singh presented the most coherent account of the incident at Pachpera within the discourse of faith and sentiment. Three segments of the interview with him are given below. English words in italics convey the respondent's own emphasis.

(1)

NS: Ganga Sahib, he was digging his *neem* tree. While he was digging under the *neem* tree, a idol was found. And the whole village assembled. They thought—thought it as a gift of God. *Ab*—it is a question of faith!

PRB: Hm. Of course.

NS: *HaN*. It is a question of faith. In rural areas, these things carry much—much weight.

PRB: Yes—

NS:—an idol has been found. They considered it the—as a gift of the God. The whole village assembled. And the persons of other villages also assembled. And they thought that a temple should be erected and that idol should be established in this new temple. It was done.[4]

(2)

I met the District Magistrate, Mr. K. B. Mani. And I—put up one point: *mane*, "I am at a loss to understand why the police party has chosen *this* procedure, of breaking the lock, of breaking the gate, and taking away the idol from the temple in so sensationally ma— matter. It is a matter of *feeling*. Why the police party adopted this procedure I have not understood till now. And why the police party didn't show any written order of any court of taking away the idol from the temple: this is also a secret—er—not understandable for me also. And the third one: why the police chose the *28th* night to take away that idol from the temple, while on the next day, on 29th of May 1983, there was a poll for the election of the *pramukh*, so important an election? Why the police did not wait for 30th? *So* sensational a matter, regarding the idol, regarding the temple, in our society, in India, temple is considered as very sac—sacred place, *gurdwara* is considered as sacred place, mosque is considered as sacred place. Anything happens with *these* sacred places, naturally the feelings are hurt of the people. [PRB: Of course, yes.] *To*, why the police—did choose the night, the darkness of the night, and the night of 28th? while on 29th there was a poll for the election of the block *pramukh*: *so* important an election?[5]

(3)

PRB: So—throughout this whole time, when the court case was going on, the dispute was going on, about the idol, you didn't go and try to mediate and reach a peaceful solution?

NS: I tried.

PRB: You did.

---

[4] *Source Text for Theft of an Idol, Created from Interviews and Segments of Interviews Carried out in 1983* [hereafter referred to as *Idol Text*], p. 23 (fifth interview, taped). I have eliminated references to the dates of these interviews for the sake of preserving the anonymity of interview respondents.

[5] Ibid., p. 29 (fifth interview).

NS: I tried. Er—both the parties met me, and I tried my level best to get some solution. But—on both the sides there was the question of feelings.[6]

Clearly, Nihal Singh's account of the discovery of the idol by the villagers, of the actions of the police, and of his own failed efforts to mediate in the dispute over the idol center around matters of faith, sentiment, feelings. The discovery of the idol under the *neem* tree was considered to be "a gift of God": "It is a question of faith." These things, Nihal Singh averred, carry a lot of weight in the rural areas. The whole village assembled and so did persons from other villages. They decided immediately to erect a temple for it.

The Jains found out about the discovery of the idol and claimed it as their own. The case was referred to the police. While litigation was still going on, however, the police went at night with a large force to take the idol from the village. Nihal Singh cannot understand why the police would adopt such a procedure in "a matter of *feeling*" of a type known to be so momentous in Indian society. He tried to mediate, but could not help the situation because it was a question of *feelings*.

Alternative accounts of the attitude of the villagers toward the idol seek to discredit their proclaimed faith and the authenticity of their sentiments. One alternative account presented by the Jains, given in more detail below, places the motives of the villagers elsewhere, in a search for profit. However, their attempt to do so contains internal contradictions. The Jains say they offered to make a *mandir* for the Pachpera villagers for any idol they wanted, of Shiva or another representation of Shiva within the Hindu faith, provided they returned their idol. The Jains in this way are challenging the villagers, implying that if they are true Hindus, they should worship idols of their own faith, not of the Jain faith. This argument, however, is hardly a conclusive assault on the alleged faith of the villagers, for we would have to know more about how they claimed to perceive the idol and about the significance of their alleged "discovery" of it, which itself, Nihal Singh has informed us, was considered by them to be an act of God.

The second inconsistency in the Jain attack on the villagers' faith concerns the value of the idol. The Jains themselves insist that the idol is not *ashtadhatu* (an alloy of seven precious metals that would make it worth hundreds of thousands of rupees). They claim it is worth only Rs. 1,000. However, if the idol's monetary worth is so low and the villagers constructed a *mandir* for it at a cost of Rs. 20,000, then it would seem that faith rather than profit constituted their true motive.

A second effort to discredit the motives of faith and sentiment of both the Lodhas and the Jains on the matter was made by Nawal Kishore Gauri, who

---

[6] Ibid., p. 30 (fifth interview).

placed the incident in a political context. He argued that the issue became an explosive one only when the politicians became involved, that, far from acting as mediators, they instigated it. If it was a matter of sentiment, he argued, how can one explain the fact that the dispute lingered on from February through May and did not explode earlier?[7]

Faith, in this reading, must be something spontaneous. If it were a matter of faith, both the Lodhas and the Jains would have acted immediately, the first to worship the idol, the second to retrieve it, and there would have been a confrontation and an explosion between the two groups. Since the explosion happened only later, on this logic, the whole incident was manipulated by the politicians for their own purposes.

The Perspective of Profit

Several accounts of the incident support an entirely different point of view from that of Nihal Singh, namely, that the villagers were motivated by a desire for profit, not at all by faith, sentiment, or feeling. This reading, however, depends upon whether the idol was *ashtadhatu* or was perceived by the villagers to be *ashtadhatu*.

The account provided by the villagers concerning the value of the idol fits within a context of profit seeking rather than faith. They think the idol is *ashtadhatu*. Moreover, they claim to believe that the Jains were in cahoots with *dacoit*s (armed robbers) and the police to recover the idol and that they paid large sums of money to the criminals and the police as a bribe to them to come to the village to do so.

Gauri's account, however, which places the incident primarily within a political context, disputes the profit motive, but is inconsistent. He claims that the Lodhas first tried to find out if the idol was *ashtadhatu*. Since it was not, they decided to install it in a temple. The assumption here, however, must be that the villagers were initially motivated by the desire for profit and that faith came second. The idol would be fit for worship and for the expense of constructing a *mandir* for it only if it was worthless.

This account, however, is contradicted by the persisting belief of the villagers that it is *ashtadhatu* and by the fact that they did install it in a temple, nevertheless. An explanation more consistent with a profit motivation for the villagers' actions would be that they did believe it was *ashtadhatu* and that they built a temple and installed it in order to provide a basis for them to continue to keep it. Sometime in the future they could then sell it.

Gauri, however, is clear and insistent on the point that the idol is not only not *ashtadhatu*, but that it is "a very, very, *very* ordinary thing." Yet he himself said he knows that the villagers collected Rs. 20,000 for construc-

[7] Ibid., p. 15 (fourth interview, taped).

tion of the temple and expenses to purify it. Station Officer Gauri's account, therefore, fails to explain the actions of the villagers.

The Jain account of the motivations of the villagers is similar to that of Gauri and also places them within the perspective of profit. It is also internally inconsistent.

PRB: How did the villagers of Pachpera come to have the *murti*?

JAIN RESPONDENTS: It was just a drama. They had actually found it much earlier, and tried to melt it down, file it, anything to take out the gold. They took it to a jeweler's shop.

PRB: So the story of finding it when digging beneath the *neem* tree is a bogus story?

JAIN RESPONDENTS: Yes.

PRB: Do you think the villagers stole it? How did they come to have it?

JAIN RESPONDENT: Right now it is in the *thana*. . . . The whole thing was concocted.[8]

In the Jain account, therefore, the villagers' "discovery" of the idol was just a drama and a lie. They had tried to melt it down, file it, somehow take out the gold. They even took it to a jeweler's shop. It was actually from the jeweler, the Jains say, that they learned of the "discovery" of the idol. Moreover, the Jains say that the villagers did not report the matter to the police right away, as the latter claimed. It was actually the Jains who first reported it to the police. The Jains believe also that the villagers from Pachpera, who worked in the temple in 1975, probably stole this and other idols at that time. Insofar as the construction of the temple by the villagers is concerned, it is simply a ruse. The account of the Jains is coherent and consistent, except for the fact that they say that the idol is worth only about Rs. 1,000. Their account makes sense, therefore, only if the villagers were so ignorant as to persist in their belief that the idol was *ashtadhatu* even after having taken it to the jeweler's shop.

The account given by the police in the *thana* is consistent with those given by Gauri and the Jains.

PRB: Does the *murti* show signs of being melted or filed?

Police: It shows signs of being filed. They thought it was gold. When they found out nothing could be done with it, they installed it in a temple because they were adamant about not giving it back. But if it was gold they would have melted it down. The court had declared that the idol belonged to the Jains.[9]

---

[8] Ibid., p. 36 (sixth interview, reconstructed from notes).

[9] Ibid., pp. 47–48 (seventh interview, reconstructed from notes).

The police, therefore, support the Jain account that the *murti* was filed to ascertain whether there was gold in it. If gold had been found, the police believe, the villagers would have melted it down. Although it turned out not to be gold, the villagers installed it in the temple because they didn't want to give it back.

Once again, however, the inconsistency remains in an account framed solely within the context of profit motivations: The villagers stupidly persisted in their belief against all evidence that the idol was *ashtadhatu* and spent their own money to build a *mandir* in which to install it and worship it. When I asked the police where the idol was, I was informed that it was right there in the *thana*. However, when I asked if I could see the idol, I was informed that I would have to get written permission from the District Magistrate.[10]

The ultimate source of authority and "truth" in the districts of India today, as in British days, is the District Magistrate. He is supposed to see all, know all, and remain incorruptible. If these assumed characteristics of present-day district magistrates are accurate, then the District Magistrate's account is of particular value. The latter's account in Aligarh during my inquiries was framed entirely and uncompromisingly within the discourse of profit, as indicated in the summary of his remarks.

> The DM was . . . asked to relate the story of the incident in Pachpera
> village. He said it concerned a stolen idol of Lord Mahavir, which
> had probably been stolen by people in the area of the village. Seven
> years after the theft it was said to be discovered on a farm. The vil-
> lagers were told that it was worth 7 to 8 *lakh*s,[11] so they shouldn't
> part with it. There was no question of religious sentiment here,
> only the money. . . .
>
> PRB: Who told them it was worth 7 to 8 *lakh*s?
> DM: Someone in the village.
> PRB: So you think the villagers had no faith.
> DM: No.
> PRB: But they built a temple for it, which must have cost 10 to
>   12,000 rupees.

---

[10] Lack of time and a concern that such a request would appear strange and place me beyond the bounds of a conventional scholar engaging in research on local politics prevented me from pursuing this line of inquiry further. In any case, it would have proven nothing for me to have seen it myself. Even if I could distinguish an idol of *ashtadhatu* from one worth a thousand rupees, it is not possible that the police would show me an idol of *ashtadhatu*, having informed me that it was not. If I were to be shown an idol of little value, that would tell me nothing since it could indicate either that the police account was true or that an idol of *ashtadhatu* had been surreptitiously replaced by a relatively worthless one.

[11] One *lakh* is 100,000.

> DM: He's a rich person, the farmer who built the temple.
>
> DM: Kewal Singh, the *pradhan*?
>
> PRB: Yes. After the Mahavir idol, they can put another idol there, one of Shiva.[12]

In sum, according to the District Magistrate, it was a matter of money for the villagers, not religious sentiment. The idol is not *ashtadhatu*, but the villagers thought it was. The construction of the temple provides no evidence of the villagers' faith, that they were willing to spend their own money for the sake of worshiping the idol, because (1) the *pradhan* is a rich man and can afford it; (2) the temple can be used in any case; they can put another idol in it, one of Shiva.

The District Magistrate's account is consistent with that of Gauri, the Jains, and the police in the *thana*. He has added only the figure of an unknown villager who convinced the others that the idol was *ashtadhatu*. The account, however, like the others that find meaning only in the search for profit, is internally inconsistent. Who is this unknown villager whose authority on the matter of the composition of idols is considered by the villagers to be superior to that of the jeweler to whom they took it? If the *pradhan* is a rich man, why does he become involved in an attempt to hold on to an allegedly valuable idol, which is presumably to be sold in defiance of the decision of a court? Finally, the fact that the *pradhan can* afford to build a temple does not explain *why* he should do so.

The final account that explains the incident in terms of profit seeking comes from the sitting MLA, Shah Ahmad, who gave a coherent statement on two matters. The first concerns the illogicality of the desire of the villagers to retain the idol.

> Now this was a new kind of thing, this finding of an idol. And there is not a single Jain in that village. No Jainis [*sic*] at all. It is only of Lodhas. And they believe in the *sanatan dharma* [traditional Hindu faith]. So they should have returned the idol to the Jains. But they thought, "This idol will be instrumental in bringing in a lot of wealth to us. And this way, by installing it in a temple, we will also be saved from being accused of the theft of the idol." This is why Nihal Singh advised them [to build the temple and install the idol there].[13]

With similarly impeccable logic, Shah Ahmad explained concisely why he was sure the idol was *ashtadhatu*.

> PRB: I am surprised to hear that the *murti* is *ashtadatu* because so far everyone we have spoken to has said it is not *ashtadatu*, it is only worth a thousand rupees.

---

[12] *Idol Text*, p. 50 (ninth interview, reconstructed from notes).

[13] Ibid., pp. 57–58 (tenth interview, taped, translated from Hindi).

SA: No, I don't have full knowledge of this, that's the truth. However, I feel the idol must be *ashtadatu*. If it were not *ashtadatu*,
such a big fight over it would not have taken place.[14]

Shah Ahmad's account is the only one of the statements made within the
narrative framework of profit that is completely consistent internally. The
villagers thought the idol was *ashtadhatu*. By installing the idol in a temple,
they would avoid a charge of theft. At some later date, they could sell it.
Shah Ahmad believes the idol is *ashtadhatu*. He said in the interview also
that the Jains themselves said it was *ashtadhatu*. From the standpoint of
profit, the idol must be *ashtadhatu*, otherwise why would there be such a
fight about it?

Although Shah Ahmad's account is internally consistent, it is not free
from the potential taint of an account constructed to serve his own interests.
Since the Lodhas of Pachpera are known to be supporters of his principal
political rival, he would want to blame them anyway. It may or may not be
true that the Jains told him the idol was *ashtadhatu*. If they did, they lied to
either Shah Ahmad or me. The Jains, however, would have no reason to lie
to Shah Ahmad, to tell him that the idol was *ashtadhatu* if it were not. They
might, however, have reason to lie to others, including me, if the idol were
ashtadhatu and they were, in fact, in complicity with Gauri and the police in
the raid to recover it. Shah Ahmad, however, by admitting that the idol was,
in fact, *ashtadhatu* logically could not have been in complicity in the raid.

The Perspective of Caste and Community

The predominant context in which violent incidents in South Asia have been
placed during the past two centuries is the discourse of caste and community. One form of Orientalism in South Asian studies has involved a denial
of the importance of the individual and his or her actions, a reification of the
categories of caste, religion, language, and the like, and the placing of most
social, political, and economic conflicts in a context of interethnic rivalries
and antagonisms. In this discursive formation, any incident involving persons from different castes or communities is perceived as a mere extension
of preexisting divisions, one event among many in a succession of ongoing
encounters between groups, the individuals in them and their interests representing nothing important.

Several statements of the persons interviewed in connection with the incident at Pachpera fit within the interpretive context of caste and community.
For example, the litigation concerning the rightful possession of the idol was

[14] *Nahin, ab yeh—iske bare men meri jankari nahin hai, yeh to kya—asal baath kya hai.
Waise, ashtadatu ke woh murti hai. Agar ashtadatu ke na hoti, to itna bada jhagra par nahin
hoti* (ibid., p. 63 [tenth interview, taped]).

said to have been a case of Lodhas against Jains. It was also noted by several respondents that the Lodhas were supported during the period between the "discovery" of the idol in February and its "recovery" in May by a Lodha politician, Nihal Singh.

However, within the context of group relations in the Madrauna area, the Jains are of little consequence. In that wider context, the litigation between Lodhas and Jains is unimportant. What matters rather is the violent termination of the conflict by the police. In the discourse of caste and community, the violent conclusion is related to other incidents of violence in the area involving Lodhas from other villages, other castes, and the police.

A few statements were made, for example, which suggested a connection between the incident at Pachpera and another confrontation between villagers and police that occurred in 1980 in a village known as Nangla Lodha. Both the villages are dominated by Lodhi Rajputs, as is the constituency as a whole and the Madrauna *thana* area. In the area, Brahmans are the second largest caste. Lodhas and Brahmans are at odds. Brahmans, it was said, can never accept Nihal Singh as their representative. Station Officer Gauri claims that Nihal Singh, for his part, has always been against Brahman police officers. In this claim, Gauri, who is by caste a Tyagi from Meerut district, that is, from a caste whose status as Brahman is not universally accepted there, is identifying with the Brahmans of the Madrauna area.

Police and villagers fought in Nangla Lodha also. The police got the worst of it there. It is logical to conclude, therefore, that the police have reason to fear the Lodhas. The person in charge of the police station at the time, whose skull was cracked in the Nangla Lodha incident, was a Brahman. In Gauri's view, there is always trouble when a Brahman is in charge and especially when he attempts to take tough action against Lodhas. In this connection, Gauri also claimed that there is a higher incidence of criminality among the Lodhas.

As for Nihal Singh, Gauri notes that he was involved in supporting the Lodhas in both incidents. Up to a point, Gauri noted, Nihal Singh had taken the same position as he with regard to the idol, namely, that it should be returned to the Jains. However, as the following quotation suggests, ultimately Nihal Singh's caste ties prevailed.

> PRB: But Mr. Nihal Singh had up to this point been taking the same position as you were taking?
> NKG: Yes.
> PRB: That the idol should be returned to the Jains?
> NKG: No. Earlier. Earlier he was of the view that this idol should be returned to the Jains. But later . . . he never allowed his community to go against him, because . . . majority of the voters are of . . . [his] community. So he just thought it better to select a lesser

evil. [I see.] That is why he became silent. [Uh-huh] So—And that is why the MLA, Mr. Shah Ahmad, who is sure that Lodhi Rajputs would never support him, and Jains are coming towards his side so he must—take the opportunity to clinch their votes.[15]

In the context of caste and communal relations in this part of the Aligarh countryside, therefore, the incident at Pachpera is merely one among others of its type in the area in which the incidents themselves are of no particular importance. The "truth" of any of these incidents cannot be isolated, for they are embedded within ongoing conflicts between caste groups, in which the police are implicated as well. The politicians are merely secondary actors in this context, limited in their freedom of action by their need for the support of particular groups.

However, yet another voice demands a hearing in this context. It emerges from Nihal Singh, who insists there is no connection between the incidents at Pachpera and Nangla Lodha. According to Nihal Singh, the villagers were beaten by the police in Nangla Lodha as well. A judicial inquiry had been held on the matter, but the report had not been made public as yet. Nihal Singh, however, was certain that the report would show that it was again a case of police misbehavior.

The Perspective of Law and Order: Litigation, Police, Criminals, and People

Although, as noted above, the Pachpera villagers explain the violent conclusion of the dispute over the idol in terms of the profit motivations of the police and the Jains in cahoots with criminals, their overall interpretation fits within another framework, that of law and order. From their point of view, however, there is no law or order in the countryside. Rather, the people are the victims of the police, who are no better than marauders, seeking opportunities to extract income from the villagers and not hesitating to use force to do so. The Pachpera villagers' account in the context of law and order, like the previous account within the narrative framework of caste and community, places the incident at Pachpera as merely one among many in an ongoing sequence of connected incidents linked by police malfeasance.

The Pachpera villagers connect the incident in their village with a previous experience they had in February, involving a kidnapping of someone from the village by *dacoits*. These same *dacoits*, it was said, came again to the village to steal the idol, but this time the police came with them. The *dacoits* were hired by the Jains, who also agreed to pay Rs. 130,000 to the police and the PAC to take the idol from the village. During the fracas, the

---

[15] Ibid., p. 14 (fourth interview).

villagers fled, but the police and the *dacoit*s fought among themselves over the idol.

The villagers, of course, insist that they were merely innocent victims throughout. They had found the idol accidentally and they told the District Magistrate and the police about their discovery. They claim they were told they could keep the idol and make a temple for it. This claim is supported by Gauri's account that one Jain gentleman did come to the village and tell them that, if they constructed a temple and installed the idol there, there would be no objection, but that the Jains later wanted it back.

Gauri's account also refers to visits of Jains from "other places" than Madrauna, who came to Pachpera, visited the temple, and complimented the Lodhas on installing the idol, whereas the local Jains demanded the idol back. The Jain account, however, is that they offered to construct a *mandir* for the villagers for any other idol than their own in order to get theirs back and that Gauri approved the building of the temple and even asked the villagers to collect Rs. 50 from each house and show the money to him. They deny that they were themselves divided, some saying the idol was theirs, others saying it was not. On the contrary, they insist that the idol was theirs and that they have always demanded its return.

Insofar as the Pachpera villagers are concerned, however, it is clear that they built a *mandir* for the found idol and no other. They insist that it belonged to them, that they intended to worship it, and that the idol was stolen from them. They link what they perceive to be the theft of their idol to police misbehavior in the area generally. They claim that the police regularly implicate people in false cases and that they wanted to do so in the Nangla Lodha incident that had happened two years previously.

The Pachpera *pradhan* claimed that, in that incident, the subinspector involved had wanted him to support him in implicating people there falsely, but the *pradhan* had refused to do so. According to the Pachpera villagers, what actually happened at Nangla Lodha was that a *dacoity* (an armed robbery by a gang of five or more persons) had been committed in the village, a complaint was lodged by the Nangla Lodha villagers in the Madrauna *thana*, but the subinspector did nothing about it. The subinspector instead came to the village at night with a constable and three *dacoit*s, but the constable and the subinspector were beaten up by the villagers.

The Pachpera villagers, therefore, connect these two incidents—their own and that in Nangla Lodha—as being part of the same pattern of police and criminals joining together to attack innocent villagers. They have, therefore, a consistent account linking these two events in one contextual framework, just as Gauri links them in another.

There are, however, two weak points in the Pachpera villagers' account. One is that the allegation that the *dacoit*s, the police, and the Jains were in cahoots and that the Jains paid Rs. 130,000 to the police and the PAC to take the idol from the village is, as Gauri says, "only a rumor." The second is that, aside from Nihal Singh, nobody confirms the villagers' accounts of complete innocence in this matter.

For example, whereas the villagers say they found the idol accidentally and they told the District Magistrate and the police about it, most other accounts, including that of the villagers in the neighboring village of Manauli, say that the Pachpera villagers found the idol and decided to make a temple for it, but the Jains found out about it. Moreover, no sensible person who has had any contact with contemporary north Indian village life can believe that the villagers found an idol that they believed to be worth hundreds of thousands of rupees and that they rushed to the District Magistrate and the police, whom they consider to be in cahoots with *dacoit*s, to tell them about their find!

There is some difference and some agreement between the accounts given by the Pachpera and the Manauli villagers concerning the incident at Nangla Lodha. The Jatavs in Manauli village, whose *pradhan* witnessed the Nangla Lodha incident, claim that the villagers there beat up the police to take revenge for the inaction of the subinspector, who had failed to get the guns back from the *dacoit*s who had stolen them from the village earlier. However, both the Pachpera and Manauli villagers agree that the police had failed to take proper action with regard to the previous *dacoity*. They differ only in emphasis. The Pachpera villagers claim it was all innocent villagers being attacked by the police in cahoots with *dacoit*s. The police were beaten up when the villagers defended themselves.

The differences in interpretation of the Nangla Lodha incident by the Manauli villagers, however, were sufficient to antagonize the Pachpera *pradhan*. As a consequence of that antagonism, they claim they were forced to join politically with Shah Ahmad. However, since then, they had changed sides again and were with Nihal Singh and the Lodhas politically.

The accounts given by villagers from Pachpera and Manauli suggest that they both have a similar perspective on the realities of law and order and political life in the countryside, which contain two salient features. One is that there is no law and order in the countryside. Rather there are sets of forces operating in pursuit of their own interests, which include *dacoit*s, police, villagers who belong to distinct castes and communities, and politicians. These forces do not operate on opposite sides of a dichotomous boundary separating the mechanisms of law and order from those of criminals, but are integrated in relationships in which criminal actions bring some or all of them into play with unpredictable results. In this context, a criminal act does not necessarily or even likely lead to a police investigation, a report, the filing of a case, pursuit of the criminals, and their being hauled up before a court. Rather, it provides an occasion for the testing of relationships and alliances or for the forming of new ones. In the ensuing encounters, force and violence are always a possibility.

Accounts by others involved in the Pachpera and Nangla Lodha incidents, however, persist in demarcating two spheres: law and order, on the one hand, and criminality, on the other hand. Within the context framed by this dichotomy, the police may err, may even step across the boundary from one side to the other, but the idea of a boundary is maintained in most explanations by nonvillagers of what happened in both cases.

Thus, Gauri defends the course of action taken by him and the police solely within the context of the need to keep in the forefront the necessity for avoiding a breakdown in law and order. He says, therefore, that although he received the orders on May 20 to take the idol, he decided not to do it then because of the difficult law-and-order situation that would be created in a Lodha-dominated area during the *pramukh* elections the day after Nihal Singh had gone on a hunger strike against him. After Gauri went on leave, his second officer went to the village on the 26th, saw that there would be resistance to a police attempt to recover the idol, and decided against acting. On the night of the 28th, however, the same officer went again with a large force of PAC and RAC as well as with his own force. The officer went at night with this force, it is said, because the search warrant came at night.

However, it strains the imagination to believe that the police, having delayed a week for the sake of maintaining law and order, decide to act immediately in the night when the search warrant comes. Clearly, a large, diverse, and well-armed force had been collected in advance. It stands to reason that such a major action was preplanned and that, if the police moved immediately the order came, it was because it was convenient for them to do so at night when they believed they would be able more easily to execute their task.

The harshest indictment of the police actions came from Nihal Singh, whose account of the recovery of the idol is close to that of the villagers except that it maintains the distinction between appropriate and inappropriate police action and the placement of the police across a boundary separating them from society.

> NS: If the police authorities had any—order of any court, to recover the idol from the temple, police party or the authorities *must* have gone in that village in the *daylight*. [PRB: Of course.] They should not have gone there—in the darkness of the night, like thieves, like *dacoit*s. And they should not—have fired bitterly, just to terrorize the villagers.
>
> PRB: Hm.
>
> NS: One—ox—was killed by the—bullets of the PAC. Had that . . . ox not come—er—in between the police firing and the villager[s], I think two, three, four, five villagers must have got—er—gunshot injuries, and they should have—have—perhaps have lost—lost their precious life. One *subedar*, Kaushal Singh, lost his life. And it is an unfortunate incident; it was the *precious* life, in my—opin-

ion. But this precious life would have been . . . saved, if the police party had acted wisely. If the police party had not gone there in the darkness of the night like thieves, if that party had any written order of any court, the party should have gone in the daylight. They didn't—er—like to go there in daylight, I don't know, it is still a . . . secret for me, *why* the police chose the darkness of the night, and chose the procedure like thieves, to recover that idol.[16]

In Nihal Singh's view, in this quotation and elsewhere in the interview with him, the police acted improperly. They went with a large force in the darkness of night, though litigation was still going on. The villagers, for their part, having previously experienced a kidnapping, fired in self-defense, thinking it was a gang of *dacoit*s coming to loot the idol or the village itself.

It was a clear case of police misbehavior. The police went in the night like thieves. Nihal Singh claims they had no court order. In any case, they should not have fired so "bitterly." Moreover, he claimed elsewhere in the interview that they went to the village again, this time with Gauri himself, on the 29th and looted it.

In Nihal Singh's view, therefore, there is proper and improper police behavior. He does not describe the police, as the villagers do, as a separate force operating for their own reasons in their own interests. Moreover, he describes the villagers' response also within the narrative framework of law and order, in legalistic terms: They acted appropriately under the circumstances, in self-defense. He does not present the possible alternative view that there is warfare in the north Indian countryside and that villages such as Pachpera are armed camps within it.

However, when I pressed him to generalize from the Pachpera incident to the general situation in the countryside, Nihal Singh placed police misbehavior into a wider pattern.

PRB: Such incidents have become more common in recent years? (Pause)
NS: *Yah to*—This can't be said that it has become more often. But— as the attitude of the—police authorities, particularly police working in police stations: I am not speaking of—er—SP or SSP or DIG or IG, but particularly the police which is working in the police stations. And—which has the closest and the direct link with the local public. Their attitude is not very much desirable. Persons are harassed, terrorized; even innocent persons are implicated in false cases. And—*known goonda*s, *known* antisocial elements— move freely. (Pause) Law-and-order situation—has badly deteriorated.
PRB: It has. Hm. Since how long?

---

[16] Ibid., p. 25 (fifth interview).

NS: Still there is a terror. Terror in the—in *my* constituency, and—
particularly. Generally speaking there is terror, harassment, uncertainty of life and property, this—feeling prevailing everywhere;
people are not certain of their—safety.[17]

In these remarks, Nihal Singh comes closer to the village perceptions, but
there is still a mental distinction being made here, which was not present in
the statements of the villagers. That is, Nihal Singh, though he is describing
a virtual Hobbesian world in the north Indian countryside—or at least in his
constituency—nevertheless continues to posit against it a countercondition:
a civil society in which there is no terror, known criminals do not roam
freely, there is law and order, and innocent villagers are not harassed. The
question is whether this distinction exists only in the minds of public figures,
agents of the state, and social scientists who interview them and prod them
to make it, and is, therefore, a merely imagined state remote from the everyday realities of rural life.

Nihal Singh's political rival, Shah Ahmad, also presented a view of the
violent conclusion to the drama at Pachpera within the discourse of law,
order, and criminality, but one that discards the idea of innocent villagers.
On the contrary, according to him, the Lodhas are a criminalized caste.

SA: Amongst these people, 10 percent are criminals: they steal trans-
formers, motors, tubewells, indulge in *dacoity*; the major portion of
them indulge in such activities. Even murders they may be committing.[18]

In his account, the villagers were ready and waiting for the police. The
police could not go to recover the idol during the day because they were
waiting and because this is a Lodha-dominated area. The implication, therefore, is that a considerable massing of armed men from the Lodhas of the
village and the surrounding area could reasonably be anticipated in daylight
to prevent the police from recovering the idol.

Shah Ahmad, moreover, sees a link between the Pachpera incident and
the one at Nangla Lodha in that both involved Nihal Singh and the Lodhas.
He does not see a connection between these two incidents in the sense that
the police retaliated in Pachpera for the beating they had received in Nangla
Lodha. Rather, both incidents, he avers, were created by Nihal Singh, who
"is quite habitual of doing such things." Nor are the villagers innocent. He
claims that the Commission of Inquiry on the Nangla Lodha incident found
the villagers at fault. Nihal Singh, for his part, uses these incidents to hold
protest meetings, which then become occasions for him to collect money.

---

[17] Ibid., p. 34 (fifth interview).
[18] Ibid., p. 65 (tenth interview).

Shah Ahmad's account at this point also becomes part of the perspective of profit since the two incidents are linked by Nihal Singh's greed.

When Shah Ahmad was asked if it was a fact that the officer in charge of the Pachpera incident was suspended after the attack, he said yes. When asked why, he said he did not know. Clearly, Shah Ahmad was willing to speculate and draw conclusions on matters on which he had little or no knowledge if they fit his interpretation, but not on those that fell outside it.

Shah Ahmad's account within the framework of law and order versus criminality places the blame squarely on the Lodhas. He claims that the Lodhas oppose all station officers who are not of their caste. Moreover, there is a high percentage of criminality among the Lodhas, many of whom are themselves *dacoits*. It is they, therefore, who want to control the police for their own purposes.

Shah Ahmad discounts completely the idea that the criminal behavior was on the part of the police, including Gauri. He insists rather that such a large action could not have been carried out by the police on their own. It had to have been done on the orders of the District Magistrate and the SSP. It could not have been otherwise.

Just as the Pachpera villagers' accounts and that of Nihal Singh are consistent with each other, so the account by the Jains is consistent with that presented by Shah Ahmad. They say that the police went on the 28th because they had search warrants and orders from the District Magistrate. The warrants had been delayed because of Nihal Singh's hunger strike. Otherwise, the *murti* could have been recovered on the 21st. They say that ninty policemen went, a force that was necessarily so large because the villagers were prepared and well-armed.

The Jains and Shah Ahmad naturally support the police action and consider it to have been justified under the circumstances. Shah Ahmad, moreover, insists that the action could not have been undertaken by the police on their own, but had to have been done on the orders of the District Magistrate and the SSP.

The man who was SSP, Aligarh, at the time of the interviews had been posted to the district after the incident. His remarks, therefore, may be taken as unprejudiced in relation to this situation. They were clear and direct. The police were wrong to go at midnight and with such a large force. They should have waited for the court cases to finish. They should have considered that religious sentiments would be hurt by their actions.

The views of the District Magistrate, who was present at the time, were similar. The police action was wrong: It was "ill-timed" and "an error of judgment." The subinspector was suspended as a consequence. Although the District Magistrate blamed the police, he exonerated Gauri who, he noted, was not there at the time. The District Magistrate, however, placed the blame for the incident on Shah Ahmad as well as the police. It is not clear from the District Magistrate's account, however, how such a large action could have been mounted without his own detailed knowledge of it in advance.

If the District Magistrate did not know in advance, suspension of the subinspector would have been an appropriate response even had there been no mishap. If, however, he did know in advance, there would be grounds for believing that he himself approved of it. His exoneration of Gauri, whose absence at the moment of the action needs further explanation, would then suggest the possibility that the subinspector was a scapegoat, perhaps even a paid scapegoat, for a plot involving all those who deny that the idol was *ashtadhatu*.

It is not, however, mere inconsistencies in the accounts, mysterious absences, and inadequate explanations that abound within the narrative framework of law and order and criminality, but utterly different perspectives on the existence of law and order. It is doubtful that such a concept has any meaning at all for the villagers in the area, not necessarily because there is police terror in the countryside and, therefore, a state of lawlessness, but because power relations in the countryside include the police, criminals, politicians, and the use of force and violence as everyday instruments of persuasion and compulsion. In this context, the concepts of law and order and criminality are smokescreens, word-weapons of attack and defense in the game of explaining or justifying incidents of violence that reach the attention of the wider public, the media, and foreign scholars. It is necessary, therefore, to look finally within the context of politics which, in Madrauna, integrates the police and the district authorities within a single network of power relations.

The Perspective of Politics

Running throughout most of the accounts of the incident at Pachpera is a juxtaposition of the fact that canvassing of support for the *pramukh* elections scheduled for May 29 was in progress throughout the month of May. Several persons interviewed also made a direct connection between the *pramukh* elections and the violent conclusion of the struggle for possession of the idol. The villagers of Pachpera claim that Shah Ahmad and Gauri were conspiring to work together to persuade villagers in the area not to vote for Nirmal Singh, a Lodhi Rajput, the candidate backed by Nihal Singh. The trade-off between these two men was that Shah Ahmad wanted Gauri's support in the elections in return for which Gauri wanted Shah Ahmad's support in getting an official inquiry against him withdrawn. Nihal Singh was in turn opposed to Gauri for his alleged interference in the elections and staged a *dharna* (sit-down demonstration) to demand his removal from the scene.

The Pachpera villagers were supporting Nirmal Singh and another candidate backed by Nihal Singh for *zila parishad* (district board) representative from the same *panchayat samiti* (block development council). The latter candidate was a Jat. The Pachpera villagers, therefore, were part of a wider alliance of backward castes in the area seeking to gain control over the local *panchayat samiti* and influence within the *zila parishad*.

Gauri, for his part, claims he was but an innocent victim caught in a cross-fire between two political "giants." One of these giants, Nihal Singh, had gone on a hunger strike and had issued a pamphlet to get him transferred. Nihal Singh did this, Gauri claims, in order to "unite his own community," which had been divided and, therefore, ineffective in corporation elections (elections to the urban local government bodies) held on May 8. It should be noted that Nihal Singh went on his hunger strike on May 19 and, according to Gauri, the order to take the idol from the village was passed on the 20th. However, Gauri says he could not take the idol on that day because it would have been too big a law-and-order situation considering the dominance of the Lodhas in the area. Gauri says he was then transferred and, after receiving the notice of transfer, left the station to take three days' leave. Moreover, Gauri claims he himself now wanted to leave the area because Nihal Singh ("one of the giants") was against him.

In Gauri's view, situated in a political narrative, the ultimate reason for the magnification of the incident over the idol was neither faith nor profit nor caste and community in itself, but the political struggle in which caste considerations were embedded.

> NKG: Actually, neither all the Jains wanted to take it [the idol] back, nor all the Lodhi Rajputs wanted to keep it back, to keep it there. But sizable community—sizable number of Lodhi Rajputs and sizable number of—of Jainis[*sic*]—er—just on the instigations or on the backing of both the leaders, in—at the—in the last stages, er— they spoke for it. Otherwise there was no difficulty. Had it been so much sentimental, *to* why the matter was lingering on since February 1983, up to May last? Had it been so sentimental, it would have happened—very early. Or quite early. *To, yah to*, after the two giants came into the—struggle, face to face, then it was there. Otherwise—er—neither religious, nor sentimental, nothing of the sort; now anybody can attribute any—any cause to it. But in my opinion definitely—er—later on it turned to be a fight between two political persons.[19]

Thus, Gauri, who claimed that the idol was not *ashtadhatu*, but that the villagers believed it to be so, discounted the faith of the villagers in the first instance as an explanation for their desire to hold on to the idol and also as

---

[19] Ibid., p. 14 (fourth interview).

an explanation for the expansion of the conflict to the level of police–village warfare. In order to accept Gauri's interpretation, one has to believe that Nihal Singh either had no faith in the faith of the villagers or used their faith or their greed to encourage them to hold on to the idol, to stand together in defense of their right to retain the idol, in order to build the solidarity of the Lodhas for political purposes against the Brahmans in the area who were working to defeat Nihal Singh's candidate in the *pramukh* election. Gauri, eager to avoid the major confrontation that ultimately did occur, chose not to take the idol when the orders came because of the threat involved to law and order at the time. One has also to assume, therefore, that the decision to take the idol in the night a week later was either designed to prevent such a major law-and-order problem or was deliberately done to create a major law-and-order problem to promote the interests of Shah Ahmad and his Brahman supporters by giving a good drubbing to their local rivals, Nihal Singh and the Lodhas. In this way, the Lodhas would be threatened and Nihal Singh discredited as their protector.

The latter interpretation at any rate is consistent with Nihal Singh's view of the matter. Nihal Singh was clear in his belief that Shah Ahmad and Gauri were conspiring against him in order to disturb the election scheduled for May 29, the day after the incident occurred. The Pachpera *pradhan* was known to be supporting the candidate of Nihal Singh in the *pramukh* election. Shah Ahmad and Gauri thought that the surrounding villages would be terrorized by this incident and would be afraid to go to the polls. Gauri was supporting the Brahman candidate for *pramukh*.

The Pachpera incident, according to Nihal Singh, was also part of a general pattern of Gauri terrorizing the Lodha *pradhan*s and openly canvassing on behalf of the Brahman candidate. So, Nihal Singh went on a hunger strike against Gauri on May 20. He terminated his hunger strike on the 25th upon the promise of the then SSP, made in front of a large public crowd, to transfer Gauri and investigate the charges against him. Gauri responded with a conspiracy and made the plan to attack the Pachpera village. Gauri was anyway, according to Nihal Singh, a corrupt police officer, who was taking bribes of from five thousand to seven thousand rupees daily.

Nihal Singh's account here is coherent and consistent. He must have been angry with Gauri for working against him. Otherwise, why would he go on a hunger strike? Gauri's response no doubt would be that Nihal Singh was staging a drama in order to "unite his own community." But, then, why this particular drama directed against Gauri unless Gauri was both an obstacle to him and a nuisance to his supporters in the countryside? Nihal Singh's claim is that Gauri was acting both corruptly and politically and, by implication, that Gauri had to act politically to protect his ability to continue to collect corrupt income, presumably by harassing the Lodha villagers.

On the specific question of political involvement in the Pachpera incident, the villagers claim that Nihal Singh played no role in the dispute. Yet Nihal Singh, as an ex-minister and, therefore, as a potential future minister in a non-Congress government—a man, therefore, locally considered to be influential—would have been one of the first persons to be approached by the parties involved. Gauri claims that the Jains, who had previously been followers of Nihal Singh, approached him first. According to Gauri, Nihal Singh had tried to get the idol restored, but the Lodhas refused to take his advice. Nihal Singh then changed his view and supported the Lodhas on the basis of caste, a decision that would also protect his political base among the members of his own community.

What about Shah Ahmad, the sitting Congress MLA, alleged to be the most important political figure on the other side of the dispute, the other "political giant"? The Pachpera villagers believe Shah Ahmad was against them. According to Gauri, the Jains approached Shah Ahmad after failing to get satisfaction through Nihal Singh. Shah Ahmad, as the incumbent MLA at a time when his party, the Congress, was in power, was in a position to approach the state government on the matter and allegedly did approach the chief minister on their behalf. According to Gauri, Shah Ahmad was sure the Lodhi Rajputs would never support him and, since the Jains were "coming towards his side," so he took "the opportunity to clinch their votes." Although this account appears logical, a problem with it is that the Jains are not politically significant, having very few votes, though they are presumed to be moneyed and, therefore, potential financial contributors to local politicians.

The Jains, however, say that they did not ask for Shah Ahmad's help, but they did go and tell both Shah Ahmad and Nihal Singh about the appearance of the idol. According to their account, Nihal Singh did not take much interest in the case because, he said, it was a religious issue. The Jain account here confirms the consistency of Nihal Singh's statement that it was a religious issue. The Jains, however, despite their own apparent religiosity, did not actually believe Nihal Singh's justification for not involving himself in the incident. Rather, they claim that Nihal Singh in fact identified with the villagers on a caste basis. As for Shah Ahmad, the Jains claim he gave them no help.

However, the SSP, the only prominent official or public figure who could not have been involved in the dispute because he had not yet been posted in the district when it occurred, partly supported Gauri's political analysis of the situation. According to him, both Nihal Singh and Shah Ahmad were politically involved indirectly—Nihal Singh for obvious reasons of identification with the Lodha villagers and Shah Ahmad because he wanted Jain support. Still, the SSP's statement falls short of Gauri's interpretation that it was the politicization of the dispute and the involvement of the two political "giants" in the issue that caused it to get out of hand.

Again, therefore, we must ask about the involvement of the other political "giant," Shah Ahmad, whose complicity must be established in order to give credence to Gauri's political analysis of the magnification of the dispute over the idol. Shah Ahmad clearly has been Nihal Singh's principal local political rival. He has had a history of election contests against Nihal Singh, all lost until then except for the previous (1980) legislative assembly election. Shah Ahmad claimed that the Lodhas, the largest caste in the constituency, were the *only* group against him. The group of idols taken from the Jain temple were all stolen by thieves from Pachpera, a village only of Lodhas.

Logically, therefore, if Shah Ahmad were to become involved in the dispute, it would naturally be on the side opposed to the Lodhas. Yet Shah Ahmad claims that the Jains did not approach him, but the chief minister of the state directly. Shah Ahmad did admit that he himself also approached the chief minister in order to get the idol back for the Jains. However, he claims "he went from the justice point of view." Shah Ahmad supported the Jains for reasons of justice whereas Nihal Singh, he claims, took a casteist position. Shah Ahmad, by his own account, "had no hand behind it and . . . was just backing a just cause." Nihal Singh, in contrast, is not only a casteist, but allegedly takes a lot of money.

Insofar as the *pramukh* elections are concerned, Shah Ahmad noted that Nihal Singh had launched a hunger strike. However, he claims that Nihal Singh did this fearing that his candidate was going to lose the election because sixteen Lodha *pradhan*s were supporting the candidate of Shah Ahmad in these elections. Nihal Singh's *dharna*, therefore, was a diversion to win back the support of the Lodhas for his own candidate. However, Shah Ahmad claims that when the chief minister heard about Nihal Singh's *dharna*, he stopped Gauri's transfer.

Herein lies the solution to the mystery concerning why the Jains think Shah Ahmad did not intervene when Shah Ahmad says he did. Apparently, Shah Ahmad did intervene, but not really or primarily on behalf of the Jains, but on behalf of Gauri. Gauri, he claims, was "not pro-Congress or pro-anyone." If we are to believe Shah Ahmad's protestations of his concern for justice, the explanation for his intervention then would be his desire to protect a good officer being threatened by a corrupt former MLA, Nihal Singh. Alternatively, Shah Ahmad found Gauri useful and intervened to keep him there to help him neutralize the local power of the Lodhas in general and with particular reference to the *pramukh* election.

The political account is coherent and internally consistent. Contradictions in the accounts of the various participants are easily explained away. For example, we do not have to disbelieve Shah Ahmad's statement that he intervened only in the pursuit of justice to note that it also served his interests to have Gauri retained and the idol returned to the Jains.

The problem with the political account, however, is that it provides a broad context only, not an explanation for the climax. We must keep in mind that a mini-war was launched in the countryside between the local police and provincial constabulary, on the one side, and the villagers of Pachpera, on the other side, that both sides were prepared for it, and that all knew that lives would be endangered if a confrontation occurred. By the account of the senior administrative officers themselves, wrongdoing was involved. A police officer was suspended for initiating the action. The villagers fought at the risk of their lives and property to retain the idol. How do we explain the actions of those who finally engaged in warfare for possession of the idol? The political explanation falls short here and we must probe further to determine why the incident culminated in major violence.

"WHO DUNNIT?"

The Villagers?

Did the villagers bring it all upon themselves by their thievery and their clear intent to offer armed resistance? If so, why?

The villagers are clearly lying about some things. For example, they did not report the discovery of the idol, which was reported to the police by the Jains only after the jeweler told the Jains about it. They may also be lying about the manner of discovery of the idol.

Speaking in favor of an accidental discovery of the idol is the lapse of seven or eight years between the original theft of several idols from the Jain temple and the discovery of the idol under the *neem* tree in village Pachpera. Speaking against it is the likelihood that someone from the village stole it and put it there in the first place, it being highly unlikely that a person from another village could bury a substantial (probably two-feet high) idol deep in the ground without being noticed. For that matter, the burial of such an idol would probably have involved more than one person in any case. Therefore, it is possible that the idol was brought forth because some person or persons in the village needed or wanted some cash.

The villagers clearly thought—and persist in thinking—the idol is *ashtadhatu*. Both the jeweler's and the police accounts indicate the villagers were after money. Therefore, the construction of the temple becomes a ruse and the villagers brought it all on themselves.

On the other hand, the history of most faiths and religions suggests there is no incompatibility between faith and the quest for profit, indeed that they are often closely linked. Melting down the idol would surely bespeak a lack of faith. However, having failed in converting the idol to money, why should we then dispute the sincere desire of the villagers to worship it?

Nihal Singh?

The fact that Nihal Singh launched a hunger strike suggests: (1) he felt deeply and sincerely that Gauri was working against him; (2) he was committed to using peaceful methods. After the incident at village Pachpera, he enlisted the involvement of MPs from other parties, which suggests he had nothing to hide. The idea that he instigates violent incidents in order to hold public meetings thereafter, ostensibly to protest but actually to collect money for himself, is too far-fetched to take seriously.

The Police?

It is conceded by the highest authorities in the district that the police misbehaved. But why?

No one is known to have seen the idol since the incident. It was allegedly locked up in the *thana*, suggesting the possibility that the police, as stated by the Pachpera villagers, wanted the idol for their own profit. However, it would seem highly unlikely that they could get away with such a theft, which would involve the complicity of the judicial authorities as well as the District Magistrate and the SSP, and would ultimately be found out by the Jains.

The idea that the police retaliated in village Pachpera specifically because of their earlier beating in Nangla Lodha can be ruled out because the incidents were too far separated in time and the personnel involved were different. However, it is quite possible that the local police did not at all mind giving a good beating to the Lodhas because of their general troublesomeness, if not criminality, in the area. The issue of caste antagonisms between the police and the backward-caste Lodhas also might be a factor here.

It is probable that the village was, in fact, looted on the 29th. The police would certainly be in a mood for revenge as well as profit after having an armed battle with the villagers in which they lost one of their men. Moreover, the pattern of police returning to a village to loot it after an incident of this type is common throughout north India. However, the opportunity for loot, which is certainly a classic motive for warfare—and this is, of course, warfare—does not seem a sufficient explanation for their initial action, though it cannot be ruled out.

Gauri and Shah Ahmad?

We come back, then, to the political explanation and specifically to Gauri and Shah Ahmad, who seem to have the only adequate reasons for instigating such a situation. Gauri had ample reason to wish to take revenge upon Nihal Singh. If Gauri had been making money in Madrauna, he had reason to be angry with Nihal Singh for depriving him of his income. Even if he were not, Nihal Singh's hunger strike demanding his transfer would provide sufficient grounds for taking revenge. An attack upon a Lodha village in the midst of the *pramukh* elections would be one form of revenge, a demonstration that the biggest man among the Lodhas in the area and an ex-minister could not prevent an assault upon his caste fellows and his supporters.

My interview with Gauri and other reports of his behavior suggest duplicity. His account is too smooth and subtle, too detached. He suggested to the villagers that they build a temple for the idol and "show him the money." What could this mean? Either that he instigated the villagers to hold on to the idol in order to make mischief or that he would allow them to construct a *mandir* and install the idol in it if he were rewarded with some money for his complicity. Moreover, the Jains claim he told them they should be happy their religion is spreading, suggesting his original complicity in the idea of the villagers keeping the idol.

However, if Gauri was originally complicit with the villagers on the matter of retaining the idol in order to make money for himself, how could he be responsible for the violent recovery of it, especially since he was not present during the incident? Speaking for his culpability is his identification with the Brahmans in the locality—despite the fact that, as a Tyagi by caste, he is in no way related to them—and his general hostility to the Lodhas. He blames the Lodhas for being unwilling to tolerate a Brahman station officer. His whole analysis of Brahman–Lodha conflict, though probably accurate as a description of the underlying political conflict in the area, suggests his alliance with the Brahmans and, therefore, with Shah Ahmad. It should be especially noted in this connection that, in his statement that he was caught in a conflict between two political "giants," he speaks *against* Nihal Singh but not against Shah Ahmad. Therefore, it is logical to conclude that Gauri, under attack from Nihal Singh and in alliance with Shah Ahmad, engaged in a plot with other police officers, possibly the suspended subinspector, to recover the idol on the night of May 28.

The missing link in this explanation for a man whose discourse moves between interest and politics is his own profit motive. The villagers must either have refused to pay Gauri a bribe to retain it or Gauri must have decided, as the villagers themselves suggested, to steal it for himself. Acceptance of this interpretation of Gauri's complicity depends upon whether or not the idol was in fact *ashtadhatu*, but Gauri's involvement can be explained in either case. If it was not *ashtadhatu*, then the failure of the villagers to pay him a bribe and his local political involvements provide a sufficient explanation. If the idol was *ashtadhatu*, that fact would merely strengthen the case for Gauri's profit motivation.

As for Shah Ahmad, his account is the least believable of all. He protests too much his passion for justice in this case. The Brahmans are his natural allies in the constituency. Their support was his only way to maintain the advantage over Nihal Singh that he gained at last in 1980 after several defeats by him and the Lodhas. Every local politician who wishes to maintain his dominance in an area must control the police so that he can protect his friends and punish his enemies. The Lodhas are Shah Ahmad's main enemies in Madrauna. Therefore, political logic suggests a deal must have been stuck between him and Gauri.

Only Gauri and Shah Ahmad, therefore, had sufficient reasons to precipitate the incident at Pachpera. It is not believable that a subinspector acted alone. Gauri must somehow have been behind it. Shah Ahmad would have no reason to be unhappy about it. He certainly shed no tears for the Pachpera villagers after the incident. By his own account, he had intervened with the chief minister of the state, presumably on behalf of either the Jains or Gauri, certainly not for the Lodhas. Shah Ahmad, therefore, provided tacit support and possibly protection from above for the action even if he was not a coconspirator. The police forces would have had their own reasons to act: An attack on village Pachpera provided them an opportunity to give some Lodhas a beating as well as an opportunity for loot.

Unanswered Questions

At the center of the drama stands the idol with one question begging an answer: Was it *ashtadhatu* or not? No one is known to have seen the idol since the incident, though it was supposed to be in the *thana*. Of those who have actually seen it, only the villagers continue to believe it is *ashtadhatu*. Shah Ahmad also believes it is *ashtadhatu*, but he has not seen it.

It is logical to suppose, however, that Gauri would insist that the idol was not *ashtadhatu* if he were intent upon stealing it. However, it is less easy to explain the insistence of the Jains that it was not *ashtadhatu*. We cannot, of course, challenge their own faith by asking, as Shah Ahmad did, why anyone would expend so much effort to recover the idol if it were not *ashtadhatu*. We must presume that even if the idol were of small value, the Jains would, for reasons of faith, want it back. On the other hand, we cannot dismiss the villagers' claim that the police, the Jains, and a gang of *dacoit*s were in cahoots to recover the idol for its monetary value. If it were truly valuable monetarily, the Jains might well be willing to pay a reward to the police for its recovery, an even stronger token of their faith. If they were complicit, however, and especially if they were shocked at the violence that accompanied the recovery of the idol, they would want to hide their own complicity by denying that the idol had any monetary value. How can we believe, however, that the Jains would want to sell their own idol in the marketplace? Surely, they would want to reinstall it. However, the villagers desecrated the idol by attempting to file it down, rendering it unsuited for reinstallation.[20] Logic, therefore, without being dependent upon profit motivations alone and without discounting either the faith of the villagers or that of the Jains, suggests that the idol was in fact *ashtadhatu*.

The second difficult question concerns whether there was actually an organized political conspiracy to enact this incident. Perhaps it just happened as a result of the converging of the diverse motives of Gauri, Shah Ahmad, and the police. It is unlikely that it just happened without calculations concerning the reactions of all relevant parties. There is enough evidence in the accounts of those with knowledge of the incident to indicate that each of the principal participants was acting and reacting to the actions of others. Shah Ahmad may have approached the chief minister on behalf of the Jains or on behalf of Gauri, but there is no doubt where his sympathies and antipathies lay nor any doubt that Gauri was fully aware of them. It is, therefore, not really critical to an understanding of the situation to know whether there was a conspiracy. To convict a person, one must know the details of his secret actions. To understand a situation in its political and social context, it is sufficient to know the effects. The effects suggest a tacit, if not an explicit, collaboration between Gauri and Shah Ahmad for profit and political reasons.

CONCLUSIONS

Reconstruction

The first conclusion is that things are never as they seem. Presentations and re-presentations of incidents such as that at village Pachpera are designed to make a case. By the time I arrived on the scene, everyone's case had already been prepared. Lawyers had also been involved, which means that the guilty—the villagers as well as Gauri and Shah Ahmad—had already been coached.

However, even without coaching, when an incident such as a theft of an idol enters the public arena in a heterogeneous society, many individuals, groups, and agencies become involved. When such an incident involves persons of different faiths or castes, the possibilities for intensification of conflict and enlarging of its boundaries increase. In contemporary India, the enlargement of the boundaries of conflict also brings into play the multiplicity of values and discursive formations that pervade society. A local theft then becomes an incident to be placed in a broader context and struggle takes place among the parties involved to capture the incident and place it in one's favored narrative framework.

There are two favored public standpoints in contemporary India for interpreting this type of event. One involves an inversion of the discourse of law

[20] I am indebted to Shyam Benegal for suggesting this point to me.

and order and criminality in which incidents of this type are interpreted as examples of police brutality enacted against disadvantaged groups. The placement of an incident in this context, however, requires that the groups allegedly brutalized belong to recognized disadvantaged groups *and* that the incident occur at a time when external political forces can conveniently take advantage of it, such as instability in the state government or an impending election. The incident at Pachpera, however, occurred only at a time of local—not statewide or national—elections. Its interpretation, therefore, was confined within the local political context.

Moreover, the Lodhas occupy an ambiguous status in the hierarchy of advantage and disadvantage in contemporary Indian society. They are generally considered to be a "backward caste" intermediate between the elite castes and the lowest castes in ritual status, in the educational attainments of their members, and in their access to prestige government employment. However, their modern history has involved the claim that they are not backward castes, not Lodhas but Lodhi Rajputs. Moreover, their claims aside, they do constitute in their area a dominant caste in the anthropological sense, that is, in their numerical size, control of land and economic resources in the area, and local political influence.

An additional point to note in this connection is that, Marxist or other Left rhetoric aside, the "common people," the villagers, are not always or even generally innocents harassed by a police force looking for victims. The police are often looking for victims, for money, for profit in rural north India, and will take it where they can find it. However, their victims, the "common people," are often not only not innocents but are themselves seeking ways of making money, taking known risks in order to do so. The Pachpera villagers—for those in the area who discount their faith or the accidental discovery of the idol—are considered thieves, who initially stole the whole lot of idols removed from the Jain temple in 1975. It is at least known that they were well armed and prepared to fight to retain their possession, however acquired.

The second favored discourse in India for the interpretation of incidents of violence is communalism. Interethnic incidents of violence are often seen as involving competing religions claiming priority for their worship, their sacred site, their idol. Had the incident at village Pachpera involved Hindus and Muslims and had it developed into a Hindu–Muslim "riot," it is virtually certain that this latter interpretation would have prevailed.

The incident at village Pachpera, however, is curious in this respect in that it appeared to involve competing claims for the right to worship the *same* idol—curious, but not unique. In the 1920s the Sikhs in the Punjab launched a massive movement to regain control of their *gurdwaras* from Hindu *mahant*s, a high point in a continuing movement to restore and retain a Sikh identity separate from that of the Hindu majority of India. Conflict of this sort has occurred in isolated cases between Hindus and Jains in India as well.[21] In both the Sikh and Jain cases, fundamental issues concerning the boundaries between Hinduism and other religions that have arisen in India in the past alongside of or as offshoots of Vedic, Brahmanical, or popular Hinduism underlay the disputes. It is a general tendency among Hindus, expressed politically as well by the BJP and other organizations associated with the RSS and militant Hindu nationalism, to claim that all these other religions are part of Hinduism. This claim, seen by some as an example of Hindu toleration, is more often seen by practitioners of the non-Hindu religions as threats to their distinctive beliefs, practices, and identities, and to their constitutional rights to worship as they choose in temples of their own under their own control. The issue of the propriety of the Lodhas worshiping a Jain image was raised during the dispute over the recovery of the idol. It cannot, however, be said to have been a major issue in the dispute, which revolved around possession of the idol rather than its appropriate worship.

In any case, the incident at village Pachpera cannot be reduced to a simple explanation. Rather, it provides a window to the realities of rural life in contemporary north India. Those realities do indeed include the pervasiveness of faith and religious sentiments as powerful forces in the countryside where the boundaries between different religions and religious practices are often blurred. Pervasive also is the desire for profit. It is, however, a mistake to think of the two as occupying different realms.

Islam and Calvinism, among other religions, may place more or less severe restrictions on the unbridled pursuit or enjoyment of profit. Other religions, however, including Hinduism, build in the pursuit of profit as legitimate ends and gods devoted to watching over that pursuit. Calvinism, of course, also considers business success in this world to be one among several signs of grace. Clearly, religion often pays in one way or another and sometimes spectacularly so, as among many notorious religious preachers in the American south and many Hindu godmen who come to America to bring their messages and amass wealth. In rural north India as well, in religious shrines, in pilgrimage centers, the pursuit of religion and profit are intertwined.

---

[21] On November 26, 1954 Hindu worshipers placed a Shivling (representation of the god, Shiva) in a Jain temple in Ratlam in the state of Madhya Bharat, now Madhya Pradesh. This Shivling was placed in the temple by a local government official to replace an idol previously removed from it, allegedly stolen from it. Hindus claimed the stolen idol had been a Shivling and that the temple, therefore, was a Hindu temple whereas the Jains claimed it was a Jain deity, not a Shivling. The temple was thereafter, in effect, taken over by the Hindu community. The state and district authorities backed the Hindus and even posted police officers at the temple to prevent Jains from worshiping there. The Jains filed suit for removal of the idol, which was upheld in court; *Tejraj v. State of M. B.*, AIR 1958 Madh. Pra. 115 (V 45 C 46), Indore Bench, pp. 115–28. I am grateful to Gary Jacobsohn for bringing this reference to my attention.

Faith as well as profit can make liars of men. If the logic of the argument above is accepted, at least one side among the devotees of the idol are lying about it and probably both are lying. The villagers believe the idol is *ashtadhatu* and claim they wish to worship it, but they tried to melt it down. The Jains claim it is not *ashtadhatu*, but they must be saying so to divert attention from their own devious misdoings in their efforts to rescue a monetarily valuable idol from its entry into the market for such idols in north India. Since no one is known to have seen the idol since its "recovery," it is likely that it is now safely ensconced and well attended in the home of a devotee or collector in Bombay or abroad.[22]

Caste and caste antagonisms also remain powerful forces in the north Indian countryside. In the political account of the climax in the dispute over the idol, Lord Mahavira fell victim ultimately to the local conflicts between Lodhas and Brahmans. In that dispute, the idol was merely a pretext in the struggle for dominance between political rivals with their bases in two antagonistic caste groups.

Moreover, the struggle between these two groups was not over control of the idol but of the police. Caste and caste antagonisms are used in the north Indian countryside primarily for the purpose of building the political power necessary to control economic resources, but also to maintain political dominance generally. The latter inevitably means maintaining control of the police.

The police are a central element in the countryside, whom the politicians strive to control. In Madrauna, the dominant castes and their most important leader could not control the police, who chose to identify with the Brahman caste rivals of the Lodhas and the Congress, the then ruling party in the state and the dominant party in the state and country for most of the post-Independence period. The Congress had retained its hold in the countryside for so long partly by using the police, which it was generally in a better position to do than its rivals because of its control over the state government.

As for the law and the judiciary, they are of little consequence in the countryside, though lawyers and judges are certainly important. Law and the judiciary as abstractions have little meaning in rural north India, where lawyers and judges are highly politicized and judicial decisions are often for sale. The law and the judiciary are there as a facade to be manipulated, to provide legitimacy for the actions of the authorities or the police or to harass one's rivals or to gain time in a dispute.

Rule in the countryside is not based on abstractions but on control over resources and safety. It is a Hobbesian world, in which security and safety are not provided by the state, but are themselves values—that is, valued

---

[22] There is a flourishing trade in stolen *ashtadhatu* idols in UP for sale in Delhi, Bombay, and abroad; see *Times of India*, July 9, 1985.

objects—integral to and inseparable from the struggle for power and influence.

The Incident at Pachpera
and Contentious Categorization in Indian Society

While rule in the north Indian countryside is not based on abstractions, it is
inseparable from the battle of discourses, which is not a struggle over words
only but a struggle for power, for the placement of incidents of violence in
their "proper" context. Different contextualizations empower particular persons and groups. The rhetoric of faith ostensibly empowers the faithful and
the manipulators of their faith. The discourse of profit may or may not empower those whose primary goals are the pursuit of profit, depending upon
whether the profit motive is valued or devalued in the prevailing talk about
it.

These two perspectives are generally placed in opposite realms, as cri-
tiques of each other. The discourse of faith is often seen as a cover for a
reality of the pursuit of profit. The perspective of profit may be used to
expose actions justified in terms of faith. But those who speak solely from
within either narrative framework dissemble for, as noted above, faith and
profit are intertwined in one way or another in many religions, if not all. The
saintly search for the life of simplicity in poverty, removed from the endless
drive for material acquisitions, would have little meaning if the reality were
not the opposite among the faithful themselves.

The perspective of caste and community is the favored context in which
incidents of violence and struggle for power generally are placed by contemporary social scientists of India. Placed within the broader framework of
political competition, it provides the most satisfying contextual explanation
of the incident at Pachpera and the core of the political reconstruction provided above. Yet this discourse, too, is a construction and a weapon in the
battle of discourses in contemporary India.

The rhetoric of caste and community is used as a critique in a secular
society. It describes a "reality" that is simultaneously criticized and accepted. It is, as noted earlier, a categorical explanation that may disguise
and certainly always simplifies, covering a variety of personal and political
behaviors. It substitutes popular values, which are said to be deplorable but
entrenched in the lives of the people, for individual responsibility and culpability in acts of wrongdoing. It diverts blame from the politicians for instigating violence between communities or between the police and villagers.
The politicians after all are secular, striving to pursue justice but hamstrung
in that pursuit by popular attitudes.

The rhetoric of politicians also can be presented in different ways. The
politicians claim to pursue justice, to protect the people from police brutal-

ity, to respect their beliefs, to promote their welfare. They are, of course, at the same time their own worst enemies in every democratic society, constantly accusing each other of doing the opposite. Their accusations against each other make it that much easier to blame the politicians for everything, thus turning attention away from, for example, police misbehavior or bureaucratic incompetence and corruption. It obviously works the other way as well. Politicians attempt to distract attention from their own misdeeds, failures, and corruption by blaming the bureaucrats and the police for the pervasive violence and corruption in contemporary Indian society.

Finally, the discourse of law and order also works as its own double. From the side of the authorities, it may be used to justify repression of all sorts. Entire villages may be raided in the dead of night, their inhabitants harassed and beaten, their property and stocks of grain looted on one pretext or another, in this case in the name of the recovery of an idol either worth nothing or valuable enough to be coveted by all the thieves in the vicinity who have become aware of its existence, including the police.

From the side of the people, the rhetoric of law and order may be inverted. The argument then is that law and order have been violated or no longer exist because the police have been criminalized, the judiciary corrupted, and the people brutalized and harassed. This argument, not entirely or always false, is nevertheless useful as a justification for all sorts of criminality and thievery perpetrated by ordinary people protected by politicians.

Most of all, the perspective of law and order masks not only its virtual absence, but the operations of an entirely different game or games. The premises of this explanatory framework constitute obstructions that keep those games out of sight. They assume the existence of a multiplicity of dichotomies, of sets of competing values that exist in pure states: justice and injustice, law and order and police misbehavior, caste and religious communities and a secular state, the state and its institutions and society.[23]

In fact, however, the proclamation of these dichotomies is part of the game that hides the lack of such clear-cut boundaries. Justice called for the swift recovery of the idol and its restoration to the Jains. The existence of multiple power relations and idioms to describe them in rural north India, however, transformed the idol from its character as the property of the Jains to a potential object of worship or profit or political advantage for an array of groups, among whom the Jains were the least important and whose rights soon became quite secondary.

---

[23] The proliferation of such dichotomies by both social science analysts and those they analyze in developing countries is emphasized in works by Timothy Mitchell, focusing on Egypt. See especially *Colonising Egypt* (Cambridge: Cambridge University Press, 1988); "Everyday Metaphors of Power," *Theory and Society* (1990): 1–32; and "Problems with the Theory of the State," paper prepared for the seminar on "State and Society: Authority and Legitimacy in the Modern Arab World," unpublished.

The laws, the lawyers, and the judiciary are instruments in the economic and political conflicts in rural north India. The politicians stand between these laws and the order they are supposed to produce for the benefit of the people. The police do not merely act upon the orders of the court, but are allied with the politicians and seek opportunities for themselves as well, to make a living from the implementation of the laws and the orders of the courts.

Nor does the secular state and its values exist above or separate from the castes and communities in Indian society. The so-called secular politicians cannot function effectively in India's political order without using caste and community as mobilizing devices. With tongue-in-cheek, they criticize each other for doing what they all do. Local caste and communal leaders in turn gain economic benefits and political access by identifying with particular political persons, groups, and parties. They also hope to gain safety and freedom from the implementation of laws that go against their interests.

Finally, there is no rigid separation between state and society. Rather, there are groups included and groups excluded and outside the state, groups and individuals with the ability to operate within the state, and groups and individuals with little or no influence who must use intermediaries to gain access to those with power and influence. The agents of the state—the police, judicial, and bureaucratic personnel—identify or ally with the politicians, with caste and communal groups, and with powerful individuals across the boundary between state and society.

Life is simplified in Western capitalist societies where, despite the persistence of a multiplicity of values and faiths, two public discourses have become dominant: interest and justice. The pursuit of one's individual self-interest is approved within sets of rules that establish limits but offer few behavioral alternatives. Group and other collective interests and values do not provide alternative modes of behavior but only limits, which have to be protected against constant encroachment from individuals in pursuit of their self-interest.

The state may pursue justice to rectify persistent inequalities and imbalances between groups that prevent individuals from pursuing effectively their own interests, but has little sanction to go further. A clearer boundary is maintained between state and society by the enforcement of a limited set of rules established by the state authorities, which ignore the contexts in which legal and illegal acts are perpetrated and the values that motivate them. On one side, interest and rights, on the other side, justice and right, at least in theory. The rest—faith, sentiment, community—are not the business of the state and are not allowed to cloud its business.

In India, in contrast, faith, sentiment, and especially community constitute major social constructions that intervene between the interested individual and the justice-pursuing secular state. I have shown how caste was brought into play in the theft of an idol in rural Aligarh district and how its existence provides a framework within which a multiplicity of individual and group interests was pursued across the boundary between state and society. There is a grander construction that has operated in modern Indian society, that of religious communalism, particularly Hindu–Muslim communalism. Later chapters show how that construction and the discourse that perpetuates it operate pervasively in north India as a cover for the political ambitions of elites and as a smokescreen to draw attention away from the consequences for its people of the policies of the modern Indian state and its leaders.

The incident at Pachpera, however, did not fit into this grander construction nor into the other dominant public narrative of police brutality for reasons already mentioned above. It remained, therefore, a local incident, not covered by the press or manipulated by external politicians and parties for broader purposes. It is my purpose to show in the rest of this volume that many incidents that do get placed within broader contexts in contemporary Indian society and expand into "communal" conflagrations are little different in origin from that which took place in Pachpera. In fact, most such incidents that bring in the wider public and external agencies and authorities begin with more trivial sparks and involve fewer interested parties than the Pachpera incident. The preexistence of a framework of meaning, of opportunities to make use of such incidents for wider political purposes, and of interested persons and groups alert to those opportunities are essential prerequisites for the transformation of local, often trivial events into ideological confrontations between whole communities.

Chapter 4

RAPE AT DAPHNALA

The Setting

The town of Daphnala[1] lies within the Nakoda tahsil in the north-central part of Meerut district, seventeen miles from Meerut city, the district head-quarters, on the border of Muzaffarnagar district. It is a bazaar town, officially designated as a town area, a census status indicating that it is neither a village nor a full-fledged urban place. There is a weekly market. The town also is known for its numerous mango groves.[2]

The population of less than eleven thousand people is fairly equally divided between Hindus and Muslims. Before Independence, the place was a *qasbah* town dominated by Muslim landlords. The most prominent political family is descended from Muslim *zamindar*s, whose holdings were concentrated in the town and in four or five surrounding villages.

Politics in Meerut district, as in several other western UP districts, including Aligarh, has had two prominent features since the 1970s: increasingly frequent and severe communal violence centered primarily in Meerut city, on the one hand, and a rural politics dominated by conflict between the Jat cultivating castes and its allies against the Brahman and Rajput cultivating castes and their allies. The former gave their allegiance overwhelmingly to Chaudhuri Charan Singh, whose home district this was. Charan Singh was the most important leader of the Jats and of the backward castes in the state of UP during his long career first as a Congress politician, then as chief minister of the first non-Congress government in the state in 1969, and ultimately as prime minister of India for a brief period in 1979. After his departure from the Congress in 1969, his party, later known as the Lok Dal, replaced the Congress as the dominant political force in the district.

Party competition in Meerut district up until 1980 was dominated in all rural constituencies by the Lok Dal and the Congress. The BJP, a party of militant Hindu nationalism widely perceived also as a communal, anti-Mus-

---

[1] To preserve confidentiality, the names of the sites and persons involved in this case and of my respondents have been changed. However, in the interests of authenticity, I have not altered the name of the district.

[2] *Meerut: A Gazetteer*, vol. 4 of the *District Gazetteers of the United Provinces of Agra and Oudh*, ed. H. R. Nevill (Allahabad: United Provinces Government Press, 1904), page reference eliminated to preserve anonymity. [Hereafter referred to as *Meerut Gazetteer*].

lim party, was at that time insignificant electorally in all constituencies in the district except Meerut city and Meerut cantonment, where it displaced the Lok Dal as the main rival to the Congress.

Communal politics, as elsewhere in UP and in other parts of north India, had until then been centered in the city, in the district headquarters of Meerut. Two major riots occurred in the 1980s, the first in 1982 just before the incidents described in this chapter. Moreover, the Meerut city riot of 1982 provided a contextual background for the events that unfolded in Daphnala in July 1983 and influenced their course.

Daphnala town is situated within the boundaries of the Niwaspur Legislative Assembly constituency reserved for Scheduled Castes and is adjacent to the Dhanapur constituency. At the time of the incident in Daphnala, the MLAs from both constituencies belonged to the Congress. The MLA from Dhanapur then was Syed Sirajuddin. He and his relation, Syed Nuruddin, were the most important politicians of the area at the time and were men of influence in the Daphnala Town Area Committee as well. The BJP had virtually no electoral strength in either constituency at the time.

Meerut district and the area around Daphnala have had a history of competitive religious proselytizationthat that began in the late nineteenth century with the introduction of several Christian missions, including an American Methodist Mission. There is even a rather remarkable and locally famous church maintained until today in good condition in the nearby town of Dhanapur. The Arya Samaj also built a lasting base among a segment of the Hindu population from the time of Swami Dayanand Saraswati's visit to Meerut district in 1878.[3] However, there has never been any strong Muslim proselytizing or fundamentalist movement in the district, though there is a *dargah* (Muslim shrine) in the town of Daphnala where an annual religious fair has been held for a long time.[4]

Daphnala has never experienced significant communal tension between Hindus and Muslims. Syeds Sirajuddin and Nuruddin are traditional Muslim politicians supported politically by the Muslim voters of the area, but they have launched no revivalist, fundamentalist, or other communal movements to solidify Muslim sentiment. Among the educated Hindu population of Daphnala and the nearby and more important town of Nakoda, there was in the early 1980s a small cadre of BJP party men with Arya Samaj and RSS backgrounds, but with a limited political base. Therefore, despite the relatively even balance in the populations of Hindus and Muslims in Daphnala, there was no particular reason in 1982 to anticipate any communal disturbances here.

[3] *Meerut Gazetteer.*
[4] Ibid.

INCIDENT AT DAPHNALA: DRAMATIS PERSONAE

A YOUNG HINDU GIRL

AN OLD MAN

THREE MEN (alleged culprits), two Muslims and a Hindu

DR. SENGUPTA, another old man, Ayurvedic physician in Daphnala

DR. RAM PRASAD KHOSLA, another Ayurvedic physician in Daphnala, member of the RSS and the BJP

SYED SIRAJUDDIN, sitting MLA (Cong-I), Dhanapur constituency

SYED NURUDDIN, former chairman, Daphnala Town Area Committee, a close relative of Sirajuddin

TIMOTHY MATTHEW, District Magistrate, Meerut District

VARIOUS POLICE PERSONNEL

THE STORY

In the late afternoon of July 7, 1983, an old Hindu man was seen weeping in the streets of Daphnala. He stopped outside the shop of a *halwai* (halva-maker), where a crowd gathered to hear his complaints. In the midst of his sobs, his story emerged. He cried that he had come by bus from the adjacent district of Muzaffarnagar with his daughter, but that she had been kidnapped at the bus stand in Daphnala. He appealed to the crowd, to the people of Daphnala to help him find his daughter, asking them to be on the lookout for a girl in a green blouse and painted pink sari and to send her here to him should she be spotted. As he was making his appeal to the crowd, one man coming from Dumka reported that he had seen a girl on the road to Dumka with three men following her. This man said he accosted the three and asked them why they were bothering the girl. That night, the old Hindu man proceeded to Dumka to search for his daughter, but she was nowhere to be found.

The scene in front of the *halwai*'s shop took place near the dispensary of Dr. Sengupta, an old man who took the other's grief upon himself and befriended him. When no trace of the girl could be found, Dr. Sengupta went to see the most prominent public person in Daphnala, the ex-chairman of the town area committee, Mr. Nuruddin, whose son-in-law, Syed Sirajuddin, was the then sitting Cong (I) MLA from Dhanapur constituency. Dr. Sengupta told his news to Mr. Nuruddin and expressed his feelings that "this is a very shameful thing for this town that a girl has been kidnapped from this place, from this town."[5]

---

[5] *Rape at Daphnala: Text for the Drama, Created from Interviews and Segments of Inter-*

Mr. Nuruddin, a practical man, asked Dr. Sengupta whom he suspected to be responsible for the kidnapping. Dr. Sengupta said he had no idea since he was a heart patient and rarely left his own area. He asked Mr. Nuruddin to call the old man to ask whom he suspected. The old man was brought to Mr. Nuruddin's place, where he gave three names: two Muslims, Rafi and Dudhu, and a Hindu, one Pahalwan.[6] Mr. Nuruddin proceeded to the local police station to complain about the situation. The police then began an investigation of the matter.[7]

In the meantime, news of the incident having spread through the town, Dr. Ram Prasad Khosla, an Ayurvedic physician, an Arya Samaji, a member of the RSS, and a local activist of the BJP, was apprised of the alleged kidnapping by "two prominent personages"[8] of the town, who brought him the news when he arrived at his dispensary in Daphnala from his hometown of Nakoda on the morning of the 8th. Dr. Khosla was told that the old man had come with his daughter from Malapur village in Muzaffarnagar district. The girl was said to be abnormal, half-witted, and was being brought to a village in the vicinity for treatment. However, when the bus stopped outside a mango grove, the girl asked the old man "to get some mangos for her." When he returned, the girl was gone.[9]

In the meantime, the police had already arrested both the witness who had claimed to see three men following the girl and the alleged culprits, who were said to be known *goonda*s (toughs). However, they had kept the witness under arrest, but released the alleged *goonda*s. The "prominent personages" who came to inform Dr. Khosla of the incident and of the police action asked his advice. Dr. Khosla advised them to mobilize local opinion and to gather a number of people from the area to go to the police station to demand an inquiry into the matter.

Following Dr. Khosla's advice, a group of twenty to twenty-five people reached the police station the evening of July 8, whereupon the witness was released and the *goonda*s were again arrested. The *goonda*s were thoroughly beaten by the police during the investigation, during which they admitted that they and eight other men had raped the girl, but they refused to reveal where she was being kept.[10] Rumors of the alleged gang rape now spread throughout the town, leading to an increase in "public tension" concerning

---

views Carried Out in Meerut District [hereafter referred to as *Rape Text*], p. 113 (sixth interview). The dates of my interviews have been eliminated from the notes to preserve the anonymity of my respondents.

[6] My interviews throw no light on the question of how the old man would have known the names of the alleged culprits, a point that casts doubt on his veracity.

[7] *Rape Text*, p. 113 (sixth interview, taped).

[8] Ibid., p. 17 (fourth interview).

[9] Ibid. (fourth interview).

[10] Ibid., p. 20 (fourth interview).

the matter. It was also reported that two of the police constables and a third local policeman were in cahoots with the *goondas*.[11]

On the evening of the 9th, several local people informed the District Magistrate, Meerut, of the incident in Daphnala. He in turn contacted the subdivisional magistrate (SDM), Nakoda, and instructed him to go immediately to Daphnala to investigate the situation there and find out the truth.[12] The SDM arrived in Daphnala that same evening at 6:30 P.M. July 9, being a Saturday, was the weekly market day in Daphnala. There was, therefore, a larger crowd of people than usual in the town, including many from the surrounding area. Those gathered in Daphnala were now angry about the incident and about the rumored involvement of the police on the side of the *goondas*. Consequently, by the time the SDM reached the police station in Daphnala, an angry crowd of 2,500 to 3,000 people was already assembled there, shouting demands for the return of the girl or the handing over of the culprits to them.[13]

At the scene at this time were the responsible and prominent public figures of the town, including Dr. Sengupta and Dr. Khosla. These men conferred with the police authorities, who asked them to give them time to do their investigative work on the case and to use their influence to disperse the crowd. Dr. Khosla addressed the crowd and requested them to disperse, and then left on his motorcycle to return to his home in Nakoda.

By the late evening, however, there was again a large crowd of people outside the police station in Daphnala. A confrontation between police and people occurred, involving an exchange of brickbats, culminating in a police *lathi*-charge[14] upon the crowd and a police firing in which some people were said to have been hurt. In the midst of the melee, some persons from the crowd broke the window panes of the SDM's jeep.

On the morning of the 10th, the superintendent of police (SP) and the District Magistrate arrived on the scene along with five or six truckloads of PAC men. The DM conducted an investigation, including administering a beating to the three men being held in custody, after which he called the prominent public men to discuss the case with them. The prominent citizens of Daphnala present on this occasion included Dr. Sengupta, Dr. Khosla, and Mr. Nuruddin. The DM informed these men of the results of his investigation so far, namely, that there was a girl who had been raped and that the *goondas* in custody had admitted their complicity, but had refused to disclose the girl's location despite the beatings they had been given. The DM said he would do his best to find the girl, but that he could not promise

[11] Ibid., p. 21 (fourth interview).
[12] Ibid., p. 22 (fourth interview).
[13] Ibid., p. 25 (fourth interview).
[14] A *lathi* is a bamboo stick, the Indian police baton.

success. Nor could he obtain further information from the *goonda*s who had been arrested, since they were extremely tough men and had been beaten thoroughly without revealing the girl's location. He issued orders also for the suspension or punishment of four police constables and subinspectors suspected of collusion with the *goonda*s.

In the meantime, a huge crowd said to number between eight thousand and ten thousand[15] people had gathered at the police station.[16] On the request of the DM, several responsible citizens of the town, including Dr. Khosla and Mr. Nuruddin, addressed the crowd and asked them to disperse, remain peaceful, and allow the authorities to pursue their investigation of the case.

The DM and the SSP then combed the area in search of the girl without success. They also brought the girl's father to the police station and then went to his residential village of Malapur in Muzaffarnagar district. There they learned that the so-called father of the girl was not only not her father, but was not married nor was his own father married. In fact, he had bought the girl as a prostitute and was probably on the move with her in order to sell her. When they returned to the police station, the DM and the SSP learned that the so-called father of the girl had escaped from custody and was now gone without a trace.

By the morning of the 11th, therefore, the attitude of the district civil and police authorities had changed completely. They were no longer in sympathy with the alleged victims of the *goonda*s and were now most concerned with controlling the crowd that had been mobilized in connection with the incident. The police began to say that there had never been any girl and that the whole case was false.[17] Therefore, their attentions were directed toward the public men who had been most involved in the incident, Dr. Sengupta and Dr. Khosla.

Dr. Sengupta was suspected of complicity in harboring the alleged father of the girl, but was not arrested. Dr. Khosla, however, was charged with throwing brickbats at the police *chowki* (station) and was put in jail in Meerut city. Before his arrest, however, he and his supporters in the Arya Samaj held a meeting attended by eight hundred to nine hundred people in which an action committee was formed to demand that the police continue their investigation of the case and be compelled to produce the girl. Anticipating police action against them, they also prepared a plan to offer themselves for arrest should any of their number be arrested on false charges. Dr. Khosla and seven of his supporters were arrested on July 13.

Following the plan of the action committee, approximately 150 people

---

[15] I suspect that all the crowd figures given to me concerning this incident are exaggerated given the size of the town itself.

[16] *Rape Text*, p. 35 (fourth interview).

[17] Ibid., p. 46 (fourth interview).

offered themselves for arrest at the police station on the 14th. However, the DM responded instead by keeping the *satyagrahis* standing in the scorching July heat without water and refusing to release them until they signed a paper promising not to engage in further protest activities. On the same day, a procession of "around six thousand people" marched through Daphnala shouting for the release of Dr. Khosla and for the recovery of the girl.[18] Dr. Khosla and his supporters remained in jail until they secured bail from the High Court in Allahabad on August 5. A crowd of four hundred to five hundred people were present at the time of their release to garland them.

After his release from jail, Dr. Khosla organized some meetings of opposition party leaders in an effort to keep public attention on the case. However, no success was achieved in drawing wider attention to this local situation. The *goondas* who had been arrested were released on bail. The girl and her so-called father were gone. Cases were pending at the time of my visit against the organizers of the protests, Dr. Khosla and his supporters.

Issues and Questions

The incident at Daphnala in July 1983 contained most of the elements required to produce a Hindu–Muslim communal riot. That fear was clearly uppermost in the minds of the superior authorities of the district, particularly the District Magistrate. Instead of a communal riot, however, the incident was turned into a confrontation between the authorities and the police, on the one hand, and the public, on the other hand.

As in the case of Theft of an Idol, the precipitating incident, the alleged rape of a girl by eleven men, receded into the background as hostilities developed between the police and the public. Also, as in the Pachpera incident, the centerpiece disappeared: No one in Aligarh admits to knowing where the idol is and no one in Meerut admits to knowing the whereabouts of the girl or her "father." Just as it is not definitely established whether the idol was *ashtadhatu*, so it is not certain that the girl was in fact raped or was offered on payment for the use of the men or for purchase by them. It is likely from the circumstances of the drama staged by the "father" that the girl at least was kidnapped and that he either received a payment for use but lost the girl altogether or he received nothing at all.

There are two important differences, however, between the incidents at Pachpera and Daphnala. One is the fact that the latter incident took place in a town on the day of its weekly bazaar when large numbers of people could be mobilized quickly. The second is that the incident, as already noted above, had the potential for conversion into a communal riot. What, then, prevented its conversion? What can be learned from this incident about

18 Ibid., p. 65 (fourth interview).

Hindu–Muslim relations and the conditions under which communal riots develop in such situations? Why did it become instead a police–public confrontation? What can be learned from this incident about the relations among the authorities, the police, the public, and public men in a bazaar town in north India?

VIEWPOINTS AND VOICES

The Authorities

The District Magistrate of Meerut at the time of the Daphnala incident was Mr. Timothy Matthew, a Kerala Christian. He was, therefore, an outsider by place of origin and religion whose neutrality and impartiality on communal matters were never in doubt. In fact, Matthew had been brought to the district toward the end of the vicious communal riots of the preceding year in Meerut city to bring them under control. He was also the kind of officer whom one often meets at this level of administration in India, one who declares openly that communal riots can be prevented and controlled if the administration acts properly and who is willing to stake his personal reputation on his ability to do so.

As soon as he was informed of the developments surrounding the incident at Daphnala, especially the rising tension in the town, Matthew clearly felt there was a potential for a communal riot, which he was determined to prevent. His own brief account of the circumstances places the incident unequivocally in the context of Hindu–Muslim relations. He saw the situation as of a piece with similar incidents that led to communal riots elsewhere.

In fact, Matthew referred to the incident at Daphnala, which was fresh in his mind at the time, in response to a general question concerning his personal analysis of the reasons for communal riots in India in general. He responded by saying that it is something like international politics, where every communal leader thinks that he can come to the brink, exploiting potential situations of communal conflict for political advantage and risking violence in the process. In Daphnala, he noted, a girl was kidnapped and raped. Some persons said that the men who raped the girl were Muslim and that the girl was a Hindu. These people exploited the situation. They lodged a complaint and later they damaged the SDM's jeep. They were arrested and a police officer was suspended. Later, however, it was found that the girl was not of good character, that she was a prostitute.[19]

In the DM's mind, therefore, towns such as Daphnala contain communal political leaders—in this case Hindu communal leaders—ready to exploit ordinary criminal incidents in which Hindus appear to have been harmed by Muslims. Often, however, the facts are otherwise: In this case, whether

[19] Ibid., p. 1 (first interview, from notes).

kidnapped and raped or not, the girl was a prostitute and, therefore, was not a "Hindu girl" victimized by "Muslim rapists." In Matthew's view, the facts are ambiguous, but the actions of the Hindu communal leaders are not.

The acting SSP at the time of my visit made similar remarks. He, too, cited the incident at Daphnala as a typical example of how communal riots begin. He drew the conclusion also that communal riots "don't have any concrete base."[20] In other words, the precipitating incidents that lead to communal riots have nothing to do with Hindu–Muslim relations.

One of the characteristic problems faced in acquiring precise, detailed knowledge of local events such as these and their contexts in north India is that the responsible authorities who have to deal with them also tend to disappear, like the idol and the girl. They are suspended or transferred by higher authorities, often on the demand of local politicians and their influential friends in the district headquarters or state capital. Although my interviews were conducted just after the release of Dr. Khosla and his supporters from jail, several persons who had personal knowledge of the events were already gone.

Thus, when I went to interview the station officer, Nakoda, I found that he had been there only a week and that the incident, therefore, had occurred before his posting to Nakoda. His account, therefore, differs in minor details from that given by other district civil and police authorities. It is, nevertheless, of value because of its overall conformity with the latter. That is, there is a consistent "police view" of this incident and others like it. The station officer's (SO's) account is given below.

> PRB: Now, . . . I have heard in Meerut talking to . . . Mr. Nepal Singh and other officers and the District Magistrate and so forth that there was an incident in Daphnala. Do you have knowledge of this incident?
>
> SO: It was before my posting. It was [a] very unfortunate incident. The way it was produced, that incident, the way it was told to people, was wrong. First, it was said that some people had kidnapped a man's daughter. But, after investigation it was found that the person who said that his daughter had been kidnapped was involved in the business of buying and selling girls, in that racket, and the girl whom he had bought was also that type of girl and she also deceived that person. And once he was standing somewhere and that girl asked him to go and buy some bananas for her. And when that person went to buy the bananas, this girl ran away. And then he said that his daughter has been kidnapped and all. And then the people who put forth the issue before the police and the general public were not good. [. . .]

[20] Ibid., p. 2 (second interview, from notes).

The main person behind this agitation was Dr. Ram Prasad. He had
around 250 to 300 followers and these people threw brickbats and
stones on the police and even overturned the jeep of the [SDM].
And then the police arrested these people and whomever they could
get hold of. And then also they filed a case against the people who
had kidnapped the girl. So, they were also arrested.

PRB: And what is the position now? [. . .]

SO: Now everyone is released on bail. [. . .]

PRB: Now, . . . what happened to the station officer who was there?
Was he transferred because of this incident or not?

SO: I have heard that he did not give prompt information to the
higher authorities. He was transferred for that reason.[21]

The view expressed in these and other statements by the police is that an
unfortunate incident occurred, but more unfortunate was that the people
were misinformed about it. False rumors were spread, which were taken up
by irresponsible people such as Dr. Khosla. These people also engaged in
hostile actions against the police and were arrested for their part in them.
The station officer was suspended not because of his complicity with the
*goonda*s, but because he did not give prompt information to the higher authorities. Failure to give prompt information on such a matter was particularly serious in their eyes because of the danger of a communal riot, which
it was the highest priority of the district authorities to prevent.

It is noteworthy that even Dr. Khosla, who was quite bitter and angry
about his treatment by the police and the District Magistrate, acknowledged
that the latter's actions were motivated primarily by his concern to prevent a
communal riot. When I asked him to explain the DM's actions, particularly
his treatment of the crowd before the police station, he gave this response.

Because the DM was convinced that here Hindu–Muslim riots are being pro-
moted, therefore, when he saw a procession, he determined that there should be
no Hindu–Muslim riot, that's why he terrorized us in this way. The DM is able
to accept any kind of tension in the area, but he cannot tolerate a communal
riot. Therefore, he became agitated, the burden was placed on him, these Congress leaders and the police officials and this Baldev Singh Talwar, the CO
[Commanding Officer], all these officials tried to convince him [of the danger].[22]

---

[21] Ibid., pp. 3–8 (third interview, from notes).

[22] *KyuNke . . . DM ke dimag meN yah bat daldi thi ki yahaN par Hindu–Muslim riot kara ja
raha hai, us ne julus ko samajh ke dekha ki Hindu–Muslim riot to nahiN ho rahe, is liye ham
log* terrorize *karo jaise ho sakta ho. DM . . . kar sakta hai apne kahiN bhi kshetra meN tens.,
Hindu,* communal riot *pasand nahiN kar sakta. Is liye wah* agitated *ho gaya, us ke dimag meN
bat dali gayi, in Congress (I) ke* leaders, leaders *ne dali aur* police *ke adhikaroN dali aur yah
Baldev Singh Talwar jaise adhikaroN dali, CO ne* (ibid., p. 75 [fourth interview]).

Dr. Khosla's justification of the DM's actions, however, did not extend to the police officers at the local level, against whom he and others involved in the incident had harsh words to say. It is necessary, therefore, to examine the attitudes of the public men who took up the issue before the police, to see how they viewed the rape case, whether they considered it a communal matter or a matter of general public concern. It is also important to consider how the public viewed the police actions and why such large crowds massed at the police station and vented their anger upon the police and the SDM's jeep.

Public Men: Dr. Ram Prasad Khosla

Dr. Ram Prasad Khosla is the public man who, in the eyes of the police, stood at the center of the disturbances that occurred in connection with the alleged rape of the girl in Daphnala. Although he maintains his primary residence in Nakoda and his dispensary in Daphnala, his natal place is a village on the outskirts of Daphnala, where I interviewed him. The population of this village is one-third Muslim and was dominated in the past by Muslim *zamindars*. Dr. Khosla, a Brahman, had been elected *pradhan* of the village the previous year in an election in which the Muslim vote was divided between the candidates of two Muslim factions. Dr. Khosla, however, claims that he had also received support from Muslims in the past, including some Muslim support even in the last election.

Dr. Khosla had been an active and prominent member of the district Jan Sangh/BJP throughout his political career and had been alternately president and general secretary of the district party. As noted above, he was also an Arya Samaji and a member of the RSS. His public political career, however, had been restricted because the Niwaspur Legislative Assembly constituency in which he resided had been converted to a reserved Scheduled Caste constituency. Although he contested in Niwaspur in 1962 when it was a general constituency and came in second after the Congress candidate, he had to confine his local electoral ambitions thereafter to village and *panchayat samiti* (local council) elections.

According to Dr. Khosla's own account of the events, he was first informed about the abduction of the girl by "two prominent people who had come to seek his assistance."[23] By the time he was informed, the police had also been notified, the girl's "father" had been to the police station, the three *goondas* and the witness had been arrested, the witness had been detained, and the *goondas* had been released. Dr. Khosla advised the people who came to see him to gather a larger group of people and go to the police station. He said that he himself at first remained aloof. When, following his

[23] Ibid., p. 18 (fourth interview).

advice, the first group of concerned citizens, numbering twenty to twenty-five persons, went to the police station, the police released the witness, rearrested the *goonda*s, and began their interrogation of them.

The question of the communal identity of the three *goonda*s was not raised by Dr. Khosla except in response to my own questions. He gave their names as Rafi, Dudhu, and Pahalwan. When I asked if they were all Muslims, he said that "two were Muslims and one was their servant." Nor did he mention that the girl was Hindu until I asked him. The only communal suggestion in his response at this point was to note that the Hindu in the group (Pahalwan) was their servant, which would make him subordinate to the Muslims as the prime actors in the rape of a Hindu girl. Dr. Khosla's own account focused on the question of the behavior of the police.

Dr. Khosla's chief complaint was that the police had not taken any action initially and that, when they did, several were revealed to be in cahoots with the *goonda*s. The police were said to have been advising the *goonda*s not to reveal where the girl was being kept. The implication, obviously, is either that the police themselves were also enjoying the use of the girl or that they were being paid to allow the abduction and sale of the girl to proceed or both. The suspension of the constables and other local policemen was placed by Dr. Khosla in the context of their misbehavior in this regard, rather than in the context of their failure to inform the district authorities of a potentially dangerous communal situation.[24]

Dr. Khosla also attributed the rising tension among the people on the day of the Saturday market to their anger at police inaction and misbehavior,[25] not to rising Hindu–Muslim animosity. At the same time, it is also evident from one statement that Dr. Khosla made in this context that the rape situation was considered to be of special concern for the Hindus of the town. This concern is evident in the feelings he expressed in connection with the visit on Saturday evening by eight or ten "prominent people and some young people" who came to him that evening to ask him to come to the police station where the SDM had also come. He said: "Whenever there is any crisis in the Hindu religion, then the people rush to me. And whenever I am in crisis, I face some problem, then they don't support me. . . . Otherwise, at that time, there was not any question of Hindus and Muslims. Both were equally angry. . . . Both were agitated equally."[26] This agitation allegedly among Hindus and Muslims equally had now spread to a crowd of 2,500 to 3,000 people assembled at the police station on that Saturday evening.

Whether it is true that Hindus and Muslims were equally agitated, the ambiguity in Dr. Khosla's remarks is a common response among militant

[24] Ibid., pp. 21, 32 (fourth interview).
[25] Ibid., p. 23 (fourth interview).
[26] Ibid., p. 24 (fourth interview).

Hindus in situations such as these. A Hindu girl has been raped by Muslims. It is a crisis for Hindus. Hindus and Muslims, he says, are equally agitated about it. How, then, can Dr. Khosla and others like him be considered fomentors of communalism when they perceive members of the other community as on their side in an issue involving a criminal act by Muslims against a Hindu girl? The unstated implication must be that these were "good Muslims," noncommunal Muslims, who have not been misguided into perceiving this situation in communal terms.

It is, however, by no means clear that Hindus and Muslims were equally in the crowd on that Saturday evening or even that there were any Muslims in the crowd at all. Other accounts dispute the presence of Muslims in the crowd. All that is certain is that the anger of the crowd that Saturday evening was directed toward the police and was expressed in the hurling of brickbats and the damage done to the SDM's jeep.

Pursuing the theme of Hindu–Muslim unity against the police, Dr. Khosla also noted that, on the day after the Saturday night fracas, "many prominent people, . . . even including Muslims, like Nuruddin"[27] came to the police station to discuss the situation with the District Magistrate. On that occasion, Mr. Nuruddin also was said to have expressed his feelings concerning the abduction and alleged rape in noncommunal terms. He was reported to have said that "this is a dirty spot, this incident is a dirty spot on our Daphnala."[28] It was framed, therefore, as a matter of civic concern and shame for the reputation of the town and its people generally. Mr. Nuruddin also joined with Dr. Khosla and other public men at this time in appealing to the people to disperse and allow the authorities to do their work.[29]

The authorities also sought to assuage the anger of the people against the police on this occasion by suspending or disciplining four policemen.[30] However, when the police did their investigative work and the authorities discovered that the whole incident was a grand fraud in which they and the public both had been fooled by a wily old pimp, their anger turned against the public men who had aroused the people. Some among the latter were threatened with police action, others with withdrawal of licenses to conduct their businesses, and others, including especially Dr. Khosla, were arrested on charges of throwing brickbats at the police station and damaging the SDM's jeep.

In response, Dr. Khosla's hostility toward the police deepened. He did not believe the police when they "started saying that there was no girl here and this is a false case." He claimed that the police were saying this because

[27] Ibid., p. 30 (fourth interview).
[28] Ibid., p. 33 (fourth interview).
[29] Ibid., p. 35 (fourth interview).
[30] Ibid., p. 36 (fourth interview).

one of the three "culprits . . . was a relative of Mr. Sirajuddin and Nuruddin." When I asked what kind of relative, he responded "that there are so many relations among the Muslims, so [it is hard to say], but there was some relation."[31]

An action committee was organized by the local Arya Samaj in which Dr. Khosla was made the convenor. Its purpose was to compel the police to continue to pursue their investigation in order to recover the girl and to find the "father" who had absconded. It was also formed in anticipation of police action against the protest organizers. Dr. Khosla claims that, at the Arya Samaj meeting at which the action committee was organized, "both Hindus as well as Muslims were present."[32]

Hindus and Muslims, it was argued, were now united against the police, who were failing to do their duty and were preparing false cases against people. Dr. Khosla went to the extent of quoting Justice A. N. Mullah, a Muslim High Court justice, who had once said that—in Dr. Khosla's quotation of him—"if there is any gang of *dacoit*s and thieves in UP, that is police."[33]

The hostility of the police toward the protest organizers and Dr. Khosla in particular is brought out well in his account of his arrest. The commanding officer who arrested him prefaced the arrest with the remark that "I want you to become a leader. And I'll make you a leader." He told Dr. Khosla that he wanted him to "become more popular among the people."[34] In the Indian context, this is a jibe against politicians whose reputations and leadership during the nationalist movement and in many post-Independence movements and agitations as well were made by courting arrest or otherwise being arrested and thereby being perceived by the public as heroes sacrificing their freedom for the sake of some public good.

The hostility of the authorities and their intent to humiliate the protest organizers also is suggested by Dr. Khosla's account of his imprisonment. Instead of being placed in the somewhat more comfortable jail setting usually provided to political detainees, Dr. Khosla and his colleagues were placed together with "murderers and criminals and *dacoit*s."[35] When they applied for release on bail, the district judge rejected their appeal. The judge was reported by Dr. Khosla to have "said in his judgment that these people are a headache for the administration." He also gave his opinion that "to maintain peace and normalcy, it is necessary to keep these people longer in jail."[36] Their stay in jail did, however, contribute to their popularity with the

---

[31] Ibid., p. 46 (fourth interview).
[32] Ibid., p. 53 (fourth interview).
[33] Ibid., p. 54 (fourth interview).
[34] Ibid., pp. 56–57 (fourth interview).
[35] Ibid., p. 61 (fourth interview).
[36] Ibid., pp. 65–66 (fourth interview).

people, as the commanding officer had anticipated since, as is customary in such situations, they were upon their ultimate release from jail greeted and garlanded by a crowd of four hundred to five hundred people.

As noted above, the DM also dealt harshly with the people who were not put in jail, breaking up the antipolice movement by ordering a *lathi*-charge against the crowds and compelling people to stand exposed in the sun without water until they signed a bond.

For his part, Dr. Khosla persisted up to the time of my interview with him in his belief that the police had misbehaved and that they had not pursued the case properly. He noted that "the police have neither recovered the girl nor the father . . . nor do they want to recover the father of the girl."[37] Confronted with the police argument that the girl was nothing more than a prostitute and the father a girl-slaver, his response was that the police should nevertheless "produce that girl." Why do they not want to produce the girl and the father? he asked. He conceded that he had also inquired concerning the situation and that it was true that the girl was not the man's daughter, that she was bought.[38] He said, nevertheless, that she was just a girl.[39] Moreover, if it is true that the "father" was in the racket of buying and selling girl(s), "then why did the police allow [him] to go?" "And if the person was guilty and he was involved in such a racket, then why was he not arrested?"[40]

Instead of pursuing the investigation of the case, recovering the girl, and catching the "father," the police were busy concocting false cases against Dr. Khosla and others. The allegedly false complaint against him "for throwing stones on the police *chowki*" was prepared "by the suspended subinspector," who had already been suspended at the time of Dr. Khosla's arrest. Dr. Khosla argued that if "this subinspector was guilty," then "why, on his instructions, was I charged and a complaint lodged against me?"[41] Moreover, the subinspector's complaint had been filed against him on the 9th. Dr. Khosla had seen the District Magistrate in Meerut on the 11th. On the 12th, he met the police inspector, Nakoda. On the 13th, he met the SDM, Nakoda. Why, then, was he not arrested at any of those meetings with high police officers of the district? Why did they arrest him only on the evening of the 13th? Dr. Khosla's explanation is that there was a "conspiracy" among the police to arrest him and that the complaint against him was backdated to make his arrest possible. These facts only prove the truth of Justice Mullah's statements that "the police is a gang of *dacoits*."[42]

Dr. Khosla also insisted that there was a conspiracy between the police

[37] Ibid., p. 69 (fourth interview).
[38] Ibid. (fourth interview).
[39] Ibid., p. 70 (fourth interview).
[40] Ibid., p. 71 (fourth interview).
[41] Ibid., pp. 71–72 (fourth interview).
[42] Ibid., pp. 73–75 (fourth interview).

and the local Congress leaders to arrest him and get him out of the way during this incident not only because a relation of one of the Congressmen was supposed to have been one of the culprits but because "the leaders of Congress (I) consider that he is a stumbling block in their way."[43] Mr. Nuruddin, he claimed, had tried to implicate him in a false case of conspiracy to murder someone fourteen years before.[44]

At the end of the interview, I confronted Dr. Khosla directly with the charge that he was a communalist and a fomentor of Hindu–Muslim tension, which led to the exchange given below.

> PRB: And then, of course, ah, you must know that the police, some people say that you are [a] notorious communalist and causing Hindu–Muslim *jhagada* [conflict].
>
> Dr. K: I said that ten years ago, Muslims in this village had voted for me for *pradhan* and I was elected. And I reside in a village of Muslims. In my village until now there was no Hindu–Muslim feeling. In my constituency until now there was never the tension of a Hindu–Muslim riot. Until this Daphnala case there was no case of Hindu–Muslim [tension]. When there was a strike on the 9th demanding the recovery of that girl, both Hindus and Muslims closed their shops. And both Hindus and Muslims wanted that girl to be recovered. There was no question of Hindu–Muslim [feeling]. Some Congress leaders gave this incident a communal color because they wanted to save their relative. And the police officers who wanted to save their own people. And, on this ground, they sent me to jail and gave this thing a communal color. There was no . . . communal question in this area.[45]

At the very end of the interview, Dr. Khosla also remarked that "any man, any Indian, will be agitated on the question of the rape of a girl." It was, therefore, never a Hindu–Muslim issue at all.

Public Men: Dr. Sengupta

The story began with Dr. Sengupta, who discovered the old man weeping outside his dispensary. Dr. Sengupta is a practicing Ayurvedic physician whose practice, however, was restricted at the time because of his advanced age and his heart condition. Dr. Sengupta has played no role in local politics, but he described himself as a person who had been a Congressman all his life, from the days of Mahatma Gandhi, who had great respect for the

---

[43] Ibid., p. 76 (fourth interview).
[44] Ibid., p. 77 (fourth interview).
[45] Ibid., p. 74 (fourth interview).

Nehru family, and who would remain a Congressman until the end of his life.

Dr. Sengupta began his account of the incident with the statement that it "was not a communal thing."[46] After he discovered the old man and heard his story, he did the logical thing and took him to see Mr. Nuruddin, the most prominent Congress politician of the town and a Muslim.[47] He told Mr. Nuruddin "that this is a very shameful thing for this town that a girl has been kidnapped from this place, from this town."[48] Mr. Nuruddin responded by reporting the matter to the police.

When, the next day, a crowd of around "thirty to forty people came" to his dispensary to ask what had happened in the case, he "again rushed to Mr. Nuruddin,"[49] this time accompanied by the crowd that had come to see him. On this occasion, Mr. Nuruddin said that he had done what he could, but that "this gathering is not going to affect me." Whatever he could do, he said, he could and would do.

I asked Dr. Sengupta if this gathering of people comprised Hindus or Muslims or both. He said: "This I can't say."[50] He responded similarly to the same question about the big crowd that gathered the next evening in front of the police station, which he, along with the other public men of the town, asked to disperse peacefully.

PRB: Were they Hindus or Muslims or both?

Dr. S: This I can't say, [but] up to that time this was not a communal thing.[51]

I also asked Dr. Sengupta if the crowds that began to gather during these first days had any leader. He said that they had none,[52] rather "that everyone was a leader and nobody was willing to listen to anybody."[53] When I asked specifically how Dr. Khosla had become involved in the incident, he responded that Dr. Khosla had become involved in the same way that he had, by some people who had gone to tell him about it.[54] He also confirmed that Dr. Khosla as well as Mr. Nuruddin addressed the crowd at the police station, requesting them to disperse.[55]

The strong impression that comes out of the interview with Dr. Sengupta and his account of the incident is that he is a kind and sympathetic man,

---

[46] Ibid., p. 109 (sixth interview, taped).
[47] Ibid., p. 111 (sixth interview).
[48] Ibid., p. 112 (sixth interview).
[49] Ibid., p. 113 (sixth interview).
[50] Ibid., p. 114 (sixth interview).
[51] Ibid., p. 116 (sixth interview).
[52] Ibid., p. 113 (sixth interview).
[53] Ibid., p. 115 (sixth interview).
[54] Ibid., p. 117 (sixth interview).
[55] Ibid., p. 120 (sixth interview).

who was moved by the apparent plight of the old man whose "daughter" had been abducted. He said that whenever he sees "anybody grieved," he also "becomes grieved." Moreover, when he learned later from the SSP that the scene put on by the old man "was just a drama," he was deeply hurt and felt defrauded. He even spoke in a childlike manner, saying in effect that he had learned his lesson and that "now whenever I see any person who is grief-stricken, I will not help him."[56]

Dr. Sengupta also suffered the indignity of being accused by the police of harboring the old man. He had taken him in for a night or two after he had found him weeping in the street and had then brought him to the police station where he stayed until his escape. After his escape, by which time it had been discovered that he was a girl-slaver, the police came to Dr. Sengupta in search of the old man and accused him of hiding him.

At this point, Dr. Sengupta went to see Dr. Khosla. When I asked him why he did not go again to Mr. Nuruddin, he said, "Because at that time Mr. Nuruddin had lost his confidence." When I asked him why, he said that, after the police visit to the old man's village and the latter's escape, Mr. Nuruddin "made this thing communal."[57] It is not clear how Mr. Nuruddin turned the incident into a communal one except that he now cooperated with the police rather than with the citizenry and that he may also have cooperated to the extent of providing the names of eleven citizens, all of whom happened to be Hindu, who were accused of throwing stones at the police station and damaging the SDM's jeep.[58]

Dr. Sengupta felt quite aggrieved by Nuruddin's behavior toward him in connection with the case. He remarked that these people from former *zamindar* families think they are the natural rulers. He said that Mr. Nuruddin abused him verbally for his part in the incident. I asked him why, knowing Nuruddin's character, he went to him in the first place. He responded by saying that he did so to insure that the incident did not become communal in any way. I asked why he thought the incident might become communal, if that meant that he, Dr. Sengupta, knew from the beginning that the girl and the man were Hindu. He said he did know that because the woman's dress indicated that she was a Hindu.

At the same time, Dr. Sengupta was emphatic that he never thought about the incident in communal terms. He had said earlier in the interview that he never thought about whether the girl was Muslim or Hindu. "I had thought that this is just the prestige of this town and something should be done."[59] He said further:

---

[56] Ibid., p. 124 (sixth interview).
[57] Ibid., p. 127 (sixth interview).
[58] Ibid., p. 128 (sixth interview).
[59] Ibid., p. 129 (sixth interview).

I never took this issue as communal. I thought that it is an insult for this town, of which I am also a citizen. So that's why I took up this case and I was interested. Because I am not communal. Because, being a Congressman, I am not communal. I believe in all religions.[60]

Despite the inconsistency in Dr. Sengupta's account concerning his awareness of whether the girl was Hindu or Muslim, there are no grounds to doubt his sincerity in this regard. As an old Congressman and a Gandhian, he said categorically: "Until my death I will not tolerate anything communal and even if I have to sacrifice my life, I will do that to stop communal [conflict]."[61] To the extent he thought about the religion of the girl, he thought to prevent its becoming a communal matter by going to the most prominent public figure of the town, a Muslim, in order to treat the incident as a civic, rather than a communal matter, a matter of concern for all the people of the town, whether Hindu or Muslim.

Moreover, like Dr. Khosla, he continued to believe, even after the fraud was discovered, that the police should pursue the case.

> Dr. S: There was a rumor that this girl was bought. Then I thought that, okay, this is all right because this is a very bad crime that the girl has been bought. And the people who have sold that girl, they should also be punished severely. And then the father of that girl should be also punished.
>
> PRB: The so-called father.
>
> Dr. S: Yes. And then the real father of the girl should be also punished because he had brought up that girl and then, after twenty-five years, [he sold that girl]. I don't bring up my son or my children to sell them in future.[62]

Also like Dr. Khosla, Dr. Sengupta believes that the police misbehaved in this case.[63] They were allegedly hesitant at first to arrest Rafi, one of the men presumed to have been involved in the kidnapping. The presumption in the town, shared by Dr. Sengupta, was that the policemen who had been suspended had taken money from Rafi.

Public Men: Mr. Sirajuddin and Mr. Nuruddin

Mr. Sirajuddin, the sitting MLA from Dhanapur constituency at the time, was a physician trained in an integrated course of the traditional Muslim system of medicine and Western medicine. He had received his education

[60] Ibid., pp. 136–37 (sixth interview).
[61] Ibid., p. 136 (sixth interview).
[62] Ibid., p. 130 (sixth interview).
[63] Ibid., p. 137 (sixth interview).

from the Aligarh Muslim University, after which, in 1969, he returned to Daphnala, where he practiced allopathy (the Indian term for Western medicine). Mr. Sirajuddin was then an enormously fat man, living in a relatively grand old *zamindar*'s bungalow, with a courtyard entry in which several visitors lazed about.

Politically, Mr. Sirajuddin had been a Congressman loyal to Mrs. Gandhi throughout his political career. He had gone to jail in 1977 in connection with a protest on behalf of Mrs. Gandhi after she had been suspended from Parliament during the Janata regime. Sirajuddin had been given the ticket to contest the Dhanapur Legislative Assembly constituency through the patronage of Mohsina Kidwai, a prominent Muslim Congresswoman, then the MP from Meerut constituency. Sirajuddin's recruitment was clearly part of the general policy pursued by Mrs. Gandhi of maintaining a strong base within the Muslim minority in north India. He was, therefore, a Muslim politician recruited by another Muslim leader as part of the general Congress strategy at the time of maintaining and strengthening the Congress links with the Muslim community and winning their votes.

Sirajuddin's account of the kidnapping and alleged rape of the girl, paraphrased below, contains factual elements found in the reports given by Dr. Khosla and Dr. Sengupta, but the interpretation and emphasis given to some aspects of the incident, especially to Dr. Khosla's role in the matter, are quite different.

> An old man came to Daphnala by bus with a girl. At the bus stand, the girl asked the old man to get some mangos for her. When he returned, she was gone. She wanted to get rid of that old man. After her disappearance, the old man came to town and said that his mad girl had disappeared. Some people complained about the matter. It was then discovered that the girl had talked to Mr. Rafi Siddiqi, Mr. Pahalwan, a Hindu, Mr. Lakhan, a sweetmaker, a Hindu, and Mr. Kamma, two Hindus and two Muslims. A man said that the girl had talked to them. The police then arrested three of the men, Mr. Lakhan having gone somewhere else. And the police beat them.
>
> The public here and then Dr. Ram Prasad, an RSS leader and a BJP leader, wanted to create a communal riot. And Dr. Khosla told the public that a Muslim boy took a Hindu girl. On the night of 7th July, the public surrounded the police station, stoned the SDM's jeep, turned it over, and tried to burn it. They also tried to beat the driver. They even fired on the police with local-made pistols. Then, the police dispersed the crowd with a *lathi*-charge.
>
> Then, the DM and the SSP came here to inquire about the girl. The SSP personally beat the three men and the police beat them again and again to get them to divulge the whereabouts of the girl. But, they said nothing. The DM and the SSP then suspended two constables and one subinspector of the Daphnala police station.

Because of the stoning and burning of the SDM's jeep, the government registered a criminal case against eleven people, including Dr. Ram Prasad, who is the leader of the BJP and RSS, which want communal riots. His politics and the Jan Sangh and BJP politics are to promote communal riots in India. In this case, the police arrested Dr. Ram Prasad and three other members of the BJP in the evening of 13th July. Upon the arrest of Dr. Ram Prasad, some religious people came here and asked the police to arrest them also.

Some time afterwards, the DM, Mr. Matthew, personally came here to see the situation and bring it under control. He personally detained about 150 people and released them only after five hours. And the DM personally led a *lathi*-charge on the public. And he only released the people after taking personal bonds from them for payment in rupees to insure that they do not again indulge in violence.

In the meantime, the police had gone to the old man's village of Malapur, where his own younger brother revealed that the old man was not married. It was also disclosed that the girl was bought. And nobody [in the village] knew whether she was Muslim or Hindu. It was after this discovery that people belonging to the BJP were arrested. When the DM came to Daphnala a second time, then everything was over. When the people realized that this girl was bought and she was a prostitute type of girl, then people left the agitation. And this agitation was launched by the BJP only to foment a communal riot.[64]

Sirajuddin and Nuruddin confirm the role initially played by the latter in the case and the attitude of Dr. Sengupta at the time. Nuruddin said that Dr. Sengupta came to him and said that the girl must be found because "it is very shameful for this town" that such a thing has happened here. So, he said, he did go with Dr. Sengupta to take the old man to the police station.[65] Moreover, it was on Nuruddin's initiative that the arrests of the three alleged culprits were made.[66]

Sirajuddin, however, felt entirely differently from Dr. Khosla and Dr. Sengupta about continuing the police investigation once the fraud had been discovered. He saw no point in it, in fact. As for the girl, he said that prostitution was her profession. Girls in her profession in this area come from a place called Dhampur. They are sent to places like Daphnala for whatever reason and, "after some time, they escape [back] to the same place, they go back to Dhampur."[67] Early in the case, Sirajuddin felt that the girl must be found, but when he learned that she was not a good girl, that she was rather "a very bad character," then he lost interest in the matter. In fact, he came to the view that the girl had escaped on her own and that the

---

[64] Ibid., pp. 89–91 (fifth interview, taped).
[65] Ibid., p. 100 (fifth interview).
[66] Ibid., p. 92 (fifth interview).
[67] Ibid., p. 93 (fifth interview).

case against the three alleged culprits arrested for kidnapping and rape was a false one. Mr. Nuruddin agreed with his brother on this matter and said that the three men arrested were actually guards protecting the mango garden.[68] Sirajuddin even went to the extent of questioning the gender of the girl. He said that "some people say that girl was both male and female" and that, without the sari, one might not have considered her a girl at all.[69]

I asked Nuruddin why Dr. Sengupta kept the old man in his house for three days. He said it was only out of sympathy because he did "not understand that old fellow." At this point, the only humor to be expressed on this case was interjected in the following exchange.

> PRB: So the old fellow simply befooled everybody.
>
> N: Yes, everybody. [Laughter] Not only the people, . . . [but] an IAS officer and an IPS officer also. [Laughter] . . . An IPS officer was sitting [at the police station] when that old fellow came and the IPS officer said, "Have a cup of tea." But, the old man said, "No, I can't take it [mocking the old man's tone]. When my girl will come, then I'll touch this cup of tea." The IPS officer talked to the old man for half an hour, urging him to take some tea until finally he agreed. It means the old man also made a fool of that IPS officer. [. . .]
>
> PRB: And what was your impression? He befooled you also?
>
> N: No. I was suspicious. But, here is a man—I was suspicious, really—but I cannot address a single word against him because there is a great impact in the public mind [because] a mad girl has been taken. I cannot utter a single word [because of the way the old man was crying about his little girl].[70]

Sirajuddin also confirms the belief of Dr. Sengupta that he and his brother took the side of the police thereafter. He said that he felt that the people who had burned the police jeep and thrown stones at the police station were rightfully arrested.[71] They were rightfully arrested also, he felt, because "these people tried to arouse this communal sentiment among the masses."[72] When I asked Nuruddin if the crowd that attacked the police station were all Hindus or a mixed crowd of Hindus and Muslims, he said they were "all Hindus." Muslims were not taking any interest in the case once the police had arrested those three persons, although he did acknowledge that, before the arrest, Muslims also had sympathy with the alleged plight of the old man

---

[68] Ibid., p. 99 (fifth interview)

[69] Ibid., pp. 97–98 (fifth interview).

[70] Ibid., pp. 101–02 (fifth interview).

[71] Ibid., p. 95 (fifth interview).

[72] Ibid., p. 96 (fifth interview).

and his girl.[73] He also said later that persons from the Jat caste living in the town area had taken a great part in the case.[74]

I asked Nuruddin if Dr. Khosla was one of the persons who attacked the police station.

> N: Yes, of course. He is . . . practiced in this [kind of thing].
>
> PRB: But, some people say he is a communalist, but isn't it a fact that he lives in a village with Muslims and is *pradhan* of this Chota Gram village, which is dominated by Muslims?
>
> N: No, . . . if . . . the Muslims . . . are dominating, then [how] can he succeed in that place? Both the Muslims and Hindus are equal in that place. . . . He contested the election, Muslims were defeated, and he secured votes. . . . He is also dominating and others also are dominating.[75] [. . .]
>
> PRB: [So], you say . . . he was actually participating in the [attack on the police station].
>
> N: Why not? Openly.
>
> PRB: Openly. Throwing brickbats himself?
>
> N: Abusing. [Saying], "Take it. Take revenge."[76] [. . .]
>
> PRB: And before the arrest, did Dr. Ram Prasad arouse the crowd or the crowd was aroused by its own feelings?
>
> N: That was on a market day and he had invited [people from] several local villages to come.
>
> PRB: So it was Dr. Ram Prasad from the beginning.
>
> N: Yes.
>
> PRB: He initiated the whole thing. [. . .]
>
> N: Ram Prasad . . . tried to make it communal.
>
> PRB: But he failed.
>
> N: . . . We advised people. Why are you so interested? Go back, go to your houses, don't participate. Persons who are guilty have been arrested. What is our interest? Let the police punish them.[77]

On the question of the political rivalry between Sirajuddin and his brother, on the one hand, and Dr. Khosla, on the other, Sirajuddin acknowledges that there was a political feud between them. He said that "because we are powerful and we are MLAs and we have won the elections of block *pramukh* (president) and all, so just to give the Congress a bad name, these people do all sorts of things."[78]

---

[73] Ibid., pp. 104, 107 (fifth interview).
[74] Ibid., p. 106 (fifth interview).
[75] Ibid., p. 103 (fifth interview).
[76] Ibid., p. 104 (fifth interview).
[77] Ibid., p. 109 (fifth interview).
[78] Ibid., p. 94 (fifth interview).

Nuruddin, however, dismissed the allegation made by Dr. Khosla that he had filed false cases against him years before.

> N: Not, not a single [case], why? He is nowhere. I think . . . he can't do, . . . what can he do against me? I think that he is not so powerful. And then . . . why [should I be] so interested? He is only a layman, just like other doctors.[79]

There is not much doubt, however, that Nuruddin and Sirajuddin, on the one side, and Dr. Khosla and his supporters, on the other side, represented distinct political interests resting on different communal support bases. By Nuruddin's reckoning, the Muslims of the area were then "80 to 90 percent . . . with Congress."[80] The reason given was that the Congress had no hatred for the Muslims, the implication being that the BJP did have such hatred. For the latter reason, of course, the Muslims also "have no sympathy with Jan Sangh [BJP] nor attachment with Jan Sangh."[81] For similar reasons, Nuruddin argued that the Muslims had no sympathy with the Lok Dal, although the latter statement was not factually correct at the time for Meerut district as a whole, where the Lok Dal did get some electoral support from Muslims.

Insofar as Daphnala is concerned, however, the underlying political dimension to the incident described above is the differentiated political support base among Hindus and Muslims of Dr. Ram Prasad and the brothers Sirajuddin and Nuruddin. Dr. Ram Prasad, with his base of support among the Hindus of the area, which he required to challenge the dominance of the Muslim leaders of Daphnala, is perceived by Sirajuddin and Nuruddin as a communalist Hindu leader bent upon fomenting a communal riot in order to get political advantage from it among his fellow-Hindus. This view was also part of the general Congress ideology of the time, shared with Hindus in the party. For example, in the local area, the sitting Congress MLA from the reserved constituency of Niwaspur had the same view of the incident as Sirajuddin and Nuruddin, as indicated in his account of it paraphrased below.

> PRB: Now, I have been to Daphnala and I hear that there was some incident there, . . . *jhagada* between the police and the people.
> MLA: This incident took place because one man had bought a girl from outside and that girl escaped from that place, Daphnala. And there are a few people . . . belonging to Jan Sangh, they spread the rumor that they have taken, some people have kidnapped a Hindu

[79] Ibid., p. 105 (fifth interview).
[80] Ibid., p. 106 (fifth interview).
[81] Ibid., p. 107 (fifth interview).

girl. Whereas the people who kidnapped that girl, they were both
Hindus and Muslims, two Hindus and two Muslims.

And then the people were misguided and attacked the police.[82]

[. . .]

PRB: Isn't it a fact that the police misbehaved?

MLA: When the people started throwing stones at the police, then, to
save their lives, the police also became very tough.

PRB: Why the police officers were suspended?

MLA: They were suspended because they had misguided the administration. And they did not inform authorities in due time.

PRB: Isn't it a fact that in the first few days, both Hindus and Muslims were involved in this and that it was not a communal thing?

MLA: No. Only Hindus were involved. Muslims were not involved.
And only because of this communal feeling, the question of [police
use of] force came.

PRB: And who was behind this communal feeling?

MLA: There is one *pradhan*, Dr. Ram Prasad, Jan Sangh *pradhan*,
who instigated and who gave importance to this.[83]

On the other side, Dr. Ram Prasad felt that Sirajuddin and Nuruddin, in
cahoots with the police, were protecting the Muslims involved in the incident, were trying to prevent his own political ascendance, and were intent
on maintaining their support base among the Muslims by turning this incident into an affair of the Hindus rather than of the citizens of the town
irrespective of their religion. It is on the foundation of such materials as
these that some communal riots have taken place in other towns in western
UP and elsewhere in India.

This kind of differentiated political support base underlying communal
divisions in north India was not a matter of local personalities only. It was
part of a widespread effort made by the Congress under the leadership of the
Nehru family to maintain a Muslim "vote bank" in the state legislative and
national parliamentary elections and of the Jan Sangh/BJP to challenge it by
building a stronger counterbase among Hindus. These efforts to consolidate
and to counteract the consolidation of the Muslim vote behind the Congress
in north India figured in many incidents of the sort described above in the
1970s and 1980s. Congress, being the dominant party in the state and the
country during most of these two decades, sought to present itself as the
protector of the Muslims against the Jan Sangh/BJP leadership, which in
turn was always presented as bent upon creating communal tension and fomenting communal riots. Since the Congress was the ruling party for the
most part during these decades, the predominant administrative/police ideol-

---

[82] Ibid., p. 143 (seventh interview, taped).
[83] Ibid., pp. 146–47 (seventh interview).

ogy was the same: Communal elements, especially among the RSS/Jan Sangh/BJP, are out to foment communal riots and this must be prevented by quick, stern administrative measures. The formula was used in Daphnala and no communal riot occurred. It remains to discuss how far the Congress/ police alliance in situations of this type actually prevented communal riots by considering again the alternative view of this incident offered by the BJP leader and by Dr. Sengupta.

CIVIC PRIDE AND COMMUNAL PASSION

Dr. Ram Prasad Khosla, an office-bearer of a militant Hindu party considered by its opponents to be communal and anti-Muslim, and Dr. Sengupta, a Congressman committed to secular values, both insist that the issue raised by the abduction and alleged rape of a girl in Daphnala was a civic one. They also concur that there were fundamental moral issues at stake. A young girl was abducted and allegedly raped. The fact that she was a prostitute does not reduce the heinousness of the crime. Moreover, if she was a prostitute who was being bought and sold, not only the girl-slaver who was transporting her, but her true father should be found and prosecuted for his immoral treatment of his own daughter in bringing her up to become a prostitute.

The fact that these immoral doings were brought to light in Daphnala by an even more heinous act of rape raised, in the statements of Dr. Khosla and Dr. Sengupta, a question of civic pride. How could such a thing be allowed to happen in the town without the persons involved being discovered and punished? The police, however, did not act properly. They were accused of being corrupt and involved in exploiting the girl and protecting her alleged assailants. The people of the town, therefore, became enraged not because the girl was a Hindu and her assailants or abductors Muslims, but because the police had not only failed in their duty, but were themselves guilty. The incident in Daphnala, therefore, became a confrontation between a morally enraged public and a corrupt police force.

How far can one accept this view of the incident and the motives of Dr. Khosla, Dr. Sengupta, and the crowds? As far as Dr. Sengupta is concerned, his statements, his secular ideology, his personal sympathy for the apparent plight of the old man, and his initial efforts to seek the help of the Congress Muslim leaders of the town bespeak a sincerity and integrity that I can find no grounds to challenge. The case of Dr. Khosla, however, is more difficult. His statements and actions require more detailed scrutiny because of some ambiguities in them and because of their correspondence with some general attitudes and approaches of members of the RSS and BJP to such matters in other parts of north India.

Dr. Khosla's statements—and his actions even more so—differed from those of Dr. Sengupta. Dr. Khosla wishes it to be known or believed that he has good relations with Muslims in his village and that he obtains Muslim votes in local elections. Like most BJP people at that time, he wished to be perceived as noncommunal. At the same time, he remarked at a point early in his long narrative account of the incident and his involvement in it "that whenever there is any crisis in the Hindu religion, then the people rush to me." The statement suggests that Dr. Khosla, in incidents such as these, is perceived not merely as a civic man, but as a Hindu public man who defends the Hindu religion. From the beginning, therefore, there was at the least an undercurrent in Dr. Khosla's own account of this incident that an outrage had been committed in the town of Daphnala upon a Hindu girl, which presented a crisis for Hindus, if not for "Hindu *dharm.*"

Now, a concern to protect Hindus is not in principle incompatible with broader civic concerns. However, the identification of the alleged victim from the beginning as a Hindu girl places the burden for a demonstration of civic consciousness in the matter upon the Muslims. Hindus will more likely be outraged if it is reported that a Hindu girl has been raped than will Muslims. Moreover, when it is also reported that two of the alleged assailants were Muslims, the Muslims of the town are likely to want to be quiet under the circumstances, fearing that they will be blamed collectively.

The BJP charge against Muslims in India in general is that they do not behave as Indians. Here is a case where Muslims might behave as Indian citizens, outraged equally with Hindus over the rape of a girl. Moreover, Dr. Khosla claims that Muslims did in fact behave in this way initially, that there were Muslims as well as Hindus in the crowds in the early stages. Although the latter fact is disputed by others, it is important that Dr. Khosla professes to believe it. It suggests that he did not intend to turn the incident into a Hindu–Muslim confrontation.

At the same time, there is no question that Dr. Khosla perceived himself to be not just a public man, but a Hindu and a politician. In contrast to Dr. Sengupta, who went alone to present the case to Mr. Nuruddin, Dr. Khosla's first response upon hearing the news was to stay back himself, but to advise those who reported the incident to him "to mobilize opinion, . . . assemble people of this area and then go to the police *chowki.*" This may be interpreted as the response of a political man who believes in numbers rather than in his own personal political influence. It may also reflect the reality that, as an opposition politician holding no important local or state public office, he could not approach the police directly with any assurance of an adequate response. Certainly he could not approach Nuruddin, his political rival.

Dr. Khosla appeared only when the crowd had already gathered at the police station. By his account, his only important action at the time was to speak to the crowd in order to help calm people down. However, his own initial actions from behind the scenes encouraged the gathering of the crowd in the first place. He himself said that he decided to stay back initially, because he thought "that unless I come for the real thing, I should not involve myself in this because of my own political career." In other words, if he acted personally in a potentially troublesome situation—from the point of view of either Hindu–Muslim or police–public relations—it might harm his political career. However, if it developed into a major public issue, then it would be appropriate for him to appear personally. His actions, therefore, also are open to interpretation as an effort to exploit a potentially useful occasion for political mobilization of opinion—particularly, and probably exclusively, Hindu opinion—which might be turned to the advantage of his party and of his own future political career.

In communities with histories of interethnic tension, there is a thin line between mobilization of one's own community for defense of its perceived interests, rights, culture, or religion and communal mobilization directed simultaneously against another community perceived to stand in the way. If one chooses to take Hindu political persons such as Dr. Khosla at their word, that they mobilize their community on moral or cultural or religious matters without seeking to offend other communities, that they even try to bring others along on some matters such as those that involve basic morality or civic or national pride, then the attitudes and actions of the authorities against them amount to victimization and denial to them of their legitimate political rights in a democratic order. The view of the authorities in this case and in many others of its type, however, is that such people are deliberately bent upon creating communal tension and even riots.

It is likely that, in some circumstances, the Hindu activists are acting honestly as Dr. Khosla claims he was doing. In other circumstances, the perception of the authorities is the truer one. In the incident at Daphnala, it appears clear that Dr. Khosla was willing to take the risk that communal tension might be created in the town as a consequence of his mobilization of Hindu opinion and that the district authorities were not willing to do so and opted instead to suppress the trouble that was beginning and to incarcerate its alleged promoters.

The issue framed here has some parallels with issues raised in recent studies of British responses to urban protests in the nineteenth century. In studies by Kumar, Freitag, and Pandey, the authors have noted the tendency of the British authorities to read potential or actual communal conflict into situations that had little or nothing to do with religion and religious passions, to see cultural mobilization by one community as a threat to the other, and to perceive, sometimes retrospectively, such movements as antitax protests as communal disturbances.[84] It is evident from the above account that the same type of thing happened in Daphnala.

---

[84] Nita Kumar, *The Artisans of Banaras: Popular Culture and Identity, 1880–1986* (Princeton, N.J.: Princeton University Press, 1988); Sandria B. Freitag, *Collective Action and Community: Public Arenas and the Emergence of Communalism in North India* (Berkeley: University

The authorities in Daphnala reacted to an incident that outraged the moral sensibilities of its citizens and aroused among some of them a concern for the town's reputation by treating the organizers of the movement as communalists bent upon fomenting a communal riot, which they were constrained to act to prevent. Like the British, the authorities in this case and in many others of its type see the society that they administer as divided into compartmentalized and often hostile caste and religious groups subject to outbreaks of interethnic or interreligious violence that they must always be alert to prevent.

What alternative do the authorities have in such situations as those in Daphnala and to what extent do their own attitudes contribute to the communal atmosphere they seek to control? The authorities could, of course, and did in Daphnala take the same position as the protesters, averring that the alleged rape and abduction were criminal acts irrespective of the religion of their perpetrators. Everything possible would be done to find and prosecute the culprits.

However, the case fell apart, the girl was never found, the alleged culprits were released, the old girl-slaver was presumably out still plying his trade, and the incident ended in the violence of a police–public confrontation instead of a communal riot. There are two possible conclusions suggested by this result. One is that, as in the case of British rule in India, the rulers of contemporary India have lost legitimacy. The authorities, particularly the police, are seen as corrupt. The people have no faith in them. Consequently, any situation of this type is likely to lead to either communal or police–public violence because of the incompetence and corruption of the police rather than because of the intent of the politicians.

Another possible explanation, however, is that there is no real gulf between state and society, police and public. Rather, they are closely intertwined. Following up the District Magistrate's view, a game of brinkmanship is being played in which everyone knows the rules. Hindu opinion is mobilized with the foreknowledge that Hindu–Muslim tension and violence may result. When the latter result appears imminent, the authorities play their role of riot prevention while the politicians proclaim their belief in communal harmony, moral values, and justice for all irrespective of religion. The police know the politicians can benefit from harassment by them to enhance their popularity. The citizens and the politicians know that police corruption and criminality are extensive, but police reform is not high or even present on their list of political goals. It is control of the police and the authorities for themselves and their parties that they seek, whereupon all will be set right by the purity of their own intentions and directives.

In the meantime, however, nothing is set right, at least in cases such as

---

of California Press, 1989); Gyanendra Pandey, *The Construction of Communalism in Colonial North India* (Delhi: Oxford University Press, 1990).

these. The incident at Daphnala, the theft of an idol in village Pachpera become occasions for political mobilization and violent confrontation in which the precipitating events become incidental to the grander political issues that surround them. In the smoke and thunder, the criminals leave with their loot or their prostitutes, the police make money, the politicians win votes. Some win, some lose. Some people, some police get injured or killed. In communal riots, many innocent people suffer and die. A few policemen are suspended, most are transferred to another post, but hardly any ever spend time inside a jail or even lose any pay.

COMPARISONS AND CONCLUSIONS

Ambiguity surrounds both incidents discussed in this volume so far as well as the consequences that followed upon them. In the incident at Pachpera, the manner of discovery of the idol, its value, and its final whereabouts remain unknown. In the incident at Daphnala, the girl had no name, doubt was cast even upon her gender, some questioned whether she was Hindu or Muslim, normal or abnormal, a victim or just a prostitute plying her own profession and escaping from her pimp. Ambiguity also surrounds the consequences of these incidents. We do not know for sure why the theft of an idol from a Jain temple in Madrauna town led ultimately to a pitched battle between the police and the villagers. In Daphnala, we do not know what led the crowd to attack the police station, whether the motivation was communal passion or moral outrage against the police or a combination of the two.

Yet it is out of such ambiguous materials that mob violence and Hindu–Muslim riots are created. It is for this reason that the SSP's remark that communal riots have no "concrete base" is relevant. In these two cases, no communal riot occurred. However, if Muslims had been involved in the incident at Pachpera and if the wrath of the crowd had not been directed against the police in Daphnala, it is easy to imagine the transformation of these incidents into communal riots.

Although ambiguity surrounds both the precipitating incidents and their consequences, it is not difficult to identify the underlying political dimensions and the political interests that surround them. The Congress was the dominant political force in both the Madrauna and the Daphnala areas at the time of these two incidents. A Congress government was in power in the state as well. The police, therefore, were also subject to the authority of the Congress.

Although the Lok Dal was the principal opposition in the rural areas in both districts, the BJP was either a strong opposition force (in Madrauna tahsil) or an aspiring political force (in Daphnala) in the particular segments of these two districts in which the incidents occurred. In both cases also, the local Congress MLAs were Muslims. In the incident at Pachpera, however, there was no question of a Hindu–Muslim confrontation.

In Daphnala, in contrast, the issue of Hindu–Muslim relations was present from the beginning. The very fact that Dr. Khosla and Dr. Sengupta both proclaimed emphatically that the incident was not a communal matter testifies to their concern that it could well have become one. Moreover, it is evident that the issue of the preservation or mobilization of a communal political base among Hindus and Muslims underlay the concerns and attitudes of the BJP/Arya Samaj people, on the one side, and the Muslim politicians of the town, on the other side.

Therefore, even if no one intended to foment a communal riot in Daphnala, the incident inevitably became tied up with the political question of who might benefit from or be harmed by a public demonstration. It is also clear that the Muslim politicians had nothing at all to gain and everything to lose from a public demonstration, especially one that might turn into a communal confrontation. Only the BJP, as an aspiring political force, stood to gain from a political mobilization, whether based on civic or communal issues. Finally, the communal element in the situation at Daphnala is evident in the interpretations given by opposed sides to the motives of their rivals. Both sides proclaimed their own lack of communal motivations, but insisted that the other side was motivated by communal considerations.

The absence of an impartial and honest police is a second major factor in both the Pachpera and Daphnala incidents. Dr. Khosla and Dr. Sengupta both blamed the police, perceiving the issue as a police–public confrontation. The police were perceived as in league with the culprits. It is evident also that both Dr. Khosla and Dr. Sengupta perceived that the police would not act without the intervention of the dominant Congress politicians in the town. The police for their part took shelter against these charges and perceptions by condemning the local non-Congress leaders as communalists bent upon fomenting a communal riot. They were aided in this tactic by the fact that both the local Congress politicians and the district authorities took the same view. It is evident once again, therefore, as in the case of the Pachpera incident, that the police, the local authorities, and the judiciary do not stand above or apart from the local political process, from society, and from intercommunal relations but are implicated in them all.

A few remarks on the local political leadership will also throw some further light on the broader significance of this potential communal situation. The three public men interviewed represent three quite different political ideologies and practices. Dr. Khosla, an RSS and BJP man, is a militant Hindu nationalist whose primary political orientation is toward the Hindu community upon whose support his political future depended. The brothers Nuruddin and Sirajuddin were descendants of the traditional Muslim leadership of this *qasbah* town, but lacked the traditional authority of their predecessors. They acted as practical politicians seeking mainly to prevent the non-Congress politicians from gaining any political advantage from the situation through the mobilization of public opinion. They castigated Dr. Khosla as a communalist, but they revealed no desire to take advantage of the situation to mobilize Muslim opinion in any way. Nor was the situation one in which they could easily do so. Dr. Sengupta was also a Congressman, but of a different breed, devoted to the nationalist ideals of the Congress of the pre-Independence period, a noncommunal man who believed wholeheartedly in Hindu–Muslim cooperation in a secular political order.

Nowhere in this picture do we find the contemporary bogey man of religious fundamentalism, either Hindu or Muslim, pitting one "fanatical" religious community against another or against the modern secular state. What we do find, however, is that British–Indian construction of Hindu–Muslim communalism lurking in the background, providing a context into which local events involving members of the two communities are easily placed. It is a context that displaces other alternatives, in this case civic consciousness. It is worth noting, however, that even in western UP, in a district noted in the 1980s for two of the most vicious communal killings witnessed in India in that decade, an alternative context was available into which the rape of a girl was placed by local public men and possibly by the people as well in the large crowds that assembled in protest. It is also evident, however, that the communal context, rather the whole discourse of communalism, its ideology and practices, was the predominant one in this situation, particularly in the minds and actions of the authorities. The practices prevalent in this discourse, which include techniques of police response and political mobilization, may turn an everyday incident into a communal riot or may work to prevent one. In either case, they provide the framework that structures the events and the interpretations of them that become dominant in official accounts and in the media as well, when the latter become involved in them.

Chapter 5

HORROR STORIES

IN 1969 Mrs. Indira Gandhi, prime minister of the country at the time, split the Indian National Congress and declared her wing of it the rightful heir of the old united party. The split left her party—dubbed Congress (R)[1] by the press—with a majority of the Congress MPs in Parliament but in a minority in the Lok Sabha as a whole, dependent for the maintenance of her government upon the support of the Communist Party of India (CPI) and the DMK, a regional nationalist party from the state of Tamil Nadu. Her rivals in the other wing of the Congress, the Congress (O), were in control of most of the state party organizations.

However, Mrs. Gandhi moved quickly to establish alternative bases of support for her party and for her leadership by appealing directly to the people of the country, particularly the poor and the minorities, attempting to bypass the state party bosses who had previously been thought to be indispensable to mobilize the electorate and win elections for the Congress. Mrs. Gandhi's party manifesto and her election speeches offered numerous programs especially for the rural poor and landless, protection for the Muslim minority against violence upon their lives and property and preservation of their religious and educational institutions, and protection for the Scheduled Castes and other poor backward castes and tribals against discrimination, exploitation, and victimization at the hands of the dominant castes in the villages.

Her first appeal in which such programs were offered to the broad electorate in the 1971 elections resulted in a landslide victory for her wing of the party, establishing it decisively as the effective heir of the original Indian National Congress. The principal slogan of her campaign in 1971 was *garibi hatao* (abolish poverty). After her successful election campaign, a whole range of new institutions and agencies were created by the central government to implement programs in the rural areas to help the poor.

However, Mrs. Gandhi's landslide victory in 1971 left her feeling insecure and still without a stable organizational base in the country. Instead of

[1] The designation Congress (R) referred to the fact that the wing of the Congress controlled by Mrs. Gandhi requisitioned (hence the R) a meeting to combat the dominance of the group designated as the organizational wing, which emerged from the split as the Congress (O). It was not long, however, before the Congress (R) came to be referred to as the Congress (I) for Indira.

striving to build a new grassroots party organization in the country, Mrs. Gandhi sought to consolidate her power by destroying the party institutions of the rival Congress and by continuing to appeal directly to the people of the country for their support against the alleged attempts by the old party bosses to thwart her efforts to improve the conditions of the poor and by communal forces such as the RSS and Jan Sangh to foil her efforts to protect the minorities. Feeling insecure and acting without a strong organization to support her, Mrs. Gandhi took more and more power onto herself and relied increasingly upon a narrow group of personal advisers drawn from the Nehru household and upon her young son Sanjay. As she did so, opposition leaders and dissident Congressmen began to mobilize public opinion against her alleged authoritarian tendencies and actions and began to have some successes during the mid-1970s, when the industrial economy was faltering and the agricultural economy was not yet producing sufficient surplus to avert scarcity conditions in some parts of the country.

In the midst of the campaign that had been building up against her and also began to draw covert sympathy from some dissident Congressmen, an election tribunal in Allahabad decided in a case filed against her by one of her opponents in the 1971 election that she and her campaign managers had violated the election laws and that her election was, therefore, null and void. Mrs. Gandhi's response to the nullification of her election included, in addition to legal countermoves, the famous June 1975 declaration of Emergency in the country, the jailing of all significant opposition leaders, and the establishment of an authoritarian regime, which lasted for two years.

Mrs. Gandhi claimed that the Emergency was necessary because of the economic conditions in the country and the dangers posed by external and internal enemies of the Indian state. She offered as a solution for the problems a twenty-point economic program, in which five points explicitly addressed the problems of the landless and the "weaker sections" of the people. Her son Sanjay also offered his own five-point program, of which one point, family planning, was ultimately to contribute heavily to the downfall of the Congress after the relaxation of the Emergency and the holding of general elections in 1977.

Despite her continued efforts to offer programs to improve the lot of the poor in the country, measures taken under the sponsorship of her son Sanjay Gandhi antagonized the very groups upon which a great part of her political base had been built, namely, the Scheduled Castes and the Muslims. The Scheduled Castes in north India particularly were antagonized by the family planning program introduced during the Emergency in which the principal method used was male sterilization through vasectomy. Civil servants were given sterilization quotas to fulfill, which they allegedly accomplished by forcing Scheduled Castes and other poor people to accept vasectomies. Muslims were antagonized by another program supported by Sanjay Gandhi, the

beautification of Delhi, which involved the demolition of squatter settle-
ments in the city occupied by the poor, the Scheduled Castes, and Muslims.
Muslims were especially antagonized by this program because of a violent
incident at the Turkman Gate involving a police firing in which several Muslims were killed. The Imam of the Jama Masjid in Delhi also turned against
the Congress and mobilized Muslims against it in the 1977 elections because
some of the squatter huts demolished were owned by him.

While in jail during the Emergency, the principal opposition leaders from
the leading political parties in the country succeeded in laying the basis for
the creation of the famous Janata Party, which, to the surprise of most people, offered a united opposition to contest against the Congress in the general elections called for January 1977. The election manifestos of the two
principal opposing forces, Congress and Janata, emphasized more than ever
before promises to pay special attention to the needs of the disadvantaged
groups, especially the poorest in the land. The Janata Party leaders also
emphasized in their campaigns the alleged atrocities committed against
Scheduled Castes and the poor during the sterilization campaign and against
Muslims at the Turkman Gate and elsewhere during the Emergency regime.
These appeals succeeded in drawing away from the Congress its two largest
"vote banks" and contributed significantly to the Janata victory.

The Janata Party that came to power after the 1977 elections was torn by
leadership conflicts from its inception and fell apart because of these divisions in July 1979. During its time in power, the Janata government had
many achievements to its credit, most notably the nearly complete restoration of the pre-Emergency political and civil order. The Janata government
also continued and extended the programs for the rural poor begun during
Mrs. Gandhi's decade in office.

During the Janata period in office, there were several major communal
riots, notably in Aligarh and Moradabad districts in western UP. There were
also reports in the press of various incidents of alleged atrocities committed
upon Harijans (Scheduled Castes) and backward castes in different parts of
north India. Several stories appeared about such alleged atrocities committed
against Harijans in Meerut district, focusing on the Jat area, which provided
the main political base of Chaudhuri Charan Singh, the Union home minister. Similar accounts came out concerning atrocities against Harijans in several villages in the eastern UP districts of Gorakhpur, Basti, and Azamgarh.
One of the worst incidents of this type occurred in village Belchi in Patna
district of Bihar state in July 1977, during which eleven Harijans and three
persons from lower backward castes were killed.

Mrs. Gandhi, now leader of the opposition in the Lok Sabha, and Congress politicians generally did their best to focus public attention on these
incidents of alleged atrocities supposedly committed by dominant castes
upon the Scheduled Castes and lower backward castes and argued that such

attacks had increased since the Janata Party took power. Mrs. Gandhi visited several of the places where such incidents had taken place to express sympathy to the victims or their families. The Janata government in most cases denied either that attacks on Harijans had increased or that the incidents themselves, where they had undeniably taken place, had anything to do with atrocities against Harijans as opposed to ordinary land disputes or criminal activities or gang warfare.

Whatever the truth about these incidents of communal violence and killings of lower-caste persons in the rural areas, the Congress attempt to place the blame for them upon the Janata government had some success. The Congress task was made easier by the fact that the former Jan Sangh was a major component in the Janata coalition. Moreover, the Janata itself split apart on the pretext that the allegedly Hindu communal RSS continued to control the former Jan Sangh members of the Janata coalition, who allegedly continued to act in a communal manner. The second large component in the Janata coalition was the former BLD, commonly also referred to as the Lok Dal, a party led by Charan Singh, with its principal base among the middle agricultural castes of UP and Bihar. Mrs. Gandhi and the Congress had some success also in portraying these middle-caste supporters of Charan Singh and the former BLD as the principal exploiters and perpetrators of atrocities against the Scheduled Castes and lower backward castes.

In the parliamentary elections of 1980, called as a consequence of the collapse of the Janata government, the Janata Party split into several segments. This loss of unity and the return to the Congress of many of its lost voters among the Muslims and the Scheduled Castes were the two most important factors in the return of the Congress to power during that election and the installation of Mrs. Gandhi once again as prime minister in January 1980.

However, non-Congress parties remained in power in the state governments in most of the Indian states and in the two most populous and politically important north Indian states of UP and Bihar. Within a month of her return to power, in January, news reports began to appear concerning a major incident of violence in village Narayanpur in Deoria district of UP, which borders on Bihar. By the end of January and the first week of February, virtually all large circulation newspapers in the country were carrying headline stories focusing on police atrocities in the village of Narayanpur, which was said to be inhabited mostly by Muslims, Harijans, and persons from lower backward Hindu castes. The atrocities alleged included mass rape of the women, police beatings and torture of the men, and plundering of the village.

Mrs. Gandhi, Sanjay Gandhi, and numerous other Congress and non-Congress leaders visited the village to ascertain what had happened there and to express their sympathy with the plight of the villagers. After their visits,

Mrs. Gandhi and her son declared that the non-Congress government in UP had no right to continue to exist in the light of its failure to prevent this incident. On February 18, the President of India, on the advice of the Prime Minister, dismissed the UP government and nine other state governments and called for elections to be held in them in June.

The incident at Narayanpur, therefore, stood both as a pretext for the dismissal of the remaining non-Congress state governments and as a symbol of the differences between the Congress and its opposition, the one standing up to protect the minorities, the poor, and the lower castes, the other portrayed as their oppressors. During her years out of power, Mrs. Gandhi clearly gained the advantage against the Janata Party and its successor fragments in this symbolic struggle. The questions I want to discuss in this chapter concern, first, the relationship between the political uses made of these incidents of violence and the context in which they are placed, on the one hand, and what can be reconstructed concerning the actual events that occurred in Narayanpur and other villages in which such incidents have taken place. Second, since the declared goals of the Congress and the non-Congress parties have for long been to take measures to protect the minorities, the Scheduled Castes, and the lower backward castes from discrimination, exploitation, and violence perpetrated against them by the locally dominant landed castes, I want to consider what effect the symbolic elevation of these incidents of alleged atrocities upon the "weaker sections" of society has had in protecting them. I do so by contrasting two incidents and the attention/lack of attention given to them: Narayanpur and a similar case in another district of UP, which occurred in 1982 and which, as far as I have been able to determine, received no media attention whatsoever. The second case will be taken up in the following chapter.

DEORIA DISTRICT: THE LOCAL POLITICAL CONTEXT

Deoria district lies in the northeastern corner of the state of UP on the border with the state of Bihar and with Nepal. In the conventional division of the state's districts, it belongs to the group known as the Eastern Districts. These districts have since Independence been considered among the very poorest in the state, with little urbanization, virtually no industry outside of the two urban places of Gorakhpur and Varanasi, and an agriculture based primarily on intensive monsoon-dependent paddy cultivation on very small plots of land. In the years after the Green Revolution, agricultural production improved and cropping patterns changed, especially with the introduction here as elsewhere of the new high-yielding varieties of wheat. Deoria district, once considered the poorest of the poor Eastern Districts, also experienced significant growth in agricultural productivity, aided by the completion of a massive irrigation project in the northern part of the district.

Narayanpur is situated in this somewhat more prosperous northern part of the district, where sugarcane and paddy are the major crops and the new varieties of wheat also are grown.

Politically, this district has been marked by intense interparty competition since Independence where, even in the heyday of Congress hegemony in the state, there was a strong Socialist movement. Congress support in this district, as elsewhere in the state, has been based primarily on the elite castes of Brahmans and Bhumihars, on the one hand, and Scheduled Castes and Muslims, on the other hand. The vast middle section of agricultural castes has always provided the central core of support for opposition parties, the Socialist parties in the 1950s and 1960s and the agrarian party of Charan Singh initially known as the BKD, then the BLD, then the Lok Dal, which absorbed the social base of the former Socialist parties in the 1970s. Interparty competition in this district, whatever the names of the contesting parties, has largely reflected the struggles between the elite castes and the middle agricultural castes for control of local institutions of power and patronage.

Always a major stronghold of non-Congress parties, the district returned all its elected representatives in the 1977 elections, including the three MPs and twelve members of the state legislative assembly, from the Janata Party. Largely because of the intense intercaste and interparty competition in this district, political leadership and authority in it has been always fragmented. After the national split in the Janata Party in 1979, the MLAs elected on the Janata Party ticket were divided between supporters of the Lok Dal and the rump Janata Party.

In the 1980 Lok Sabha elections in Deoria district, the Congress succeeded in wresting from its opponents all three MP seats. As in many other districts of north India at the time as well, Mrs. Gandhi's son, Sanjay, had established linkages with selected local political leaders during the Emergency. Those who had been loyal to Mrs. Gandhi during the Janata period remained in the favor of the central leadership of the party. The most prominent local leader of the Congress allied with Sanjay Gandhi was C. P. N. Singh, scion of the most important ex-*zamindari* estate in the district. His leadership was not, however, accepted by many older Congressmen of the district, who resented his rise to prominence through his association with Sanjay Gandhi. The Congress, therefore, like the opposition, was internally divided in Deoria district in 1980.

Narayanpur village falls within the legislative assembly constituency known as Ramkola, which in turn was a segment of the Lok Sabha constituency of C. P. N. Singh. The two polling stations that encompass the village of Narayanpur divided their votes in the Lok Sabha election principally between the Congress candidate, C. P. N. Singh, and the Lok Dal candidate, a Muslim. The candidate who polled the next highest number of votes in these polling stations was a Brahman who belonged to the rump Janata Party. The village of Narayanpur, therefore, like the district as a whole, was divided in its political inclinations more or less as one would expect a village containing a population mostly of Scheduled Castes, Muslims, and some Brahmans to divide.

THE MANIPULATION AND CONTROL OF INCIDENTS OF VIOLENCE

Incident at Narayanpur:
Local Violence as a National Symbolic Resource

The Narayanpur incident differs in two important respects from those presented in the two preceding chapters. In this case, the "basic facts" concerning the origins of the incident that led to a police–public confrontation and police violence against the villagers were well documented. Second, the Narayanpur incident received extensive media coverage and was placed in a specific interpretive context by the Congress leadership and the media: police violence and atrocities committed against the "weaker sections" of society.

Disagreement centered on two aspects of the situation. How severe was the violence committed by the police and against which persons in the village were violent acts perpetrated? What was the relationship between the dominant interpretive context into which the incident was placed and the "facts" of the case?

On January 11, 1980 an old woman of the village, a grandmother and sole support of two grandchildren, was run over and killed by a bus owned by a local private transporter. People of the village and the surrounding area besieged the bus and driver and demanded compensation for the death of the old woman. During the tumult, police arrived and persuaded the villagers to allow the bus and driver to leave the scene on the understanding that the bus owner would pay just compensation to the family members to bring up the surviving dependent children.

However, by January 14 the villagers had received no compensation. So, when another bus belonging to the same owner came by on that day, the villagers stopped it and prevented it from moving, saying they would not allow the bus to move until they received the promised compensation. Police from the Captainganj police station arrived, but a violent struggle between them and the villagers erupted when they attempted to intervene. It was reported that the fracas began when one of the villagers accused the station officer of having taken a bribe from the bus owner. After some time, police reinforcements reached the scene from the Hata police station. Senior police officers of the administrative subdivision and the district as well as the local MLA also arrived thereafter. A large force of PAC (Provincial Armed Constabulary) men later reached the spot. In the negotiations that ensued, the police offered to take the villagers to the Captainganj police station, where the issue of compensation would be settled. The villagers were afraid of what might happen to them at Captainganj police station and proposed instead that they go to the Hata police station.

At the Hata police station, an agreement was reached in which the bus owner was to pay Rs. 5,000—the standard money value attached to a poor person's life in those days—in compensation to the surviving family members for the upbringing of the children. However, the police then detained a number of the male villagers—variously estimated at between eleven and fourteen persons—at the Hata police station, where they were beaten and grossly abused. They were then taken to the Captainganj station for further beatings and humiliation. Finally, they were put in the Kasia jail.

That night, the night of January 14, a police force of nearly one hundred men from both police stations, reinforced by PAC-men, descended on the village and committed further acts of violence, the precise nature of which was disputed, but which allegedly included further beatings, molestation of women, looting of property and money, and even killing and torture. It was reported that another sixteen men from the village also were arrested and taken to the Captainganj police station. The two batches of arrested men were released within a week or two. Within three weeks, Rs. 5,000 were paid to the villagers for the care of the children.

PRESS REPORTS

The first accounts of the incident at Narayanpur in the national English-language press appeared on January 29. The *Times of India*, picking up on a statement made in the UP Vidhan Sabha (Legislative Assembly) by a minister in the Janata government reporting that police and PAC personnel had committed "mass rape and plunder" in the village "resulting in the death of two persons," featured the story under the headline, "Mass Rape, Plunder by UP Cops." An *Indian Express* story appeared on the same day with a similar headline, "Mass Rape Incident Rocks UP House." These two stories reported that "mass rape, loot, torture and brutality" as well as "plunder" had been committed by police and PAC personnel in the village and that two persons had lost their lives during the police attack on the night of January 14.

Within forty-eight hours, Sanjay Gandhi reached the village. He was quoted in the press as follows: "Mr. Gandhi said what had happened in Narayanpur was unprecedented. 'There was not a single girl or woman in Narayanpur who was not raped. Nor was there a single man who was not beaten up. To cap it all, there is not a single house which was not looted.'"[2]

---

[2] *Indian Express*, February 1, 1980.

Two days after Sanjay Gandhi's visit, stories were published in the press, citing a police report on the incident acknowledging police misbehavior, including "atrocities on the villagers," but denying that any "mass rape" had occurred.

The following day, the press reported that the prime minister would make a personal visit to Narayanpur, which the state chief minister criticized as an improper interference by the central government upon the prerogatives and responsibilities of the state government in the matter. Nevertheless, Mrs. Gandhi reached the village on February 7 with a large entourage of state Congress leaders. During her visit in the village, she met privately with several women in their huts, with no observers from the press present and with all men in her entourage explicitly forbidden to participate.

The *Patriot* published a detailed account of Mrs. Gandhi's visit to the village, her meetings with the villagers, and her own responses to the stories she was told under the headline, "Horror Stories of Narayanpur."[3] Describing the village as a "sleepy hamlet of Harijans, Muslims and a sprinkling of Brahmans," the correspondent remarked that the villagers had become "aware of its new found role in national politics" and had "become used" to the stream of visitors—including major public figures as well as journalists and television camera crews—since "the orgy of police violence and perversion" that had been visited upon it. Writing apparently without tongue in cheek, the writer of this report also noted that "the men, women and children of the small village have . . . learnt through repeated practice to narrate their tales of woe in brief emotional sentences, crying as they speak." The reporter did, however, note the irony involved in the presence in this village recently subjected to police atrocities of a huge armed police force of some five hundred men, including reinforcements from surrounding districts as well as PAC *jawan*s (youth, lower ranks), and the fact that villagers and police worked together to make the necessary arrangements to receive the prime minister and her entourage.

When she reached the village, Mrs. Gandhi moved systematically from house to house among those that had been selected for her visit and chalk-marked to guide her on her way. She listened as the old women and men and the children of the village narrated tearful accounts of beating of the men and looting of money. Though the meetings with women who recounted tales of molestation were closed to the men, one police woman present reportedly said that, at one house, "Mrs Gandhi heard in grim silence a shocking tale of rapes and molestations." In another hut, Mrs. Gandhi was greeted by "a lot of women . . . already wailing loudly." After consoling the women, they spoke to her of "mass rape and the terror" they had faced. Similar tales were allegedly recounted in other houses, of which

[3] *Patriot*, February 10, 1980.

the worst was the narration of "the repeated rape by policemen" of a "barely" fifteen-year old "and recently married" girl who had not yet gone "to her husband's house." The account noted that "this rape case was among the ones that even the preliminary police inquiry of the State Government had to acknowledge as genuine." The last house she visited was that of "old Jumman," whose age was said to be somewhere between sixty and eighty years, who had died a week after he had been "severely beaten up by policemen in their raid."

This story also paid close attention to Mrs. Gandhi's demeanor, which was reported to have grown increasingly "grim" and "determined." At the conclusion of her tour of the village, Mrs. Gandhi addressed a public meeting at which she attacked the leaders of the UP government, saying that they were either "not human if they are not moved by this" or else "they think that the villagers . . . are not human." She said these state leaders were "trying to hide this brutality," which could not be tolerated. Consequently, "they have no moral right to rule." She also promised the villagers that "the guilty [would] be punished." After concluding her speech, Mrs. Gandhi "left the village amidst tears and cheers."

The personal visit of the prime minister to the village notwithstanding, police and law and order remained a state subject in India's federal system. Punishment of those responsible for police atrocities in the village, therefore, remained the responsibility of the state government. However, it was clear from her remarks after her tour of the village that Mrs. Gandhi included the state government itself among those most responsible for the outrages committed in Narayanpur. In a letter to the chief minister of UP released to the press on February 17, Mrs. Gandhi placed the Narayanpur incident in the broader context of reported widespread atrocities against Harijans in the state, which the state government had failed to treat satisfactorily. On the same day, the president of India, acting on her advice, dismissed the UP government and dissolved its legislative assembly along with eight other state governments in the country and imposed President's Rule upon them in preparation for new state legislative assembly elections.

No further news reports concerning the Narayanpur incidents appeared in the press thereafter until two-and-a-half years later, in August–September 1982, after the report of a judicial commission appointed to investigate them had been presented to the UP government, now under the control of the Congress. On September 11, 1982 the *Hindu* published the news concerning this report under the headline, "An Embarrassment to Congress (I)." Its story noted that the report had been presented to the UP government on July 3, 1981, but not made public at the time. Instead, it was forwarded to the CID (Criminal Investigation Department) for its comments. The CID delayed for six months, until January 21, 1982, before transmitting its comments. The report was then translated from English into Hindi and forwarded to the state government press on February 23, 1982. Four months later, on June 22, the printed report was transmitted to the state government in time for the monsoon session. However, it was not laid on the table of the UP Legislative Assembly until August 30, 1982, a day before the end of the session, making it impossible to hold any legislative debate or discussion of its contents.[4]

However, the press discovered the contents of the report, which "concluded that there was no evidence, written, oral or circumstantial, to substantiate the charge of mass rape of women by policemen in Narayanpur . . . on January 14, 19[80]." Nor did the commission uncover "any evidence of the death of any person as a result of the police beating" nor "any substance in the charge that the police plundered the village or looted any villager." At the same time, the commission did support the charges of beating and torture of the men of the village in the Hata and Captainganj police stations "on the night of January 14" and "indicted two station house officers, three sub-inspectors, and ten constables" for their alleged parts in carrying out these illegal acts committed against twenty-seven persons of the village.[5]

For the most part, and overwhelmingly so, the national English-language press acted as handmaiden for the Congress and for Mrs. Gandhi in drawing attention to the Narayanpur incident, giving credence to every charge made concerning the atrocities committed in the village and upon the villagers of Narayanpur, and in criticizing the state government. The countless headline stories virtually exhausted the repertoire of available synonyms in the English language to describe the violent incidents in Narayanpur and at the police stations, the favored terms having been atrocities, brutalities, excesses, crimes, horrors, outrages, perversions, carnage, terror, and torture. Favored adjectives were heinous, horrific, and unspeakable. These terms were used to describe specific alleged incidents of beatings, destruction of village property, looting of money and valuables in the village, and mass rape.

Although back-page denials that some of these events had actually occurred were printed as well as statements of non-Congress politicians that the Narayanpur incidents were being used by the Congress leadership for political purposes, the overall impression conveyed by the press was that the charges were either completely or virtually true. In its account of Mrs. Gan-

---

[4] *Hindu*, September 11, 1982. Despite repeated efforts on my part, I have not been able to get hold of this report, which is supposed to be lodged in one of the libraries administered by the government of UP.

[5] *Asian Recorder*, October 22–28, 1982, p. 16,851.

dhi's visit to Narayanpur, the *Patriot* buried the muttering of the police assigned to the village for the occasion—that "the incident had been exaggerated, politicalised"—in the reports on the "horror stories" told to Mrs. Gandhi by the villagers.[6] Since Mrs. Gandhi's charges that the state government had been attempting to "hush up" the incidents were given much prominence, many readers would in any case have discounted the published denials of their occurrence as part of this "hush up."

Although it soon became obvious that not every woman in the village had been raped, as Sanjay Gandhi had alleged, the press had committed itself by its headlines and its sycophancy in relation to Mrs. Gandhi to the idea that mass rape had occurred in the village. Thus, the CPI (Communist Party of India) paper, the *Patriot*—the party and paper both being fellow-travelers of Mrs. Gandhi at the time—justified the mass rape charge as late as February 9, by which time considerable doubt existed that any such event had occurred: "There are at least three practically confirmed cases of women raped by the police and armed constabulary. Unconfirmed cases total to nearly 15. While it is not true that every woman from 10 to 60 was raped, even four cases are mass rape, and 16 more so."[7] When, two-and-a-half years later, the contents of the inquiry commission on the Narayanpur incidents were published in which the charges of mass rape or of any rape whatsoever were dismissed as without foundation, the BJP leader, Mr. Atal Bihari Bajpai, was reported to have said that "it was noteworthy that the commission had said that not even oral complaints [of rape] were filed against the policemen."[8]

A second image conveyed by the press reports is that the "unspeakable horrors" were committed by the police on "innocent" victims, including women and children, the most innocent of all.[9] The police were portrayed as "predators" and "marauders," the victims as "hapless." The virtue of the villagers was contrasted with the "beastliness" of the police. Thus, though it is common knowledge that a raped woman in an Indian village often becomes a pariah to her own kith and kin, a *Patriot* correspondent reported that a "young," "good looking" woman whose "robust figure drew the attention of the policemen"—and quite obviously that of the correspondent as well—who supposedly had all raped her, continued to be showered "with affection" by her tailor husband.[10]

Associated with the image of innocent villagers is the image conveyed about this type of village. In some press reports, Narayanpur was described

[6] *Patriot*, February 10, 1980.

[7] Ibid., February 9, 1980.

[8] *Hindu*, September 11, 1982.

[9] *Times of India*, leader, February 9, 1980.

[10] *Patriot*, February 13, 1980. This quaint vignette is further suspect since showering one's wife with affection in public is not an Indian custom.

as a "sleepy village" awakened from its slumber by the bus accident and the incomprehensible brutality suddenly unleashed upon it thereafter.[11] This sleepy village, moreover, had been isolated from the turmoils of Indian life. There had never before this incident "been any dacoity, murder or any quarrel meriting police intervention." Despite the fact that the village has "a mixed population of Hindus and Muslims," its people know nothing of communal animosities and, therefore, "did not witness any violent frenzy even during the worst days of communal rioting."[12]

The caste and communal composition of the village also was noted in the press several times, namely, that its residents were primarily Harijans and Muslims, with a few families of Brahmans. The press, however, dutifully followed Mrs. Gandhi in this respect also, which was simply to note the caste and communal composition of the village without implying that "caste issues" were in any way involved in the incident except that this was another case of atrocities committed against the "weaker sections" of the people, particularly Harijans. Thus, the *Patriot* found it simply one among the so-called mysteries of the Narayanpur incidents "that most of the victims are Harijans or Muslims."[13] There is, of course, nothing mysterious about the fact that the victims in a village containing mostly Harijans and Muslims were mainly Harijans or Muslims.

The press, however, found it not at all mysterious that both Sanjay Gandhi and Mrs. Gandhi should have chosen this village—above all others in which such incidents occur in Indian rural life with sufficient frequency—to bring the problem of police brutality and the alleged incompetence of non-Congress state governments in dealing with it to the attention of the press and people of the country. It was, of course, because of the very convenient fact that the village consisted predominantly of Harijans and Muslims. It allowed Mrs. Gandhi and her loyal press to place the incidents at Narayanpur in the broader context of the general rural problem of atrocities against Harijans, which had allegedly become more rampant than ever under Janata rule, and in the context of communal violence against Muslims.

The *Patriot*, therefore, noted in its leader on Narayanpur that the role played by the state administration in supporting the PAC—which had "been turned into a brutal force in the past few years"—and trying to hide its crimes there was of a piece with its support for the "cruel and communal" activities of the PAC in dealing with "communal riots in Aligarh and elsewhere" in which the PAC was generally believed to have been pro-Hindu and anti-Muslim and to have killed innocent Muslims.[14] The *Patriot* did pub-

[11] *Times of India* and *Patriot*, February 10, 1980.

[12] *Patriot*, February 13, 1980. As a matter of fact, Deoria district in general has been relatively free of communal incidents in modern Indian history up to the present.

[13] Ibid., February 9, 1980.

[14] Ibid., February 11, 1980.

lish as well, but in a small and inconspicuous piece in a center page the next day, excerpts from a letter sent by the president of the UP Muslim League to the president of India, in which he also bemoaned the fact that "minorities and Harijans" were "the worst sufferers of police atrocities in Narayanpur." However, he went on to say that it was not only the fault of the government of UP, but of "the system . . . created over the decades by Mrs Gandhi and her party."[15]

The *Hindu*, too, contributed to the placing of the Narayanpur incidents in the context of atrocities against Harijans and Muslims by printing a report that apparently was completely false that, in addition to the raping of the women of the village during the January 14 assault, the police and PAC personnel left "an elderly Muslim man and a Harijan woman" lying dead. The very choice of the victims, the most hapless imaginable, one from each category of the "weaker sections" and, among the weaker sections, the weakest of all, an old man and a woman, itself gives the clue that the choice was made by the Congress and its press rather than the police. This paper also reported that "newsmen found the body of the Muslim still lying even after three days as the residents did not dare to perform his last rites."[16] One can only wonder what might have prevented the residents of Narayanpur from doing so. It is clear enough, however, that most Muslims who read these lines would have been enraged and would have considered it an insult to Islam for the state police to have created a situation in which it proved impossible for Muslims to fulfill the religious injunction to give honorable burial to their dead. It is likely that they would have been so enraged that they would not have seen through the evident ruse involved in this kind of reporting, which has Goebbelsian qualities.

One mystery that the press did not comment upon is why Mrs. Gandhi chose not to emphasize caste issues in this incident, that is, to place it in the context of police brutality against the villagers as opposed to assaults by the dominant or upper castes against the Harijans. There are many precedents for doing so, most notably the charge that the PAC in western UP is not merely an anti-Muslim Hindu police force, but one allegedly dominated by the Jat caste of Mrs. Gandhi's long-standing political foe, Chaudhuri Charan Singh. The caste issue as such could not, however, be brought forth in this case because the subinspector in charge of the Hata police station, who probably ordered the raid on the village and the beating of its men, was a Brahman, with the very obvious Brahman name, Chaturvedi. The Congress in UP at the time was Brahman-dominated. Moreover, in the symbolic battle between the Congress and the non-Congress parties over who was most responsible for atrocities committed against the Muslims and Harijans, Mrs.

[15] Ibid., February 12, 1980.
[16] *Hindu*, February 9, 1980.

Gandhi's position was that it was always the backward castes such as the Jats and never the Brahmans who did such things.[17] Although press reports occasionally did mention the name of this subinspector, there was never a hint that the assault launched against the villagers had anything to do with caste prejudice.

Reports that the villagers initially assaulted the police were placed in the middle of stories otherwise devoted to tales of the unprovoked assaults and brutalities of the police upon their victims. Moreover, when press reports appeared that the police themselves had filed complaints against the villagers, it was also noted in these stories either that the complainant(s) had been suspended,[18] implying their own guilt and casting doubt on their own assertions, or it was implied that the police had filed cases against the villagers as a ruse to cover up their own misdeeds. Sometimes the press did give credence to the alleged assault by the villagers upon the police who, it was reported, then became determined to pay the villagers back. Such reports then went on to describe atrocities committed by the police upon the villagers that went far beyond any "reasonable" vengeful counterattack. One story even reported that, however brutal these counterattacks were, they fell short of what might have happened, for one overzealous police constable was allegedly barely held back from setting fire to the village huts and, presumably, to whomever among the villagers remained inside them.[19]

The *Patriot* correspondent who visited the village on February 8 had difficulty explaining "why the police were so brutal although the provocation, if any, was hardly of the magnitude or gravity to deserve" such a response. He could think of no other explanation except the tautological one that the police brutality had to be placed "in the context of general police administration in the huge State" of UP and the increasing breakdown of law and order in it. He concluded with the following general observation: "'The police here are not policemen or keepers of the peace. They are marauding gangs, just like the criminals,' says a senior observer in Lucknow. A trip . . . to Narayanpur confirms it manifold."[20]

The English-language press, like the general body of English-speaking intellectuals and professional people for whom they write, were hostile also to the state government of UP—and of Bihar as well, where another quite different type of incident of village violence occurred and was featured in the press around the same time. Although the state government intervened in the Narayanpur incident before the central government became involved and although the incident itself was brought to national attention through an ad-

[17] Personal interview with the author on March 26, 1978. Mrs. Gandhi, of course, was a Brahman.

[18] E.g., *Times of India*, February 10, 1980.

[19] Ibid., February 10, 1980.

[20] *Patriot*, February 9, 1980.

journment motion in the UP Legislative Assembly, the press more or less completely supported the attacks of Mrs. Gandhi upon its inefficiency and its ultimate responsibility for what happened at Narayanpur. The *Times of India* charged that the state government, instead of administering "exemplary punishment to the guilty," had acted "in a cavalier manner."[21] The paper did not explain how, in a parliamentary system with an established police and judiciary, the state government could identify the guilty immediately and administer "exemplary punishment" to them.

The *Patriot*, in its leader on Narayanpur under the heading "SICK STATES" (referring to both UP and Bihar), dismissed the objections of the UP chief minister to Mrs. Gandhi's visit to Narayanpur. In response to the chief minister's charge that the prime minister's visit was an infringement on the proper relationship between the center and the states, the leader remarked that the chief minister had "bandied about" words like "autonomy" and "federalism" "as if the power of the States are so sacred that rape, murder and torture can be committed by the peace-keeping organs of the State with immunity from outside intervention."[22]

THE ACCOUNT IN THE UP VIDHAN SABHA (LEGISLATIVE ASSEMBLY)

Far from hiding the incident at Narayanpur, the members of the state Legislative Assembly and those from Deoria district in particular as well as the state cabinet were their own worst enemies in exposing its full details in the state legislature. The proceedings of the Vidhan Sabha on January 28, 1980, were completely blocked by the persistence of its members by means of a privilege motion and a calling attention motion to expose fully the events that had occurred in Narayanpur. All the charges against the police and the descriptions of atrocities and brigandage that had occurred in that village and in the nearby police stations were recorded in the legislature that day as well as some that the English-language press obviously thought too horrific or disgusting to print. The debates in the legislature also call attention once again to the tenuous relationship between politicians and police, on the one hand, and the fundamental hostilities between police and people, on the other hand.

It is evident that the police were completely out of political control in this incident. Despite the fact that the Janata Party had won all the seats from Deoria district in the 1977 legislative assembly elections, no stable structure of local political power had been established in the district. Moreover, the Janata MLAs had not been able to assert control over the police. In fact, it was revealed during the legislative assembly debates that several of the legislators from Deoria district had complained about both the SP, Deoria, and

[21] *Times of India*, February 9, 1980.
[22] *Patriot*, February 11, 1980.

the station officer, Captainganj, Lakshmi Narayan Chaturvedi, during the parliamentary elections that had just been concluded. They were charged with being pro-Congress and the chief minister was requested to transfer both of them. However, the chief minister told the Legislative Assembly that he had not been able to make the transfers during the election, which would have gone against the procedures normally followed and supervised by the Election Commission of India, whose permission would have had to be sought.[23]

That the local police, whether because of their Congress connections or otherwise, were totally out of the control of the local, elected Janata politicians is evident from the statements made in the Assembly by MLAs from both Deoria district and the adjacent district of Gorakhpur, who visited the scene. Sri Janardan Prasad Ojha, Janata MLA from Gorakhpur district, reported that when he visited the village, the local MLA, Bankey Lal, a man who had represented this constituency for four terms, "was present there at that time and he said that if I say anything about the police, then the police will take out my eye, then who will save me?"[24] The low esteem in which Bankey Lal was held by the police was evident from the fact that most of the beatings of the people in the police stations of Hata and Captainganj as well as the looting of the village and the alleged rapes occurred immediately after he had arranged a settlement of the issue of payment in the Hata police station on the 14th. His account of what transpired after he left is given below.

At 8:30, a Congress car arrived at my house. The Congress people said, "Bankey Lal, the Narayanpur people have been kicked and beaten, their beards plucked, and they have been made to drink their own urine in the *thana*." A lot of people were arrested and taken to Captainganj. I also got into the car and went to Narayanpur. When I arrived this time, the police were posted on every road. As the P.A.C. men saw me, they aimed their rifles at me and threatened to shoot me. The *daroga*s [subinspectors] of Hata and Captainganj along with their fellows sacked the entire village. I then went over to Captainganj where the people had been locked up and put in the *thana*. There I saw that each and every person there had been beaten with shoes, their beards had been plucked, when they asked for water those people were made to drink their own urine, at the time for doing *namaz*, those people were stripped and beaten, *lathi*s were stuck in their anuses and in the village the police people looted and abused [the people] in such a manner that I cannot speak about it. [. . .]

[23] Statement of the chief minister, Sri Banarsi Das, on January 29, 1980, in *Uttar Pradesh Vidhan Sabha ka Karyavahi: Adhikrta Vivarana* [hereafter referred to as UP Legislative Assembly Proceedings], vol. 343, nos. 2–4 (January 25–29, 1980), pp. 254–55. All quotations from this source cited below have been translated from the original Hindi by me or Mr. Michael Moses.

[24] Statement of Sri Janardan Prasad Ojha, UP Legislative Assembly Proceedings, p. 259.

The things I saw today [that day] are enough to cause humanity also to weep. The sins which the policemen have committed are beyond description. The villagers are annoyed with me as to how this could happen in spite of me. It was a blot on me. I was helpless. I am ready to resign my membership of the Legislative Assembly. I just cannot describe the atrocities of the policemen.[25]

As for the relations between police and people, which make such everyday incidents so inflammable, the account given by a government minister from Deoria district, Sri Mohan Singh, also of the Janata Party, conveys their character. According to his statement, the villagers "reported the matter" of the killing of the old woman at the Captainganj police station on the 11th, but the police did not come to the village for that purpose at all, but only "at 5:00 in the evening" after the villagers "intercepted" the second bus and "just to ask who intercepted the bus" and to "order them to set the bus free," while promising them also to take care of the matter with the bus owner, Sri Gupta. Moreover, the minister reported that the subinspector and the bus owner were in collusion, which "delayed matters" concerning the settlement of his payment.

Two further days passed before the next incident of interception of a bus by the villagers. In the meantime, according to the minister, the villagers collected funds for the cremation of the old woman, but the police insisted that the dead body had to be taken by them for a postmortem. The body was placed in a rickshaw, the police drove off with it and with the money for the cremation expenses and had the body thrown into a canal along the way, pocketing the cremation money.

In the minister's account, the next bus interception and the brawl between the villagers and the police occurred on the 14th. When the news of the police–public fight was transmitted to the "District Headquarters," the SDM (subdivisional magistrate) of Salempur, one B. K. Gupta, "arrived with a truckload of policemen." It was after the arrival of this force that the villagers were persuaded to go to the Hata police station for a settlement of the matter. The manner in which the settlement was reached at the police station is also of some interest.

There were CO Padrauna and the Captainganj police over there. Under the prevailing circumstance, Sri Gupta was asked in their presence to pay Rs. five thousand as compensation. Sri Gupta said that people were crushed by his bus every other day, and if he went on compensating like that he would be sold out/ broke. He offered to pay a sum of Rs. three hundred. SDM, Hata threatened that he would not allow his bus to ply on that route. Sri Gupta said that he had his connections in the top rank and no one could stop his bus from plying on that route; he would not pay more than Rs. 300. After much persuasion, how-

[25] Statement of Sri Banke Lal, UP Legislative Assembly Proceedings, p. 264.

ever, did Sri Gupta accept SDM, Hata and Sri Bankey Lal as a *panch* (council). The *panch* decided that Sri Gupta should deposit Rs. 5000 in the children's name, and a[n additional] sum of Rs. 3000 should be collected [by the villagers] and put in a Fixed Deposit in the children's name. It was also decided that both the pass books should be entrusted to SDM, Hata, and the children should live on the interest from that amount till they came of age. So, this was decided.

The minister, after reciting once again the details of the atrocities upon the villagers that followed, closed his account by placing the blame upon the Congress (I), noting "that quite a few members [of the Legislative Assembly] have observed that the . . . Sub-Inspector canvassed for the Congress (I)" during the just-concluded parliamentary elections. He went on to add the following remarks.

Since the Congress (I) came to power at the Centre (Delhi), it has boosted such people's morale and . . . a few officials, instigated by them, are creating such a condition of law and order to defame the state government and disturb the public life here. Therefore, I wish to appeal to all of you that, considering the human point of view, a most stern action should be taken against such people. And the House must sympathise with the families of all those who have suffered.[26]

The minister's closing remarks were challenged by a Congress (I) member, who retorted "that if false blames are laid on other parties to conceal the incompetence of the administration, it will not be tolerated."[27]

It is evident from the several accounts given above in the state legislature that the police, in addition to their "normal" desire to take revenge on the people for an attack upon their forces, also must have borne resentment against the Janata legislators from the district. The latter had already demanded the transfer of the SP and had made known their displeasure with the subinspector of the Captainganj police station as well.[28] Therefore, the common police practice in north India of obtaining financial benefit from the misfortunes of the villagers was here reinforced by both the desire for revenge and the opportunity to embarrass the Janata politicians who had been making their life difficult in the district and in the locality.

It is also evident that the villagers acted with understandable rage against

[26] Statement of Sri Mohan Singh, Minister of State for Small Industries, UP Legislative Assembly Proceedings, pp. 268–70.

[27] Remark of Sri Gulab Sehra, UP Legislative Assembly Proceedings, p. 270.

[28] A transfer from one police station or from one district to another may appear to be a minor matter, but it is well known that police officers routinely pay substantial sums of money to their superiors for particular postings that they must make up through collecting of sufficient illegal income during their stay in such a posting. If they are transferred before they have done so, they suffer considerable financial loss—well beyond their official salaries—and must again seek out a lucrative posting by the usual means.

the police for their failure to have any concern about the incident of the death of the woman and for their arrival on the scene only to protect the interests of the bus owner. Further, they mistrusted the honesty of the police, expected them to demand bribes, and believed that the subinspector had in fact taken a bribe from the bus owner. The callousness of both the police and the bus owner, who was said to have exclaimed that he would go broke if he had to pay Rs. 5,000 for every person killed by his bus drivers, certainly also would have enraged the villagers.

Moreover, the final financial settlement also appears suspicious on its face. Why should the villagers be required to put up Rs. 3,000 for the children as well? Why is it the business of the police and the bus owner to make such a demand upon them? Perhaps the police mistrusted the sincerity of the villagers and thought they simply intended to pocket the Rs. 5,000 for themselves. Requiring them to come up with some money of their own and placing it together with the Rs. 5,000 in a fixed deposit account would, in this reading, demonstrate the villagers sincerity and insure that the money would be there for the children when needed.[29] On the other hand, the entrusting of the payment from the fixed deposit account to the SDM, Hata, increased to Rs. 8,000, leads one to the supposition that the interest from the account, which was to go to the upkeep of the children, might have to be shared between the police and the villagers and that the larger sum would make the division more appreciable.

The exchange between the police and the bus owner at the Hata police station is also of considerable interest, revealing as it does so clearly the relationships between persons of substance, as opposed to ordinary villagers, and the police. Bus owners may argue with the police, challenge their threats, and threaten to bring to bear upon them their influence in higher quarters with no fear of being beaten.

While the feelings of shock and outrage expressed by the members of the UP Legislative Assembly over police brutality appear to be genuine, they did not allow their sentiments to make them entirely forgetful of the political implications of the incident. The Janata members exposed fully the incidents which, as it turned out, brought them down, but they also sought to blame the Congress (I) and the police, who were said to be Congress (I) supporters, for the attacks on the villagers.

Finally, the process of casting blame, engaged in by both sides, but most effectively by the Congress (I) on this occasion, serves to divert attention from any serious consideration of remedies. The ultimate solution proposed

---

[29] One may also note here a similarity between this police demand upon the villagers of Naryanpur and that of Nawal Kishore Gauri, the station officer involved in the Pachpera incident recounted in chap. 3, when he advised the villagers to collect some money to build a temple for the idol and show the money to him.

by the chief minister of UP was ludicrous. He pointed out in his remarks in the Assembly that incidents of this type occur every day; people are killed by buses and cars on village and city roads, and the automatic response of the people is to attack the drivers and burn their vehicles. He took the position, therefore, that though such police brutality as occurred in Narayanpur could not be tolerated and must be dealt with severely, "we must also ensure that if there were such an incident, a road accident in particular, the people must not take law in their hands, otherwise it would not be easy to safeguard them."[30] The people, therefore, are also to blame.

Every car and bus owner in north India knows what the chief minister meant by making such a statement. It would be a rash person indeed who chose to stop his car and get out to express his chagrin to the villagers after an incident involving the death of a person and, even more seriously, the death of a cow. But to preach the observance of "the law" in such circumstances is a travesty of the situation. The unfolding of the events in Narayanpur reveals how much of a travesty it is, for the chain of events that occurred there is inevitable, law or no law, given the negligence and corruption of the police, the knowledge the villagers have of their negligence and corruption, the links between the police and important men, and the ties between police and politicians. The solution is not "law and order," or other such meaningless abstractions, but immediate action and instant justice. No court proceedings are required in a case of this type, where the basic facts are known, the persons responsible are known, and the price for a person's life is well established.

POLICE ACCOUNTS

Police accounts of the Narayanpur incident confirm that police personnel misbehaved. They acknowledge that the police acted dishonestly and thoroughly beat the men of the village, but they deny all other charges. News reports of police response to the charges made against them at the time quoted "senior officers" as claiming that the charges against them were exaggerated, most particularly on the matter of rape and loot. They claimed especially that no woman in Narayanpur was raped. They also asserted that the original cause of the incidents was that "the people had violently stopped the bus, assaulted the police and beaten up constables."[31]

Moreover, the police statements convey a quite different view of the village and its inhabitants and of the motivations of some of the politicians who became interested in the incident. For example, a senior police officer[32] of Deoria district in 1982, a disinterested and intelligent Muslim officer, who

[30] Statement of the chief minister, Sri Banarsi Das, UP Legislative Assembly Proceedings, p. 273.

[31] *Patriot*, February 9, 1980.

[32] Title and name of officer masked to preserve confidentiality.

had not been posted to the district until after the incident, gave the following summary account of it.

> The majority of the people of Narayanpur are Muslims. They are militant and rowdy in the sense that, in case of any minor incident like the killing of a chicken by a car, they may try to extract five times the price of that chicken. In [the] 1980 incident, an old woman was run over by a truck [*sic*] and she died instantaneously. People gathered around the truck and started bargaining with the truck driver over the question of compensation. Meanwhile, police arrived on the scene and a compromise was reached. Money was paid to the subinspector who gave only [a] small proportion of that amount to the villagers. The villagers were enraged and subsequently beat up two policemen. In retaliation, a contingent of police force was sent to Narayanpur, who mercilessly thrashed the people of Narayanpur. All the men were beaten. After this, two cases were filed, one by the villagers against the police and [the] other by the police against the villagers. A commission of inquiry was set up which absolved the police of any guilty act [of rape]. It observed that the villagers were guilty of beating up policemen and the rape of Harijan women was a case of fabrication by the villagers. Subsequently, a Thakur minister visited Narayanpur. He looked at that issue from a microscopic level in the sense that he wanted to get the removal of [the] Brahman subinspector from that police station. The matter was brought to the notice of the State [Legislative] Assembly. After this, many politicians visited Narayanpur.[33]

This police account differs in important respects, though not completely, from the Congress/media version. In contrast to the press version, the villagers are not seen as innocent or hapless. They are militant, rowdy, and liars.

Second, corresponding to the press reports of the time, the police are described as corrupt (having taken part of the money paid in compensation to the villagers for the death of the old woman) and brutal (having beaten the villagers "mercilessly"). This part of the account, however, differs from the press reports in that it eliminates the mystery. It is matter-of-fact. An accident occurred, an old woman was killed, the villagers demanded compensation, compensation was paid, a dishonest subinspector took his share, the villagers became angry and thrashed the police, the police returned and paid the villagers back in beatings many times over. The fact is that there *is* nothing unusual or unexpected in any of this except the extent of the beatings administered and the details of the humiliation inflicted upon the villagers in the police stations, which the SP did not mention in his account. The latter aspects, however, would fit well enough into this account if it is

---

[33] *Horror Stories Text* (first interview, from notes, in Deoria on October 15, 1982).

accepted also that the villagers were a militant and rowdy lot. Under those circumstances, more severe police beatings and humiliation of the villagers make a kind of "sense."

One further aspect of the SP's account here was not mentioned at all in the press, namely, a caste factor, but one that had nothing to do with the atrocities. The UP minister who corroborated in the Legislative Assembly the charges against the police, and particularly the role played by the Brahman subinspector, was a Thakur[34] who wanted to remove the latter. The reasons are not given in this officer's account, but they will be explored further below.

The principal difference between the press account and that of the police, as well as that of the report of the inquiry commission, is the contention that no rapes at all occurred nor were there any deaths. There is also no hint in these accounts that the beatings that took place had anything to do with the fact that the victims were Harijans or Muslims.

The first police inquiry into the incident was reported in the press on February 3, before Mrs. Gandhi's visit. This was a preliminary inquiry ordered by the chief minister of the state and conducted by a deputy-inspector general of police, who visited the village along with the secretary, Harijan and Social Welfare Department.[35] Although the two men heard reports of at least one "shameful incident" of police misbehavior with two young women, they discounted the reports of mass rape. They confirmed that the police had "entered the houses of villagers and beat up men, women and children," but they also declared "that it was not a fact that all people in Narayanpur village had been beaten up." However, in their ten-page report, they did criticize the conduct of the station officers in charge of both the Hata and Captainganj police stations and acknowledged that the police and PAC personnel "had committed atrocities on the villagers." These atrocities, which had already been reported in vivid detail in the proceedings of the UP Legislative Assembly, were described as treatment that was "inhuman, barbarous and shameful" and "a disgrace to society." The report called for a further inquiry by the CID into the entire incident.[36]

The crime branch of the UP police also conducted its own investigation of the incident. As a result, criminal cases were filed against twenty policemen for "murder, dacoity, and molesting women." It was reported also that the crime branch specifically accused the Hata station house officer with deliber-

[34] Thakur is used interchangeably with Rajput to refer to persons from this cluster of upper castes. Thakur is really the common title used for persons of this caste grouping, as Pandit is for the Brahman castes.

[35] Generally misreported in the press at the time as the Commissioner for Scheduled Castes and Tribes.

[36] *Times of India*, February 3, 1980.

ately organizing the assault on the village on the night of January 14 in
retaliation for the alleged beating by the villagers of policemen at the village
earlier in the day.[37]

However, as already noted above, the judicial commission appointed to
investigate the Narayanpur incidents absolved the police of the charges of
mass rape and murder. The commission did, nevertheless, confirm that the
police, including the Hata subinspector, were "guilty of wrongful confinement and merciless beating of some villagers." At the same time, "it also
held some villagers guilty of attacking policemen on duty." As a result of
the commission's report, the most serious charges against policemen of rape
and murder were withdrawn, but the cases against the police "for wrongful
confinement and beating of villagers . . . continued in courts."[38] A search of
the Indian press has revealed no news reports on the ultimate conclusion of
these cases.

THE ACCOUNT OF THE VILLAGERS

Accounts given by the villagers to various persons who came to the village,
including the present writer, are detailed and consistent on the matter of the
beatings and indignities they suffered. My own visit to the village took place
on October 26, 1982. It occurred in an unexpected and unplanned way. I
had stopped by the side of the road at the sight of a beautifully harvested
crop of paddy lying neatly in the fields. I and my informant began to ask a
Lohar (low caste) *kisan* (cultivator) engaged in tying up the bundles questions about the paddy crop. After a while, I asked the name of the village
and was told it was Narayanpur. I asked if it was the very Narayanpur in
which the incidents had taken place and was told it was. I then began to ask
questions about the incident. As the Lohar was responding to my questions,
a tall bearded Muslim man strode up with a scythe in his hand, motioned to
the Lohar to shut up, and proceeded to take over the telling of the story,
which is given below.

> RESPONDENT: A little ahead from the place where we are standing
> [an old woman] was crushed to death by a bus. The villagers
> stopped the bus. She had two small grandchildren and her son and
> daughter-in-law had already expired. They were Kahar [caste of
> water carriers]. They stopped the bus and the bus driver went to
> Gorakhpur. The owner was some Mr. Gupta. And the bus driver
> said that he'll bring the owner. And that owner came and contacted
> the SO, Lakhsmi Narayan Chaturvedi, and he bribed him. They
> kept on waiting for that owner so that they can be paid some

[37] Ibid., February 14, 1980.
[38] Citations from the *Hindu*, September 11, 1982; see also *Asian Recorder*, October 22–28,
1982, p. 16,851.

money for the cremation. The police came with the owner and they started beating the people. Four policemen and one *daroga*. . . .

PRB: Why [did] the police [come] and beat them?

RESPONDENT: Many people had collected and police did not like this and they started beating them, they started caning them. And the villagers resisted and they pushed them [back]. So, from here, officers from Hata and other places came and they were taken to Hata bus stand on the pretext that they will be paid money by this owner and a *panchayat* [council], a [group from the] village *panchayat* had gone as well, and Vakil Khan, who is here, he was member of that *panchayat*, he also went to Hata, on the belief, which was told to them, that they will be given money by the owner for the cremation of that old lady. The MLA of this area was also present there. And the MLA, along with the officer, they left it on the decision of these two persons, and it was decided that rupees 5,000 would be paid for the cremation of the old woman and the upbringing of these two children. Money was to be paid after two to three days. Eleven members who were representing the *panchayat*, along with the two children, had gone to Hata, and when the decision was taken that they will be paid five thousand rupees, the owner of the bus left and they were surrounded by the police and kept in surveillance and even were not allowed to urinate outside. They were asked to urinate in the place directed by the police. . . . They were kept under surveillance . . . till other people who were involved had left. From two to five o'clock, they were kept under surveillance.

PRB: Until which people left?

RESPONDENT: The MLA and others who were trying to mediate, and along with the owner. Then, at night, when they requested that they should be allowed to go, the police said that you'll have to sign at this place and they signed, in fact they put their thumb impression, some of them put thumb impression and some of them signed . . . and they were asked to sit in a queue. After that, policemen came and they asked their names, their names were called out, and whoever responded was caned, was beaten up. One Mr. Johare, . . . his legs were tied and they were, he was suspended by two policemen and just below the foot, they were hit with *lathi* [long staff], . . . at the arch and ball of the foot. They were hit with *lathi*s. They kept on beating others at their will until they became more or less half dead. Their hands were tied behind their backs and they were made to walk and they boarded the bus and those who were unable to board the bus, they were still thrown into it . . . and Mr. Vakil Khan's watch was taken away by the policemen, wristwatch, and Habib Khan's six hundred rupees were taken away. They had to sit under the seats of the bus[39] and whenever they tried to get out, the police beat them with their *danda*s [sticks]. They were taken to Captainganj police station and they were again beaten. The police stashed away even their matchboxes, whatever they had, to the extent they even took away their matchboxes.

Then the people from Ramkola, Hata, and places around Narayan-pur, including *goonda*s and police, they were sent to the village, and those *goonda*s, along with the policemen, they came to the village around 11:00 o'clock at night and after that they started beating people mercilessly and they took some of the people away to the Captainganj police station where they again kept on beating them and, on the way, they also kept on beating. They were beaten so mercilessly in Captainganj that one Mr. Qutubuddin Khan of this village, his leg was fractured. Ghaffar, tailor, also fractured his leg. And after these two people had their legs fractured, they were, there was some calm, they were given some relief. Early in the morning, at around 4:00 A.M., they took out four people from the cell and it was very cold outside and they were made naked and made to lie down flat on their stomach on the floor and four police-men—then their hands and legs were held tightly—policemen stood on their legs and hands and then they were beaten up on their back with shoes and slippers. They were lined up again and their beards and moustaches were pulled and, if they tried to shake their head, then they were hit on the face flat with hand and it was so terrible that if I hit you at this moment in that way, you will become un-conscious. Then they were put in Kasia jail. In fifteen to twenty days, that old lady, five thousand rupees was given to the family of that old lady, which included the two children as well.

[Questioned further on the matter of police torture, the villager responded as follows.] When one Mr. Lallan Pandey was given a cup of tea, so, while the cup was in his mouth, it was hit by the hand and they were made to drink, they were given urine to drink. They were told to drink their own wine. . . . When this incident happened, Banarsi Das, the ex-CM [chief minister], who was CM at that time, he made an announcement that anyone who has been affected will be given five thousand rupees, which was not paid to them.[40]

[39] For those who have never ridden on an Indian country bus, let me simply note here that to be made to sit *under* the seats is itself an act of brutality.

[40] *Horror Stories Text* (second interview, taped, October 26, 1982). The specific forms of beating and torture described in this interview and allegedly administered by the police in this case are common in north Indian police stations, documented in numerous human rights reports

This account given by the villagers of their encounters with the police is consistent as far as it goes with virtually all other accounts of the incident that appeared in the press and in the UP Legislative Assembly—except in one respect. The one respect in which it is contradicted by other accounts is the absence in the statement of the villagers that they beat the police on the morning of January 14 and, thereby, provoked the retaliation. I did not obtain from the villagers accounts of rape and killing in the village. However, I and my informant did not complete the interview because we both felt somewhat nervous at the manner in which the scythe-carrying respondent was beginning to illustrate with physical gestures the tortures and humiliations he and others had suffered at police hands.

Therefore, despite the decisive conclusions of the commission of inquiry, there remains some doubt concerning whether mass rape or any rape was committed in the village and whether any person was killed or died as a consequence of police beatings. The latter would seem unlikely since it is rather harder to hide from a commission of inquiry the deaths of two people than it is to demonstrate conclusively the occurrence of rape. No medical examinations of the women of the village were ever done to determine whether any of them had been sexually assaulted. Mrs. Gandhi's testimony to the effect that they had been so assaulted is subject to doubt both because her interviews with the women were held in private and because it was clearly in her own political interest to believe that it happened. Finally, the very future of the village and its families became endangered by the nationwide publicity given to the charges of mass rape. Consequently, the villagers themselves became reluctant to press the claim that all or any of the women of the village had been raped because, as one of them put it very early in the official and unofficial investigations of the matter, "Why do you want to take our statements [on this matter], who will marry our daughters afterwards?"[41]

Consequently, we can take as facts or virtual certainties the beatings, humiliations, and torture of the villagers in the police stations and a repetition of the beatings and some destruction and looting in the village on the night of January 14. It is virtually certain also that the villagers, despite their denials, beat a couple of policemen on the morning of January 14, thereby provoking the savage retaliation they suffered. At the same time, it is also highly likely that the villagers were correct in their belief that part of the money due them was being siphoned off by the police and understandable that they feared they would receive none of it. It appears also that the ferocity of the attacks on the villagers was exceptional, greater than in the case of village Pachpera or in the town of Daphnala. Since there was not much

---

and, in part, by my own personal observation.

[41] UP Legislative Assembly Proceedings, p. 257.

money at stake here,[42] the only rational grounds for explaining its ferocity lie in the image conveyed by the police of the villagers, namely that, contrary to the press accounts, the men of the village were not hapless victims, but a militant and rowdy lot.

Whether the attacks in Narayanpur were more ferocious than in Pachpera or Daphnala and whether mass rape or any rape took place, the patterns in all three cases are similar. A theft, a rape, or an accident occurs that draws the attention of people, politicians, and public. Lack of trust between public and police leads to provocation of the police by the public, followed by police retaliation with larger numbers and with firepower. In the commotion, the precipitating incident or the object of the original quarrel recedes into the background. The idol disappears, the raped girl in Phalauda is gone, the children in Narayanpur ultimately receive Rs. 5,000 in some kind of trust, but hardly any attention is paid to them otherwise.

However, what distinguishes the Narayanpur case from the others is not the specific horrors and atrocities that were committed nor the rapes, if there were any, but the publicity that it received and the political context in which it was placed. That context was mentioned in the introduction and has been present in the background of all the discussion so far presented. It must now be considered.

THE POLITICAL CONTEXT

Two aspects of the political context of the Narayanpur events are discussed here. The first is the evident close connection between the parliamentary election results that brought Mrs. Gandhi and the Congress back to power in New Delhi and her search for a convincing pretext to dismiss the UP government and the other non-Congress state governments as well and hold new legislative assembly elections in them. The second is the relationship between the Narayanpur incidents and the attention that had been given in the preceding years to the problem of atrocities committed against Harijans and to police atrocities in general against the so-called weaker sections of society, including poor Muslims. These latter questions in turn are related to the interparty competition for the votes of the Scheduled Castes and Muslims.

The announcement of the parliamentary election results and the swearing in of Mrs. Gandhi as prime minister of the country once again occurred virtually on the very days when the incidents took place at Narayanpur, that is, between January 9 and January 14. During those days, all the national newspapers of the country were filled with news of the election results and of their consequences for the future of the non-Congress governments in the states. It was generally accepted among the non-Congress party leaders that

---

[42] However, one member of the UP Legislative Assembly claimed that Rs. 200,00 worth of "stuff" had been looted from the village (UP Legislative Assembly Proceedings, p. 259).

the victory of the Congress had been brought about principally by two factors: the disunity among the former principal components of the Janata coalition and the failure of the non-Congress parties, particularly the rump Janata Party, to hold on to the support it gained among "the poor and weaker sections" in the 1977 elections.[43] Having lost the parliamentary elections because of their disunity, two of the parties formed out of the wreckage of the Janata coalition, the rump Janata Party and the Lok Dal, sought to repair the rift between them in order to retain control over the governments in the states where non-Congress governments remained in power. At the time, the Janata Party held office in six north Indian states and Gujarat whereas the Lok Dal was the governing party in UP.

The leaders of both parties anticipated that Mrs. Gandhi would seek to do what they had done after the massive Janata victory in 1977, namely, dismiss all the state governments in which the opposition (then, of course, the Congress) held power on the grounds that they no longer represented the wishes of the people. However, they sought to distinguish the situation that existed in 1980 from that in 1977 when, it was argued, the Congress had not only manifestly lost the support of the people, but its state governments were in power only because their lives had been extended by constitutional amendments that the Janata had promised to annul. It was also noted even in a newspaper that otherwise supported Mrs. Gandhi that the Congress vote had not "risen substantially in the Hindi-speaking states"[44] so that it could not be argued that the Congress had achieved a mandate in those states comparable to that achieved by the Janata Party in 1977. Whereas the Janata Party had won all eighty-five Lok Sabha seats from UP in 1977, the Congress won only fifty-one in 1980. In fact, in UP, the Congress had polled barely above 36 percent of the vote in the Lok Sabha elections in 1980.

Consequently, although Mrs. Gandhi naturally wished to follow the Janata precedent of 1977, her justification to do so did not appear so clear as that of Janata in 1977. Moreover, she was naturally eager to avoid accusations that she was a dictator bent upon restoring her authoritarian rule. Further, as a practical matter, the Lok Sabha election results in UP did not indicate that the Congress would be able to have as great success in new legislative assembly elections as it had in the Lok Sabha elections. It was noted, for example, that in a majority of the assembly segments of the Lok Sabha constituencies, the principal non-Congress parties had run ahead of their Congress (I) opponents.[45] These results confirmed that opposition disunity had been the principal factor in the Lok Sabha election results, but they also suggested that the various non-Congress parties were still able to

[43] *Times of India*, January 10, 1980.
[44] Ibid., January 23, 1980.
[45] Ibid., January 16, 1980.

defeat the Congress on their own in the smaller legislative assembly constituencies.

The government of UP, politically the most important state in the country, was particularly vulnerable since the Lok Dal held only 164 seats in a house of 425 members. If the government fell of its own, Mrs. Gandhi's task would be immensely simplified. However, the non-Congress leaders instead made her task more difficult. The chief minister, Mr. Banarsi Das, summoned the legislatures of both houses to meet and called for a vote of confidence on January 23. In the meantime, negotiations took place between the Lok Dal and Janata Party leaders that led to an agreement on the part of Janata to support the existing government in UP in exchange for the Lok Dal's continued support for the Janata government in Bihar.[46] Nearly all other parties, whose leaders and members were obviously not eager to fight new elections, also decided to support the confidence motion. On January 23, therefore, the UP government received a strong vote of confidence from more than 80 percent of the members in the legislative assembly.

Mrs. Gandhi initially kept mum concerning her intentions. There was also some division within the party on the advisability of going to the polls again in some states, particularly UP.[47] However, a majority of the members of the executive of the organizational wing of the national party, the Working Committee, and of the organizational wings of the state parties and of the Youth Congress as well as the state legislators in UP and other states favored new elections and soon began to call openly for the resignation or dismissal of the non-Congress governments in the states in which the Congress had heavily defeated its rivals.[48] The results of the confidence motion in UP on January 23 had stalemated this demand.

However, on the very day on which the UP government survived its confidence motion, a small story appeared in the Gorakhpur edition of the Hindi newspaper, *Jagaran*, in which a local CPI peasant leader was quoted as having said that PAC forces had attacked the village of Narayanpur, looted it, and damaged its standing crops. It also reported that the PAC had remained deployed in the village since January 14. Two days later, on January 25, having sent a correspondent to Narayanpur, *Jagaran* led with a full report on the alleged mass rape, looting, and beating of the villagers.[49]

On January 27 the chief minister of UP said at a press briefing that he had asked for a full report on the incidents at Narayanpur and that he had sent one of the members of his council of ministers, Mohan Singh, who was also

[46] Ibid., January 14, 1980.
[47] Ibid., January 16, 1980.
[48] Ibid., January 19, 20, and 21, 1980.
[49] From a reconstruction of the chronology of reporting on the Narayanpur incidents in the *Times of India*, February 10, 1980.

an MLA from a constituency in Deoria district, to the district to conduct a personal inquiry. On the next day, as noted above, the deputy speaker of the UP Legislative Assembly admitted an adjournment motion on Narayanpur during which all the alleged atrocities committed in Narayanpur and at the Hata and Captainganj police stations—and some that were not reported— were described by a Janata MLA from Gorakhpur who had also visited the village. Mr. Mohan Singh also intervened in the discussion to corroborate the stories that had appeared in *Jagaran*. It should be noted that, up to this point, all the revelations and inquiries were made and conducted by or on leads provided by non-Congress politicians in and out of the UP government.

It was not until January 29, after the matter had already been revealed in the UP Legislative Assembly, that the national press and the leading English-language dailies picked up the story and featured it on their front pages. Two days later, Sanjay Gandhi visited the village, found the horror stories that had been revealed to be insufficient and enlarged upon them, and immediately linked the atrocities that had been committed against the Narayanpur people to the fate of the UP government, calling for its resignation.[50] Mrs. Gandhi then announced her decision to pay a personal visit to the village.

The chief minister responded to this announcement by characterizing it as an interference in the autonomy of the state. He also claimed that the state government had already taken necessary action by suspending two police subinspectors, transferring a senior officer, and ordering a judicial inquiry into the events. He also reported that a team sent by the state government, including a deputy inspector general of police and the secretary, Harijan and Social Welfare Department, had concluded that the police and PAC did commit atrocities against the villagers, but found no evidence of mass rape. The state government was also reported to have appointed a Deoria district judge to make an inquiry into the happenings at Narayanpur and to present a report within three months.[51]

On February 7 Mrs. Gandhi visited the village, expressed her shock and outrage at the atrocities committed against the people there, accused the state government of trying to "hush up" the atrocities, and remarked that it was extraordinary that the chief minister had accepted the police version of the events. She also linked the incidents with the fate of the UP government by saying that it no longer had any right to remain in office. The chief minister responded by saying that her charges of a "hush up" were false, noted that Mohan Singh had been sent to investigate, said that twenty-five

[50] *Times of India*, February 1, 1980.
[51] *Data India*, February 4–10, 1980 and *Times of India*, February 3, 1980.

policemen had now been transferred and cases had been registered against them, senior police officers had been transferred as well, and each of the victims had been given payments of Rs. 5,000.[52]

Despite the press linking of Mrs. Gandhi's reactions to the Narayanpur events with her statement concerning the illegitimacy of the UP government, the prime minister denied that her visit to Narayanpur had anything to do with its future. She said there was in any case a very strong demand for the dissolution of the UP Legislative Assembly. In other words, she was quoted as saying that the government of UP no longer had any right to rule because of the Narayanpur incidents, but that her personal visit there had nothing to do with the future of the government.[53] This statement was, of course, utterly disingenuous since the dissolution of the state government could follow only upon her advice to the president of India.

The UP chief minister responded to the reports of Mrs. Gandhi's statements concerning Narayanpur by saying that it was evident she was "making political capital out of a human tragedy." Former prime minister Charan Singh, now leader of the opposition in Parliament, also said that Mrs. Gandhi obviously intended to use the Narayanpur incident as a pretext for removing the state government.[54] The untouchable leader and head of the Janata Party, Jagjivan Ram, also visited Narayanpur along with a lady MP of his party, who could also be in a position to speak to the women as Mrs. Gandhi had done. The latter said that the women had not declared to her outright that they had been raped. They had said that they had been "dishonoured" which, she noted, might or might not mean that they were in fact raped. In any case, Jagjivan Ram added his voice to those of other opposition leaders who found no justification in the Narayanpur incidents for the dissolution of the UP Legislative Assembly.[55]

In the meantime, the state government continued its investigations. Twenty police personnel were charged with various crimes, including molestation of women. The crime branch of the state police was instructed to conduct an inquiry. Preliminary reports of their inquiry were released confirming the deliberate organization of the raid on the village by the Hata police station officer. The state government also ordered a judicial inquiry into the incidents to be carried on by a judge of the High Court of the state.[56]

These efforts and actions on the part of various opposition leaders and the state government to head off the impending dissolution of the UP government were of no avail. On February 18 the news appeared that the government of UP had been dismissed, the state legislature dissolved, and the state

[52] *Data India*, February 4–10, 1980.
[53] *Patriot*, February 8, 1980.
[54] *Times of India*, February 9, 1980.
[55] Ibid., February 13, 1980.
[56] Ibid., February 14, 1980.

placed under President's Rule in preparation for new legislative assembly elections.[57]

The importance of the Scheduled Caste and Muslim vote in interparty competition, especially in north India, has already been noted above. It has also been previously noted that, ever since Mrs. Gandhi's 1971 election campaign, the major political parties in India have sought to present themselves as the better protectors of the interests of the "weaker sections" and to portray their rivals as unable to control violence and other forms of harassment against the Scheduled Castes and Tribes, the poor, and the Muslims. The principal method of demonstrating the latter point has been to draw public attention to major incidents of violence that could be attributed to one's rivals. This competition for control over atrocity propaganda was especially evident in connection with the Narayanpur incidents and in the arguments used by party leaders to attack and defend each other on the issue.

The interparty propaganda on the subject of atrocities against the weaker sections was particularly intense in January 1980 because of the way in which the Scheduled Caste and Muslim votes had been perceived as having fluctuated in the 1977 elections away from Mrs. Gandhi and the Congress and partly back to the Congress in 1980. All parties were engaged in some self-analysis of the election results from this point of view during the weeks in January after the Lok Sabha election results had been declared and as the Narayanpur incidents were occurring. For example, the rump Janata Party, whose head was the Scheduled Caste leader, Jagjivan Ram, held a meeting of its national executive on January 9. At that meeting, it was reported that the executive committee felt that "the party failed to impress on the people its concern for the poor and weaker sections in contrast to its success in this direction under the leadership of Mr Jayaprakash Narain in 1977."[58] The Janata Party had failed to do so despite the fact that it appealed to the Scheduled Caste voters partly by promising that, if the party emerged victorious, Jagjivan Ram would become the prime minister of the country.

Insofar as UP was concerned, however, it was noted that the Janata Party polled miserably among Scheduled Caste voters, whose votes appeared to have been divided between the Congress and the Lok Dal, with the former retaining the larger share of them.[59] There was a consensus in the press and among the political parties that the restoration of a large part of its base among the Scheduled Castes and Muslims was of major importance in the

[57] Ibid., February 18, 1980.
[58] Ibid., January 10, 1980.
[59] Ibid., January 10 and 13, 1980.

Congress victory in UP, in addition to the division of the votes of the non-Congress parties. However, the Lok Sabha results were not so favorable for the Congress in UP as to indicate an easy victory in that state should state legislative assembly elections be held. Consequently, there was not only some doubt in the minds of Congress leaders about dismissing the UP government, but it was also considered important to keep up the momentum of support-building among the Scheduled Castes and Muslims in case such elections were to be held. The principal method for doing so—for the Congress as for other parties—was for each party to draw attention to atrocities committed against Scheduled Castes and Muslims the responsibility for which, or the failure to take appropriate action in relation to which, could be attributed to others.

So, even before the revelations concerning Narayanpur, the president of the UP Congress organization submitted a memorandum to the governor of the state claiming "that the Lok Dal government had failed to protect the minorities and Harijans" and that, as a result, "there was a sense of insecurity among them."[60] The Janata Party leaders, who were in competition with the Lok Dal in UP and Bihar, also criticized the Lok Dal government in UP for similar reasons in connection with an incident involving the murder of some Scheduled Caste voters in Amroha constituency. They accused the government of failing "to protect the weaker sections of society."[61] The Lok Dal responded to both these accusations within three days first, by mobilizing a delegation of twenty Scheduled Caste MLAs who submitted a counter-memorandum to the governor in which they denied the Congress charges that atrocities had been committed against Harijans during the Lok Dal rule of the state. They pointed out also that the Lok Dal had won a majority (ten out of eighteen) of the constituencies reserved for Scheduled Castes to the Lok Sabha from UP, which, they said, demonstrated that the Lok Dal "enjoyed the support of the majority of Harijans in the state." On the same day, the Lok Dal chief minister announced that payments of Rs. 5,000 each would be made to the dependents of Harijans who had been killed in violent incidents during the Lok Sabha poll in the district of Moradabad, including the incident at Amroha.[62]

One of the ironies of the Narayanpur situation was that, while exposing it themselves, the Lok Dal leaders in the UP state government sought to displace blame for it onto the Congress by arguing that the local police officers, including the Hata station officer, Lakshmi Narayan Chaturvedi, were Congress supporters whose purpose was to disrupt law and order in Deoria district because the non-Congress parties had the support of the weaker sections

[60] Ibid., January 20, 1980.
[61] Ibid., January 21, 1980.
[62] Ibid., January 23, 1980.

of the population there. The Lok Dal MLA of the constituency, Bankey Lal, claimed "that police officers of his area who belonged to the upper castes wanted to punish voters, mostly Muslims, who had supported him in the previous assembly elections." Mohan Singh, whose corroboration of the reports of police atrocities against the villagers of Narayanpur greatly embarrassed his own government, sought to blame the Congress for the incident. He charged that state government officials sympathetic to the Congress had been trying to "destabilise the Lok Dal ministry" and that the incident at Narayanpur had been instigated as "part of that design." The chief minister, Banarsi Das, took the same position, asserting in the state legislative assembly that "he had heard complaints that the police administration in Deoria was acting in a partisan manner," that is, on behalf of the Congress.[63] However, the Congress propaganda machine, which brought the prime minister herself into the fray, proved far superior in this contest to that of the Lok Dal.

In the contest for supremacy in relation to atrocity propaganda, the rhetoric of attack included a recitation of the most gory incidents of violence committed against Scheduled Castes, Muslims, and others under the regime of one's opponents. The rhetoric of defense involved efforts to distinguish the violent incidents that occurred under one's own regime by characterizing them as minor in comparison to those that occurred under the opposing regime. In the wake of the Narayanpur incident and Mrs. Gandhi's personal visit to the village, the rhetoric of attack and defense also included accusations against the previous prime minister or chief minister of not showing sufficient sympathy for atrocity victims by personally visiting the site of the atrocities and, of course, of not taking appropriate and expeditious action or even of attempting to "hush up" the incidents. At a meeting of Congress workers held just after her visit to Narayanpur, Mrs. Gandhi responded to the objections of the chief minister to her visit there by chiding him for not doing the same, saying "it was the duty of the chief minister to visit the village and ascertain the facts." She then went on to recite a list of places where atrocities had been "committed on the people" in states ruled by non-Congress governments in the previous years: "Belchi, Aligarh, Kanpur, Jagdishpur, Purnea and Nadia and asked why the people in power then did not visit these places to provide relief to the people."[64]

The *Patriot* reported on the same day that Mrs. Gandhi was shocked that "instead of being outraged by the recent police atrocities on villagers" in Narayanpur, the chief minister should have tried to hide them. Moreover, despite the fact that various state officials and ministers had already visited

---

[63] Ibid., January 29, 1980; see also their statements from the UP Legislative Assembly Proceedings quoted above in nn. 23–26.

[64] Ibid., February 8, 1980.

the village on the orders of the chief minister, Mrs. Gandhi was also reported to have said "it was extraordinary that the Chief Minister, instead of
going to Narayanpur himself or sending someone else to ascertain facts,
should have accepted the police version, though it was the police, or at least
some of them, who were responsible for the incident." She then went on to
accuse the chief minister and other state government officials of a lack of
humanity or of harboring the feelings "that the villagers of Narayanpur are
not human beings."[65]

Whatever action was taken by the state government in Narayanpur also
was dismissed as useless or inadequate. When the state government announced that a district judge of Deoria had been ordered to hold an inquiry
into the Narayanpur incidents, Mrs. Gandhi responded that it "would serve
no purpose" because an impartial inquiry could not be held by officers from
within the district. She accused the state government of "laxity in dealing
with the incident" and went on to say that "the villagers were living in a
state of shock and nothing had so far been done to restore confidence there."
On the contrary, she charged that "the police were still harassing the villagers and hundreds of them had been implicated in a number of cases."
Moreover, she claimed that "about a dozen persons arrested [from Narayan-
pur] were still in jail."[66]

The *Times of India* added its support to Mrs. Gandhi's charges of state
government inaction on Narayanpur with a leader on February 9:

> It is clear beyond doubt that the U.P. government might not have taken, but for
> Mrs Gandhi's visit to the village, even the limited action it took against the
> police officials in question. For only after she had announced her travel plans
> did U.P.'s Inspector-General of Police and other senior officers bestir them-
> selves and suspend those of the alleged culprits who were still strutting around
> Narayanpur and intimidating the already terrified villagers into keeping quiet.[67]

The editorial completely ignored the fact that the matter was brought to
national attention only because of the discussion of it in the UP Legislative
Assembly and that Sanjay Gandhi and Mrs. Gandhi learned about Narayanpur only because of its exposure by non-Congress politicians and ministers
in the UP government itself.

The *Patriot* followed a similar line, placing the attitude of the UP government in the broader context of its alleged protection of the PAC, which was
even then widely perceived as an anti-Muslim force in communal riots in
western UP. Pointing out that the PAC had been involved in Narayanpur as
well, the newspaper said that the state government had "not only failed to

---

[65] *Patriot*, February 8, 1980.
[66] *Times of India*, February 1, 1980.
[67] Ibid., February 9, 1980.

control" the PAC, but had protected it and that the chief minister himself had at first attempted "to hide its crime."[68]

The rhetoric of attack on the Narayanpur atrocities also included statements implying that these were the worst incidents of the type ever witnessed in the country. An *Indian Express* editor wrote in a leader on January 30: "Even to a country inured to excesses committed on its weakest sections, the police atrocities on the poor villagers of Narayanpur in Deoria district of U.P. must have come as a shock."[69] The strongest statement on the matter was that of Sanjay Gandhi, previously quoted. In that same statement in which he said that every girl and woman had been raped, he also was reported to have said that "what had happened in Narayanpur was unprecedented."[70] Mrs. Gandhi also was quoted as saying that she doubted "if there has been any other instance of such magnitude since Independence."[71] To the opposition charges that worse incidents had occurred under her own regime, Mrs. Gandhi replied that these incidents, including police firings at Sultanpur and Muzaffarnagar "which took place in 1976 . . . are negligible in comparison with what happened in the Pantnagar police firing [during the Janata period in 1978] or now in Narayanpur."[72]

The view of the opposition leaders, of course, was quite the opposite. Jagjivan Ram's position was that the Narayanpur incident had been "blown out of proportion" for political purposes. However "painful" the incident was, it did not reflect an "abnormal law and order situation" in the state, for "such things" did happen "in changing societies."[73] Chief Minister Banarsi Das accused Mrs. Gandhi of pretense, of shedding "crocodile tears" over the plight of the Harijans, which "only added insult to injury."[74]

Former Prime Minister Charan Singh, head of the Lok Dal and leader of the opposition in Parliament, responded to the charges made by Mrs. Gandhi after her visit to Narayanpur. At a news conference, he sought to expose Mrs. Gandhi's intention to use the Narayanpur incidents as a pretext for dismissing the UP government by saying that it seemed that in her view, "a single 'shocking incident' was enough to prove that the government in U.P. could not be carried on in accordance with the provisions of the Constitution." He then went on to counter Mrs. Gandhi's list of atrocities committed during non-Congress rule with a list of those committed during her tenure and that of various state Congress or Congress-allied governments: Muzaffarnagar in 1976, where forty-four Muslims had been killed while

[68] *Patriot*, February 11, 1980.
[69] *Indian Express*, January 30, 1980.
[70] Ibid., February 1, 1980.
[71] *The Hindu*, February 9, 1980.
[72] Ibid., February 9, 1980.
[73] *Indian Express*, February 12, 1980.
[74] *Statesman*, February 19, 1980.

resisting vasectomies during the Emergency; Ferozabad in 1972, when forty-eight Muslims had been killed in a demonstration concerning the Aligarh Muslim University; and the infamous incident in Tanjore district in 1968, where "42 Harijan women and children had been burnt to death in broad daylight." Charan Singh's list of the most notorious incidents pointedly included the most prominent ones involving the two largest potential voting blocs of Muslims and Harijans.[75]

Charan Singh also responded to the criticisms against Chief Minister Banarsi Das for not visiting Narayanpur by asking why she had not visited Muzaffarnagar—"only 65 miles from Delhi"—in 1976 nor dismissed any officer nor held "any inquiry" nor dismissed the state government then ruled by the Congress. The actions of the state government in relation to Narayanpur, he implied, shone in contrast to her nonresponse in connection with Muzaffarnagar. In response to the news of the Narayanpur incident, he noted that three government ministers and the vice president of the Lok Dal had gone to the village, the DIG (deputy inspector general) and the SP had been transferred, "three police officers and 26 constables were suspended," and a judicial inquiry had been ordered. In addition, monetary payments had been made to the victims.[76]

However, it was Mrs. Gandhi who had the last words to say on Narayanpur and atrocities against Harijans. On the day the dissolution of the UP and eight other state legislative assemblies was announced, the *Times of India* printed, in the text of the same story in which this event was reported, the following letter of Mrs. Gandhi to the UP chief minister on these matters.

Dear Shri Banarsi Das,

I am astonished to receive your letter of the 28th January in which you have expressed your inability to take action for giving protection to Harijans who want to return to their homes as I did not give any details about such people. As I mentioned to you in my letter dated January 22, several groups of Harijans from different parts of Uttar Pradesh have been coming to me to relate their tales of woe regarding intimidation and harassment by certain caste groups. The number of such persons has been so large that it would be impossible to take statements from all those who come to see me. The question of atrocities on Harijans during the elections in U.P. was raised in Parliament also, [by] the Congress (I). With such widespread complaints, I should have thought it would have been simple for you to locate the affected villages and take necessary action. You should ascertain why such complaints do not reach you and you are not kept informed.

I have received written representations from some residents of Makhmapur village in Muzzafarnagar district and Behla Hajipur village in Ghaziabad dis-

---

[75] *Times of India*, February 9, 1980.
[76] Ibid.

trict, copies of which are enclosed. These are complaints of intimidation on the polling day and the victims include Harijans also. I hope it will be possible for you to initiate some action at least in these cases.

You have drawn my attention to the machinery set up by your government to give protection to Harijans. But the fact remains that despite this machinery, the largest number of complaints of atrocities on Harijans still come from U.P. Even in Narayanpur, the response of this special machinery was most unsatisfactory.

We cannot afford to remain complacent merely by creating an administrative apparatus. It is also necessary to ensure that this machinery is responsive and effective. It is for the state government to find out why and how Harijans and other people from weaker sections are harassed and humiliated and ensure that such incidents do not recur. In such matters the political leadership in charge of the government cannot afford to wait for filing of written complaints.

Yours sincerely
Indira Gandhi[77]

PERSPECTIVES ON ATROCITIES

The rhetoric used by the opposing sides in their efforts to inflate or downplay the significance of the Narayanpur atrocities went beyond the ordinary boundaries of political gamesmanship. It was embedded within a broader structure of argument that the politicians on both sides had become accustomed to using, involving the symbolic use of atrocities as weapons against each other. More important, the rhetoric reached that stage noted by Foucault in which talk itself becomes not just a substitute for inaction, but a means of perpetuating the very system of abuses to which it draws attention.

That system of talk persists in India and contributes to the perpetuation of violence in three ways. First, it selects for attention only those incidents that are politically useful, neglecting the many others that occur day-in and day-out. Second, it misidentifies incidents as atrocities against Harijans and "weaker sections" just because it is politically useful to do so, thereby ignoring numerous incidents that do constitute atrocities of that specific type and seeking appropriate measures to deal with them. And, as a corollary to this, it also fails to address the facts and the motives of those who commit brutalities mislabeled as atrocities against Harijans. It is as if were they not labeled as such, they were not worthy of attention and action. Third, and probably most important, it fails to identify the realities of violence in the north Indian countryside and their underlying bases because it is so useful to have such recurring incidents as a symbolic resource pool from which to draw in political battles and so difficult to contemplate the social, economic,

[77] Ibid., February 18, 1980.

and institutional restructuring that would be required to prevent or limit the frequency and intensity of their occurrence. Finally, it should also be noted that, in specific cases such as Narayanpur, the public attention drawn to them may even make the situation worse in some respects for the villagers.

Consider first the matter of selectivity. Even the politicians pointed out in their verbal dance of attack and defense and the press in their analyses of the Narayanpur events that other similar events were occurring during the very time in which these events were receiving national attention. For example, a *Times of India* correspondent noted the incident at Nangla Lodha in Aligarh district, which was mentioned in chapter 3 and which occurred on January 24–25. In this case also, and with roughly similar authenticity, charges were made that police had raped women of the village, were caught and beaten by the villagers, after which "the police allegedly beat [the villagers] up mercilessly and registered cases against them." Also echoing the Narayanpur events, "a large police force entered the village on January 25 and allegedly plundered the village." Mr. Kalyan Singh, then of the Janata Party, raised the matter in the UP Legislative Assembly immediately thereafter, but it was drowned in the sea of attention devoted to Narayanpur. The same correspondent also noted that an incident had "occurred near Narayanpur within a few days" afterwards, in which "armed dacoits looted" a village "and allegedly raped a teenaged girl, leaving her unconscious."[78]

Why did these two incidents not receive the same attention from the politicians and the press as that given to Narayanpur? Why did they not all rush to these two places as well? Insofar as Nangla Lodha is concerned, a pertinent factor is that the villagers beaten there were backward-caste supporters of the Janata Party, not Harijans and Muslims. Insofar as the second incident is concerned, the police were not involved, only a gang of *dacoits*. Therefore, the state government could not be directly blamed for the incident, but only charged that it was unable to maintain law and order.

However, the question of selectivity is a much broader one than choosing between stray incidents here and there. It raises rather the whole question of the discovery, labeling, and prosecution of acts of brutality and torture committed against the poor, the Scheduled Castes and Tribes, the minorities, and the "weaker sections" of the population generally by the police or the dominant landed classes in the countryside.

A look at table 5.1, which provides statistics on "atrocity cases" committed against Scheduled Castes in the state of UP from 1974 to 1985, gives a preliminary indication of the dimensions of the problem of selectivity. During those years, the total number of offenses of this type listed in the annual reports of the Commission and Commissioner for Scheduled Castes and

[78] Ibid., February 10, 1980.

TABLE 5.1

Offense-Wise Statement of Atrocity Cases against Scheduled Castes, Uttar Pradesh
(Number of Cases Reported)

Year	Murder	Violence[a]	Rape	Arson	Other IPC Offenses	Total
1985	223	582	177	408	2745	4135
1984	213	580	176	377	2854	4200
1983	202	507	148	344	2650	3851
1982	208	457	152	327	2833	3977
1981	N.A.	N.A.	N.A.	N.A.	N.A.	3865
1980	236	149	489	282	3123	4279
1979	191	122	487	326	2976	4102
1978	219	613	188	445	4195	5660
1977	143	447	90	278	4106	4974
	(148)	(506)	(112)	(281)	(3774)	(4821)[b]
1976	N.A.	N.A.	N.A.	N.A.	N.A.	2447
1975	N.A.	N.A.	N.A.	N.A.	N.A.	4656
1974	N.A.	N.A.	N.A.	N.A.	N.A.	5791

Sources: The figures come from two annual reports, one designated *Report of the Commissioner for Scheduled Castes and Scheduled Tribes*, the other the *Report of the Commission for Scheduled Castes and Scheduled Tribes*. Both are published under the auspices of the Government of India, Ministry of Home Affairs, and published in Delhi by the Controller of Publications.

[a]Listed in earlier reports under the heading "grievous hurt."

[b]The figures in paretheses come from the commissioner's twenty-fifth report, for 1977–78, at p. 139, and are slightly different from those in the commission's report for the same year.

Tribes[79] ranged between 3,851 and 5,791. The large majority of these offenses were nonviolent, but there were also between 1,200 and 1,500 major cases of murder, violence, rape, and arson listed annually in these reports. It is obvious, therefore, simply from the very number of the cases involved and the seriousness of so many of them, that the selection of one or two cases for extensive media attention involves arbitrariness.

One might think that the media and the politicians would be most drawn

[79] Nothing better illustrates my point above—and Foucault's—concerning the political uses of talk and their irrelevance and frequent counterproductivity to action than the existence of two offices, both under the Home Ministry of the Government of India, one labeled the office of the Commissioner for Scheduled Castes and Tribes, the other labeled the Commission for Scheduled Castes and Tribes. The office of the commissioner, established by constitutional mandate, has been in existence since 1950–51. The office of the commission was established by the Janata government in 1978 to demonstrate its own special desire to protect the Scheduled Castes and Tribes. However, the terms of its appointment, its powers, and its functions were identical to that of the commissioner! Initially, two virtually identical reports also were published, one by the office of the commissioner, another by the office of the commission. Later, the reports of the commission displaced those of the commissioner.

to those cases that involve more than individual actions of murder, violence, rape, or arson, that is, large-scale attacks by the police or the landed castes upon groups of Scheduled Caste persons or whole villages, as in the case of Narayanpur. However, some of the comments noted above about cases comparable to Narayanpur that occurred around the same time but did not receive such attention, as well as the discussion of the incident at Pachpera in chapter 1 and the incident to be discussed in the following chapter, should immediately dispel that notion. It is clear that the selection of incidents of this type for public attention is a stage-managed procedure in which politicians and press work in tandem for political advantage and in which the interests of the victims are incidental and soon forgotten. The *Statesman*, an anti-Congress newspaper at the time and the only national newspaper that took a critical view of the propaganda campaign in connection with Narayanpur, put the matter in just this light.

> Narayanpur's moment of glory is over. The Prime Minister has come and gone. Other politicians will shortly come and go, perhaps even the Chief Minister will come and then go along with his Government.
>
> For a while longer tears, real and crocodile, will be shed and the dust will continue to rise in the village as cars filled with VIPs tear in. Then, Narayanpur will become another paragraph in history.
>
> These things are, however, not as important as the avalanche of allegations and counter allegations. Mrs. Gandhi talks of Belchi, Aligarh, Kanpur, Jagdishpur, Purnea and Nadia, and demands to know why "those in power then" did not bother to visit these places. Her opponents ask her the same questions about Turkman Gate, Rewasa, Pipli and Muzaffarnagar. She says there has been no law and order in the country in the past three years; they say there has been none since independence and Narayanpur recedes further and further into the background.[80]

Misidentification is the second problem produced by the talk and the official reporting on alleged atrocities against Scheduled Castes and others. How does the commission decide that a specific incident of murder, violence, rape, arson, or offense of another type should be labeled as an atrocity against the Scheduled Castes? The commission definition is simple and utterly inadequate. Atrocities against Scheduled Castes are simply any of the crimes just noted committed against Scheduled Castes.

Although the official definition does not say so, the assumption also is that these crimes are committed by either caste Hindus or other higher-status persons or the police upon the Scheduled Castes. However, this definition, even with the added assumption, eliminates any distinction between crimes committed between persons of different castes or by the police against

---

[80] *Statesman*, February 9, 1980.

Scheduled Castes that have nothing to do with caste prejudice and those that do. From some points of view, such a distinction may seem invidious. However, from another point of view, namely, the proper identification of the extent and nature of the operation of caste prejudice, exploitation, and oppression of the Scheduled Castes by other groups in society, it is a matter of some importance.

The figures in table 5.1 give no clue concerning how to sort this question out. However, for 1982 and for that year only, the commission published comparison figures on the total number and percentage of cases of rape and murder committed against Scheduled Castes as a percent of the total such cases in the state. These figures, presented in table 5.2, immediately cast doubt upon the magnitude of the problem suggested by the overall figures given in table 5.1. Although Scheduled Castes constituted more than 21 percent of the total population of the state according to the 1981 census, the percentage of murders of Scheduled Caste persons to the total murders committed in the state in 1982 was less than 4 percent and of rape less than 20 percent. There is, therefore, no evidence from these figures that such violent crimes are particularly directed against Scheduled Castes. In fact, the figures suggest quite the opposite insofar as murder is concerned.

Moreover, perusal of those incidents described in detail in the commission reports provides ambiguous evidence concerning their origins and nature. When a group of Scheduled Caste persons under the local leadership of persons of their own caste are organizing to fight for their rights against the dominant landed castes and are murdered or their families are burned alive in their huts, it would be invidious to make any distinctions concerning whether such a crime is to be defined as an atrocity against Scheduled Castes. However, when an altercation takes place between upper castes and lower castes in a village concerning the routing of a procession blocked by a person from an upper caste who had built a house that caused a narrowing of the traditional way, it is not so clear that caste prejudices are involved and that such an incident that leads to injuries against the Scheduled Castes is meaningfully described as an atrocity committed against them by upper castes.[81]

Insofar as the Narayanpur incident is concerned, Mrs. Gandhi chose not to label it as a caste or communal incident, but the stage-managing of the incident certainly led to its identification as a case of police atrocities committed against Scheduled Castes and Muslims. However, as a matter of fact, many of the victims of the police atrocities in Narayanpur and at the police station were from poorer, but non-Harijan, backward castes. Moreover,

[81] Incidents of these types are described in Government of India, Commission for Scheduled Castes and Scheduled Tribes, *First Report (July 1978–March 1979)* (Delhi: Controller of Publications, 1980), chap. 6.

TABLE 5.2

Murder and Rape Cases of Scheduled Castes in Relation to Total Such Cases in
Uttar Pradesh, 1982

% of SC Population (1981 Census)	Murder Cases			Rape Cases		
	Total Cases	Cases of SC	% of Cases of SCs to Total Cases	Total Cases	Cases of SC	% of Cases of SCs to Total Cases
21.16	5716	208	3.63	773	152	19.66

Source: Government of India, Home Department, *Report of the Commission for Scheduled Castes and Scheduled Tribes (April 1982–March 1983), Fifth Report* (Delhi: Controller of Publications, 1985), pp. 122 and 124.

completely neglected in the account of the atrocities committed against the villagers was the fact that one of the victims of the brutal attacks in the police station was a Brahman, whose sacred thread was torn apart and whose top knot was cut.[82] While these acts seem much less atrocious than those committed against the other villagers, they certainly constituted a serious humiliation for this Brahman. I could find no reference whatsoever to this insult to the Brahman in any of the accounts published in the national English-language press.

The third problem with all the talk about atrocities and brutalities is that it in a way underplays the pervasiveness of violence in north Indian rural society and its causes. The Narayanpur case was portrayed by Mrs. Gandhi and the national press as an example of the failure of the (opposition) state governments to maintain law and order and of the need for better police training. Mrs. Gandhi's remarks on the latter subject can only be described as ludicrous. She was reported as having said that an important aspect of the Narayanpur incident was "the manner in which the worst in the police personnel comes out in situations" of this type. She concluded from this observation that "flaws in police training had to be identified and eliminated." The "whole matter had to be studied."[83] In the meantime, while "it was important to keep up the morale of the police, she thought it would be "disastrous to our democracy as well as to the well-being of our people if the police get the feeling that they can get away with atrocities."[84]

After all the noise about Narayanpur created by Mrs. Gandhi and her son, filled with hyperbolic statements magnifying for political purposes brutal incidents concerning which a statement of the bare facts would have been

[82] This detail, along with all the other atrocities reported in the press, appeared in UP Legislative Assembly Proceedings, p. 257.

[83] *Times of India*, February 10, 1980.

[84] *The Hindu*, February 9, 1980.

sufficient to portray their atrocious character, the problem was reduced to an administrative one. Study, leading to identification of the problems that create situations of this type, and appropriate new training procedures were offered as the route to a solution. In other words, more talk and further administrative action were proposed.

With all the words written about Narayanpur, no answers were provided by anyone concerning why the situation turned so grim. Yet it should be clear enough what the principal elements in its development were. The first was the failure to provide immediate justice. In a situation of this type, villagers cannot be expected to behave like citizens of industrial societies, who would report the matter to the police, then call their insurance agents and attorneys and, if necessary, file suit in court. It is not that Indian villagers are not accustomed to litigation—far from it—but not in situations involving accidental, instantaneous, and unanticipated death to one of their number. Such situations call for an immediate response.

Instead, the bus owner procrastinated and offered the villagers a pittance, even by Indian standards, for a human life. By the time the police intervened on the road on the 14th when the second bus had been stopped by the villagers, the situation had become dangerous. Police intervention only made the situation worse because there was no trust between villagers and police. It was assumed the police were taking a cut from the bus owner and that the delay in payment of any amount to them was because of police corruption. An assault on the police by the villagers led to a counterattack by the police upon them in their village and at the police station.

A need for immediate justice and for a sense among the villagers that the police will not take money from them at any opportunity, including a time of tragedy and mourning, and the tendency on both sides to resort to violence in such situations are not matters that can be solved by police training. These matters require decentralization and local control of the judicial system, the transformation of the police into servants of the people rather than instruments of the state and the local politicians who control them, and the establishment of a police administration in which the members of the force receive adequate pay and career incentives, instead of depending upon corrupt income, including loot and plunder, to sustain themselves and their families.

Almost completely missing from the press accounts concerning this incident are the connections between the local police and the politicians. How could the police perpetrate an incident of this type in one of the strongest support districts for the Lok Dal? How could the local MLA have been so ineffective that, once his back was turned and he had left the police station, the local police set about to humiliate, beat, and torture the Narayanpur men, his constituents? The Lok Dal minister from Deoria district, who made his own investigation of the incident, claimed that the station officer,

Lakshmi Narain Chaturvedi, was a Congress supporter. No evidence was provided for this claim nor was any further investigation of his connections done by the press.

Yet the answers to these questions concerning the freedom of the police to misbehave as they did at Narayanpur are most likely related to the local political scene, just as they were in connection with the incident at Pachpera. However, it is not likely that the station officer deliberately created an incident directed against Muslims and Harijans in order to provide the Congress leadership with a useful tool to attack the non-Congress government in UP. Rather more likely is that he was under no effective control in a situation of political flux both within the district and in the state.

The MLA of the constituency, Bankey Lal, who first brought the incident to the attention of the chief minister, was reported to have "alleged that police officers of his area who belonged to the upper castes wanted to 'punish' voters, mostly Muslims, who had supported him in the previous assembly elections." Mohan Singh, the minister who visited the site and corroborated the atrocity and mass rape charges, blamed it upon "a section of the state government officials [who] wanted to destabilise the Lok Dal ministry." The chief minister himself claimed that he had received complaints "during the Lok Sabha elections . . . that the police administration in Deoria was acting in a partisan manner,"[85] that is to say, on behalf of the Congress. No doubt, the MLA, Minister Mohan Singh, and the chief minister would want to displace blame upon the Congress and its supporters in the state and district administration for the incident just as Mrs. Gandhi and the Congress blamed the Lok Dal government for it. However, it is possible that there was some truth to the accusations against the local administration in the sense that there may have been some enmity between the station officer, Lakshmi Narain Chaturvedi, and the local MLA. It is at least certain that the station officer neither feared nor respected the MLA. Otherwise, he could not have ordered or permitted such brutalities as soon as the MLA's back was turned.

It is at this point that the remarks of the UP Muslim League president become relevant. His position was that Harijans and Muslims were "the worst sufferers of police atrocities in Narayanpur," but he blamed not the UP government, but "the system . . . created over the decades by Mrs Gandhi and her party."[86] It is not clear what aspects of this system the Muslim League president had in mind, but the highly politicized character of police–politician relationships are certainly at the center of it. The police—underpaid, without career incentives, always on the lookout for opportunities to make money—are indeed potential marauders in the countryside who can be controlled only if there is firm political authority at the local level.

[85] *Times of India*, January 29, 1980.
[86] *Patriot*, February 12, 1980.

However, the exercise of local political control over the police does not mean that they then become a peace-keeping force. Rather, they become a partial force, avoiding trouble with the supporters of their political boss, but being relatively freer to act as they choose with those who do not support him, provided that they also do not cause political embarrassment to their boss. It is evident that this political control was completely lacking in Deoria district.

One final aspect of the consequences of excessive talk about incidents such as those at Narayanpur is that the talk itself may make matters worse, in two ways. First, as already mentioned in the case of Narayanpur, it may brand the village and its inhabitants with a stigma, in this case the stigma that all the women had been raped. More serious in general is the false impression that talk conveys that it is associated with action. There are grounds to doubt that any significant action was taken to console the villagers in Narayanpur.

It is acknowledged by everyone that compensation of Rs. 5,000 was indeed paid to the survivors of the grandmother. Otherwise, no report has ever appeared concerning their fate. However, the villager whom I interviewed in Narayanpur denied that any other compensation reached any of the other villagers. I do not know if his statement is true.

Even if the villager's statement were not true and the villagers did receive compensation for their injuries, there is something atrocious about the system of relief payments that has been worked out by the state governments, with the approval of the central government, in these matters. No one, I suppose, would want to transfer to India the procedures used in the United States for seeking justice in such cases through long court proceedings in which no upper limit is placed upon the value of a human life except what one's lawyers can persuade a judge and jury to settle upon. On the other hand, there is something dehumanizing about the system of compensation that has been adopted by most of the Indian states, which recognize that they have problems with atrocities against Scheduled Castes. Under these systems, a scheme of compensation is established, a "scale of relief," under which a human life is usually valued at Rs. 5,000, replacement of a house at Rs. 2,000, and so on.[87]

If there are grounds to doubt that the relief provided to the Narayanpur villagers was adequate, there is not much doubt that little progress has been made in such matters in general. During the year of the Narayanpur incidents, the Commission on Scheduled Castes and Tribes recorded 4,279 cases of atrocities against Scheduled Castes. In 1985 the figure was only marginally smaller. Because these figures are not based on any clear criteria for distinguishing and assessing the relative incidence of crimes against Scheduled Castes from other crimes except for the identities of the victims,

[87] These are the figures that prevailed at the time. They have since been revised upward.

one cannot draw significant conclusions from them except to note that, by the government's own account, there has been no change despite all the talk.

More telling than these figures are the reports and figures on the "disposal of atrocity cases by the courts." First, the "pendency" of such cases in the courts has risen year by year in most states with atrocity problems and, second, the percentage of acquittals has been very high. The figures for UP for 1985, the latest year for which they are available, showed that there were 15,080 atrocity cases pending in the courts at the beginning of the year, of which 2,339 were decided, leaving 12,741 still pending. Of those that were decided, only 803 resulted in the conviction of the accused whereas 1,536 cases (65.67%) ended in acquittals.[88] While there may be many reasons for a high rate of acquittals, it is possible that misidentification of local quarrels of all sorts as atrocity cases against Scheduled Castes may have a bearing upon the matter. It is at least clear that, in the majority of the cases, because of excessive delays and ultimately acquittals, the system in general does not provide justice to either the victims or the accused.[89]

[88] Government of India, Ministry of Welfare, *Report of the Commission for Scheduled Castes and Scheduled Tribes (April 1985–March 1986), Eighth Report* (Delhi: Controller of Publications, 1988), pp. 38–39 and 56.

[89] My point in arguing that a high rate of acquittals indicates an absence of justice is not that those acquitted may in fact be guilty, which is quite possible. Rather, it is that, in general, with so many cases and so many acquittals, the "justice" system is either failing to provide relief to many, perhaps most, victims or is harassing many, if not most, innocent accused persons, or some combination of the two.

Chapter 6

HORROR STORIES UNTOLD

INCIDENTS such as those at Narayanpur occur frequently in the north Indian countryside. Very few have received press coverage comparable to that given to the Narayanpur incident. Some become front-page news for a few days and are then forgotten or a judicial inquiry commission is appointed, whose report is published some years later with a brief notice in the press. Still others receive brief mention in the back pages of the newspapers, which are read by the staff of the Commissioner for Scheduled Castes and Tribes to see if atrocities have been committed against any of the latter and if further attention by the commission is warranted. However, the vast majority of such incidents are unnoticed by the press and do not warrant inclusion in any government report or document on atrocities committed by upper castes or the police against lower castes, the poor, or otherwise disadvantaged groups. In most such cases, the circumstantial differences between them and incidents of the Narayanpur type are insignificant. What varies are the local political contexts and the relationships between local and extralocal politicians. What matters is who stands to gain and who stands to lose from publicizing such events.

The incident described below, which occurred in a village called Kurman Purwa in Gonda district in central UP in July 1982, falls in the category of unnoticed incidents of local violence. I learned about it only because it was mentioned to me in an interview with the superintendent of police (SP) of the district as an example of the problems posed for police administration by the interference of local politicians and because I was in search of such tales. Yet it is similar in several respects to the incident at Narayanpur. It occurred in a village inhabited mostly by persons from lower backward Hindu castes and untouchables. The men were beaten by the police, a few women were also injured, village huts were damaged, and the village was plundered. Charges of mass rape were absent, but then it did not occur at Narayanpur either.

News of incidents of this type travels rapidly in the local environment and soon reached the ears of the local politicians. Opposition (non-Congress) politicians rushed to the scene and offered their assistance to the victims. A local Congress MLA became involved because of his hostility to the police administration in the area. The dominant Congress leader of the district also intervened in a successful effort to bring the situation under control and to prevent it from embarrassing him and the Congress, then the ruling party in the state and the country. Some opposition politicians came from the state capital, but none with sufficient stature to be followed by the press.

The violent incidents at Kurman Purwa were not magnified, distorted, and manipulated for external use in wider political arenas. I could find no reference to this incident in the press or in the proceedings of the state legislative assembly. Rather, the situation was brought under control locally and potential damage to the dominant Congress was effectively contained. Therefore, this story lacks the mystery of Theft of an Idol, the potential danger of communal conflict as in Daphnala, and the high drama of Narayanpur. It is an ordinary event, which is recounted here for that very reason: to stand in for dozens of others that occur every week somewhere in north India and to contrast with the more mysterious, the more dangerous, the more distorted incidents of this type.

GONDA DISTRICT: THE LOCAL POLITICAL CONTEXT

Gonda district belongs to the central UP districts that were formerly part of the Kingdom of Awadh (conventionally spelled Oudh). These districts have been distinguished from those in other regions of the state by low agricultural productivity and the continued economic and political importance of former landlords, particularly those belonging to the special class known as *talukdar*s, mostly large *zamindar*s accorded higher status than others under British rule. Gonda district has no major urban places and, until the establishment in the mid-1980s of a large French-built telecommunications industrial complex, had no important industry.

As in most of the plains districts of UP, Brahmans and Thakurs have been the two most important landed castes, Ahirs (Yadavs) and Kurmis the two largest and most important of the middle peasant or "backward" castes. Among other backward castes, the two largest are Koiris, mostly poor cultivators and agricultural laborers, and Kahars, traditionally water carriers, but now found in a variety of agricultural and menial occupations. Another caste of some importance and high status in the district are the Gosains, whose members include locally prominent temple *mahant*s (priests), but many of the secular members of the caste engage in trade. There is also a substantial Muslim population, particularly in the northern part of the district.

Kurman Purwa lies in the southwestern part of the district, off the main road. The nearest urban place is the bazaar town known as Colonelganj, where there is an important Tuesday cattle market. In the surrounding rural area, Brahmans are the largest caste, but the descendants of former local *zamindar*s are also important land controllers. Ahirs, Koiris, and Kahars are the largest backward castes. Kurman Purwa itself is largely a Kahar village.

In contrast to Deoria district, Gonda in 1982 was a Congress-dominated district, particularly in its southern part. Here, political control was in the hands of Anand Singh, son of the last Raja of Mankapur, the fourth largest *talukdari* estate in the district but politically the most important. Between 1956, when Anand Singh's father, Raghvendra Pratap Singh, left the Congress to form the Swatantra Party in the district, and 1967, when Anand joined the Congress and contested the legislative assembly elections from Mankapur, there was intense interparty competition between Congress and Swatantra. There had also been intense interparty competition between Congress and the former Jan Sangh in the northern part of the district. However, between 1967 and 1982, the year of the Kurman Purwa incident, Anand Singh had established himself as the dominant political leader of the district.[1] Under his leadership in the 1980 election, the Congress (I) won both parliamentary seats and nine of the eleven legislative assembly seats from the district.

Kurman Purwa falls within the legislative assembly constituency of Katra Bazaar, whose MLA at the time was a Congress Brahman politician. However, the village is also close to the Colonelganj legislative assembly constituency, whose MLA then was Umeshwar Pratap Singh, a Thakur politician. Although both these constituencies were included in Gonda parliamentary constituency represented by Anand Singh and both men acknowledged the leadership of Anand Singh, Umeshwar Pratap sought to establish his own independent sphere of influence in this area and his control over local institutions, including the local police.

INCIDENT AT KURMAN PURWA:
THE IMPORTANCE OF LOCAL CONTROL OF THE POLICE

INCIDENT AT KURMAN PURWA: DRAMATIS PERSONAE

SHARDA, a cattle dealer, Kahar by caste, resident of village Kurman Purwa

OTHER VILLAGERS OF KURMAN PURWA

DUDH NATH GOSAIN, resident of village Gonwa

RAHUL KUMAR SRIVASTAVA, a subinspector of police

SHYAM SUNDER LAL, constable

YASHPAL SINGH, superintendent of police, Gonda District

MURLI DHAR DWIVEDI, MLA

UMESHWAR PRATAP SINGH, MLA

DEEP NARAIN PANDE, attorney

ANAND SINGH, MP

---

[1] Anand was not able to establish his political dominance firmly until after 1972, when he shifted from the Congress (O) to the Congress (I) under the leadership of Indira Gandhi.

Basic Facts

Initial accounts provided to me concerning the incident at Kurman Purwa centered around the activities of the following *dramatis personnae*: the villagers of Kurman Purwa and a villager from an adjacent village, Gosain by caste, the local police, the district superintendent of police, the Congress MLA of the constituency and the Congress MLA of an adjacent constituency, the opposition parties and their leaders, and Anand Singh, the Congress MP and the most powerful man in the district. However, after this incident, the case was heard by a Special Sessions Court in Gonda, whose summary of the events enlarged the scene and the participants to include the village and inhabitants of the adjacent village of Gonwa.

As in the Narayanpur incident, the principal events are not difficult to establish, but the details and the explanations vary. Insofar as the events are concerned, it appeared from the initial accounts that a party of police and local toughs descended on the village of Kurman Purwa, inhabited entirely by persons of low- and backward-caste status, on the night of July 13, 1982, and engaged in a brawl with the villagers, whose outcome was indecisive, that is to say, the villagers gave back as good as they received. However, as usually happens in such cases and as in Narayanpur, a second and larger police party returned that night and beat the villagers, allegedly dragged the women out of their houses, and did some damage and looting. On the 17th the police returned with a decree of confiscation and allegedly removed grain and other property of the villagers. The villagers say that a number of their men also were taken to the police station that night and robbed there and that six of them were left in jail for nearly three months.

In the court proceedings, the initial scene of the action was established as village Gonwa, where persons from village Kurman Purwa engaged in a brawl with one Dudh Nath Gosain of the former village, whose stepmother rushed to the police station for help. When the police arrived, a struggle occurred between the Kurman Purwa villagers and the police during which the villagers snatched the guns away from the police and brought them to Kurman Purwa, beating them along the way. According to the court summary, police reinforcements arrived at Kurman Purwa during the brawl there, took control of the situation, and arrested six of the villagers on the spot.

Between the 13th and the 17th, the local Congress MLA, Murli Dhar Dwivedi, intervened. The police promised him that no further retaliatory action would be taken against the villagers. However, as in the Narayanpur incident, the local MLA was not able to control the police, who returned to the village on the 17th despite their promises not to do so. Anand Singh also intervened personally in an attempt to keep the situation under control. However, the local police apparently were not even restrained by his intervention.

Between July 13 and August 9, the Congress MLA from the adjacent constituency, Umeshwar Pratap, also became involved. By most accounts, the police violence perpetrated at Kurman Purwa was carried out by the local police constables on their own, without the authority or support of the station officer. Both the SP and Anand Singh wished to transfer the sub-inspector and constables involved, but retain the local station officer, whom they both considered to be a good and loyal (to them) police officer. However, Umeshwar Pratap wished to have the station officer transferred because the latter was not willing to accept his authority locally. Therefore, Umeshwar Pratap joined with the opposition to protest against the alleged police atrocities committed at Kurman Purwa.

For their part, opposition party men organized a protest meeting on July 27, on the way to which the party secretary of the local Democratic Socialist Party (DSP) was badly beaten by the police. At this point, both Anand Singh and the SP considered it best to have all the local officers, including the station officer, transferred in order to defuse the situation. When the station officer was transferred, Umeshwar Pratap withdrew from the protest, which then became entirely an opposition affair.

Opposition involvement took two forms. The runner-up candidate for MLA in the constituency in which the incident occurred, an attorney and local leader of the DSP, met with the villagers and agreed to act as attorney on their behalf. Second, in cooperation with the local Communist Party, he organized political protest meetings on July 27 and August 9, 1982. CPI and DSP leaders from all parts of the district and several state party leaders also came. The opposition leaders demanded that a judicial inquiry be held into the alleged police atrocity at Kurman Purwa, that the cases pending against the villagers of Kurman Purwa be withdrawn, and that the police personnel involved in the incidents be punished. None of the opposition demands were conceded.

Anand Singh did not intervene beyond seeing to the transfer of the officers. He clearly wanted the incident to be kept as quiet as possible. Although he was not able to keep it out of the hands of the opposition and the press entirely, it did not acquire anywhere near the publicity associated with the Narayanpur incident.

Explanations

There are three versions of the reasons for the police action in Kurman Purwa. One is that it arose out of a quarrel between a Kahar villager of Kurman Purwa and a Gosain of the neighboring Gonwa village in which the Gosain enlisted the aid of the police on the basis of friendship and/or bribery to retaliate against the Kahar. However, in this version, it is disputed whether the physical fighting began in village Gonwa or in Kurman Purwa.

The second version is that the Kahar and other villagers of Kurman Purwa who deal in cattle had a successful day at the Tuesday cattle market in Colonelganj and that the police learned that they had made some money and went to the village to rob them. The third version is that the police went to Kurman Purwa for some reason or other and were beaten by drunken villagers, after which the police returned with a larger party. In one variation on this version, both the villagers and the police were drunk.

Whichever account one accepts of the Kurman Purwa incident, there are similarities between it and the one at Narayanpur. The principal differences are in the character of the precipitating incidents that produced the police–village battles. In Narayanpur, an accident precipitated a quarrel between the villagers and the police in which it is not at all clear who struck first, though there is not much doubt that the police struck last and hardest. In Kurman Purwa, initial accounts of the incident suggested an unprovoked attack by the local police on the villagers, precipitated in most versions by enmity between persons of neighboring villages of different castes. However, in the version accepted in the court proceedings, the origin of the police–village confrontation is similar to that in Narayanpur: A quarrel occurred in village Gonwa between the Kurman Purwa villagers and the police that led to an exchange of blows after which a larger police party descended upon Kurman Purwa either to rescue two of their number or to take vengeance or both.

Here, then, were materials for a case to be made of police atrocities committed against persons of backward- and low-caste origins. However, such an issue can be expanded only through collaboration between locally knowledgeable politicians and interested outside leaders. Since the Congress controlled the constituency and the district, it was in the interests of the local MLA and Anand Singh to keep the issue quiet and to settle it peacefully, without further fuss. They were prevented from doing so by the activities of a renegade Congress MLA, whose sole interest in the matter was to get the local police officers who refused to obey him transferred, and by the local opposition politicians, who naturally wished to capitalize on the issue.

The Congress MLA's activities were stopped by satisfying his demands. Anand Singh, at first reluctant to transfer the station officer, ultimately agreed to do so after the police attacked the opposition demonstration in Colonelganj and when it became clear that the local police were continuing to harass the villagers. The activities of the local opposition could not be stopped, but they were not deeply threatening because the opposition parties involved were the least effective ones in the politics of the district and the state. The two leading opposition parties in UP, the Lok Dal and the Bharatiya Janata Party (BJP), had no interest in becoming involved in an incident from which other parties stood to gain.

The account of this incident given by a senior police officer of the district at the time was that it began as an "unfortunate incident" in which some of his constables were beaten by drunken villagers of Kurman Purwa, who also grabbed the guns of one of the constables. Police reinforcements were sent, they "recovered the gun," and they arrested a number of people of the village.[2]

This merely "unfortunate incident" was magnified and distorted because of the involvement in it of Umeshwar Pratap Singh, the Congress MLA of the adjacent constituency. According to the same police officer, Umeshwar Pratap had prevailed upon him to transfer the station officer of the Colonelganj police station, but he had refused to do so. So, when the Kurman Purwa incident took place, the MLA "came with a story" that the police had broken open the village houses, "molested women and raped them and all this sorts [*sic*] of nonsense." The local opposition leaders also became involved and organized a procession and demonstration. Umeshwar Pratap allegedly "manipulated some confusion in that procession," which made it necessary for the police to charge the crowd with *lathi*s (sticks) during which some people were injured. Because of the police *lathi*-charge, the SP now had no choice but to transfer the station officer.

In the early 1980s, particularly after the Narayanpur events, all persons involved in incidents of this type were aware of the advantages and disadvantages of magnifying and exaggerating the extent and character of police action. Between the time of the Narayanpur incident and the one at Kurman Purwa, another famous story of police atrocities committed on innocent villagers had come from a village known as Siswa in Basti district. Here, as in Narayanpur, it was alleged that the police had committed mass rape, looted the houses, and molested young girls. This incident was dramatized by the BJP and by Maneka Gandhi, the estranged daughter-in-law of Indira Gandhi, who had gone into opposition politics and who played her role in this village by mimicking her mother-in-law and visiting the place personally to show her sympathy. This incident, which was very much in people's minds at the time of the Kurman Purwa brawl, was also in the mind of the senior police officer whom I interviewed in Gonda. He began his account to me of the Kurman Purwa incident by referring to the Siswa situation and declaring that Umeshwar Pratap had deliberately set out, only for the purpose of getting the station officer transferred, to magnify and distort the events at Kurman Purwa to make it appear similar to Siswa.

Insofar as the details of the brawl are concerned, the police account presented in court was that a complaint was received at the Colonelganj police station at 9:10 on the night of July 13, 1982, that twelve or thirteen persons

[2] Interview in Gonda on November 14, 1982.

had surrounded the house of Dudh Nath in village Gonwa. The complaint was received by Subinspector Rahul Kumar Srivastava, who took his sten gun, thirty-three cartridges, and constable Shyam Sundar Lal along with him to the site. At village Gonwa, the two police officers found Dudh Nath's house surrounded by a crowd of men led by one Sharda of village Kurman Purwa. They were armed with spears, at least one knife, and *lathi*s and were attempting to break down Dudh Nath's door. When the two police-men tried to stop the action and one of them fired in the air, they were in turn assaulted by the crowd, the gun and cartridges were grabbed, and Sub-inspector Srivastava and Constable Shyam Sundar were taken to Kurman Purwa. Police reinforcements were summoned and arrived at Kurman Purwa, where they rescued both police officers, one of whom, Shyam Sun-dar, was badly injured.

Thus, the police account in brief is that they were called to intervene and stop a threatening brawl between two groups of villagers. In the course of their attempts to do so, they were assaulted by the villagers of Kurman Purwa and two of their number were injured, one of them seriously. A larger police party came to rescue their colleagues and arrested the drunken villagers of Kurman Purwa who had been criminally misbehaving. From the point of view of the senior police officer interviewed, the incident was merely an "unfortunate" one in which no atrocities were committed. Its magnitude was exaggerated because of the machinations of Umeshwar Pratap Singh, whose sole interest in the matter was to get the station officer transferred. The SP was quite conscious of the potential embarrassment to him and to his career and to the ruling party in the district and the state if the incident acquired the same notoriety attached to incidents such as those at Narayanpur and Siswa. However, he clearly saw the attempt to fit this inci-dent into that category as purely politically motivated.

THE ACCOUNT OF THE VILLAGERS OF KURMAN PURWA

The story told to me and to the court by the villagers of Kurman Purwa is entirely different from the police account. Their tale is that a dispute had occurred between them and Dudh Nath Gosain after the Tuesday cattle mar-ket in Colonelganj, where one of them, Sharda, had taken a calf to sell. The villagers admit that the calf had gone grazing into Dudh Nath's fields and that they had quarreled about it. Someone from Dudh Nath Gosain's side went to the police station to lodge a complaint against them and paid the police officers a bribe of Rs. 1,000 to come and raid their village. The police arrived unexpectedly, began shooting, looted nearly Rs. 10,000 from Sharda and his sons and other villagers, and arrested six people. Later, they came back and arrested twelve more people.[3]

---

[3] Interview in village Kurman Purwa on November 20, 1982.

According to the villagers, Sharda is a known cattle dealer who goes around to the moneylenders before the Tuesday market and borrows money from them to buy bullocks, which he then sells at the market. So the Gosains of village Gonwa, particularly Dudh Nath, knew that he had a substantial sum of money on his person from his sales at the market, they told the police, and the police came with that knowledge to steal his money.

The police later returned to the village with a decree of confiscation, went inside the houses, dragged the women out, beat them, broke open the houses, and took away everything that could be moved: cattle, goods, grain. They even took ornaments from the women's bodies. The profits from the police depredations were then divided between the Gosains and the police. They arrested twelve villagers, beat them up at the police station, and then put them in jail. Six of them were kept in jail for nearly three months.

On questioning whether they managed to give a few blows to the police, the villagers said they did so only when the police removed the ornaments from their women's bodies, at which point they all "ganged up against the policemen and started beating them up." The villagers also admitted to having in their possession a gun taken from the policemen. They claim that one of the women whose ornaments were removed had grabbed the gun from the police. They also claim that, at the time of the incident, they did not know whether the people who attacked them—who, they say, numbered about twenty-five—were policemen or *dacoits*.

Asked if they had received any help from the local politicians, the villagers said that both their own MLA and Umeshwar Pratap Singh had come to the village, made inquiries, and filed complaints on their behalf to higher authorities. However, they said that, despite their intervention, the police had kept coming back to the village, three or four times, to harass them. They had also retained Deep Narain Pande as attorney to represent them and defend them in the court case filed by the police against them.

Thus, the villagers of Kurman Purwa present themselves as wholly innocent victims of a police raid on their village for purposes of loot. They admit only to having had a quarrel with Dudh Nath Gosain of village Gonwa on a relatively minor and quite common matter concerning a calf grazing in his field. They accuse Dudh Nath and the police of being in collusion and of having divided the spoils of the police attack. They admit to having beaten the police, but only when the honor of their women was threatened. They claim it was one of the women who grabbed the subinspector's sten gun.

Since the villagers had already retained an attorney and the case was before the court when I arrived, the villagers' account was well prepared. Their story of the police raids, the beatings they received, and the confiscation of their goods is believable and was accepted by other persons not directly involved in the incident. However, the story they tell of the circumstances that precipitated the police attack and the grabbing of the sten gun are not believable and were not believed by two judges who heard the case on separate occasions.

THE "TRUTH" OF THE COURT

In Western societies and those like India, whose political, legal, and judicial traditions have been established upon a Western base, considerable sanctity is attached to judicial proceedings for arriving at the "truth" of criminal and other illegal actions. Complaints are sometimes heard as well in such societies, particularly in the United States in the past and India at present, that the judiciary does not stand apart from society or from the specific cases that come before it. Sometimes, it is charged that the proceedings are influenced by false cases concocted by the police, through bribery of witnesses, and through purchase of the judges. A broader question also arises concerning whether the judiciary, any more than the police, can stand apart from the society and reach decisions in disputed matters free from the prejudices and partialities prevailing among the people whose actions they must judge.

The case concerning Kurman Purwa was heard three times, in two preliminary bail hearings by sessions judges in Gonda, and ultimately by a special magistrate, also in Gonda. The initial hearing occurred soon after the incident in response to a motion for bail by Sharda, who had been in jail since the night of July 17. He and others of the village were being held in connection with various charges arising out of the incident filed by Subinspector Rahul Kumar Srivastava against them.

It is in this preliminary hearing that the story first appeared that the original site of the incident was village Gonwa. This was the charge of the prosecution, that is, of the local police, whereas all accounts provided to me by the district authorities and politicians referred only to an altercation that occurred between persons of two adjacent villages followed by a police attack on the residents of village Kurman Purwa. The latter also claimed in court that the account that the brawl began in village Gonwa was a prosecution fabrication. The additional sessions judge referred to these and other discrepancies in the accounts of the case as "imponderables" that were under investigation by a commanding officer from the Criminal Investigations Division (CID) and found it unnecessary to reach any conclusion concerning the accuracy of the competing accounts in order to reach his decision on the matter of bail for Sharda. Sharda's bail application was rejected, but only on the grounds that the situation remained too tense to permit his release because of the danger that further violence might then erupt between the opposed sides.[4]

---

[4] In the Court of III Additional Sessions Judge, Gonda, Criminal Misc. Case No. 715/1982, *Sharda* [son of Ram Phal, resident of Kurman Purwa, post office Gonwa, police station, Colonelganj, Gonda] v. *State*, Order of July 26, 1982.

The additional sessions judge took note of the claim by Sharda's attorney that the incident at Kurman Purwa was comparable to "the much publicised Siswa episode," but he dismissed the comparison. He noted that even the defense had not claimed that any rape had been committed in Kurman Purwa.

However, the judge's dismissal of the comparison with Siswa is revealed more in the whole tone of his summary of the circumstances surrounding the incident. Although he indicated his belief that there had been "some high-handedness" in the case, implying that the situation had gone beyond one of normal law enforcement, it is clear that he saw the circumstances more as farce than as atrocity. The decision, rendered in English, was laden with pseudo-Shakespearean language. The police were referred to as "myrmidons of the law." The doors of the poor village huts at which the police arrived and to which they were also allegedly forcibly brought after being beaten up by the Kurman Purwa villagers were referred to as "portals." The villagers did not curse and abuse each other and the police, but "hurled invectives." They did not beat, kick, cut, and shoot, but "plied their weaponry." Making fun of the Kurman Purwa villagers' claims that it was the women of the village who grabbed the police sten gun, the judge noted that the defense case assigned this role to the "muliebrity,"[5] who were being portrayed by the Kurman Purwa villagers as if they were "Amazons."

The summary of the case given six-and-a-half years later in the decision of the special judge was written in a less florid and more serious tone, but it also did not place the Kurman Purwa incident in the same category as the incidents at Siswa or Narayanpur. Like other local knowledgeable people, the court traced the origins of the incident at villages Gonwa and Kurman Purwa to a long-festering dispute between Dudh Nath of village Gonwa and the residents of Kurman Purwa, "brokers in the sale of oxen," concerning the grazing of the latter's cattle on the fields and crops of Dudh Nath. In connection with this dispute, a petition had been filed with both the SP and the District Magistrate on the day previous to the melee, requesting the intervention of the authorities to prevent Sharda and others from grazing their cattle on Dudh Nath's fields and complaining that the former were "after his life and seeking an opportunity to murder him." According to the latter, the accused appeared at his door with spears, knives, and lathis, saying "Catch hold of the sala[6] and take him home. This bastard always goes to the police station and puts up a petition."[7]

---

[5] A word that sent me to the *OED*, where I discovered that the judge's knowledge of English vocabulary was greater than my own and that it referred to womankind.

[6] Literally "brother-in-law," but used commonly as an abusive term roughly equivalent to "swine" in English.

[7] In the Special Court of the Sessions Judge, Gonda, review numbers 432/83, 218/1984, *State v. Sharda Prasad* [s/o of Ram Phal] *and others*, and review number 219/84, *State v. Ram*

The court did not reach any decision on the precise words used by the
accused, but it ultimately did accept the prosecution's charge that the Kurman Purwa villagers arrived at Dudh Nath's door and threatened him and
that the incident began there. The discrepancy between the accounts of the
actual initial site of the first brawl does not appear of great importance when
it is noted that the distance between Dudh Nath's house and Kurman Purwa
is only about two hundred yards. Legally, however, it was a matter of great
importance for the prosecution to establish that the initial aggressors were
the villagers of Kurman Purwa and that the police came to village Gonwa at
first to protect Dudh Nath's life against an illegal and threatening assemblage. The judge accepted their contention, but at the same time reached the
conclusion that the statements of Dudh Nath and others whose complaints
were recorded at the Colonelganj police station on the evening of July 13
and thereafter were "exaggerated" and that one of their statements concerning the breaking down of Dudh Nath's door was false.

The court did not reach a decision concerning the site at which and the
precise circumstances under which Subinspector Rahul Kumar Srivastava
and Constable Shyam Sundar were injured. It was sufficient for the court to
decide that they were in fact injured in the course of their attempt to prevent
a breach of the peace by the Kurman Purwa villagers at Dudh Nath's residence. The judge satisfied himself that the latter part of the prosecution's
case against the Kurman Purwa villagers was well founded and that the
police did not collude with Dudh Nath in putting up a false case. His reasoning in this respect deserves especial note since it also helps explain the
subsequent actions of the police in this and other incidents of its type. It is
given below.

> The two injured witnesses will never spare those persons who assaulted them,
> especially a police sub-inspector and constable [will not do so]. Even with the
> motive of protecting their dignity, a police sub-inspector and constable will
> neither inflict nor state false injury on their person. Under the circumstances
> there is no justification whatsoever not to believe the evidence of these wit-
> nesses. They will neither falsely implicate innocent people nor spare those who
> assault them. Even in this respect the evidence of both the above witnesses is
> acceptable.[8]

The judge's reasoning here is cogent. It is also fair to both sides. It is
assumed that the police will not inflict injury upon themselves nor implicate

---

Dulare, decided on February 13, 1989. I am grateful to Deep Narain Pande, who provided me
the court judgments in these cases and also to Professor T. P. Singh of Patna, who translated
faultlessly the texts of the judgments for me from handwritten Hindi full of technical legal and
judicial terms, a task that was far beyond my capabilities and that of everyone else I approached.

[8] Special Court of the Sessions Judge, Gonda, Judgment, para. 29.

innocent people in false cases as a means of extracting vengeance. The reasoning does not impute high integrity to the police. Rather, it assumes that they have other methods of dealing with persons who attack them—they will not "spare those who assault them." In this way, the judge added another piece of evidence to establish the "truth" that the police officers had been attacked and injured by the villagers of Kurman Purwa while attempting to carry out their duties and that their behavior was not such as to warrant actions of self-defense on the part of the Kurman Purwa villagers. However, it also implies that they probably used more than sufficient force in their subsequent visits to the village to rescue the besieged and injured officers, retrieve the snatched gun, and confiscate the village goods.

The judge's fairness to both sides in this matter is also indicated by his criticism of the prosecution in his judgment for recording the crime of the accused—the "snatching of the sten gun, musket, bullet and bag"—"in exaggerated manner." Despite the injuries to Constable Shyam Sundar, the judge relieved the accused of the charge of intent to murder him. He accepted only the accusation that their intention was to prevent them from carrying out their duty. Consequently, he found the accused guilty of assembling for the unlawful purpose of giving Dudh Nath a beating and for assaulting the police party that came to rescue Dudh Nath, but he considered these relatively "minor" offenses. For these offenses, the accused villagers were given two concurrent but suspended sentences of six months' rigorous imprisonment. In other words, they were found guilty of the relatively minor offenses with which they had been charged, but not of the charge of illegal possession of arms—that is, of the sten gun and bullets they had grabbed from the subinspector and constable in the first melee—or the more serious charges of intent to murder either Dudh Nath or the police officers and they were not required to serve any further time in jail.

It needs also to be noted that the statement quoted above that the police will not "falsely implicate innocent people" was not meant by the judge to apply universally to police behavior in India, but only to the question of retaliation against an assault upon them. In other respects, the judge's comments on police behavior in this case and in general were not complimentary. Although the judge did not accept the accusations of the defense that Dudh Nath and the police were in collusion from the beginning against the Kurman Purwa villagers or that the police were "under the influence of liquor," he passed several other unfavorable strictures against them.

The police were reprimanded for producing two disreputable and unbelievable witnesses to support one part of their charges against the accused, persons with known criminal records who had made frequent appearances in previous cases as witnesses for the police. The judge remarked in this connection that "it is a matter of regret that the police has only such a sympathiser who is their friend in need." The judge also dismissed the account of another witness for the police side as unreliable on the grounds that the person in question "was himself accused in a case" and, therefore, "became a witness to appease the police." The judge also noted that the police had to resort to the use of such witnesses because they could not produce any reliable ones, a matter he attributed to the fact that "witnesses do not want to become witnesses of an occurrence. They want to keep themselves away from such circumstances where there is probability of enmity with any side or of becoming a prey to its wrath. This tendency has become stronger because the police has failed to protect the common man."[9]

The judge also criticized certain aspects of the police investigative work as negligent. However, his strongest strictures concerned the failure of the police to produce a principal investigative witness from their own side, Inspector Nagendra Prasad Rai of the CID. Not only did this witness—who was by then serving in another district—not appear, but he ignored repeated summonses to do so and was supported in his defiance of the court summonses by his superiors. Inspector Rai's investigation was considered to be of substantial importance in determining the site of the initial brawl that allegedly took place at Dudh Nath's house and led to the gun-snatching and beating of the two policemen. The judge concluded that the prosecution side did not want their own witness to appear and that they gave "frivolous reasons" for preventing him from being examined. Therefore, the real reason behind the failure to produce their witness must have been that he had become "hostile to prosecution or was won over by the accused," that is, he had become "a witness hostile to his own side." The judge reached this conclusion despite the fact that he had also noted that Inspector Rai's examination of the facts of the case were "careless" and "cursory" and were done in a manner merely to confirm "all the actions of the previous investigating officer, Shri Ram Kripal Tripathi," the Colonelganj station officer. The judge noted that the unsuccessful attempt to produce Inspector Rai before the court caused a full year's delay in the court proceedings and put the "accused . . . to mental and financial trouble" as a consequence. He used this circumstance as part of his justification for the order suspending the sentences of the accused.

The strictures passed against the police in this case are not uncommon in Western judicial proceedings. What is uncommon in contemporary Western proceedings is a situation of this type in which the police in a local quarrel act from the beginning in a manner partial to one side, in this case Dudh Nath of village Gonwa. This issue was left unresolved by the court in its final decision. Yet, for our purposes, it is the most important question,

---

[9] Decision of Special Court of the Sessions Judge, Gonda, Judgment, para. 27. These remarks about both witnesses and police would apply as well in the United States, as every American reader will immediately observe.

which will affect how one perceives the police in north Indian society. Are the police to be seen as an agency placed above society, which acts to enforce the law, to identify transgressors and to punish those who take the law into their own hands but sometimes misbehave? Alternatively, should the police be perceived as participants in the quarrels and social conflicts of local society, who happen to be provided with arms by the state or, further, as semi-independent armed bands acting for their own ends, sometimes in collusion with particular local groups?

The court attached great importance to determining the site of the original brawl, namely, whether it took place at Dudh Nath's house and was, therefore, initiated by the Kurman Purwa villagers or in Kurman Purwa, where it would have had to have been initiated by the police. As I have already noted above, all accounts of the incident given to me a few months after its occurrence failed to mention Dudh Nath's house as the original site. That can have one of three implications. The first, that all my informants were misinformed themselves, can be dismissed since one of them was the SP himself.[10]

The second possible implication is that the actual site of the original brawl was not considered of much importance in assigning responsibility or blame. Such fights are common in the close quarters of local village societies, the opposed parties had a history of enmity and quarreling, Dudh Nath's house and village Kurman Purwa are only a short distance apart. Therefore, what does it matter where the fight actually began? What mattered in most accounts given to me were the relationships among the participants, namely, the enmity between the two sides and the role of the police which, in most accounts, assumed that they acted on behalf of Dudh Nath, that they were on his side.

However, modern judicial proceedings do not consider the whole context of a dispute in determining whether a law was violated and by whom. Consequently, neither side could actually present for serious consideration by the court the sources of the antagonisms between them, the actual causes of the quarrel. In fact, one side, that of Dudh Nath, was in effect represented by the police because the case became one of the state versus the villagers of Kurman Purwa. The quarrel between two parties, as has happened in every case discussed so far in this volume, turned into a confrontation between one side and the police.[11] The burden of the court proceedings for both sides then became one of establishing not the cause of the quarrel, but its site, from

---

[10] The associated possibility that I misheard or failed to note this information myself has troubled me, but I find it difficult to believe that I failed to note it seven or eight times, including in some taped interviews.

[11] It should be kept in mind that my focus is on police–public confrontations. I am not suggesting that all such local quarrels in which the police become involved inevitably become transformed in this way, only that all police–public confrontations of which I have detailed knowledge do begin in this way.

which it could then be decided legally who was the aggressor, who took the law into their own hands. Therefore, the sources of the antagonisms between the two sides, the actual causes of the quarrel could only be presented as part of the evidence to determine who was responsible for initiating violation of the law. However, the accounts given to me attached no importance to these legal issues. They stressed instead both the local and the broader political contexts.

The third possible implication of the absence of information concerning the original site of the quarrel in the accounts given to me is that it did not in fact originate there. It follows from this implication that the Kurman Purwa villagers were correct in their defense argument that a false case had been instituted against them and that they were merely innocent victims of police marauders in collusion with their enemies from village Gonwa. The judge took great pains to sort this matter out and satisfied himself that the original site of the quarrel was village Gonwa. He was not satisfied with all the evidence presented on the matter, but found insufficient reason to doubt the prosecution arguments and sufficient reason to doubt the accounts of the Kurman Purwa villagers, which did not seem to him to hold up.

However, even if one assumes that the entire case was not falsely put up and that the original site of the quarrel was Dudh Nath's house, the judge's strictures against the police leave little doubt that they did strive to concoct a detailed account of the case by using false witnesses and by preventing the testimony of an inspector whose account might have gone against them. In a word, they had no credible witnesses, they were acting on the side of Dudh Nath, and they pursued the Kurman Purwa villagers at the very least to wreak vengeance on them in repeated attacks and harassment of them in their village and in the proceedings of the court. In this case, although the judge decided that the villagers of Kurman Purwa were not mere innocent victims, he concluded that the matter had been exaggerated and they had suffered enough, and he released them from their prison sentences.

In short, therefore, it is difficult to conceive of police forces in north Indian rural society as impartial agents of law enforcement from above. One way or another, through their own malevolent designs, through their relationships and alliances with specific local groups, or through the hostilities they themselves develop against local people, they are part of the local society and are partial agents in local quarrels.

What about the judiciary itself? Do we look here for that impartial authority from above whose "responsibility" it is, in the words of the presiding judge of this case, "to carefully examine [the] evidence and find out the truth"? If so, what is the nature of this "truth"?

Both judges who heard this case, whose decisions were available to me,[12]

---

[12] I have the petition for bail of the accused Kurman Purwa villagers for the second bail application as well, but not the written decision of the judge.

appear to have set themselves apart from it. The first judge clearly found the stories told in court to be a matter of amusement. The second painstakingly sorted all the verbal, medical, and other circumstantial evidence to arrive at the "truth" and chastised the police and their higher authorities for obstructing the judicial proceedings. There appears on the face of it, therefore, to be no grounds for doubting the impartiality of the court.

At the same time, it is clear that the "truth" that the court established was at best a partial and a surface or superficial truth, incidental to larger truths that determine the course and consequences of local quarrels in village India: whether and how they develop into pitched battles involving the police fighting on behalf of one side against another and whether and how they come to represent broader social and political issues. The courts had the last word in the Kurman Purwa case, as did a commission of inquiry in the Narayanpur case. In both situations, judicial proceedings determined that the extent of the fighting and damage to persons and property and/or the police atrocities committed had been exaggerated.

However, the last word in the Narayanpur case was of little importance in comparison to the political uses made of it just after the occurrence, when the Congress leaders sought to draw larger "truths" from it concerning police atrocities and the victimization of backward, poor, and minority persons in north India. No such larger "truths" were allowed to emerge from the Kurman Purwa incident, which resolved itself into a matter only of determining whether further punishment was to be inflicted upon the Kurman Purwa villagers seven years after they had been beaten and harassed by the police. I believe that, in both cases, important "truths" were ignored or paid scant attention, those that lie between the mere establishing of who broke which laws, on the one hand, and the grand abstractions of political elites who distort and manipulate social conflicts in such a way as to insure their perpetuation in a controlled manner, always in the belief that they can prevent their occurrence while their political rivals cannot. These intermediate "truths" are well known to local political participants and observers and are discussed in the next section.

THE POLICE, THE PUBLIC, AND THE POLITICIANS

The first truth ignored by the court in Kurman Purwa concerns control of the police, which was at the heart of the incident from beginning to end. The local knowledge of my informants was that the police intervened in the village quarrel on behalf of Dudh Nath, with whom they had good relations. It is important to stress at this point that the police do not automatically come to any village upon request, even where there are good reasons to believe that a breach of the peace is taking place. It is usually necessary in such circumstances, as in all dealings with government authorities and agencies in India, that the persons filing a complaint be known to the police.

Often enough, it also means that a payment is made or has been made in the past or that some profit is likely to come to the police for doing their duty.[13] It can be assumed, therefore, that at the very least the police were sympathetic to Dudh Nath and that they went to his village or to Kurman Purwa to protect him or act on his behalf.

However, the police often also act on their own, particularly in two types of situations: when there is money to be made or when they have been beaten. It was charged that the police were after money that Sharda, the cattle broker, had in his possession. This fact was never established and was not believed by local informants. However, there is no doubt in anybody's account of the events that the police received a bad beating from the villagers in their first appearance and that they then acted in retaliation. Indeed, it is quite likely that this was the primary motivation for most of the subsequent police beatings and harassment of the villagers. It is unlikely that they began with the intention of looting the villagers for they would have then come with a larger force from the beginning, as they did in Pachpera. Therefore, it appears that the police acted initially on behalf of Dudh Nath for friendship or money and secondarily in retaliation against the Kurman Purwa villagers for the sake of their own prestige and dignity.

Once the police acted on their own, the important issues became local control over the police and "damage control," the prevention of the capturing of the event by politicians out of power, and its external use for wider political purposes. At this point, the issue became one of whether the Colonelganj station officer should be transferred, according to Umeshwar Pratap Singh's demand, but initially opposed by the SP and the political leader of the district, Anand Singh.

Umeshwar Pratap's reasons for wanting to transfer the station officer were clear to everyone involved. He had a notorious reputation for making money from the local peasantry through his influence in the nearby cane union and cane factory, which made it possible for him to distribute illegal *parzis* (certificates) for cane growers to supply cane to the factory for crushing, from which he took a share of the profits from the growers. For this kind of activity and other activities of an allegedly criminal nature, Umeshwar Pratap needed to have the police under his thumb.

It was admitted that Umeshwar Pratap was engaged in a struggle with the SP over control of the local police and that he sought to have the station officer transferred in the aftermath of the Kurman Purwa incident.[14] Moreover, his desire to control the local police was transparent from the explanations given for his differences with the SP. The astonishing remark was

[13] On these matters in general, see David H. Bayley, *The Police and Political Development in India* (Princeton, N.J.: Princeton University Press, 1969), chap. 11, esp. pp. 288–93.

[14] Interview in Gonda district on November 16, 1982.

made that his main difference with the SP was that the latter, who was the official appointing authority for the local constabulary and the superior police officer in the district, interfered too much in police activity![15] Moreover, although Umeshwar Pratap is a Thakur by caste, the complaint made by his side was that the SP was guilty of casteism in appointing mostly Thakurs as *darogas* (station officers). The complaint was also made that the SP "disturbed" the police administration through his management of the transfer and postings of *darogas*. He had a clear record of having put any *daroga* he wished in charge.[16] Umeshwar Pratap thought that, in general, the powers that SPs had to appoint, post, and transfer local police officers were too great.

When a respondent was asked to explain, given all the complaints Umeshwar Pratap had about the then SP, how the latter had managed to stay on in the district for the unusually long term of three years, he attributed it to the "kindness of Raja Anand Singh." He noted that in the year previous to the current SP's appointment, seven SPs had come and gone because Anand Singh did not like them and, therefore, they could not remain in a district of which he was the leader. However, Yashpal Singh, the then SP, remained so long in the district because he was the "obedient dog" of Anand Singh.

When questioned if Umeshwar Pratap had asked Anand Singh to get rid of the SP, the respondent volunteered that he had opposed Anand in connection with the Kurman Purwa incident. In fact, he went further and said that, even though he was in the same party as Anand Singh, he did not like him and that he "certainly did oppose him in the Kurman Purwa episode."[17] He acknowledged, however, that both ultimately were on the same side in the Kurman Purwa episode and that, because of Anand Singh's intervention, the station officer was transferred along with the constable and police inspector accused of misbehaving in Kurman Purwa. Anand Singh's intervention and the transfer of the station officer led to Umeshwar Pratap's withdrawal from further involvement in the affair. However, he remained unhappy with the SP with whom, it was said, he could never get along because "the SP supports his department, whereas [Umeshwar Pratap] supports the public."

The exchange with this respondent illustrates clearly and rather starkly the importance and the dynamics of the struggle for control of the local police. Local political leaders who strive to maintain control over an entire district must find viable candidates to contest elections to the Legislative Assembly and Parliament. Viable candidates in most constituencies must have some political weight and resources of their own. They must have a good reputa-

---

[15] *Inka* interference *bahut zyada hai* . . . police activity *meN*; interview in Gonda district on November 16, 1982.

[16] *Yah SP ko yah pura* record *hai ki jis daroga ko chhahe, usko charge de de*; interview in Gonda district on November 16, 1982.

[17] Interview in Gonda district on November 16, 1982

tion in a locally important caste, come from a well-known former landlord family, have acquired a reputation for looking out for the interests of particular disadvantaged segments of a constituency, or the like. In recent years, criminal connections and a fearsome reputation of causing harm to one's enemies as well as supporting one's friends has come to matter a great deal as well in many north Indian constituencies.

The more advantages a potential candidate has, the more his relationship with the leader of the district becomes a bargaining one. In the case of a strong leader such as Anand Singh, who controlled the ticket selection process for Congress candidates from his district, the balance is weighted heavily in his favor for, without the ticket, even candidates with local influence of their own can rarely win elections nowadays as independents or on the ticket of inconsequential political parties. Umeshwar Pratap accepted the dominance of Anand Singh in the district, bowed to his leadership of it for the sake of getting the ticket, but wanted freedom to be the local boss in his own area. At the least, an MLA wants to be sure that the station officers in his area will not cause him political trouble and will be receptive to his requests for assistance to him and his supporters as needed. In the case of more ambitious persons such as Umeshwar Pratap, who are engaged in dubious if not illegal and criminal acitivities, they want the police to be completely subservient to them and their interests.

However, if every local MLA had unchallenged authority over the police in his area, there would be no overall political or administrative control in a district, which would come to be dominated and, in many cases, tyrannized by local "police lords." In this instance, Umeshwar Pratap went to the extent of appealing directly to the chief minister of the state over the head of his local political leader, Anand Singh. Ultimately, however, it was Anand Singh who decided, for his own reasons, to have the station officer transferred.

Insofar as the district as a whole is concerned, the SP has the authority to appoint and transfer the local station constabulary and inspectors. However, this authority does not necessarily carry the actual power to do so. In Gonda district in the 1980s, that power was shared with the local political leader of the district, Anand Singh. In the absence of such a powerful district leader, the SP's authority would be hostage to the power and influence over higher authorities of individual MLAs. Since the SP can be transferred by the state government, those in the district with influence in the state government can get the SP transferred. If he is in a district where he and his family are comfortable—or where he is making money—his authority over his own staff in the district is limited by the ability of local political leaders to get him transferred.

Clearly, a struggle was in process for control over the police in the area where Umeshwar Pratap wished to be the dominant force at the time the Kurman Purwa incident occurred. He had no interest in the matter beyond seeing to the transfer of the station officer nor is it likely he had the slightest sympathy with the Kurman Purwa villagers, who were not even voters in his constituency. As soon as his goal had been achieved, he withdrew from the matter.

Umeshwar Pratap's withdrawal left the fate of the villagers in the hands of Anand Singh, the police, and the courts unless the opposition parties in the district could draw sufficient attention to the case to bring outside forces into play. This they sought unsuccessfully to do.

The leader of the opposition agitation to draw wider attention to the Kurman Purwa incident was a local attorney by the name of Deep Narain Pande. He had contested the legislative assembly elections for Katra Bazaar constituency, in which Kurman Purwa falls, in 1974, 1977, and 1980. He won the seat on the Congress ticket in 1974 before Anand Singh had consolidated his control over the district Congress organization. He switched to the Janata Party and won the seat again in the Janata landslide of 1977, but was defeated in the 1980 election on the ticket of a splinter Congress organization, the Congress (U), whose leader in the state was H. N. Bahuguna. In 1984, two years after the Kurman Purwa episode, he contested against Anand Singh for the Gonda parliamentary constituency and was defeated in the massive Congress landslide of that year in which Anand Singh polled the second highest vote percentage in the state after Rajiv Gandhi.

I was informed that Deep Narain Pande identified with the cause of the Kurman Purwa villagers and appeared to believe in his heart that the police had misbehaved with them and that they had been unjustly treated. At the same time, he was clearly not a disinterested observer. He was an active non-Congress politician at the time seeking to establish and maintain a political base for himself in the southern part of the district from which he hoped also to challenge the dominance of Anand Singh.

I was told that Deep Narain believed that police atrocities had been committed against the Kurman Purwa villagers and that the incident began when the subinspector, Rahul Kumar Srivastava, and the constable in company with him went to the house of Sharda in village Kurman Purwa in a drunken state to steal money from him. He acknowledged that a "scuffle" then took place in which the two policemen were beaten by the villagers, after which the police returned to the village and committed their atrocities in retaliation.

As for Umeshwar Pratap Singh's role in the incident, this respondent remarked that his involvement was a consequence of "his own personal grievances against the police." Because Umeshwar Pratap was in league with criminals, he would naturally be at odds with the police and want the police to "be under his guidance." However, in the Colonelganj area, the local police had rebelled against Umeshwar Pratap's dominance. The Kurman Purwa events came in the midst of this tussle between Umeshwar Pratap and the police, which he then turned to his advantage.

However, it deserves note that Deep Narain had no complaint against the SP, despite the latter's friendly relationship with Anand Singh. More important, despite the fact that his own party workers were *lathi*-charged by the police when they organized a political procession to protest against the alleged police atrocities in Kurman Purwa, his complaints were directed only against the local police. In this respect, he and the opposition made common cause with Umeshwar Pratap, though for a different reason. That is, in Deep Narain Pande's view, the local police were out of control, but he was satisfied with the district police administration headed by SP Yashpal Singh.

To protest the police atrocities, Deep Narain Pande organized the procession of July 27 and a public meeting on August 9 in which, however, only the insignificant political parties in the district participated: his own Democratic Socialist Party, the Communist Party (CPI), and a splinter Congress group. The principal non-Congress party in the district, the BJP, did not participate. Speakers at the rally on August 9 included several state leaders of the CPI and the DSP as well as local former MLAs and party workers. A local Communist organizer claimed that ten thousand people attended the rally on August 9, which is most likely a highly exaggerated figure.

Although the Communist Party organizers worked closely with Deep Narain Pande, it is clear from the account of one of them that they took this occasion as an opportunity to demonstrate their ability to mobilize party workers and the public. The meeting of August 9 was described as "a brilliant success." The local CPI man whom I interviewed spoke with pride that the party's opponents claimed that "the entire show was captured by CPI." Although he acknowledged that the CPI had hardly any organization in the Colonelganj area, he thought that the people there were impressed by their contribution to the rally, "were sympathetic towards us," and "appreciate our strength, courage, sincerity, and integrity."[18]

Unlike Deep Narain Pande, the CPI was completely hostile to the police, including the SP, Yashpal Singh. In my CPI respondent's view, police atrocities are not isolated incidents. Rather, "by nature, police is atrocious" and "cannot be just."[19]

Despite their efforts and claims, the opposition achieved virtually nothing for the Kurman Purwa villagers through their political activities. As noted above, they demanded that a judicial inquiry be held into the happenings at Kurman Purwa, that the cases against the villagers be withdrawn, and that

---

[18] Interview in Gonda on November 17, 1982.
[19] Interview in Gonda on November 17, 1982.

the police personnel involved be punished for having looted the village and beaten the villagers. None of these goals were achieved. The only goal achieved was the transfer of the police personnel and ultimately the local station officer, a goal held by the opposition in common with Umeshwar Pratap. However, once this goal was attained, Umeshwar Pratap then sought to sabotage the opposition agitation by circulating a pamphlet among the people declaring that now that the local police had been transferred, all their grievances had been taken care of and justice should now be allowed to take its course.[20]

After August 9 no further publicity was given to the Kurman Purwa incident. Justice then took its course in the manner described above. Deep Narain Pande remained as the attorney for the villagers for the next seven years, their only source of external aid. Through his advocacy of their case, they avoided further punishment for the events of July 13, 1982. He himself was satisfied with the final decision of the sessions judge. However, the effort to enlarge the importance of the incident at Kurman Purwa, to turn it into a symbol of police misbehavior, and to use it to expand the support base of local non-Congress parties and politicians failed utterly because of the actions of Anand Singh and because no important external forces could be brought to bear on the case.

Anand Singh clearly played the critical role in defusing the Kurman Purwa situation. He was able to do so because of his close working relationship with the SP who, according to Umeshwar Pratap, continued in the district because of the "kindness" of Anand Singh, the leader of the district. All persons involved in the incident whom I interviewed acknowledged the part played by Anand Singh. The terms used over and over again to describe his part was that he succeded in having it "hushed up." He opposed the police actions that had taken place there, but he wanted to keep everybody quiet. "Because of him, everybody kept quiet, became quiet, and that's how he managed the whole affair [and] got the police officers transferred."[21] Anand Singh "supported the police. He wanted to hush up the entire matter."[22] The villagers, too, acknowledged the importance of Anand Singh in the matter for, when I interviewed them, they said that, in addition to the work being done on their behalf by their attorney, inquiries were going on under the auspices of the commissioner of Faizabad division and also under Anand Singh, whom they referred to as the Manakapur Raja.

As for Anand Singh, he felt that the police had in fact misbehaved, but that the station officer whom Umeshwar Pratap wanted transferred had done nothing wrong. However, I was informed that he did agree to the transfer of

[20] Interview in Gonda on November 17, 1982.
[21] Interview in Gonda district on November 16, 1982.
[22] Interview in Gonda on November 17, 1982.

the station officer because he felt this was the only way to prevent the opposition from taking advantage of the situation. If he did not agree to the
transfer of the station officer, then the whole matter "would just drag on and
on and the opposition would be in a position to continue to make capital out
of it."[23] It was also said that, in general, he tried to play down the whole
incident and advised the national leaders of the party who wanted to come to
the village not to do so and not to let it get expanded in this way.

Anand Singh succeeded in gaining control of the situation for three reasons. First, at the time he was the dominant political leader in the district.
He had good relations with the SP, with whom he worked out the final
decision to transfer all the police officers, including the station officer, from
the Colonelganj police station. Second, the Vidhan Sabha was not in session
so that the opposition lacked a legislative forum to dramatize the issue. The
press showed no interest in the matter, depriving the opposition of any public forum beyond their own processions and rallies. Third, the opposition
parties who organized the agitation were of no consquence in the politics of
the district and had little strength elsewhere in the state. Mrs. Gandhi was in
power in New Delhi and had shed all her tears in Narayanpur two years
earlier. Her daughter-in-law, Maneka, had shed her tears in Siswa. There
were, therefore, none left to shed tears for the villagers of Kurman Purwa.

Nor did this case, any more than the Narayanpur case, qualify for the
attention of the Commissioner for Scheduled Castes and Tribes. One of the
victims of the police assault was a Pasi, a Scheduled Caste, but the principal
accused in Kurman Purwa were not from Scheduled Castes. Consequently,
the villagers of Kurman Purwa were left to defend themselves with the aid
of a lone local attorney. The case dragged on for seven years until its "truth"
was established by the court and the villagers were relieved of the threat of
further punishment.

HORROR STORIES TOLD AND UNTOLD

It is probable that police atrocities were committed against the villagers of
Narayanpur and that the beatings and humiliations inflicted upon them were
greater than those inflicted upon the villagers of Kurman Purwa. However,
this "truth" is of less significance than the general pattern revealed in the two
cases, for the Narayanpur incident was merely somewhat worse than the
normal warfare that takes place at the local level between the police and
villagers from time to time, from village to village. Kurman Purwa represents more the norm than does Narayanpur.

It is this "truth," of the relative normalcy of the events at Narayanpur and

[23] Paraphrased quotation from my recall of conversation in Mankapur on November 22,
1982.

Kurman Purwa, which is masked by the exaggerated rhetoric used to describe the few cases that transgress the accepted boundaries of violence and atrocity in north India, which the politicians and the press seek to expose for their own benefit. On the other hand, this truth is also masked by the silence that is imposed upon the myriad cases of its type represented in the Kurman Purwa incident. Thus, rhetorical manipulation of violence and local control of violent incidents, talk and silence about them contribute equally to the persistence of the institutions and practices that perpetuate them.

The "truth" of Narayanpur was never told in all the talk about it. We learn of it through Kurman Purwa. We never learned of the complex relationships among the local police and politicians in the Captainganj police station area of Deoria district in which Narayanpur is situated because they were masked by the higher politics of state and country, of the struggle for power in UP and in India as a whole, in which the occurrence of police atrocities was a useful weapon for one side. Just because the Kurman Purwa incident was not expanded, because we are able to ask why not, we learned of the dynamics of local police–politician–criminal–public relationships, which were probably similar in Narayanpur.

From these two stories and from the others in this volume, we have learned several important "truths." The first concerns the partiality of the police, the fact that they are often, probably generally, implicated on one side or the other in local disputes. They may sometimes be on the side of the victims rather than the aggressors or the exploiters of the poor, but they do not stand apart from society as representatives of an impartial, progressive, and secular state.

Underpaid, overworked, provided with no decent working conditions and no status except that which they achieve by lording it over the poor and disadvantaged segments of society, from which some of them also come, they use their positions to make a decent living for themselves and their families through petty and larger bribes, through extortion, through linkages with local criminals or *dacoit* bands and complicity with them in thefts of all sorts. The principal obstacle to their conversion into marauding bands operating under the cover of state authority is the control exercised over them by local and district politicians. However, this control is also partial in two senses: It is only partly effective and it is exercised for the benefit of the controllers.

Local control is only partly effective because the dominant politicians are interested primarily in insuring that the police act partially, helping them and their friends and not their enemies. They are not interested in the ties that exist between subinspectors and constables, on the one side, and people like Dudh Nath Gosain, on the other side—as long as those relationships do not lead the police into the commission of politically damaging atrocities against persons who can be portrayed by their rivals as innocent victims. No one would have cared much if the police had been able quietly to take Sharda down to the police station, frame a false case against him, and beat him up to their hearts' content. However, the villagers of Kurman Purwa, mostly from Sharda's family, were not prepared to let that happen and a brawl ensued. In such brawls, when the police are hurt, as we have seen in this case and the others in this volume, they retaliate powerfully, unsparingly, and viciously. If they are sufficiently angered, they go out of control and cause embarrassment to their political patrons. When that happens, they are normally transferred to another part of the same district, where their behavior is unlikely to change. In more serious cases, they are sent to the "lines" for a while, out of active duty until the publicity dies down and they can be returned to their normal activities in another police station.

Political control is partial also in another sense. It favors the controller, his friends and supporters, and is neutral or to the disadvantage of his enemies and their supporters. Important people from elite and dominant castes with strong ties to the politicians who control the police may walk with ease, safely and securely, wherever they wish. They may walk into any police station where the writ runs of an important politician who controls the police and to whom they are connected, sit and drink tea with the station officer, request and receive his help in matters big and small. Even lesser folk may do so if they are well connected.

However, ordinary people without political connections, voters from villages where the vote has consistently gone against the winning party, and even important people of high status, if they are linked to rivals of the locally dominant police patron, may be ignored or treated badly in the local police station. False cases may be instituted against them at the behest of their political controllers. In political campaigns, the workers of the non-dominant candidates may be beaten by their rivals while the police stand aside.

In a well-run district or locality where there is a dominant political leader, incidents such as that at Kurman Purwa will either not occur or will be kept quiet—more likely the latter, for village brawls happen all the time and the police will often get involved on one side or the other. In such a well-run district or locality, the function of the police is to give the appearance of peace and order, not its reality. In such districts, local conflicts will be resolved through the peaceable intervention of politicians and/or through the long, tedious judicial process.

The Kurman Purwa and Narayanpur incidents demonstrate the importance for the appearance of peace and order in the countryside—and hence the national political importance—of effective local control over the police. In the Kurman Purwa incident, as in Narayanpur, the police broke free of all political constraints, thereby providing the potential for a symbolic political issue of state and national importance focusing on police atrocities and victimization of middle- and low-caste people. The incident appears to have had little to do with caste victimization except in the general sense that the subinspector and constable who were beaten were upper-caste and the villagers backward- and lower-caste people, but nothing is known about the caste composition of the larger force that descended on the village in the later assault. However, both incidents reveal the local police in a characteristic mode—implicated directly in local conflicts, open to bribery, capable of looting and harassing innocent persons and of vicious retaliatory actions against those who are not so innocent, and a potential danger to the exercise of state and national power when they cannot be controlled effectively at the local level and cannot be used to restrain and conceal potentially embarrassing situations rather than creating them.

Chapter 7

KALA BACHCHA: PORTRAIT OF A BJP HERO

Kanpur City

Kanpur city, situated on the southern bank of the Ganges River in the east-central plain of Uttar Pradesh (UP), is the ninth largest city in India—with a census population of 2.1 million in 1981—and one of its most important industrial centers. It is also the largest city in UP as well as its most important industrial town. Although Kanpur was a "small township" with a population above fifty thousand by the mid-nineteenth century,[1] its rapid growth in population and manufacturing began after the Mutiny of 1857, when it was partly laid waste and thereafter rebuilt. It began in this phase, like Bombay and Calcutta, essentially as a British trading and industrial center, rather than as a traditional Indian city.

Although Kanpur's industrial growth began with leather goods, which continue to occupy an important place in its production, it was cotton textiles that soon provided the bulk of its industry and employment. As Kanpur expanded, especially during the two World Wars, its industrial base diversified considerably, notably in ordnance, chemicals, and metals and engineering. Diversification continued in the post-Independence period, with considerable expansion in "light engineering, transport equipment, electrical goods, chemical based industries, cold storages and fruit and vegetable preservation etc."[2] However, this expansion and diversification have taken place simultaneously with a considerable decline in the number of textile factories and an enormous decline, more than 50 percent in the 1970s, in employment in the textile industry, Kanpur's industrial mainstay.

Kanpur experienced steady growth in both population and industrial and commercial development—except for the influenza decade of 1901–11—but it underwent phenomenal expansion after 1931. The population literally doubled between 1931 and 1941, when it reached nearly half a million, then increased by another 50 percent between 1941 and 1951, fed both by the enormous industrial expansion that occurred during World War II and by the influx of refugees from Pakistan after 1947. Population increase returned to a more modest and declining rate of growth thereafter: 37.7 percent from

---

[1] S. N. Singh, *Planning & Development of An Industrial Town (A Study of Kanpur)* (New Delhi: Mittal Publications, 1990), p. 35.

[2] Ibid., p. 17.

1951 to 1961, 31.3 percent from 1961 to 1971, 28.5 percent from 1971 to 1981 and 28.3 percent from 1981 to 1991.[3]

Unfortunately, despite the declining rate of increase in the growth of population, industrial expansion since Independence has not kept pace with it. Moreover, the industrial base has been changing from previous dominance by large-scale industry, principally cotton textiles, toward smaller industrial and commercial units.[4] Though smaller, these units are not especially labor intensive. The consequence, though there may be other contributory factors such as increases in the female–male ratio[5] and in the proportions of children in the total population, has been a steady decline in the percentage of the working to the total population of the city. That percentage was as high as 45.4 percent in 1911. It had already declined to 37.3 percent by 1951 and continued to decline, to as low as 29.6 percent in 1971 and 27.5 percent in 1981.[6]

There has been a corresponding decline in the proportions of the total population engaged in manufacturing industry—from 25.3 percent in 1945 at the end of the war to only 10.2 percent in 1971.[7] The decline in employment has been partly a consequence of measures of "rationalization" introduced in the textile and other large industries in this period to increase efficiency in the older industrial plants of the city. In addition, as already indicated, the principal growth sector industries do not provide as much employment as the traditional textile–based industries which, despite their increasing prominence in the industrial life of the city in terms of numbers of factories, still provided only about 25 percent to 26 percent

[3] *Census of India, 1981*, Series 1: *India*, Part II-A (ii): *General Population Tables*, by P. Padmanabha and *Census of India, 1991*, Series 25, *Uttar Pradesh*, Paper 1 of 1991, *Provisional Population Totals*, by Vijender Paul.

[4] For example, in the period between 1953 and 1979, the most dramatic increases in numbers of registered factories occurred in chemical-based industries and metal and engineering, where the numbers of factories went from 18 to 46 and from 103 to 299, respectively, and employment from 1,058 to 5,085 for chemicals and from 3,703 to 11,103 in metal and engineering industries. In the same period, the number of textile factories increased from 28 to 52 in 1971, then declined to 45 in 1979 while employment decreased in the entire period by more than 50 percent from 51,084 to 25,796. The number of workers per factory in 1979 works out at 66.9 for chemicals, 36.8 for metal and engineering, and 573.2 for textiles (Singh, *Planning & Development of An Industrial Town*, p. 17).

[5] That is, the number of females in the population has been increasing over the decades such that the sex ratio of females per 1,000 males stood in 1991 at 839 compared to 812 in 1981. To the extent this reflects an increase in the family population in the city, with the women staying at home, it could mean as well an increase in the nonworking population. However, it would also indicate increased stability in the population not reflected in other measures of economic and demographic change.

[6] Rajendra Kumar Awasthi, *Urban Development and Metropolitics in India* (Allahabad: Chugh Publications, 1985), p. 13; and *Census of India, 1981*, Series 1: *India*, Part II-B (i), *Primary Census Abstract: General Population*, by P. Padmanabha.

[7] Awasthi, *Urban Development*, p. 14.

of the industrial employment while textiles provided 61.7 percent in 1975.[8]

As in other major industrial cities in India, there is also a large and largely indeterminate population of casual labor, that is, workers not attached permanently to particular shops or factories. One estimate, based on census figures that combine construction workers with other categories is that this population contains about 34,000 people. The "other categories" include those "employed on regular basis" by the railways, public works and military engineering services departments, contract and temporary workers in the textile mills, and those seeking "loading-unloading work" on a daily basis through labor contractors. Most of these people are recent rural migrants, working for low wages, living and sleeping in the open or in meager facilities provided at the work site, at the railway station, or on the sidewalks.[9] In fact, more than half of the population of the city are immigrants, the vast majority of them from the rural areas of the state.[10] Most of the rural immigrant population in Kanpur is male, though the female–male sex ratio has been rising in recent decades, from the very low sex ratio of 762 females to 1,000 males in 1971 to 839 in 1991.[11]

Kanpur began as a planned British city with a large cantonment area, providing generous drill and living space for the military and their families; the most prosperous upper-class families enjoyed spacious parks and broad streets; several middle-class residential areas boasted large houses set on broad lawns. The city gradually became known more for its congested central area and its slums. Nowadays, more than half of the city's population is crowded into the central section, situated between the two more spacious areas of Civil Lines and the cantonment. Most of the *mohallas* (residential areas) in this central section are now classed as "slums or 'blighted areas.'"[12] In addition, a very large proportion of the population of the city now lives in what are known as "labour colonies" and *ahatas*. The latter, mostly "owned by private parties or trusts," are "single room quarters" lacking "lighting, water and sanitary facilities," and giving the appearance of "dungeons or of

[8] Singh, *Planning & Development of An Industrial Town*, p. 19.

[9] K. G. Agrawal, *Casual Labour of Kanpur: Their Living and Working Conditions* (New Delhi: National Labour Institute, 1988), pp. 9–14.

[10] Awasthi, *Urban Development*, pp. 18–19.

[11] Ibid., pp. 19–20, and *Census of India, 1991*, Series 25: *Uttar Pradesh, Paper 1 of 1991, Provisional Population Totals*, by Vijender Paul. Awasthi estimated that over one hundred thousand men in Kanpur lived "without their spouses" in 1971. I have not been able to find more recent figures.

[12] Nandu Ram, *The Mobile Scheduled Castes: Rise of a New Middle Class* (Delhi: Hindustan Publishing, 1988), p. 31.

pigeon holes in which human beings have been compelled to take shelter."[13] It is estimated that one-third of the inhabitants of the city live in these wretched accommodations, which house—not surprisingly—a large criminalized population.[14]

Both the owners of the large industrial establishments of the city and the "civic authorities" sought to increase the housing stock for the city's vastly increased population of workers at the end of the two World Wars, when "labour colonies," that is to say, housing meant specifically or primarily for industrial workers were built under the auspices of government corporations such as the Kanpur Improvement Trust and the Kanpur Development Board.[15] After World War II, for example, between 1955 and 1971, some 18,015 such quarters were built, especially in the until then sparsely populated and more open southern areas of the city.[16] Nevertheless, crowding is acute in the city, with an estimated "61.9 percent of the families" in Kanpur living in single-room tenements.[17] While this figure is well below that for Bombay (77.6%), it is well above most other cities in India. Moreover, a large population of the city lacks even the most elementary amenities of civilized life, living "on footpaths in dingy dwellings and cramped camps with inadequate lighting, no privies, open and overflowing drains, rotting garbage and excreta." In 1978 it was estimated that just above a half million of the city's population lived in slum localities, of which more than half lived in *ahatas*, nearly a third in "older slums," 8 percent in "*abadis* [semirural urban settlements] and villages," and nearly 9 percent in "new slums" situated on roadsides and beside the railway lines.[18]

Even where new housing has been constructed by the civic authorities for the benefit of the poorer classes, it is believed that "most" of such houses are then either "illegally sub-let or forcibly occupied by unauthorized persons," with the complicity of local officials, politicians, and municipal councillors. Such activities have "become a flourishing business for many such persons."[19] In Kanpur, as in Bombay and many other large cities in India and other parts of the world, there is a predatory class of slum landlords and real estate developers who seek opportunities to displace slum dwellers from their miserable hovels, gain control over the land and buildings, and use them for

[13] Noor Mohammad, *Slum Culture and Deviant Behaviour* (Delhi: Idarah-i Adabiyat-i Delli, 1983), pp. 23–24.

[14] Ibid., p. 30.

[15] Singh, *Planning & Development of An Industrial Town*, p. 35.

[16] Ibid., app. iv.

[17] Awasthi, *Urban Development*, p. 21.

[18] Ibid., p. 24.

[19] Ibid., p. 29.

rental purposes for both lower-middle-class persons and for the development of local commercial markets.

Communal and Caste Composition of Kanpur Mohallas

Approximately 20 percent of the population of Kanpur is Muslim. The vast majority of the Muslim population of the city is concentrated in the highly congested central sector *mohallas*. Moreover, within the central sector itself, the bulk of the Muslim population is further concentrated in a compact geographical section containing sixteen *mohallas* in which the Muslims comprise above 80 percent of the population, another two in which they comprise between 50 percent and 80 percent, and one in which their proportion is between 30 percent and 50 percent. In the center of this overwhelmingly Muslim area lie two census "chaks" in which Hindus are in a majority and Muslims comprise less than 30 percent of the population. There is also one other *mohalla* outside the main area of Muslim concentration in which the Muslims are above 80 percent, seven in which they are above 50 percent, and two in which they are a substantial minority.

Immediately south of the heavily Muslim areas is a broad swath of Hindu-majority localities. To the immediate south of the latter are the Grand Trunk Road, which cuts through the center of Kanpur, and the Central Railway Line, across which lie three *mohallas*, one of which, known as Babu Purwa, falls in the category of more than 80 percent Muslim, and two others—Chandmari and Juhi-Hamirpur Road—which lie in the 50 percent to 80 percent range. South of this cluster of localities, Muslims live only in scattered populations amid Hindu majorities.

Most of the city's slums also lie in the congested central sector of the city or on its borders. According to one survey research estimate, 86 percent of the slum population is Hindu, 14 pecent is Muslim, whereas 66 percent of the population of the somewhat more habitable "colonies" are Hindu and 34 percent are Muslim. Among the Hindu population, the vast majority of the population in both slums and labor colonies are of low caste, comprising 92 percent of the slum areas and 83 percent of the colony areas.[20]

Communal Relations in Kanpur

Kanpur did not until recently fall into the category of towns in UP that have developed in the post-Independence period what I call "institutionalized riot systems," in which a high level of tension in communal relations is maintained by the existence of opposed forces in one or both communities continuously alert to alleged affronts from members of the other community and

[20] Renuka Biswas, *Slum Clearance in Kanpur* (Calcutta: Sree Publishing, 1981), pp. 74–75.

predisposed to take a range of actions to deal with such affronts, ranging from complaints to the authorities to organization of processions to deliberate provocations designed to threaten or inflict harm upon persons and property of the other community. Kanpur had such a system for a time in the 1930s and has such a system now to which economic and political factors have contributed, but it has not developed out of a long tradition of communal conflict or embittered communal relations. Though there have been several communal riots in Kanpur in the twentieth century, including one of vast proportions, they have until recently been no more prominent than other types of riotous behavior in the modern history of the city.

From the turn of the century until Independence, there were a half dozen large-scale riots in Kanpur: the plague riots of 1900, the Kanpur Mosque incident of 1913, the spectacular communal riots of 1931, and three others between 1933 and 1939.[21] There was also "a minor communal riot in 1927."[22] Little is known—and no major studies have been written—of those that occurred in 1927, 1933, and 1939. Of the three well-known cases, the first involved Hindu and Muslim local leaders working together against the enforcement of the plague regulations, in the aftermath of which one Hindu and one Muslim activist were hanged by the authorities. The second involved a confrontation between Muslims protesting the construction of a road by the British authorities in the city through a site occupied by the Macchli Bazaar mosque in which a "washing place," commonly used by worshipers before entering a mosque, was destroyed. The third, the great Kanpur riot of 1931, was unequivocally a Hindu–Muslim riot, precipitated out of angry exchanges in which Hindu Congressmen demanded that Muslims observe a Congress-sponsored strike in the city in protest against the execution of the nationalist hero Bhagat Singh for terrorist activities. Hindu processionists and crowds of young men attempted to compel Muslim shopkeepers to close their shutters and made other demands for participation of Muslim passersby, which soon led to a full-scale Hindu–Muslim riot in the course of which nearly 400 people were said to have been killed, more than 1,200 were injured, 18 mosques and 42 temples were damaged, and 248 Hindu and 101 Muslim houses were burned.[23]

In the period just before and continuing after the great Kanpur riot of 1931, Freitag describes the elements in Kanpur that comprise what I call an

---

[21] Ian Wilkinson, "What Large Datasets Can Tell Us about the General Explanations for Communal Riots," unpublished paper presented at the panel on "Communal Violence in India: New Research" of the Association for Asian Studies, Washington, D.C., April 7, 1995, p. 6.

[22] N. Gerald Barrier, ed., *Roots of Communal Politics* (New Delhi: Arnold-Heinemann, 1976), p. 10.

[23] Sandria B. Freitag, *Collective Action and Community: Public Arenas and the Emergence of Communalism in North India* (Berkeley: University of California Press, 1989), p. 245; and Barrier, *Roots of Communal Politics*, p. 11.

"institutionalized riot system." The general political background of the time provided a framework for the communalization of public issues, brought about particularly by the schism between Congress Hindu leaders and Muslim political elites in the state and country that developed in the aftermath of the Non-Cooperation and Khilafat movements of 1921–22, the rise of competitive movements of religious proselytization (*shuddhi* and *tabligh*), and the acting out of these conflicts and issues in local politics. Local political leaders thus found a political interest in promoting differences between Hindus and Muslims, even to the extent of fomenting violent disturbances as a means of gaining advantage over political rivals from the other community. In a city with a large rootless and unemployed population, there were many so-called *badmash*es or bad characters available to be used by local politicians for such purposes as well as by the "Hindu merchants" of the city for their own political or economic interests. There was also the huge population of factory workers who formed a potential source for vastly enlarged riotous behavior, such as occurred when they also became involved in the 1931 riot.[24] The existence of such a "riot system" might help explain the fact that three further Hindu–Muslim riots occurred in the succeeding years to 1939, though we know little about them.

On the other hand, a contrary impression exists both in the literature on Hindu–Muslim riots and in popular impressions in Kanpur itself that the city was free of serious communal conflict for the next half century.[25] Once again, in the post-Independence period, as in the first half of the twentieth century, although several major riotous events occurred, none until the late 1980s and early 1990s could be characterized as Hindu–Muslim affairs. A major confrontation between elements of the public and the police occurred in 1959, which had no bearing on Hindu–Muslim relations; quite serious Muslim sectarian rioting between Sunnis and Sh'ias broke out in 1976; a police firing on textile workers at the Swadeshi Cotton Mills took place in 1978; and there was a massacre of Sikhs in 1984 in the aftermath of the assassination of Mrs. Gandhi by her two Sikh bodyguards. Hindu–Muslim riots as such, however, did not begin to occur until the late 1980s as a kind of prelude to the extensive rioting of December 1992.

By 1992 most of the elements of an institutionalized riot system were in place to take advantage of any incident, small or large, and raise it to the level of a Hindu–Muslim confrontation. Some of the elements of the Hindu–Muslim riot system exist at all times in Kanpur: a large and increasing rootless population for whom riotous activity provides a much needed source of employment, income, and booty and a close link increasingly common

[24] Freitag, *Collective Action and Community*, pp. 244–45.
[25] Ashgar Ali Engineer, "Communal Violence in Kanpur," *Economic and Political Weekly* 29, no. 9 (February 26, 1994): 473–74.

everywhere in north India among criminal elements, the politicians, and the police. However, the political element in the system, lacking for most of the pre-Independence period, was introduced in the late 1980s when the BJP captured political control over virtually all the legislative and parliamentary constituencies from the city.

The Changed Political Context

In the post-Independence years, politics in Kanpur city have undergone profound changes, some mirroring changes in the economy of the city noted above, others mirroring changes in state and national politics. In the early post-Independence years in Kanpur, as elsewhere in the state and country, the Congress was dominant in the city's politics. At that time, one parliamentary constituency, encompassing five legislative assembly constituencies, covered the entire city and, in one of the assembly constituencies, a small portion of the countryside as well.

In the General Elections of 1952, the Congress won the parliamentary seat and all five of the assembly seats. The opposition was divided and fragmented. The runner-up candidates in the Lok Sabha constituency and in two of the assembly constituencies were from the Socialist Party, whereas the second-place candidates in the three remaining assembly constituencies were, respectively, from the CPI, the Jan Sangh, and one Independent. At that time, when the textile industry was still in its heyday, trade union politics and labor support constituted the main political battleground. Many of the candidates from both the Congress and the Left opposition came from the trade union movement, which itself was divided among unions affiliated to the various political parties. Only in the constituency of Kanpur City (South), later renamed Govind Nagar, was the militant Hindu party, then the Jan Sangh, the runner-up candidate. This result was based largely upon the fact that a small but significant population of Hindu refugees had settled in this newly developed and sprawling southern part of the city, which gave its support for the most part to the BJS.

As a consequence of the death of the Congress Lok Sabha candidate in the middle of his term, a midterm election for the parliamentary seat was held in 1954 focusing on issues pertaining to the textile industry and labor politics. [26] The winning Congress candidate, a cloth merchant who defeated two candidates from the labor movement, resigned five months later, forcing another by-election, this time won by a Praja Socialist Party labor candidate. As a consequence of these by-elections, the parliamentary contest took on a life

---

[26] For the history of this constituency from the first to the third general elections, see Paul R. Brass, "Class and Community Voting in Kanpur City," in Paul R. Brass, ed., *Caste, Faction and Party in Indian Politics*, vol. 2: *Election Studies* (Delhi: Chanakya, 1985), pp. 280–300.

of its own somewhat separate from the lower-level battles in the assembly constituencies, becoming for the next several elections a contest between candidates from the Left with strong support in the labor movement and a candidate from the Congress, who sought unsuccessfully to recover this seat. In 1957 a CPI-supported independent candidate, S. M. Banerjee, won the seat and continued to hold it over the next three elections until his retirement from politics after his last victory in the elections of 1971.

At the assembly level, the Congress retained its dominance in the elections of 1957 and 1962, winning all seats but one in 1962, which it lost to the CPI. All the runner-up candidates behind the Congress in those elections were either from parties of the Left or independent.

The General Elections of 1967 brought intensified competition and further fragmentation of political parties in Indian politics at all levels from the Center to the states and localities. In the meantime, the textile industry had begun its decline, labor and trade union politics were losing their centrality, and new, medium-sized industries and trades were becoming more important in the economy of the city. In this changed political and economic context, including a great increase in the city's population leading to an increase in the number of legislative assembly consituencies to seven, Congress dominance was shattered and the Jan Sangh came into prominence in several constituencies. The Jan Sangh won its first legislative assembly seat in Kanpur city in 1967 from the Generalganj constituency, where the wholesale cloth trade is centered as well as many other of the city's commercial trades in which the Jan Sangh was the more effective competitor with the Congress for support than the parties of the Left.

Political fragmentation continued until the 1977 elections, the post-Emergency elections in which the Janata Party won all the Kanpur seats, including both the Lok Sabha and legislative assembly seats. This position was completely reversed in 1980 with Mrs. Gandhi's return to power at the Center. Congress won the parliamentary seat in the general elections and all five of Kanpur's assembly seats in the state elections that followed thereafter. By this time, the Janata Party had fragmented and the BJP had emerged as the new incarnation of the former Jan Sangh, winning three of the seven Kanpur assembly seats. In the Rajiv Gandhi landslide election of 1985, the Congress again predominated in Kanpur, winning all but one of the assembly constituencies, while the BJP now emerged as the runner-up in four of the seven. The rise of the Janata Dal in the 1989 elections led again to a reversal of party fortunes in which the Janata Dal won five of the assembly seats and the BJP had its first success in a Kanpur assembly contest, prevailing in Govind Nagar. The CPM prevailed in the parliamentary contest, in which the BJP was the runner-up for the first time.

The elections of 1991 and 1993 (table 7.1) once again partly mirrored changes in politics at higher levels. The struggle between Rajiv Gandhi and

TABLE 7.1
Legislative Assembly Election Results for Kanpur City Constituencies for Principal Parties,
1991 and 1993

| | 1991 | | | | 1993 | | | |
| | Winning Party | | Second Party | | Winning Party | | Second party | |
Constituency	Name	Vote %	Name	Vote %	Name	Vote %	Name	Vote %
Arya Nagar	BJP	43.34	ML	28.72	BSP	46.58	BJP	41.44
Sisamau (SC)[a]	BJP	50.47	INC	20.45	BJP	51.74	SP	21.89
Generalganj	BJP	53.00	INC	19.06	BJP	45.97	SP	38.31
Kanpur Cantt.	BJP	44.60	INC	23.67	BJP	51.47	SP	31.58
Govind Nagar	BJP	46.24	INC	26.35	BJP	47.61	INC	25.72
Kalyanpur	BJP	48.09	INC	22.19	BJP	49.77	INC	23.37
Sarsaul	JP	23.07	JD	21.66	SP	36.94	BJP	26.13

Key: BJP = Bharatiya Janata Party; BSP = Bahujan Samaj Party; INC = Indian National Congress; JP = Janata Party; ML = Muslim League; SP = Samajwadi Party.
[a]"SC" refers to the fact that this constituency is reserved for Scheduled Caste candidates.

V. P. Singh, the development of the controversy over reservation of jobs for backward castes, and the rise of the Ayodhya movement led to the destruction of the Congress organization in UP. Since the Janata Dal had, like its predecessor, also fragmented, the initial beneficiary of these changes was the BJP, which took power in UP for the first time in 1991. In Kanpur, it won the parliamentary seat for the first time as well as six of the seven assembly constituencies.

Major changes in the political context occurred between the elections of 1991 and the next elections in November 1993. These included the resignation of the BJP state government in the aftermath of the destruction of the mosque at Ayodhya and the violence that then followed in northern and western India, the continuing disintegration of the Congress in the state, a realignment of the Janata parties in which the Samajwadi Party of Mulayam Singh Yadav emerged preeminent, and the rise of a new party among the lowest castes, the Bahujan Samaj Party (BSP). The 1993 midterm elections then became a contest primarily between the BJP and an alliance of the SP and BSP under the leadership of Mulayam Singh Yadav, which barely prevailed and came to power at the state level, but not in Kanpur. In the city, the BJP won five of the assembly constituencies while the SP won one and the BSP another. In Kanpur during both the elections of 1991 and 1993, small-scale violent conflicts and minor riots occurred in connection with the electoral battles in the Kanpur constituencies between the BJP and SP candidates.

The changes that have occurred in Kanpur politics over the past nearly five decades may be summed up as follows. The early period was characterized by Congress dominance in the assembly contests and Congress-Left electoral competition at the parliamentary level. A stable, industrialized textile labor force provided the major area of contestation for electoral support in those early elections. A long middle period followed with a multiplicy of changes at the local, state, and national levels, leading first to the decline of the Left, then of the Congress. Intensified political competition occurred in these middle years at the same time that economic changes produced changes in party support bases. In the midst of these changes, the major political beneficiary in Kanpur was the BJP, whose rise has also been associated with a communalization of electoral politics in the city as in the state as a whole.

THE RIOT OF DECEMBER 1992

Between December 6 and 12, 1992,[27] in the immediate aftermath of the demolition of the Babari Masjid in Ayodhya, a major Hindu–Muslim communal riot occurred in Kanpur. This riot was in some ways similar to the post-Ayodhya riots in Bombay which, because of their vast size and the extent of the killings, overshadowed in the press the events in Kanpur that would otherwise have been front-page news. The destruction and killings in Kanpur were second only to that which occurred in Bombay in the most extensive wave of rioting in India since Independence.

This chapter presents some of the general features of the Kanpur riots, while focusing on the role of a single person, a man considered by some to be a major killer in them and by others, almost exclusively from the BJP and RSS family of organizations, to have been their principal hero. This man, known as Kala Bachcha, was killed in February 1994, provoking further riotous disturbances which, however, stopped far short of those in December 1992. In this chapter, I use the issues surrounding the rise and fall of Kala Bachcha as a point of departure from which to consider further the issues of

[27] The bulk of the information in the remainder of this chapter comes from two sets of materials: (1) thirty-eight personal interviews carried out by me with the assistance of Gyan Chaturvedi in three visits to Kanpur in July and August 1993 and in June 1994 and (2) sixty-eight typewritten affidavits submitted by victims or eyewitnesses of riotous events in December 1992 to the Mathur Commission. The interview materials will be referred to by the interview number in the sequence in which they were carried out, as "Kanpur-#n," the affidavits as "AN-nn." For reasons of discretion and confidentiality, the names of the interviewed respondents, with the exception of the deceased Kala Bachcha, have been left out and their official positions masked. However, the interviews have all been transcribed, typed, and placed in binders, which will form a permanent record should anyone wish to check the authenticity of my accounts and for future consultation by scholars under the same rules of confidentiality that I follow.

I want to express here my gratitude to Mr. Sharfuddin Ahmad, Advocate, a member of the staff of the Mathur Commission for providing me with copies of the affidavits.

explanation and representation in the presentation of accounts of riots, their causes, and their uses.

Sequence

It is virtually impossible to construct a straightforward, factual, and sequential account of the incidents that made up the disturbances that occurred in Kanpur between December 6 and 12, 1992. Such an objective account is rendered impossible first by the myriad of incidents that occurred on those days. Lack of complete information available to anyone as well as the human necessity in speech and in most forms of writing about big events to generalize mean that selectivity and screening are inherent in the process, whoever tells the story. Second, most observers of the Kanpur riots, especially those present, implicated, or politically interested in its proper representation, attribute to particular incidents, and not others, the beginnings of a chain of events that they believe make up the whole. Rather than attempt an "objective" account, therefore, this narration seeks to pinpoint the few "facts" that are not in dispute, but also notes, briefly here and in further detail later, the discrepant accounts provided by respondents and witnesses.

DAY ONE, DECEMBER 6

The people of Kanpur, as well as those in the rest of the country, were aroused by the broadcasts by both Door Darshan (the government television network) and the BBC, which appeared on the television screens after the collapse of the mosque. Door Darshan made its announcement on television at 7:30 P.M. that the mosque had been demolished.[28] Muslims became upset and began to come out in the streets, particularly in the overwhelmingly Muslim-majority areas of Chaman Ganj and Begam Ganj (also commonly referred to as Bacon Ganj or Bekan Ganj) in the center of the city, from where it is said they began "pouring out."[29] Between 7:00 and 8:00 o'clock in the evening, "a huge crowd of Muslims gathered and they started breaking the locks of the Hindu shops." The Bekan Ganj *thana* was "surrounded by a mob."[30] Muslim crowds also began to attack administrative offices and police stations and destroyed some shops and houses of Hindus in Dalelpurwa (another heavily Muslim majority *mohalla* in the center of the city) and Rizvi Market, where four or five people were killed.[31] Curfew was imposed in the evening at 8:00 P.M. in eight *thana*s in the city.[32]

[28] Kanpur #24 and AN-19.
[29] Kanpur #1.
[30] Kanpur #9.
[31] Kanpur #1 and Kanpur #9.
[32] Kanpur #1 and Kanpur #24.

Rioting spread through the night of the 6th to the morning of the 7th and on the day of the 7th from the Chaman Ganj and Bekan Ganj areas to other Muslim-majority localities, such as Faithful Ganj, Babu Purwa, and Shujat Ganj,[33] all of which fall into the 80 plus percent Muslim group, but lie across the Grand Trunk Road on the borders of the Hindu majority *mohallas*. Police vehicles moving through these areas were fired upon.[34] On the 7th, between 10 and 12 in the morning, the PAC, hated by virtually all Muslims, was withdrawn from the Muslim-majority areas where rioting had begun and replaced by the military.[35] Rizvi Road remained a scene of riotous behavior, particularly looting, up to the night of the 7th. Police also opened fire on mobs this night.[36]

The incident on the 7th emphasized by most respondents as a pivotal point in the extension of the rioting in Kanpur was the pitched battle that occurred early in the morning, around 9:00 to 9:30, in two Harijan (Scheduled Caste) *basti*s in Babu Purwa, both named after the low castes whose members are numerically predominant therein: Pasiyana and Khatikana. These *basti*s also contain some Muslim homes and families. The two Harijan *basti*s are adjacent to each other, the larger being Khatikana.

The fighting in these two localities of Babu Purwa is acknowledged by all parties inteviewed to have been decisive in the spread of rioting to other parts of the city. The differing interpretations concerning the facts and the actions of the crowds and, in particular, those of one corporator (member of the elected municipal corporation), Kala Bachcha, are discussed in detail below. The pivotal character of the events here concerns the further spread of the rioting to adjacent and more distant localities.

The 8th of December was somewhat more subdued than the previous days. Quiet was restored in Pasiyana and Khatikana.[37] Curfew was extended to further areas of the city, the military were deployed in Muslim areas,[38] which relieved tensions there somewhat, while the PAC was sent to predominantly Hindu areas. Some scattered incidents were reported from the southern part of the city on this day.

---

[33] Kanpur #24.
[34] Kanpur #9.
[35] Kanpur #2 and Kanpur #4.
[36] Kanpur #9.
[37] Kanpur #8.
[38] Kanpur #9.

DAY FOUR, DECEMBER 9

The scattered incidents reported on the 8th in the southern areas of the city were but a prelude to the massive rioting and massacres of Muslims that occurred on the 9th and 10th in the periphery of the city, in the most outlying areas of Barra and Nau Basta[39] (in which small and often isolated Muslim houses and quarters are surrounded by overwhelmingly Hindu populations) where curfew had still not been imposed. It is universally acknowledged even by BJP and Bajrang Dal activists as well as by their enemies and by the administration that the rioting in Nau Basta was begun by Hindus, incited by rumors "that so many Hindus, police, and PAC men were killed in the presence of the army" in the Muslim-majority areas and that a large mob of Muslims was on their way to kill Hindus.[40]

Several affidavits submitted to the postriot inquiry commission describing the events of this day make it clear that large mobs were roaming the southern areas in broad daylight, attacking homes, shops, and factories at noon.[41] Two hundred and six FIRs (First Information Reports) were filed in the Babu Purwa police station referring to attacks on the 9th, beginning as early as 10:00 A.M. and increasing in number through the late afternoon hours and into the night. Fourteen incidents were reported at the Govind Nagar police station on this date, which occurred between 6:00 A.M. and 9:00 P.M. Twenty-seven incidents were reported from Nau Basta police station between the hours of 10:00 A.M. and midnight (see table 7.2).

DAY FIVE, DECEMBER 10

The relative impunity with which the mobs marauded and attacked Muslim persons and property on the 9th, with little interference from the police and with the curfew honored in the breach, encouraged the mobs to spread their attacks farther and with even greater intensity. The most notorious incidents of the Kanpur riots occurred on the 10th in areas in the southern periphery of the city. As the riot went completely out of control in these areas, the governor of the state replaced the two most responsible administrative officers, the DM and the SSP, in the early morning hours of the 10th[42] with two well-known, trusted, impartial officers known for their ability to prevent riots and to control them after they had started.

Before the rioting in south Kanpur was brought under control on the 10th, however, there were a further twenty-nine incidents in Babu Purwa, thirty-seven in Govind Nagar, and 144 in Nau Basta. These incidents included

[39] Kanpur #4.
[40] Kanpur #13.
[41] AN-31 and 45.
[42] Kanpur #1.

TABLE 7.2
Date of Incidents of Communal Violence by Police Station, Kanpur City

Police Station	Date					After 10th	Not Known	Total
	6th	7th	8th	9th	10th			
Anwar Ganj	—	—	2	—	1	—	—	3
Babu Purwa	6	54	83	222	29	5	37	436
Bazeria	2	—	—	—	—	—	—	2
Bidhnoo	—	—	—	1	—	—	—	1
Chakeri	—	—	3	9	—	—	1	13
Chaman Ganj	—	—	—	—	—	—	1	1
Collector Ganj	—	—	—	1	—	—	—	1
Colonel Ganj	—	1	—	—	—	—	—	1
Fazal Ganj	—	—	1	1	4	1	—	7
Govind Nagar	—	1	5	14	37	10	1	68
Juhi	1	5	22	1	2	—	—	31
Kalyanpur	—	—	—	1	—	—	—	1
Kidwai Nagar	1	2	15	4	2	—	2	26
Kotwali	—	—	10	—	—	—	—	10
Nau Basta	—	7	7	27	144	5	21	211
Rail Bazaar	—	58	—	—	—	—	—	58
Rai Purwa	—	—	1	—	1	—	—	2
TOTAL	10	128	149	281	220	21	63	872

Source: The figures in this and the following table come from materials prepared by the staff of the Mathur Commission, appointed to inquire into the Kanpur riots of December 1992. They were provided to me by a member of that staff, Mr. Sharfuddin Ahmad.

assaults on a large crowd of Muslims seeking safety in the Hari Masjid mosque, which began on the night of the 9th and continued up to the late afternoon of the 10th, and the attack on a mosque on Hamirpur Road in Nau Basta in the afternoon.[43] The attack on the Nau Basta mosque was preceded and followed by considerable destruction in the adjacent locality of Taj Nagar. One affidavit was signed by forty-four Muslims, who claimed that their houses were "looted, burned, and demolished" in this locality.[44] Another referred to the selection and burning of fifteen Muslim houses in a locality known as Mool Chand ka Ahata.[45] Two other infamous incidents that occurred on this date were the slaughter of seven members of a Muslim family in this same locality of Taj Nagar in Nau Basta and the razing to the ground of a colony inhabited mostly by poor Muslims, known as Vijay ka Ahata.

[43] Kanpur #5 and AN-10, AN-11, AN-14, and AN-15.
[44] AN-14.
[45] AN-2.

Several interview respondents and affidavits note that the mobs on the 9th and 10th discriminated carefully between Hindu and Muslim houses and occupants, even to the extent of removing and burning the goods of Muslim occupants of multistory apartments while leaving intact those of Hindu occupants.[46] In the Chaman Nagar locality of Nau Basta, one affidavit writer reported that sixty-five Muslim houses were singled out for looting and burning. However, in one case, where the house was owned by a Hindu but occupied by a Muslim tenant, "the goods of the Muslim tenant were taken out from the house by rioters and saving the house from any loss the goods were burnt."[47] One affidavit noted that four houses, the only Muslim houses in a locality known as 24 Quarters in Naubasta, were singled out from among the larger number of Hindu houses in an organized attack by a mob composed mostly of outsiders, but guided to the Muslim houses through "the active collusion" of local residents.[48] Many also commented that the actions of the Hindu mobs on both the 9th and the 10th took place with no intervention from the PAC and the police or even with their "indulgence" and participation, again often in broad daylight.[49] At the damaged Nau Basta mosque, the PAC men were said to have "joined the rioters shouting Jai Shree Ram" along with them.[50] Several also stated that, seeing the unchecked actions of the mobs and the inattentiveness, inaction, or indulgence of the PAC and the police, they fled Nau Basta, leaving their houses and goods behind, to save their lives and those of their family members.[51] In some cases, those who escaped did so just in time, for they could observe their houses set on fire as they ran for their lives.[52]

The rioting diminished in these areas in the late afternoon of the 10th at the time of the arrival of the CRPF, but some accounts suggest that the rioting had already subsided before this force came on the scene.[53]

Statistical Summary of the Incidents of Violence

Table 7.2 gives an incomplete quantitative accounting of the violent events in Kanpur between December 6 and 11, 1992. These figures were compiled by persons working with the official commission of inquiry appointed by the government to inquire into the Kanpur riots, the Mathur Commission. They

[46] Kanpur #16 and AN-2.

[47] AN-46.

[48] AN-23.

[49] AN-2, AN-25, and AN-55.

[50] AN-38 and 41. *Jai Shree Ram* (Victory to Lord Ram) was the slogan used by processionists and crowds during the mass mobilizations that accompanied the Ayodhya movement in the late 1980s and at the time of the destruction of the mosque in Ayodhya on December 6, 1992.

[51] AN-5.

[52] AN-25.

[53] Kanpur #13.

were based on FIRs filed at the various police stations in Kanpur in the aftermath of the riots. The BJP and other militant Hindu organizations refused to cooperate with the Mathur Commission. Moreover, there is an evident bias in the materials compiled by the Mathur Commission staff toward the recording of Muslim complaints, which form the vast bulk of both the affidavits drawn upon above and the figures discussed herein. Only one or two affidavits were filed by Hindus and only a tiny percentage of the FIRs listed in this compilation referred to complaints made by Hindus. The distortion is most evident in the figures for Chaman Ganj, where rioting was initiated by Muslim crowds on the 6th. Yet only one incident, the murder of a Muslim, is noted for Chaman Ganj throughout the entire riot period and none for the first two days when it is known that serious rioting was taking place in this and adjacent areas. The compilers note in their record that the primary reason for this lack is that the principal damage done to persons and property in this area on those days was done by the police and the PAC firing upon Muslim crowds. This explanation, however, is not entirely satisfactory. The discussion below, therefore, must be read with these limitations in mind.

If we take the figures as a close approximation of the consequences for Muslims in the city of the Kanpur riots, then we can approach them with more confidence. In that respect, the figures reveal a rising crescendo of riotous activity directed against Muslims from the 6th to the 9th and 10th, with the total number of incidents reported rising from 10 on the 6th to 128 on the 7th, 149 on the 8th, 281 on the 9th, 220 on the 10th, and falling away rapidly thereafter, after which only 21 incidents were reported on a few days later in the month. These figures are also broadly consistent with the reports given to us in our interviews and presented above.

The shift in activity toward the southern and southern peripheral areas of Kanpur is also clearly revealed in these figures. Fifty-four incidents are recorded in Babu Purwa on the 7th, the day of the pitched battle in Pasiyana and Khatikana, and another 58 in the adjacent police station area of Rail Bazaar. On the 8th, the intensity of activity rises further in Babu Purwa and extends also to Juhi and Kidwai Nagar. The peak of activity in Babu Purwa occurs on the 9th, with 222 incidents recorded on that date. The number of incidents in Nau Basta and Govind Nagar also rises significantly on that date. On the 10th, the primary area of activity becomes Nau Basta, followed by Govind Nagar, with a recession in activity in Babu Purwa where, however, the number of incidents remains high.

It is evident from the figures also that the bulk of anti-Muslim riotous activity occurred within the jurisdication of six police stations in the city: Babu Purwa, Govind Nagar, Juhi, Kidwai Nagar, Nau Basta, and Rail Bazaar. Of these areas, Babu Purwa is predominantly Muslim, comprising above 80 percent of the total population. Juhi is also a Muslim-majority area, but Muslims are in a minority in the other areas. Babu Purwa and Juhi also contain several predominantly slum areas and large populations of Scheduled Castes.

ACTIONS AND REACTIONS

There is a broad consensus on the sequence of riotous behavior in Kanpur after December 6, and even to an extent on the question concerning the communal composition of the crowds at each stage. However, consensus disintegrates on matters concerning fault, provocation, and justification as well as on both general and specific motivations. The general issue of motivation concerns whether crowd actions should be considered attack or reaction, assault or retaliation. At another level, the issue also arises concerning whether motivations other than communal ones appeared during the riot and under the guise of communal attack, reaction, or retaliation.

It is generally accepted that large-scale riotous behavior began in response to the news of the demolition of the mosque at Ayodhya, concerning which reports were broadcast late in the morning of the 6th, and were followed in the evening with film footage on television, of the collapse of the structure. It is also accepted that it was large crowds of Muslims who came on the streets initially from the heavily Muslim residential areas (*mohallas*) of Chaman Ganj and Bekan Ganj.[54] The Muslims in these areas attacked and looted Hindu shops and also surrounded the *thana* of Bekan Ganj, which had to be rescued by an additional force.[55]

These acknowledged facts provided further "evidence" for the oft-proclaimed statement of militant and communal Hindus that it is always the Muslims who start riots, never the Hindus. The following statement by an ex-MLA of the BJP, a member of the RSS from his childhood days, and a member of the Bajrang Dal as well, states this position clearly.

> RESPONDENT: . . . Since Independence, since 1974 until today, whenever the riots are there in our country, those who have started [are] from Muslim community, straightaway I blame them. And everybody knows it. Hindus are never in a position and they never feel and they don't have such type of thinking that they'll go and attack somebody.[56]

While even impartial administrators will often acknowledge the "truth" of the first part of this statement, they will also note that Muslims do not usually come out in the streets in large numbers unless they are provoked by Hindus or through the communally biased, pro-Hindu, anti-Muslim Hindi

[54] Kanpur #13.
[55] Kanpur #9.
[56] Kanpur #32.

press or, in this instance, by the emotionally searing sight of a mosque being brought down by Hindu mobs to the cheers of several hundred thousand Hindus and in the presence of well-known political leaders, the police, and other armed forces, who did nothing to prevent the demolition. In fact, most administrative and police officers in Kanpur, who commented on the actions of the Muslim mobs in this first phase, attributed their actions to "resentment" at the events in Ayodhya.[57]

In the case of Kanpur, even most Muslim religious leaders and politicians acknowledge that it was the Muslims who came out first. However, the manner in which they present this "fact" and the feelings that inspired Muslims are stated rather differently by Muslim than by either Hindu or administrative respondents. A prominent Muslim cleric of the city put the matter with the most eloquence and feeling, saying that "when the Muslims discovered that the Babari mosque had been martyred, they were agitated and, in order to express the grief in their heart, they came on the streets."[58] Further justifications beyond their natural resentment over the destruction of the Babari Masjid were provided by the actions of the police and the administration. In conformity with numerous previous situations of this type in other times and places, the police and the PAC, it is alleged, responded with excessive force to control the Muslim mobs and that, specifically with respect to Kanpur, the administration in command at the beginning of the riot, both the District Magistrate and the SSP, were "of the Hindu mentality" and on the side of the "Hindu fundamentalists." Initial Muslim resentment, therefore, was now fueled by anger over police actions against them and over the perceived partiality of the district administration and police. The Muslims, therefore, "retaliated and they burned Hindu houses," "but this was a retaliatory action."[59] Although, therefore, this Muslim cleric acknowledges that Muslims were the first to come out in the streets, it is wrong to blame the Muslims for it, for reasons given in the quote below.

On the 6th of December in broad daylight, hordes of Hindus destroyed the mosque whereas the Supreme Court, the Constitution, the Government, even the BJP government were all committed to safeguard the mosque, and they destroyed not the mosque, they destroyed the Constitution of India. So did the Muslims destroy, did the Muslims take any initiative in destroying Hindu temples on the 6th of December? The initiative was taken by Hindus who destroyed the Muslim mosque.[60]

It is among Hindus, however, particularly militant Hindus, but more generally among the public and many administrative officers as well, that the

[57] E.g., Kanpur #9.
[58] Kanpur #2.
[59] Kanpur #2.
[60] Kanpur #2.

retaliation argument has become most common. Indeed, it is a fixed belief for the great majority of upper caste Hindus, reflecting not only their perceptions of riots but their perceptions of the very character of Muslims and Hindus as well, that it is always the Muslims who are aggressive, who come out in the streets first, who start the riots, who attack the Hindus first. When asked to explain the fact that, in virtually all riots in India in the post-Independence period, it is mostly Muslims who are killed, they say either that they are killed by the police who react to their riotous behavior or that they are killed by Hindus who retaliate against Muslim attacks, which is only natural. But it is something more than that for militant Hindu leaders and activists of the various political formations associated with the Sangh *parivar* ("family" of organizations linked to the RSS), who have through endless repetition created what amounts to a "big lie."

This "big lie" goes beyond imputing mere frenzied action to Muslim mobs, attributing to them deliberation, forethought, and conspiracy. BJP members will not allow that Muslim mobs came on the street only because of their emotional response to the destruction of the mosque. Rather, the news that really inspired them was that concerning the resignation of the BJP government and the dismissal of the Legislative Assembly. It was the declaration by the prime minister of India dismissing the Assembly that provided the signal to the Muslims to start the riot. Even the previous resignation of the BJP government was not sufficient to embolden the Muslims, for they might fear that the BJP government could be formed again under a new chief minister, which would take stern action against them if they started a riot. Until then, during seventeen months of BJP rule in UP when the BJP claims—against the truth—that there were no riots in the province,[61] the realization by Muslims that attempts on their part to start a riot would be dealt with severely had kept the communal peace in the state. However, once it was clear, with the dismissal of the Assembly, that the BJP government would not return to power, then the Muslims thought they could act with impunity.[62]

There is a consensus that another major event in the development of the Kanpur riot was also initiated by Muslims, namely, an attack upon Scheduled Castes living in a poor hamlet known as Pasiyana (populated mostly by low-caste Pasis) in a southern part of the city called Babu Purwa. A pitched battle between Scheduled Castes and Muslims then followed as the residents of Pasiyana were aided by crowds coming from an adjacent *basti* known as Khatikana (inhabited mostly by Khatiks, otherwise known as Sonkars, a low caste whose traditional occupation is tending pigs). How-

---

[61] Virtually all BJP respondents make this claim, ignoring the Banaras riots of November 1991.

[62] Kanpur #11.

ever, opinions on the significance to be attached to this battle differ somewhat.

Once again, the militant Hindu, BJP view of this incident presents the
Muslims in insidious, concerted, and even demonic roles. The picture presented by a prominent BJP politician from this area is that this locality is one
of so many where Hindus—not Scheduled Castes, but Hindus in general—
are surrounded by Muslims who, whenever they feel like it, plan attacks
upon them. This year, inspired by the dismissal of the UP Assembly, they
descended upon the Scheduled Caste *basti*s and committed inhuman atrocities upon the Hindus. They tied up two old persons, eighty to eighty-five
years of age, poured kerosene oil on them, and burned them to death. They
raped a young girl. They murdered many Scheduled Caste persons, surrounding them, throwing bombs at them, and then, when their victims
rushed into their houses for safety, threw chains around their houses so that
none could escape, then poured kerosene oil and petrol on their houses and
burned them to death.[63]

Out of this destruction and victimization of the Hindus in these Scheduled
Caste *basti*s, however, there emerged a hero whose actions will be discussed
in detail below, who rose up to defend the Hindu community against the
aggressive Muslims, whose name was Kala Bachcha. As we will see, accounts differ among Hindus concerning the precise nature of his heroism and
the acts for which he deserved the praise showered upon him. It is certain
only that whatever he did in the midst of the mayhem in Pasiyana and
Khatikana and afterwards in the more peripheral southern localities of the
city, even if "he may have killed some Muslims, but that would have been
in retaliation."[64]

It is also agreed that the second, most destructive and murderous phase of
the rioting occurred in the outlying southern areas of the city, where thousands of Hindus massed and killed many Muslims. Fifty of the sixty-nine
officially acknowledged deaths in the Kanpur riots of 1992 occurred in three
areas: thirteen at least in Babu Purwa, seventeen in Govind Nagar, and a
further twenty at least in Nau Basta, of whom the overwhelming majority
were Muslims. The uniform, overall BJP interpretation of the destruction
and killing in the southern part of the city is that it occurred as retaliation for
the Muslim attacks upon Hindus in other parts of the city, notably in response to the gruesome killings, rape, and arson in Pasiyana.[65] However,
according to one BJP respondent, the Hindu retaliation was not concerted,
organized, and planned but began rather as a "very panicky" reaction of fear

[63] Kanpur #11.
[64] Kanpur #33.
[65] Kanpur #11.

that the Muslims, having killed Hindus elsewhere, would do the same throughout the southern part of the city.[66] The Hindu station officer (SO) in the worst-stricken locality of the southern periphery of the city, Nau Basta, who was suspended after the riots, also supported the view that the Hindus here acted from fear that the Muslims would attack and kill the Hindus.[67]

Another view, however, from a Bajrang Dal respondent, suggested that the reaction, if not organized in the sense of being preplanned, definitely did not arise out of fear but out of a heightened morale among the Hindus, as indicated in the paraphrased statement below.

> RESPONDENT: All over the nation, riots are always started by Mus-lims, but the change that has taken place—and so it was in Kanpur this time—is that because of our high morale brought about by the good work done by the Bajrang Dal, the Hindus were able to react and to organize their reaction. The situation is that in Chaman Ganj, or areas like it, if there is only one percent Hindus in that area, then Muslims will kill half of them and loot their property. But, this time, especially in south Kanpur, the Hindus reacted to the initial attack which had materialized from the Muslims.[68]

There are further components to the BJP-RSS "big lie" concerning Hindu actions during communal riots, which draws upon "essentialist" images of Hindus. A BJP ex-minister commented upon the response of Hindus to the massing of Muslims in mixed Hindu–Muslim *mohalla*s such as Munshi Purwa and Babu Purwa, "where the Muslims . . . live in groups" and where they had organized themselves," "were offering resistance [presumably against the police]," and "were actually fighting." In these areas, where the Hindus also live in large numbers, the former minister remarked that "the Hindu community maintained its mental balance, . . . they did not lose their sense of balance. Otherwise, they, Muslims would all have been elimi-nated." Insofar as "this horrible incident . . . of the 9th [referring to the massacre of an entire Muslim family in Taj Nagar, which actually occurred on the 10th]" is concerned, by then "everyone was killing everyone." It was "uncontrolled [*anyantrit*] mobs," "who had totally ignored the administrative machinery, and the Hindu attack later on comes as a reaction to this."[69] Here is a fine example of the "Orientalist" image of the placid Hindu: always composed, mentally balanced, never on the offensive, observing calmly the rampaging mobs of "the other" community, and finally "reacting" only when the world itself has collapsed and Shiva dances.

[66] Kanpur #11.
[67] Kanpur #13.
[68] Kanpur #3.
[69] Kanpur #14.

Two Riots or One?

In the account above, I have adopted a description of the Kanpur riots provided to me by many respondents as divided into two distinct phases, the
first centered in the overwhelmingly Muslim areas of Chaman Ganj and
Begam Ganj, the second in the southern areas of the city. There are some
grounds for believing as well that these constituted two separate riots, the
first spontaneous, the second planned. However, we have seen that the predominant explanation of the spread of riotous behavior throughout large
parts of Kanpur is one of Muslim resentment upon hearing the news of the
destruction of the mosque, leading to atrocities against Hindus, followed by
Hindu reactions in the south based on resentment over the preceding Muslim
actions. There is also in most accounts an intervening phase of pitched battles between Muslim and Hindu mobs in the area of Babu Purwa, where
Hindus and Muslims are fairly evenly divided in numbers.

The term used over and over again to describe the Kanpur disturbances of
December 1992 is the Hindi word, *danga*. Only one respondent used the
word *kranti*, signifying in his mind a popular revolution. In English and
other Western languages, a larger number of terms are available to describe
such happenings as those in Kanpur. They include, of course, the term
"riot," which is identical to the term *danga*. There is also the Russian term
"pogrom," which has come to mean, in its contemporary English usage,
state-sponsored killings of members of an ethnic group, race, or religious
community in the *form* of a riotous assault by members of another, antagonistic group. When a riot or pogrom involves the systematic killing of large
numbers of defenseless people in a concentrated area, the term "massacre" is
sometimes used. On the other hand, many Black and white liberal political
activists and social scientists as well, seeking to label the rioting of Blacks
in northern cities in the United States in the late 1960s, preferred terms such
as insurrection and rebellion, which signified, like the use of the term *kranti*
in our case, more their sympathy with the rioters than a contribution to the
settlement of the issue of terminology.

None of these terms, nor indeed any single term, can satisfactorily capture, identify, and label an event so large in scale as the Kanpur disturbances, which I argue in fact is not a single event at all, but a multiplicity of
big and little events, occurring at numerous sites over a very large area.
Even the division of the Kanpur disturbances into two phases, such as has
been done above, constitutes a gross simplification of the events, though
we have seen there is some basis for it. The first phase, for example,
appears more like an unorganized riotous disturbance, the second more
like an organized, directed attack with some police complicity or indifference, for which the term "riot" is inappropriate. At the same time,
neither the term "pogrom" nor "massacre" seems adequate to encompass

all the events discussed here, which themselves represent only a selection of some of the major incidents that occurred between December 6 and 12 in Kanpur city.

One respondent, a Western-educated, analytical, and very articulate person expressed some of the problems in encompassing all these events with a single term. This respondent identified three distinct types of disturbances in Kanpur in December 1992, which can in no way be equated. These three situations can be summarized in the following graded terms: communally motivated destruction and murder by unequally matched crowds against isolated individuals and groups and their property and edifices; riots between equally matched forces; and pogroms or massacres of one group by another, in which the forces are unequally matched and the state authorities or agents are complicit through either motivated inaction or action. But our terms, however clearly or precisely defined, are themselves unequally matched to the events and their interpreters. The very events themselves are but particular acts in an ongoing struggle for power, in this case for power in the Indian state and society, which is a contest over the meaning of events, which in turn includes their labeling.

KALA BACHCHA: PORTRAIT OF A BJP HERO

We first heard the name of Kala Bachcha from a prominent Muslim religious leader of Kanpur who informed us that, in a locality known as Begam Purwa in the larger police station area of Babu Purwa, there lived a member of the municipal corporation by this name who "was instrumental in burning the houses of Muslims and also in destroying the mosque of Nau Basta."[70] At the Nau Basta mosque itself, we were told by a respondent that when the attack occurred, he and the Muslims at the site at the time could not recognize the persons in the attacking mob.

> RESPONDENT: They [persons in the crowd], they were not immediate neighbors because we could not recognize them. They were outsiders who came from the city and some of our local Hindu neighbors kept on saying that these are the men of Kala Bachcha, but we do not even recognize who Kala Bachcha is, so we are not able to say who these people were.[71]

We later learned that Kala Bachcha's name was mentioned in twenty-seven FIRs filed at the Babu Purwa and Nau Basta police stations as an accused in riot incidents in these areas, a record approached only by one other named accused, one Raghuvir Singh. Even where he was not physically present, it

[70] Kanpur #2.
[71] Kanpur #5.

was said that marauding mobs included his name in slogans as they did their dirty work, shouting "Kala Bachcha Zindabad" ("Long Live Kala Bachcha") along with anti-Muslim and pro-BJP slogans.[72]

Though he was, therefore, not alone in amassing a large number of accusations during the Kanpur riots, he was the best known and the most publicized person in the press. We were quite surprised, therefore, to find that opinions concerning his role in the riots, his whereabouts, and his actions were far from uniform. Several Muslims interviewed affirmed that Kala Bachcha had been directly responsible for many incidents of riot and murder of Muslims in the southern parts of Kanpur and downplayed his alleged role in saving Muslims in his own *basti*. On the other hand, for the BJP and militant Hindus generally, Kala Bachcha was not the principal villain of the Kanpur riots, but its bravest hero. Consequently, we mentioned his name to nearly every respondent interviewed after we first heard it and interviewed him personally as well.

We interviewed Kala Bachcha on July 20, 1993 on tape. He was then thirty-five years old. His true name was Munna Sonkar. The name "Kala Bachcha," literally "black boy" or "black child," became attached to him from his childhood when he lived with his maternal uncle, who called him, affectionately, by that name.[73] We were also told that since his family was in the piggery business and since pigs in India are mostly black and, "as a child he used to play among the pigs, so he came to be known as Kala Bachcha."[74] His parents, it is said, continued to use this name for him, which appeared in "his school certificate."[75] However, in a country where black skin, such as that of Kala Bachcha, is disdained, and where the term *kala* (black) also carries negative connotations of wickedness and fearfulness, the very name suggests a kind of negative notoriety.[76] On the other hand, it is a name sometimes used for the playful god, Krishna, who is painted at times in blue, at times in black, and for whom Kala is an alternative name.[77]

Kala Bachcha's true last name, Sonkar, is that of his caste, which is also known as Khatik, a Scheduled Caste. The predominance of Khatiks in this *basti* where Kala Bachcha lived is indicated by its name, Khatikana. Members of this caste engage in occupations considered by

---

[72] AN-50.

[73] Kanpur #8.

[74] Kanpur #37.

[75] Kanpur #32.

[76] As a relative of his put it, "his name being Kala Bacha, which is a little strange name, . . . some people used to feel strange about it," a disadvantage that had to be overcome in the early stages of his political career; Kanpur #30.

[77] See R. S. McGregor's *Oxford Hindi-English Dictionary*.

upper-caste Hindus as polluting, such as butchery and tending of pigs. Kala Bachcha himself had a piggery business at that time, comprising some two hundred animals. He was also the owner of a large, multistory building, in which some two hundred tenants were housed, in the front room of which we met him. He had little formal education, only up to fifth class. He began his political career by winning an election to the Kanpur Municipal Corporation as an independent candidate, but he soon joined the Congress party and then, being dissatisfied with the Congress, joined the BJP. He was not, therefore, an RSS member or an ideologically committed member of the BJP.

Though we knew little about Kala Bachcha's alleged activities when we met him, he was quite keen to establish certain points about them and concerning his whereabouts during the riot.

> PRB: . . . I heard that on 10th, a big *danga* broke out in Nau Basta, in South.
> KB: I know nothing about it.
> PRB: Do you know that going around, some people say that people were organized in trucks with the help of the PAC and the help of Kala Bachcha to go to Nau Basta and take revenge.
> KB: This is all wrong. . . . There was curfew all around and why would I have left my house? I didn't go anywhere.
> PRB: Why do you think such rumors would go around about you?
> KB: I'm linked up with the BJP and because the Muslims are against the BJP and I'm a political man, therefore they are out to malign me.
> PRB: Have you heard such stories? Do you know that such stories are going around about you?
> KB: Yes, I have heard about this and I have been named in various legal cases, my name has been given, I know this, but this is politically motivated and my name has been published in newspapers also in this context. But it is all politically motivated.
> PRB: But there are some legal cases against you?
> KB: Yes.
> PRB: Who has made these cases?
> KB: The Muslims have lodged the FIRs against me.
> PRB: In which *thana*?
> KB: Babu Purwa and Kidwai Nagar.
> PRB: And have you prepared a response? A written affidavit?
> KB: Not as yet. I have not replied to that as yet. . . . I had to bail myself out on the basis of these cases that are instituted against me.
> [. . .]

> I still have five or six Muslim tenants here in my building and, if you want, I can call them and they can testify that I had [not left] this place.
>
> PRB: No, I'm not any court here, just, I accept what you say, you seem like a very honest fellow, how can I dispute?
>
> KB: If you're interested, I can call these Muslims to testify whether I had taken part in any nefarious activity or whether I was here.
>
> PRB: After we finish, maybe.

At Kala Bachcha's insistence, at the end of the interview a Muslim tenant was brought down to meet us. The man came before us with a baby in his arms, appearing quite frightened with his eyes bulging. Before us, he was asked some pointed questions by Kala Bachcha concerning the latter's actions during the riots, whether he participated in them, and whether he harmed the Muslims. The Muslim man responded by saying, "No, you have not harmed Muslims, you were present [here] all the time." Moreover, he added that his children were hungry for forty-eight hours and he had the ration brought here and he called all the tenants, Muslims and Hindus, and the rations were distributed to all of them, and some money was also given to them for use in an emergency. The man further stated that Kala Bachcha stood on top of his building and declared to the mob down below that they had better leave his building intact, that he did not care if they killed people and people killed them, but no one was going to harm either Muslims or Hindus in his building.

Before the close of the interview, Kala Bachcha gave further testimonies to his innocence.

> KB: There are so many rumors about me all over and I think that, is this part of my destiny that people will talk like this about me, whereas I have done nothing but good for the people?
> [. . .]
>
> There are many . . . cases instituted against me in which they were showing me present in three places at 10:00 o'clock in the same time and, therefore, automatically, these cases were nullified, and, how could I be present in three places at one time? Do I have a helicopter that I could be physically present in three places at one time? And I do not have wings to fly either.

The sequence of Kala Bacha's alleged activities in the records in our possession is as given in table 7.3. We have complete or partial information on thirty-one incidents in which Kala Bachcha was named. Contrary to his statement to us, there is a remarkable consistency in the times and locations of virtually all incidents, a progression of movement from place to place in Babu Purwa and Nau Basta police stations, located in the southern and

TABLE 7.3

Site, Date, and Time of All Incidents in Which Kala Bachcha Was Named in FIRs, by Police Station, Kanpur City

Police Station	Date	Site	Time
Babu Purwa	7th	NA	9:00 A.M.
Babu Purwa	7th	130/335, Hata Mohan Lal Pasya	9:00 A.M.
Babu Purwa	7th	130/370, Khatikana	2:00 P.M.
Babu Purwa	7th	132/214, Babu Purwa	9:30 P.M.
Babu Purwa	8th	Bagahi Bhatta	5:00 P.M.
Babu Purwa	8th	130/008 B, Bagahi Bhatta	5:00 P.M.
Babu Purwa	8th	130/008 B, Bagahi Bhatta	Evening
Babu Purwa	8th	214/006, NLC Babu Purwa	6:00 P.M.
Babu Purwa	8th	145/009, NLC Babu Purwa	7:00 P.M.
Babu Purwa	8th	300/005, NLC Babu Purwa	9:30 P.M.
Babu Purwa	8th	300/012, NLC Babu Purwa	NA
Babu Purwa	9th	Bakar Ganj Bazaar opp. Temple	NA
Babu Purwa	9th	65/001, NLC Babu Purwa	NA
Babu Purwa	9th	253/005, Babu Purwa	11:00 A.M.
Babu Purwa	9th	347/003, NLC Babu Purwa	4:00 P.M.
Babu Purwa	9th	Hata Shastriji	6:00 P.M.
Babu Purwa	9th	130/006, Bagahi Bhatta	7:00 P.M.
Babu Purwa	9th	130/006, Bagahi Bhatta	7:00 P.M.
Babu Purwa	9th	130/006 A, Bagahi Bhatta	7:00 P.M.
Babu Purwa	9th	175/004, Babupurwa Colony	6:00 P.M.
Babu Purwa	9th	179/005, Babupurwa Colony	7:30 P.M.
Babu Purwa	9th	130/394, Khatikana	8:00 P.M.
Babu Purwa	9th	130/394, Khatikana	8:00 P.M.
Babu Purwa	9th	130/172, Bagahi, Vijay ka Hata	Night
Babu Purwa	9th	130/172, Hata Vijay Singh	NA
Babu Purwa	9th	130/172 A, Bagahi, Vijay ka Hata	Night
Babu Purwa	9th	213/002, NLC Babu Purwa	Night
Babu Purwa	9th	213/006, NLC Babu Purwa	Night
Nau Basta	9th	224, EWS, Sector 10 Duplex, Barra-2	NA
Nau Basta	10th	027, Chaman Nagar	3:00 P.M.
Nau Basta	10th	043, Chaman Nagar	4:00 P.M.

southern peripheral areas of Kanpur, which would not require a helicopter to enact. This progression by no means establishes Kala Bachcha's presence at these sites, but the progresssion is sufficiently plausible that, if there was any attempt to frame him, rather than imagining fanciful charges against him, one would have instead to suppose a rather large conspiracy among complainants to present such a consistent sequence of FIRs in these two police stations. It should also be noted that all but three of these incidents were recorded in Babu Purwa police station, Kala Bachcha's home area, where it could be expected that his name and face would have been known to at least some of the complainants. Insofar as the incidents in Nau Basta are concerned, an officer attached to that police station at the time asserted that neither Kala Bachcha nor any other outsiders came to Nau Basta and other areas in the southern periphery where Hindus started the riots.[78]

The charges against Kala Bachcha notwithstanding, all BJP respondents interviewed presented his activities between the 6th and 10th of December 1992 in a much more favorable light. One BJP respondent said that Kala Bachcha appeared first on the scene of the riots in response to the atrocities committed by the rampaging Muslim mob that entered Pasiyana, allegedly burning alive two old persons, raping and murdering a young girl, and murdering many Harijans by setting fire to their houses and then preventing their escape from the flames. Kala Bachcha, it is said, then rushed to the scene from his residence in the adjacent *mohalla* of Khatikana, resisted bravely the onslaught of the Muslim mob, and finally succeeded in stopping its violence by a particularly dramatic act. As it happened, according to his account, he was the owner of a multistory building, by far the largest in this slum, which he used partly for rental purposes. Several of his tenants were Muslims. In order to stop the violent Muslim mob, he brought forth three or four old Muslims from his building and announced to the mob that they were under his protection, but that, if they did not protect Hindus in their area or if they murdered any Hindus or burned any Hindu houses, then he would also kill the Muslims under his protection. According to the MLA, "this threatening" had a "very good impact," as a consequence of which the riotous Muslim mob stopped their activity.[79]

> RESPONDENT: I was not present in the city [during the riots], . . .
> Kala Bachcha was present. Bravely he resisted, he was the only
> person who could resist, who could threaten people that, you see, if
> you don't stop that action, I also will start against these persons
> whom I am keeping under my security. Then, not to speak of secu-
> rity, I shall see that same action [will be] taken against them also.
> His . . . threatening created pressure on them [the Muslim rioters]
> and then, under that pressure, they slowly and slowly cooled . . .
> down.

Further questioning of this MLA and other BJP respondents concerning Kala Bachcha's alleged riotous and murderous activities outside his home area of Khatikana elicited accounts that elevated Kala Bachcha's actions, giving them, and him personally, heroic quality. To every such respondent,

[78] Kanpur #13.
[79] Kanpur #11.

we asked essentially the same question, which ran more or less consistently as follows: "We have also heard about Kala Bachcha, whom you mentioned, that not only did he keep Muslims in Khatikana as hostages to prevent attacks on Hindus, but he also organized gangs to come to the southern parts of the city to attack the Muslims." Every BJP respondent, including Kala Bachcha himself, vigorously denied this allegation, but the differences in their accounts were quite breathtaking.

The first story we heard from a person other than Kala Bachcha himself, from a BJP MLA just cited, was that Kala Bachcha could not have "come out of his own area" because he had harmed himself in a heroic act of rescuing an eighteen- or nineteen-year-old girl from the roof of a burning building set on fire by some "Muslim people." In this rescue, Kala Bachcha rushed to the roof, picked up the girl, and then had to jump from the roof because the stairs were blocked by fire.[80] As a consequence of his brave action, he broke both his legs, which had to be put in plaster. We were informed by this MLA on July 21, 1993, that his legs had remained in plaster until quite recently and that even up to that date, he was not able to move about easily. When we asked if he was still unable to walk, we were told that his plaster had been removed, but that massage therapy was continuing. We did not mention to him that we had seen Kala Bachcha the previous day and that, on the completion of our interview with him, we had observed him moving about quite nimbly to a *pan* (betel leaf) shop. His general disposition on the day of the interview, that is to say, the free movement of his legs and his nimbleness afterwards suggested to us in retrospect that, if the plaster had indeed been recently removed, his recovery was quite complete by July 20, 1993.[81]

In contrast to the BJP accounts, one Muslim politician in Kanpur, who claimed intimate and detailed knowledge of the riot events in December, insisted that Kala Bachcha "was very much active physically" at that time. He asserted that there were twenty-seven cases against him, including thirteen murders. I reported that I had heard a different story, which led to the following exchange.

> PRB: They all say he never left his place in . . . Pasiyana, where we met.
> RESPONDENT: Ah, yes, Pasiyana.
> PRB: . . . that he never left that place. They all say he never left that place.
> RESPONDENT: He forced some of his Muslim tenants to file affidavit in favor of him, so long they were there.
> PRB: Yah, I have seen those Muslim tenants.

[80] Kanpur #11.
[81] Note from Kanpur #11.

> RESPONDENT: The moment they could, they could come out of
> their house, his house, they were, they could collect their courage
> to speak the truth, and he was very much involved, physically in-
> volved in killing and arson.
>
> PRB: But did he appear in Nau Basta in 9th–10th?
>
> RESPONDENT: Many places he appeared.
>
> PRB: With crowds behind him?
>
> RESPONDENT: Yes, yes. . . . In a motorcycle, he was there. He
> was leading the youngster[s] in motorcycle.[82]

It was not only Muslims, however, who alleged that Kala Bachcha had
played a destructive and murderous role in these riots. A former non-Mus-
lim, non-BJP MP, actively involved in monitoring the riot events as they
happened, mentioned his name spontaneously along with the names of several other Hindu municipal corporators who allegedly played a similar role.
However, this person found the case of Kala Bachcha in a special class for
reasons given in the statement below.

> RESPONDENT: Kala Bachcha thing is very interesting because he's
> got lots of Muslim tenants also, and he saw to it that nothing hap-
> pened to them. So, he was able to create this whole thing that, you
> know, he was protecting Muslims. And a lot of Hindus came and
> took shelter on his roof and all that. So, he was, had this thing. But
> he was very much involved in the rioting.
>
> PRB: But how do you know?
>
> RESPONDENT: Because I was able to go there and find out, and [be-
> cause] I know what type of person he is, so and so.
>
> PRB: But I mean, were there any reports coming . . . , during those
> days, that Kala Bachcha was out on his motorcycle?
>
> RESPONDENT: Not a motorcycle, in his car which has got a, he had
> put a, that revolving light, you know.
>
> PRB: *Achcha.* Oh yes, as if he is a policeman, uh?
>
> RESPONDENT: Yah.
>
> PRB: So reports came in that he was moving about?
>
> RESPONDENT: Yah, from the 7th itself.

This respondent gave no credence to the idea that Kala Bachcha protected
Muslims, insisting rather that he used the presence of his Muslim tenants,
"that whole situation very intelligently to his own advantage." This respondent remarked that his tenants were, in effect, "like hostages." When I reported that Kala Bachcha had brought one of his tenants down to me to tell
me how he protected him, the respondent remarked that "he did that, . . . he
did that with the military also. When I sent the military there to get those

---

[82] Kanpur #16.

people out, he got them to say [that], because he kept their children with
him . . . and he told them to say that they didn't want to go."[83]

Nevertheless, a very articulate defense of Kala Bachcha's actions during
the riots was made by a relation of his interviewed on June 19, 1994, some
months after his death.

> RESPONDENT: He brought a large number of . . . people into this
> building [where we were then sitting during the interview], which
> has seventy rooms and which, at that time, was inhabited by fifty
> Muslims. The register of that time would give evidence on this. So,
> Kala Bachcha brought a large number of people into this building
> to give them shelter and he was managing the riot situation because
> the police had not yet arrived in full force.
>
> PRB: He brought a large number of Hindus or Muslims or both?
>
> RESPONDENT: Both, both, Hindus and Muslims. . . . In that riot
> situation, there were Muslims who had been brought to this build-
> ing, but they had left some of their relatives behind in different
> places and no one was willing to go back, return back to those
> areas to bring the relatives back and the police was looking for
> someone to come with them and here was this man [Kala Bachcha],
> who said that I will come along, accompany the police to bring
> these people into this building. And he accompanied the police,
> these people were brought into the building, but there were so
> many of them that they could not all be accommodated. So, he ac-
> tually had tents pitched and telephoned to the BJP leaders that there
> are so many people and they have to be fed. So, these leaders came
> along with funds and support and a whole community kitchen was
> organized to feed these large numbers of victims, riot victims who
> had taken shelter.[84]

Despite the nobility of Kala Bachcha's actions, there was nevertheless
suspicion about them and charges were made against him, concerning which
his relation had the following remarks to make.

> RESPONDENT: On the 9th of December, . . . a Muslim major of the
> Indian army, the military, came around in this locality asking where
> is Kala Bachcha, asking for Kala Bachcha. And he mounted a
> search for him. Kala Bachcha was in one of the houses close by
> and he was on a staircase. When he found that a search was being
> mounted for him, he jumped from the staircase and hurt both his
> legs and, therefore, he became immobilized. He was unable to ac-
> tively move around.

[83] Kanpur #29.
[84] Kanpur #13.

PRB: *Achcha.*

RESPONDENT: On the 10th of December, almost three kilometers
away from here, in outlying areas, there was a riot situation in
which houses were burned and people were killed and this went on
for two to three days. But Kala Bachcha, who was lying immobilized because of the hurt in his legs, read in the newspapers[85] that
it was being said that either Kala Bachcha or his men were responsible for the arson and the riot in these outlying areas, whereas he
was actually hurt and he was immobilized, he could not have
moved around. But, after the curfew was lifted and the time came
to lodge the FIRs because compensation was to be given to riot victims, so a large number of people wanted to lodge FIRs. So, it was
found that they all named Kala Bachcha and his men as the key
culprit responsible for the riots of the outlying areas, whereas he
was actually lying immobilized because of the hurt in his legs.
[. . .]

PRB: . . . When he damaged his legs, his legs had to be put in cast
or he was only, uh, a sprain or what?

RESPONDENT: No, no, plaster was necessary. . . . When his legs
were hurt, they had to be encased in plaster. Both the legs had to
be encased in plaster.

PRB: And for how long the legs were in plaster?

RESPONDENT: Initially, *kachcha* plaster was put on his legs for two
or three days because this riot situation was such that proper plaster
could not be put at that time. But then, after a few days, then a
pakka plaster, the final plaster was put on his legs, actually for four
weeks. But he had this removed after two weeks and went to Lucknow and consulted some senior doctor there who once again put his
legs in plaster. So, this is how it was.

PRB: And, uh, were his legs broken or his ankle was broken, what
was it?

RESPONDENT: There was a fracture, the heelbones had been fractured. He could not stand or sit on his two legs and even he had to
be lifted in a chair to go to the bathroom.

PRB: And when was the cast finally removed?

RESPONDENT: In small stages, but the plaster continued to be on
his legs for three months and he used to get the plaster removed
and then again, the pain will increase, so he will get the plaster
done again, but all told for about three months.

PRB: And then afterwards, he continued to have some difficulty with
his feet or he was perfectly recovered?

---

[85] I did not ask how Kala Bachcha got newspapers during the curfew.

RESPONDENT: The trouble, the pain and the trouble in the legs persisted, kept on persisting until the end. It was not finally cured.

PRB: Until the end of his life?

RESPONDENT: Yes.

PRB: And did he have some limp or . . . ?

RESPONDENT: Yes, yes. . . . There was a limp until the end. Also if he would walk for a couple of hours, then the legs would get swollen and some kind of medicine would be applied . . . to remove the swelling, but this condition persisted until he died.[86]

LEADERS, CROWDS, AND POPULAR MENTALITIES

How, in the midst of all these conflicting testimonies concerning the activities of Kala Bachcha, does an impartial observer find a place to stand, to speak the truth about one person's activities and about the relevance of the activities of such a person to the development of a riot? It must be borne in mind that there was more than one Kala Bachcha in the Kanpur riots. We have already mentioned the name of Raghuvir Singh, against whom even more cases were instituted, some thirty-six, than against Kala Bachcha and whose name was associated with one of the most destructive and murderous assaults during this riot, the razing to the ground of the poor colony inhabited mostly by Muslims known as Vijay ka Ahata. There is also one Chhedi named in twenty-nine incidents, Chunna in twenty-one, Ashok Chawalwala in fifteen, Girish Chakki Wala in nine, Sarwan in eight, Anoo Chaiwala in four, and numerous others in one, two, or three incidents. Who are these people, what do they do when they are not allegedly looting, burning, and killing in riots? What is the difference between them and Kala Bachcha, whose activities were widely publicized, whose picture appeared in the newspapers, who was proclaimed a hero and rewarded for his activities by a political party, the BJP, to which he owed only a tenuous and recent allegiance? And what is the relationship between these persons and the more powerful and respectable leaders of known political parties, on the one hand, and the popular actions and resentments that allegedly sustain the small groups and large crowds that gather behind them? I take up the latter question in this section, but reserve a discussion of the former until we have occasion to examine further below the relationship between Kala Bachcha and the "family" of militant Hindu organizations operating in Kanpur.

In the literature and comment on riots and pogroms the world over in the past century, there is a broad division between those who argue that these large events are planned or engineered from behind by powerful forces, including the state itself either directly or indirectly through its agents, the

---

[86] Kanpur #30.

police and the civil administration. On the other side are those who see such events as manifestations of popular mentalities, built-up resentments that are expressed in popular actions that may even approach the scale and intensity at times of insurrection, rebellion, and revolution. Both these positions are well represented in India. Nor is there a perfect correspondence on this matter between the position adopted and the general points of view and ideological perspectives of particular political parties or the state authorities.

It is true that since Independence, whenever large-scale riots have occurred in India, the secular state authorities have tended to attribute them to preplanning by known organizations, which have been banned several times since Independence for longer or shorter periods after their occurrence. The prime target has always been the RSS and related militant Hindu organizations. Since the Indian state has claimed to be secular, however, it never bans the RSS alone, but always bans one or two Muslim organizations at the same time, the favorite being the Jamiat-i-Islami, an allegedly Muslim communal or "fundamentalist" organization. This coupling, however, is one example among many of the insincerity or hypocrisy of the actions of the state leaders after major riots. The Jamiat-i-Islami is a pathetically small and ineffective organization of orthodox Muslims in India, in no way comparable in size, effectiveness, and sway among Muslims such as the RSS has had among large segments of the Hindu population. To equate the two and automatically ban this organization every time the RSS is banned serves a double purpose. It displaces blame from the state and the ruling party for failing to prevent riots and it panders to Hindu public opinion by demonstrating an alleged even-handedness, which is not even-handed at all because it involves in effect blaming the victims equally, the Muslims and one of their organizations, for riots and pogroms in which mostly Muslims are killed.

Prominent persons and parties on the Left have tended to share the Congress view that Hindu–Muslim riots are preplanned, but they tend to blame the militant Hindu organizations more than the Muslim organizations, while nevertheless censuring Muslim "communal elements" as well. Some Left organizations at times and others consistently, notably the Communist Party of India (Marxist), have refused to form political alliances or to make electoral adjustments with the BJP because of its propagation of Hindu communalism, anti-Muslim propaganda, and Hindu–Muslim riots.

The RSS and the BJP, for their part, have also adopted the view that riots are planned and engineered, but they blame the Muslims and their organizations and the Congress, which has been the ruling party since Independence, for pandering to the Muslims, appeasing them, allowing Muslim criminals and communal elements and organizations to organize them freely for the sake of getting the Muslim votes in elections. They have insisted that if the state acts firmly against known riotous elements and groups, there will be no riots. They declared there would be none once they came to power, and they claimed—against the truth, as we noted above—that there were none under their state governments when they did come to power. The BJP charge is somewhat different from the sort made by the Congress governments at the head of the Indian state during the long post-Independence period of Congress hegemony, for the BJP is less specific about particular organizations that are alleged to plan riots. They rather tend to refer more vaguely to the Muslims in general, to criminal and communal elements, and to specific persons.

All these positions are, however, nothing but posturing. They fail to examine the actual dynamics of riots and pogroms or even the roles of particular individuals, where they come from, how they become prominent, how they act with impunity and escape prosecution or even become heroes, how they relate in practice to other persons, to particular organizations, groups, and political parties, and to the state. When all or almost all known organizations and groups are posturing without examining what is actually happening, even ignoring the conclusions of their own inquiry commissions or suppressing the reports of those—in recent years nearly all—which present a picture not to their liking, then one must presume they are all themselves somehow implicated. However, it is not my argument that all are equally implicated in the same way. Some are directly implicated in fomenting riots and in protecting the rioters after the facts. Those who are not so directly implicated—with the possible exception of a few organizations such as the CPM in Bengal—are indirectly implicated by the very hypocrisy of their talk and action in relation to riots.

In comparison with the politicians and the political leaders, those in charge of the civil and police administration and the local police as well, much maligned and often justly maligned for their own incompetence and complicity, often nevertheless have a more precise understanding of the precipitants of riots and of the local forces behind them and implicated in them. Moreover, the competent administrators are able to demonstrate their knowledge of riot dynamics and the persons and groups who foment and participate in them by preventing their outbreak at moments of high tension and bringing them to a quick and forceful end when they do break out.

Even among the civil and police administration, however, there are profound differences in interpreting riotous events on the scale of the Kanpur riots of December 1992. In our interviews, two police officers with experience of the Kanpur riots took the view that these riots involved popular action, expression of popular resentments on both sides, and even popular revolution on the Hindu side. Although the testimony of one of these officers is suspect because it seemed to reveal an identification with the actions of the Hindu rioters, that of the second reflected no such sentiments. This officer, who believes that any crowd of rioters, no matter in how many thousands or even hundreds of thousands they may gather and no matter their religion or politics, can and should be dispersed by police bullets, argued that the Kanpur riot was a popular action, played down the roles of specific people such as Kala Bachcha, and argued that the course of this riot did not suggest planning or engineering.[87] Let us leave this question aside a bit while we consider the short further existence of Kala Bachcha and the events that followed his death, after which some further comments on this topic will be made.

THE REWARD OF A HERO

It was obvious to us at the time of our initial interviews with BJP people in Kanpur after the December 1992 riots that Kala Bachcha would be rewarded for his role with a ticket (nomination) to contest a legislative assembly seat in the next state election scheduled for November 1993. Since he was a Scheduled Caste man, however, political exigencies left only two seats for which he might be considered: one constituency in Kanpur city reserved for Scheduled Castes, but already held by the BJP, and a second, a mostly rural, reserved seat on the outskirts of Kanpur, known as Bilhaur. It was the latter constituency that was allotted to Kala Bachcha.

Although Kala Bachcha failed to win the Bilhaur Legislative Assembly seat, he came within a few hundred votes of doing so.

Dead Certain: The Killing of Kala Bachcha

At 11:30 on the morning of February 9, 1994,[88] while traveling on a scooter with his relation, Ravi Sonkar, not far from his house at a crossing known as Pasiyana Tiraha, Kala Bachcha was attacked by a body of men, who threw primitive bombs at him, as a result of which he was thrown to the ground.[89] His assassins, wishing to leave Kala Bachcha certainly dead, threw "more bombs" at him, one of which hit his head, "blowing his brains out."[90] "Irate mobs" in the neighborhood reacted immediately, setting fire to homes and shops in the area and, as by chance the car of a minister in the state government happened to be passing nearby, attacking and injuring the minister and persons from his retinue, who had to be rescued from the enraged mob. Two

---

[87] Kanpur #28.

[88] Most of the references in this section come from local newspaper articles, some of them very kindly provided to me in Kanpur by Mr. S. P. Mehra. Unfortunately, in several cases, the name of the newspaper has not been noted on the clipping. In such cases, the reference is given as *Unknown*.

[89] *Unknown*, February 11, 1994.

[90] *Pioneer*, February 10, 1994. The same paper later noted in a report on the use of bombs in Kanpur that Kala Bachcha's "head was completely blown off" (April 13, 1994). This kind of reporting needs to be seen as a form of titillation, common enough in the Western press as well.

local persons were killed in this initial mob response, described in the press as "communal violence." The press further commented as follows.

Infuriated by the ghastly killing, hundreds of BJP workers and irate citizens of the area went berserk. Among those to be hurt in the mob frenzy was the Minister of State for Revenue, Mr Baburam Yadav. The minister, Mr Yadav, was on his way to Mainpuri from the state capital, and was completely caught unawares by the strong mob, which included BJP and Bajrang Dal and VHP workers, who had collected near the mortuary where Kala Bachcha's body had been taken for the post-mortem examination.[91]

The police and the district administration reportedly responded instantly to the situation, the former by rushing to the scene to control the mob, while the district administration imposed a curfew on the Babu Purwa police station area and ordered "all schools and colleges in the city" closed.[92]

This initial report on the killing of Kala Bachcha is a fine example of how misleading media reporting of such events can be, for the impression conveyed is that a spontaneous outburst of popular rage followed immediately after the killing. An astute reader may wonder how it happened that so many BJP, VHP, and Bajrang Dal leaders gathered so quickly after the killing and would then note that this assemblage of persons from militant Hindu organizations took place at the mortuary. Not until the next day, when one newspaper published an hour-by-hour account would it become clear that, in fact, several hours elapsed between the killing and the mob action during which "hundreds of BJP workers and irate citizens of the area went berserk." This berserk crowd knew very well that the car they had attacked was that of a minister of the state government and, while they grabbed and beat him, they shouted slogans against the state government and its chief minister, Mulayam Singh Yadav. Moreover, the crowd that gathered was at some unspecified point joined by several of the most prominent BJP leaders of the city, including three MLAs, two MPs, and the principal leader of the Bajrang Dal.

This same newspaper, which opened its story with the words, "Communal violence . . . erupted in Kanpur," noted later in the same report that, in Babu Purwa itself, where the killing occurred, in the Khatikana-Pasiyana area familiar to us from the events of December 1992, it was "mobs of Khatiks, the community to which Kala Bachcha belonged, [which] went on a rampage," attacking Muslim houses, shops, and persons "because of the rumour that Kala Bachcha had been killed by Muslims." Toward the end of this report, it is also noted that the District Magistrate, Mr. Kapil Deo, denied that the "incidents" were "communal," although he was reported to

[91] Ibid.
[92] Ibid.

have said that "some people were certainly trying to give it a communal colour." He added further that Kala Bachcha was a criminal and several cases were pending against him. The newspaper, however, had earlier in the same article referred to Kala Bachcha as "a BJP corporator, [who] had earned popularity during the 1993 December riots when he had organised several relief camps in Babupurwa and had provided food and shelter to hundreds of Hindus who were trapped in the Muslim-dominated areas. Kala Bachcha, who had a criminal background also, was named in the riots [*sic*] cases also, but was absolved of the charges by the police after investigations."[93]

It appeared to the district administration that the killing of Kala Bachcha and the reactions, organized and unorganized, which followed upon it had serious riot potential. Despite the prompt arrival of the police on the scene and the equally prompt removal of the body to the mortuary, crowds in the area around the killing, which was the same area from which the riot spread in December 1992, were engaged in looting, burning, and slaughter. At 1:00 P.M., it was reported, "a woman and a man" were "burnt alive." As in December also, incidents of violence occurred later in areas such as Kidwai Nagar, where shops were burned and the police had to open fire to control the mob. Incidents were being reported from other localities in Babu Purwa into the evening, including a stabbing and "bomb explosions."[94]

The district administration, wishing to take no chances of a repetition of the events of December 1992, called out the army the next day, which deployed promptly "in eight communally sensitive areas where clashes broke out" the day before and held a "flag march" in several of them. By then, four persons had been killed. Curfew was later extended to all areas of the city where incidents had occurred in December 1992 and all schools and colleges were kept closed for several days.[95] In the meantime, the district administration, which had allegedly promised to hand over the body for the last rites to the BJP, had the body of Kala Bachcha taken for cremation secretly in the early hours of the morning of February 11. Although the administration claimed the cremation was done with his family members present, BJP leaders protested at the secrecy involved and "alleged that none of the relatives of the deceased was allowed to go to the cremation spot." In protest against this administrative action, most of the important BJP leaders in the city staged a demonstration at the residence of the District Magistrate upon which they and approximately "100 persons" were arrested and taken to jail. The police also arrested the immediate family members of Kala Bachcha, who were detained for a day.[96] The former BJP chief min-

---

[93] Ibid.
[94] *Unknown*, February 11, 1994.
[95] *Times of India*, February 11, 1994.
[96] Ibid. and *Unknown*, February 12, 1994.

ister and other important state and national leaders of the party also expressed their interest in the murder and announced their intention to come to the city.[97]

Despite the curfew and the deployment of overwhelming force in Kanpur city, consisting of "six columns of the army, nine companies of PAC, four of the rapid action force (RAF) and nine of the CRPF" in addition to "the local police,"[98] "stray incidents" of arson and shooting were reported even "in curfew-bound areas" for several days following Kala Bachcha's murder. The areas from which such incidents were reported are again ones familiar to us from the December 1992 riots, Babu Purwa and Begam Purwa, though stray incidents were reported from other parts of the city as well.[99] In some cases, the reported incidents were a secondary reaction to the arrest of the BJP leaders rather than a continuing "spontaneous" expression of rage against the killing of Kala Bachcha.[100]

In fact, the BJP leadership sought to convert the occasion into a symbolic confrontation between them and the police, but to direct public hostility toward the state government.[101] By the 12th, some 353 people "had been arrested" for curfew violations and other acts.[102] The number increased to 443 by the 13th.[103] By noon of the 11th, the district administration felt sufficiently confident to allow some relaxation in "curfew restrictions."[104] However, the press continued to report the presence of "tension and mistrust" throughout the city as well as further incidents of violence, attacks of Hindus upon Muslims, as late as February 15.[105] The police, for their part, continued to discount communal motivations in the killing of Kala Bachcha, emphasizing instead the possible involvement of his own relations and the motivation of a dispute over land.[106]

Insofar as the alleged killers of Kala Bachcha were concerned, the administration announced the arrest of one of them, a man by the name of Nihal Ahmed, a Muslim.[107] A second arrest was reported the next day, of a man whose name was given as Imran, also a Muslim name.[108] Despite the fact that the arrested suspects were both Muslims, the "district authorities," in a press interview, "said that it was too early to say that the killing was [a

---

[97] *Times of India*, February 13, 1994.

[98] Ibid.

[99] *Unknown*, February 12, 1994 and *Times of India*, February 13, 1994.

[100] *Unknown*, February 12, 1994.

[101] *Times of India*, February 14, 1994.

[102] Ibid., February 13, 1994.

[103] Ibid., February 14, 1994.

[104] *Unknown*, February 12, 1994.

[105] *Pioneer*, February 16, 1994.

[106] Ibid.

[107] *Times of India*, February, 11, 1994.

[108] *Unknown*, February 12, 1994 and *Times of India*, Feburary 13, 1994.

result of] communal enmity" and "did not rule out" that it might have been a consequence of "enmity and gang war."[109] For their part, the BJP leaders criticized the police for "victimising BJP workers" and "arresting BJP leaders" instead of "Kala Bachcha's assassins."[110]

The state government also entered the picture at this stage when a minister accused the BJP of politicizing a "minor crime" and seeking to exploit "the killing of Kala Bachcha, a history sheeter [person with a criminal record], by giving a communal tinge to the case."[111] Precautions were also taken in communally sensitive districts in western UP, far from Kanpur, to assure that there would be no "fallout" in such places as a consequence of the violence in Kanpur.[112]

The killing of Kala Bachcha also became an occasion for leaders of all the principal political parties in the state to make some comment. Spokesmen for the opposition Congress used the incident to support its claim that the state government was unable to control "an unending spate of violent incidents in different parts of the state." CPI and CPM spokesmen charged the BJP with deliberately "fanning" and "encouraging caste and communal violence in the state." The principal exchanges took place between the BJP leaders and spokesmen for the state government. The president of the state BJP was reported to have "said that Mr. Kala Bachcha [had] become an eyesore for people of one community [a reference to Muslims] after he saved a large number of people from wrath of rioteers [sic] last year. A number of fake cases had been registered against Mr. Bachcha during the riots on the basis of which he was being termed a criminal." On the contrary, however, "Mr. Bachcha's neighbours considered him their guardian and not a criminal."[113] The previous BJP chief minister of the state, Mr. Kalyan Singh, gave his opinion that ISI (Inter-Services Intelligence) of Pakistan was behind the killing.[114]

The SP leaders, however, charged the BJP with "unnecessarily politicising the murder of Kala Bachcha" for the purposes of creating instability in the state, said that "Kala Bachcha was a criminal who was involved in umpteen cases of murder, loot, arson and rape," and suggested that his murder was a consequence of personal enmity against him by persons who had been victimized by Kala Bachcha previously, including his relations.[115]

However, the press reported a fundamental difference on the matter of motivation between the local police and an investigative team from the Cen-

---

[109] *Times of India*, February, 11, 1994.
[110] *Unknown*, February 11, 1994.
[111] *Times of India*, February 11, 1994.
[112] Ibid.
[113] *Unknown*, February 11, 1994.
[114] *Unknown*, February 16, 1994.
[115] *Unknown*, February 16, 1994.

tral Bureau of Investigation (CB) and the Criminal Investigation Department (CID) of the state government. The city police continued to insist that the murder of Kala Bachcha was a "routine crime," whereas the CB-CID team characterized it as a communal matter. The city police considered Kala Bachcha "a hardcore criminal who got eliminated at the hands of his rivals," while the external investigative team linked his murder to Kala Bachcha's role during the December 1992 riots and the charges against him of having "organised killings of the Muslims." The city police alleged that not only was the incident not linked to the previous communal riots, but that the person behind his murder was one Ramesh Khatik, that is to say, a person from his own caste, who had "incited five Muslims to eliminate Kala Bachcha." The press report, however, treated the police claim as "a bid to underplay the incident." The CB-CID team claimed that it was unlikely that Ramesh Khatik was "involved in the murder." Their report, as revealed to the press, was said to make the following claim.

> The murder of Kala Bachcha was conspired by a section of communal elements, who were waiting for an opportunity to settle scores. Those involved in the murder, were directly or indirectly victims of '92 violence and had made up their mind against Kala Bachcha since the violence broke out in '92 in Babupurwa.[116]

It should be evident from the newspaper accounts cited above that riot and near-riot events such as those surrounding the killing of Kala Bachcha cannot be separated from the representations of them once the media and external, that is to say, nonlocal persons, agencies, and institutions become involved in them. Representation in this case began with the first line of the first press report, "communal violence . . . erupted," and flowed into hidden interpretive reporting masked as a statement of the facts. "Irate mobs" gathered and crowds went "berserk." In other words, the spontaneous feelings of the people erupted uncontrollably. The nearly immediate arrival of large numbers of BJP workers followed by virtually the entire leadership of the party and the rest of the RSS family of organizations in the city was noted, but treated as part of the natural, emotional response. Although other press reports in the following days took note of alternative interpretations of the killing, they retained throughout a bias in the direction of reporting the matter as a communal one and an extension of the events of December 1992, universally acknowledged—though not necessarily correctly so—as communal.

It is equally noteworthy that the police, for their part, consistently underplayed the communal character of the killing. They and the district authorities insisted throughout that it would be inappropriate to jump to premature

[116] *Unknown*, February [n.d.], 1994.

conclusions on the matter, taking the position in effect that it should be treated as a criminal act and a routine one at that until evidence was provided of other motivations or a larger conspiracy. While the press reported the interpretations of the police, they did so with obvious incredulity.

Nor can the accounts of either the press or the police be taken at face value, for both have a stake in the proper representation of the situation. Aside from the obvious commercial advantages of sensationalizing and expanding local criminal events into something larger, individual reporters and the newspaper editors and owners for whom they work often have communal biases and prejudices. Even if they do not have evident communal biases, they have a bias in the direction of interpreting such events through the filter of the discourse of Hindu–Muslim communalism. Some may believe communal conspiracies need to be made public to expose the culprits from one of the communities. Others may feel they are doing a valuable service by pointing out the evil communal forces at work in the city, exposing them to view. However, since motivations usually cannot be discerned with certainty, it is best in such circumstances to concentrate on the effects. The effects of press reporting on the killing of Kala Bachcha were, plainly and simply, to blame the Muslims as a community for the killing of a person with a known criminal record and an ugly and notorious record in the December 1992 riots, portrayed predominantly as a "hero" rather than as a criminal and a killer.

Police and administrative motivations are also suspect. There is no question that the administration feared a serious riot in the aftermath of the killing and took measures to prevent one. Immediate, firm police and administrative actions were taken, including rushing to the scene, imposing curfew, and rapidly deploying overwhelming forces. Though they feared a riot, they insisted throughout on playing down the communal implications of the killing. It is natural to speculate that the police were dissembling, perhaps even concocting a case and implicating at least one Hindu in it, to demonstrate the noncommunal, criminal, and routine character of the case. However, in personal interviews four to six months after the event, both the police and administrative authorities held to their view. As one senior administrative officer put it to us, the killing of Kala Bachcha was "70 to 80 percent criminal, the rest communal" or, put in another way, "the motive of the killing was not communal though a Muslim did the killing."[117] As with the press, what matters most are not the motives but the effects of police actions, which were to localize the incident and probably thereby prevent its transformation into something bigger, a communal riot in which much property would be damaged and many lives would be lost.

It is most interesting in this context that the CB-CID team entered the

[117] Kanpur #37.

scene with a report contradicting that of the police, enlarging it into a communal event. I do not have the necessary information to explain this divergence, which went against the policy of the local administration, the police, and the state government. It is, however, to be noted that this unpublished report reached the press somehow and was used in news articles to contradict the accounts given by the local police and administration and the state government.

The actions of the BJP leaders and workers and those of other members of the RSS "family" of organizations were quite prominent in these events. It is a matter of very considerable interest also that their presence and actions on this occasion were much more prominently and precisely presented than anything these same persons and organizations did during the December 1992 riots. On this occasion, at any rate, it is important to note the immediate and continuing involvement of these persons and organizations in the events that transpired in the aftermath of the killing and their failed attempt to take charge of the situation.

It should be noted first that, whatever doubts to the contrary exist in people's minds in India or abroad, the immediate response and political involvement of the BJP and related organizations demonstrate without a shadow of doubt that there is a BJP-RSS network that gets activated immediately in such situations, including especially those with riot potential. That does not necessarily mean, however, that in this or any other specific situation, the network is activated for the purpose of fomenting a riot. Different assessments of the BJP-RSS motivations in this situation are plausible. Their leaders may have wanted to precipitate a riot or simply to keep communal fires alive or merely to embarrass the government controlled by their principal opponents, the SP and its strong and hostile chief minister, Mulayam Singh Yadav.

Whatever their motivations, however, the effects of BJP-RSS actions are clear. It is a game of brinkmanship. Note in this regard that the leaders desired a funeral procession, a provocative ritual, which all know could lead to a riot, though the purpose might have been merely mobilizational, to rally the Hindus and to display themselves at the head of Hindu popular sentiment. It is, however, doubtful that these leaders actually wanted to precipitate a riot. The very fact that they put themselves in the forefront suggests the contrary. Would they place themselves in such a position if they actually wanted to create a riot for which they would then be evidently to blame?

On the contrary, it appears more logical to assume that the BJP-RSS leaders wanted to keep tempers smoldering and to use them for the purpose of embarrassing the government. For this purpose, their presence was required. Their presence, especially that of members of the state Legislative Assembly and the national Parliament in both of which arenas they were representing themselves as the primary opposition and the government-in-waiting, transformed the killing of a local politician with a criminal record and an otherwise notorious past into something more than a local event. It expanded into a statewide party political issue between them and the state government in an effort to challenge the latter's leadership, competence, and ability to control communal violence, on which they claim to have a better record.

A final question is suggested by the newspaper accounts of the events following the aftermath of the killing of Kala Bachcha, namely, did the fast, firm police and administrative measures and the military deployment prevent a communal riot in Kanpur in February 1994? Is there, therefore, something to be learned from this situation about how to prevent a communal riot? Or, on the contrary, should the events of February 1994 be classed as a "small" riot, in which, by the way, four people were killed in addition to Kala Bachcha?

On what basis do we class events such as those in February 1994 as riots, especially as "communal riots"? Hardly anyone doubts that the events of December 1992 were communal riots, both because of their association with the feelings surrounding the demolition of the mosque at Ayodhya on the part of both Muslims and Hindus and because of the scale of the events and the pattern of targeting of victims. If one compares the scale of events of February 1994 with those of December 1992, and the lack of agreement concerning the communal nature of the precipitating incident, then the former might not be classified as a "communal riot," though it is difficult to see some of the crowd actions thereafter as something other than some kind of riot.

Administrative and Police Action in the Aftermath
of the Killing of Kala Bachcha

The family of Kala Bachcha nursed a grievance against the police administration for its actions after the riot in three respects: for their alleged initial failure to arrest the killers, for their handling of the cremation and last rites of Kala Bachcha, and for their alleged harsh treatment of members of the family.

Insofar as the actual killers are concerned, a police officer of the Babu Purwa police station had a list of six suspects, of whom five were Muslim residents of Begam Purwa and one, Ramesh Khatik, was a Sonkar and a resident of Khatikana. The police theory concerning the murder connected the killing of Kala Bachcha to the riots of December 1992, but did *not* connect it with communal hostilities, as indicated in the quotation below.

RESPONDENT: The murderers are actually among these [six] people and the background is that the number one person of the list, that is, Bhai Jan *urf* [alias] Ikram, he and Kala Bachcha were living next to each other near C.O.D. gate number 6 and during the riots of '92, Kala Bachcha had caused considerable damage to the house of Bhai Jan and also misbehaved with the womenfolk of the house. And, therefore, he nursed a grudge against him. Now, after that, there was also a situation in which Ramesh Khatik of Khatikana, who was also a neighbor of Kala Bachcha, was also for reasons of property dispute, he was against Kala Bachcha, and the other people, four people in this group, are hardened criminals whose occupation is to throw bombs and to engage themselves in criminal activities. So, Bhai Jan and Ramesh Khatik got together and formed a network with these hardened criminals and together they are the ones who did the job.

PRB: So, you mean to say it is not a communal question, it is a question of dispute between two Khatiks and these Muslim criminals have been brought in?

RESPONDENT: That is correct. I do not think it was a communal situation at all, but because Kala Bachcha had done considerable work in the Khatik community and he had a very good hold over these people, therefore it is but natural that when he was murdered, there was an upsurge of the Khatiks and upsurge in his constituency.

PRB: . . . there [were] no Muslim terrorists or organization behind them or ISI or any such thing.

RESPONDENT: Absolutely not. . . . [It was a] local, local-level [thing].[118]

The police and the district administrative authorities gave precise information also on the specifics of the quarrels between Kala Bachcha, on the one hand, and Ramesh Khatik and Bhai Jan, on the other. With respect to Ramesh Khatik, it was said he had cheated him out of Rs. 135,000 in a property purchase deal. Insofar as Bhai Jan is concerned, it was said he raped his sister. Therefore, the evidence in the view of the police and the administration was that the killing of Kala Bachcha was a revenge killing on a man who was not only a "criminal type," but a "thief" as well who made money by stealing "whatever unclaimed pigs were roaming around" to sell in Lucknow fifty miles away. It is hard to imagine a sharper contrast to the BJP portrait of Kala Bachcha as a hero and martyr than the police characterization of him as a murderer, rapist, cheat, and pig-thief.[119]

This police account, minimizing the communal aspects of the killing of Kala Bachcha, was disputed by BJP leaders interviewed on the matter. One ex-BJP MLA, a member also of the Bajrang Dal, who was prominent

[118] Kanpur #31.
[119] Kanpur #37.

among the BJP leaders who protested the killing of Kala Bachcha and the police handling of the funeral, saw the killing as an organized Muslim plot and attached responsibility to the government also for failing to protect Kala Bachcha when he had asked for such protection. He argued further that the government was actually "involved" in his killing because they knew that he could be killed, they failed to protect him, and they came out with an announcement immediately after his death that Kala Bachcha was nothing but a criminal. As for the police account that the killing of Kala Bachcha was actually just some local fracas between people in Khatikana over property, he insisted "that was a story made by the government," which was interested only in branding Kala Bachcha as a criminal. Finally, this respondent was irked by the action of the district administration in removing the body during the night after having agreed to give the "dead body to the parents of Kala Bachcha" and to allow the funeral procession to originate from the BJP party office. He noted further that he and other BJP leaders protested as well that Kala Bachcha's "mother and his wife . . . were beaten badly by the police" when they resisted the removal of the body during the night.[120]

Similar accounts were given by other BJP respondents. One MP said he had no doubt that Kala Bachcha's murder was planned because of his role in the December 1992 riots. This respondent even allowed that the murder might have had something to do with the possibility that Kala Bachcha "might have killed a few Muslims" during that riot. He, too, was angry with the district administration who, he said, had violated an agreement made in the presence not only of the local BJP leaders, but of the former BJP chief minister, Kalyan Singh, and the president of the state BJP, who came to Kanpur on this occasion, that "the body of Kala Bachcha . . . would be brought to the BJP office, from where a procession would accompany the last journey."[121]

No more evident authentication of the seriousness with which the administration viewed the situation during this night can be given than the fact that the army was called out as a precautionary measure at around the same time the body was removed for cremation. But the administrative-police measures went much further. Curfew was imposed over large parts of the city and, in the words of an additional city magistrate on duty at the time, was "very strictly imposed." Extensive "patrolling and *lathi*-charges were used to enforce the curfew." PAC pickets were placed at all especially "sensitive places." The circle officers and inspectors "were patrolling day and night" and many of the police and administrative officers "could not sleep for many days." Because of "the strict enforcement of curfew, there was no further violent episode" after the initial killings and house burnings that took place

---

[120] Kanpur #32.
[121] Kanpur #33.

immediately after the murder, although some thought that as many as 1,500 people might "get killed after Kala Bachcha's murder" in a general conflagration.[122]

Insofar as the role of the BJP and its sister organizations is concerned, it appears from our interviews that the press accurately reported their public activities. Moreover, the conclusion reached above that the BJP did not seek to precipitate a communal riot in Kanpur, but sought political advantage from the circumstances surrounding Kala Bachcha's murder, is also upheld. The BJP statements only provide further clarification of the methods and the rhetoric used to achieve their ends.

It is obvious from their actions and rhetoric that the BJP neither sought a repeat of the conflagration of December 1992 nor a genuine confrontation with the police and the administration. On the contrary, the BJP leaders were not out to condemn the district administration and the police, but to blame "the Muslims" and the state government. Although they criticized the local police and administration for *lathi*-charging Hindus instead of punishing "the Muslims," for failing to arrest the real criminals, and for violating an agreement to hand the body of Kala Bachcha over to them, they transferred the blame to the state government, arguing that the local police and administration were under pressure from the state government and its chief minister to take a pro-Muslim stance in order to gain political advantage from the situation.

The BJP-Bajrang Dal rhetoric emphasized violation of Hindu traditions, customs, and values, whose preservation they consider their special province, and Muslim culpability in the murder. Acting on the orders of the state government led by a chief minister who had already, in their view, shown himself to be anti-Hindu and pro-Muslim in practice—especially during his previous tenure in office, when his police fired upon and killed Hindus seeking to destroy the Babari Masjid in Ayodhya in 1990—the local police and administration violated the caste sensibilities of the family and the Sonkar community by having the body burned at a *ghat* set aside for another Hindu group. Further, they violated "the Hindu *shastras*" by having the body cremated at a prohibited hour. Finally, in the most outrageous act of all, they violated all decency and propriety by beating the bereaved family members who protested the removal of the body.

The BJP leaders also expressed no doubt concerning the identity of the killers, their motives, and the preplanned character of the killing. No effort at serious reasoning was indulged. The killing was a Muslim plot, supported by a pro-Muslim state government. The ISI of Pakistan might have been

---

[122] Kanpur #37.

involved, but the actions were carried out by local Muslim criminal and fundamentalist elements. It should be noted that none of the BJP or Bajrang Dal persons interviewed specified any Muslim organization by name nor could they provide a name of any known, prominent Muslim of the town whom they considered to be complicit. Indeed, they seemed to lack even the most elementary knowledge of the names of important Muslim political and religious leaders, even in their own constituencies. They seemed capable only of referring to Muslims as "the Muslims" or with the oft-repeated labels "criminals" and "fundamentalists," which strangely enough often merged in their speech into almost a combined category.

The principal BJP grievance, however, was the unwillingness of the local administration to cooperate in their efforts to magnify the murder of Kala Bachcha into a grand political event from which they could profit. They saw no impropriety in their own efforts to take over from the bereaved family the rituals pertaining to the last rites of Kala Bachcha by having the body brought to the party office, garlanded and honored there, then taken in procession to the burning *ghat* with, no doubt, a huge crowd in train. They say they had no intention or desire to precipitate a communal riot, which I believe to be true. However, in effect, what they wished to achieve was to make the local police and the local administration secure the peace while they transformed the event into a major political victory. Moreover, with a large police force securing their route and the Muslim population unlikely to be seeking a confrontation in such a situation, they could be sure there would be no violence. In effect, they sought to use the police and administration for their own political purposes and to provide a demonstration that would simultaneously cow the Muslim population of the city.

When the administration refused to cooperate with the BJP plans, the BJP leaders sought no direct confrontation with the authorities. Rather, they took the maximum political advantage they could from the situation without loss of face by staging a peaceful *dharna* at the residence of the District Magistrate and there courting arrest. In this way, they attained without risk to themselves the symbolic virtue of resistance and their removal from a scene from which they could gain no further advantage without seeking a violent confrontation through crowd mobilization in which they would be directly implicated.

There remains yet a further point in the presumed BJP calculus of political advantage and the true direction of their political attack. It was not only a question of Hindu–Muslim relations or of exploitation of anti-Muslim sentiment for the sake of consolidating Hindu support behind the party. It was also part of a broader assault on the political coalition that led to their defeat in the 1993 state legislative assembly elections and brought to power as chief minister of the state their nemesis, Mulayam Singh Yadav. The winning coalition in those elections comprised backward castes, particularly

Yadavs, Scheduled Castes, and Muslims. The Yadav and Muslim votes are beyond the reach of the BJP, but they seek to win support from other backward castes and Scheduled Castes.

The district authorities themselves saw the BJP action after the murder of Kala Bachcha in this context. They noted "that since the SP-BSP government came to power," there had been conflicts in different parts of the state between Yadavs and Scheduled Castes. Whether "organized or spontaneous," their purpose was "to tarnish the image of the party in power." The BJP was further "trying to create some incidents to take political advantage" of conflicts between Scheduled Castes and Muslims. Kala Bachcha was a person from a Scheduled Caste "killed by Muslims." Whether there had "been connivance of family members also in this killing" did not matter.

> The BJP decided to take advantage of the situation. So many leaders came here to say that . . . we have simply come because we have to come. There were also three MPs who came from Delhi. They first came to me and they wanted complete security. They visited the place during ten o'clock at night. They said to me, "You have done very nice, by not handing over body. There would have been riots." Then they went to Kala Bachcha's family and said, "Even Bhagat Singh's . . . and Chandrashekar's [heroes and martyrs of the Indian Independence struggle] bodies, were not handed over by the British police to the relatives, and the . . . bodies of martyrs, [are] not handed over to the family members. That is why, that is how they become martyrs."[123]

In effect, the authorities were saying that the BJP was playing a double-faced game: acting out a political role to gain maximum political advantage from the murder of Kala Bachcha by treating him as a fallen hero and martyr and urging the family members to cooperate with them to insure his proper elevation to that position, while making it clear to the district administration that they sought neither a riot nor a confrontation with the police over it.[124]

Why Was There No Riot in Kanpur in February 1994? Or Was There?

Most of the senior administrative personnel, journalists, and many politicians in Kanpur considered that the city remained in a high state of communal tension after the termination of the December 1992 riots. Newspapers ran articles from time to time referring to the continuing tension in Kanpur and calling the city a "powder keg" and a "tinder box" ready to blow at any moment. Some confidently predicted the outbreak of another riot in the near future. Perhaps for this reason, Mr. Kapil Deo, sent to Kanpur to save the situation on February 11, 1992, was kept on in the city thereafter and, when

[123] Kanpur #37.
[124] Kanpur #37.

time came for his promotion, was retained in the city as commissioner of the entire administrative division of which Kanpur is a part.

No more opportune or critical an occasion for another riot to erupt could have been provided than the killing of Kala Bachcha on February 9, 1994, in the very area where his heroic actions had provided the pivotal point in the development of the 1992 riots. Moreover, Kala Bachcha's killing was reported fully in the local and national press, more fully in fact than his actions in 1992, when there were so many other riot events occurring throughout the northern and western parts of the country, particularly in Bombay, to receive top billing in the press. Further, as we have seen above, the BJP made every effort to transform his death into a martyrdom, to generate a public display of grief, to organize demonstrations and processions. Finally, there was in fact some riotous behavior on the part of Hindus in the locality, who attacked and killed three Muslims and burned their houses, providing the necessary spark for a Muslim reaction. Yet nothing of the sort occurred from the Muslim side, though stern action was required to prevent further riotous activity on the part of Hindu supporters of Kala Bachcha and the BJP. Why was there no reaction from Muslims? And why was the Hindu reaction so easily constrained?

I put these questions to two respondents, one a prominent local Muslim politician, the other a non-Congress, non-BJP former MP. In the Muslim respondent's view of the matter, there were three reasons why there was no communal riot after the murder of Kala Bachcha: the victim was not an important person, for whom public sympathy could be aroused beyond his local area; Hindus, even those who were "sympathizers and supporters" of the BJP, did not agree it was "a political murder"; and the administration acted firmly to suppress "the trouble shooters" (*sic*) who set out to inflame the situation. Further, it is implied in this respondent's statement that the BJP leadership did sit down together and plan a strategy to capitalize on the situation following the killing, but that their purpose was to "make the issue [a] state-level issue." Several elements of this interpretation are contained as well in a much more elaborate explanation of the postmurder developments by our second respondent.

> RESPONDENT: . . . everybody says why didn't rioting break out.
> PRB: Yah, that's the obvious question.
> RESPONDENT: So that is the obvious question, so I think there are three or four very important things. One is that when the new government came [headed by Mulayam Singh Yadav after the defeat of the BJP in the 1993 legislative assembly elections], then, as a result, Muslims feel much less threatened, much less alienated than they were feeling when there was a BJP government. And so even though what happened was that immediately after Kala Bachcha's

killing, innocent Muslims in the neighborhood were attacked and killed, and their homes were burned . . . and looted, but there was no widespread Muslim reaction to this. [. . .]

So the fact is that there was no reaction, no Muslim reaction to these killings, and to this arson in any of the other Muslim areas. Had that happened, then you couldn't have avoided rioting, at least some rioting. If, supposing in La Touche Road there had been a reaction or if there had been a reaction in that Bekan Ganj-Chaman Ganj area [heavily populated by Muslims], but there was absolutely none because I happened to be in Bekan Ganj when the news of Kala Bachcha's death came and immediately after that there was also the news that some Muslims have been attacked, there was no . . . reaction, no crowds forming, everybody was just trying to keep very cool and just hoping . . . *kuch na hoto achcha, kuch, kuch na hoto achcha* [it's good if there's nothing, if there's nothing it's good].

PRB: So why do you think there was no reaction from the Muslims?

RESPONDENT: Because, . . . as I said, they feel that this is to some extent . . . their government or they feel, it's not that this is their government, this is a government that's not against them, and they don't feel so alienated, they don't feel so threatened. So, therefore, they don't react. . . . They hope that the government will react, that the police will react, and that the administration will react. This is a very, I think, one very important factor. [. . .]

The second thing is that the administration is of a different type also. And the police officers immediately went and forcibly took away the body.

PRB: So no procession.

RESPONDENT: And they didn't allow crowds to collect there. I mean there was, the CO there [circle officer, Babu Purwa police station] was also very, very alert and active, and he himself is a Scheduled Caste man. . . . And he was pretty tough. [. . .]

So he was there and he had been very tough in that area, you know, regularly, there'd been marked improvement, so his presence there, he knew exactly where, what should be done, and the body was taken away, and then . . . his criminal history and, in that sense, he was not . . . a big political leader, he'd become notorious. [. . .]

So there was no . . . feeling for him, I mean nobody in the city thought of him as a public figure. . . . He didn't have that kind of reputation and, uh, therefore, there was no great feeling of sympathy when he was killed. . . . Or there was no great feeling that a public leader had been lost. And the other thing is that, after the

December 6th riots and after the, you know, several bouts of curfew that we've had here, business has been so badly affected that
there was no great enthusiasm among the trading community for
*bandh*s [shop closings] and curfew and. . .

PRB: Amongst the Hindus?

RESPONDENT: Hindus I'm talking about. Everybody was just fed up
to here, had it up to here, you know. And, therefore, the BJP attempts at trying to whip up, you know, people's feelings and emotions became very transparent, you could see through it. And it was
no, they could no longer do what they'd done successfully in the
past, which is to create a certain situation, move away from it, and
then pretend that this is a public outcry or a public reaction or public sympathy, you know, they were there, well-known BJP leaders
and BJP personnel, with their identifiable [presence], and every
time there was a *dharna* or a procession or *satyagraha*, you know
that makes a lot of difference. One is that people feel, oh, this is a
people's thing, people's movement, it's not political party's activity. And the other, identifying something as the activity of a political party and, therefore, eyeing it with suspicion, and there's a
distance between people and this happening. And then again, in,
among general public also, the realizations are different, government has come, [and] it's going to get tough, you know, they
might get beaten up and might go to jail. [. . .]

So, all these things people could see were being engineered by certain political people. I'm not saying that they don't have their sympathies with these people. They have their sympathies with them.
They have their sympathies with Kala Bachcha even. But they
could not, there was no identification like there has been in the past
. . . with certain movements that they've been able to organize.
And then it became more like that. Then they went to the, after his
body was cremated, you know, early in the morning without the
BJP leaders being [informed] and all that, then they made a big
thing that, you know, Hindu sentiments were violated and all this
. . . and then they went and gave *dharna* and then they were sent
off to jail. And then it just petered out. So, it has a lot to do with
so many different things, it's got to do with the kind of people who
are in the administration, it's got to do with the change in government, it's got to do with people being tired of curfew, it's got to do
with their public perception of what Kala Bachcha was, their own
understanding that this was a political party which has lost the election trying to again, you know, all these things were generally part
of public perception, which all led to this thing not erupting. But I
think the major thing was that there was no Muslim reaction any-

where in the city. That would have immediately then made all these other things irrelevant.[125]

We have here a quite elaborate theory of the causes of riots and their prevention, which deserves to be spelled out systematically. The first element of the theory is that riots are produced by precipitating events, in this case the killing of a leader or prominent public person. One reaction then leads to another, generating a chain which, if not contained immediately, will lead to a major conflagration. In this case, the killing of Kala Bachcha did precipitate a reaction among Hindu sympathizers, who attacked "innocent Muslims in the neighborhood," killed a few persons, and burned and looted their homes. However, this first precipitating event did not produce a "widespread Muslim reaction." In effect, therefore, no second link was provided to the chain. This absence of a second stage of reaction, of course, contrasts markedly with explanations provided for the conflagration in December 1992, when Muslims reacted first to the demolition of the mosque, which was in turn followed by a Hindu reaction. It is also worth noting in this regard that the Muslims in this case demonstrated the mythical patience under provocation that the Hindus are alleged to display at all times in contrast to the Muslims, who, we have been told over and over again, always act aggressively in contrast to the peaceful Hindus, who react only after repeated provocations.

Why, then, did the Muslims not react? They felt a sense of trust in the state government and in the local authorities that the situation would be brought under control. Therefore, they felt "much less threatened." The second element in the theory, therefore, is that a combination of threats both from another group and from the state and the authorities is required or is at least contributory to the movement of a riot into the dynamics of a chain reaction. Presumably the second group moves into the streets to protect itself against further attacks because it fears the government and the authorities will not do so. Once this second stage is reached, produced by a lack of faith in the willingness of the government to provide justice and protection, then nothing can prevent "at least some rioting."

The third element in the theory is that the authorities, the administration and the police, do in fact act immediately and forcefully to remove the cause of the strong emotions, in this case the inciting presence of the dead body of Kala Bachcha to be taken out in a procession, a virtually universal precipitant of riots. Crowds were not allowed to collect. The police officer in charge of the affected area was known to be "tough."

Fourth, the precipitating emotional event lacked sufficient resonance to affect a wider population, in this case the general population. Despite the BJP efforts to make him a hero and a martyr, Kala Bachcha was generally

[125] Kanpur #29.

perceived as a criminal and there was, therefore, "no great feeling of sympathy when he was killed."

Fifth, although the press and many administrative officials had conveyed the impression that Kanpur was a "tinder box" ready to go up in flames at the least provocation, this respondent took an opposite view, namely, that businesspeople "had been so badly affected" during the previous riots that they would not respond to the demand to close their shutters and did not want to face another curfew and the attendant loss of business. Moreover, people in general had become "fed up" in the aftermath of the December 1992 riots. The implication of this argument from a theoretical perspective is that major riots do not follow upon each other at the same site, that there must be a breathing space between them for people to forget their inconveniences, to say the least.

Sixth, a rather subtle point, is that too deliberate an effort to create the conditions for a riot by an identifiable political party or organization such as the BJP, from which they stand to benefit, becomes "transparent." In this view, people do not want to be manipulated. In order, therefore, for a riot situation to develop, people must either be manipulated more cleverly from behind the scenes to produce "a public outcry" or the "public reaction or public sympathy" must itself be genuine. People must believe that they are participating in "a people's movement," not something directed by interested politicians. The Ayohdya movement gave that impression, but the killing of Kala Bachcha did not.

However, the people must also feel that the risks they take in rioting are not too great. If they feel that there is a strong chance they "might get beaten up and might go to jail," then their emotions will be tempered and a riot may not materialize. Thus, the third element in the theory, the strength of administrative and police action, comes in again as a powerful preventive even when the materials are otherwise present for a major "public reaction."

Finally, the theory comes back to the decisive importance of a second-stage reaction. If the Muslims had reacted after the initial Hindu reaction, nothing could have prevented a riot. What is left unclear here, however, is whether strong administrative action—after the first precipitating incident and the first reaction—is decisive or the sentiments and feelings of the second group are more important. Although the respondent makes the statement that, given a Muslim reaction, that would have "made all these other things irrelevant," her previous statements link the presence or absence of such a reaction to other factors. However systematic, therefore, the theory is circular.

Though it is circular, the theory conforms to much social science writing on the subject in India and elsewhere and does provide valuable insights into the dynamics of riot creation. The key variables in it are: a precipitating incident, whether or not it produces a reaction and a counterreaction, whether or not it is allowed to be dramatized through a procession or other significant ritual provocation, whether or not the authorities and police act firmly and decisively, and whether or not a widespread "public reaction" occurs spontaneously or can be generated through subtle action by *agents provocateurs*. The circularity, which makes prediction difficult and all attempts at causal theorizing on such large-scale events ultimately futile, is inherent in the dynamics of riots.

Moreover, since participants in riots are knowing actors who themselves are aware of how riots are produced or act intuitively as if they knew, the self-denying and self-fulfilling prophecies also come into play to prevent or precipitate riots. Reactions can be engineered when they would not otherwise occur. So can counterreactions. Stern and impartial administrative and police action are variables, not constants, as the theory itself recognizes. Higher authorities may want to prevent riots in particular areas, so they post "tough" officers to them, but they may also not care or even welcome riots in other areas, where incompetent or partial officers may be posted. Local politicians strive to curry favor, buy out, or otherwise control politically the station officers in riot-prone areas, who may then stand aside when a "reaction" to a provocation occurs in their area. And, of course, skilled *agents provocateurs* are master theorists and countertheorists, who may upset the most finely crafted theories concerning the causes and enlargement of riot situations. So are skilled administrators who know how to deal with such people, especially if they know who they are. In other words, such theories are part of the game, known to skilled practitioners on all sides in the schemes of brinkmanship that precede riots and near-riot situations.

Chapter 8

CONCLUSION

WE HAVE COME a long way from village Pachpera to the destruction of the mosque at Ayodhya and the communal riots in Kanpur that followed it. Were it not for the link between these two incidents in the roles played in both of them by BJP party men, one might dismiss any connection between them as another type of construction, in this case, that of the writer. However, it has been the purpose of this research from its outset to show that there is a logical link between events such as those in village Pachpera and how they are interpreted, on the one hand, and large-scale incidents of violence involving Hindus and Muslims and how they are interpreted, on the other hand. From the point of view of the design of this research and its elaboration over thirteen years, it was completely fortuitous that the destruction of the mosque at Ayodhya took place before this work could be completed and that Kalyan Singh had by then become the BJP chief minister of UP. It had all along been my intention to conclude the volume with an analysis of Hindu–Muslim riots in Aligarh and Meerut and to show how such riots have been precipitated by incidents as trivial and localized as those in village Pachpera and in the town of Daphnala. When the mosque was destroyed in Ayodhya and riots followed in Kanpur, a city that I have visited many times during the past thirty-four years, I decided to put aside the Aligarh and Meerut materials, to leave them for another book, and to conclude this volume with an analysis of the communal riots in Kanpur.

There is a problem, however, in substituting the Kanpur riots for those in Aligarh and Meerut and allowing the events in that city to stand in, as it were, for those that are precipitated by trivial incidents. In the case of Kanpur, the riot was preceded by a massive mobilization in north India of Hindu militants and Hindu faithful, by a communal political polarization between organizations claiming to represent the interests of both communities, by the involvement of all the political parties on one side or another on the issue of the status of the mosque, and by the vastly increased strength of the party of militant Hindu nationalism, the BJP, in cities such as Kanpur. Moreover, the Kanpur riots were not isolated events. They were part of a chain of riots that occurred in many cities and towns in northern and western India in the aftermath of, and in response to, the conditions created by the destruction of the mosque at Ayodhya. How, then, can the Kanpur riots be considered in any way comparable to those in Aligarh and Meerut in the years before the

Ayodhya movement or to an isolated event in the countryside to which nobody outside the area except this writer has drawn any attention?

Aside from the linkage represented by BJP personalities, there are two logical connections. The first concerns the realities and the rhetoric justifying the actions of the people, in both cases Hindus. The second concerns the process of communalization in general, the arduous and dangerous route deliberately pursued in Indian society from triviality to generality, from localization to nationalization, from faith to ideology.

In village Pachpera, Nihal Singh justified in terms of faith and sentiment the insistence of the villagers in retaining possession of an idol that the courts established had been stolen from the Jains of the nearby town. The villagers, he argued, had "found" the idol. Their discovery of it was seen as an act of God. They proceeded to worship it. Under the circumstances, it was outrageous for the police to have come during the night to take the idol, to beat the villagers while doing so, causing them to flee for their safety. The fact that the courts had determined that the idol was not theirs, that it had been stolen from the Jains years earlier, and that there were reasons to believe that some of the villagers had stolen it made no difference to Nihal Singh. The faith and sentiment of the people stood above all other considerations and could not in justice be overriden by any authority.

In Ayodhya, the same argument was used to justify the destruction of the mosque, namely, that the mass of the Hindu population assembled there was moved by faith and sentiment, by the belief that the mosque had been set upon a site holy to the god Ram, his birthplace, and that a temple to Ram had been destroyed by Muslim conquerors to build the mosque on that very site. The faith of the people had here also to be respected. In this case, quite opposite to the situation in village Pachpera and consistent with his own beliefs, Kalyan Singh, from the position of highest authority, refused to order what the courts had ordered and the police had done in Pachpera, namely, to enforce the law against a people presumed to be motivated by faith. It needs, of course, to be noted that the two situations, though alike in the minds of BJP leaders, were opposite in fact: In Pachpera, the villagers' retention of an idol that did not belong to them was justified while in Ayodhya the destruction of a mosque that did not belong to them was also justified. At the same time, there is yet another similarity in the BJP responses to the two incidents: The faith of the Jains and of the Muslims did not matter in either situation.

Does this mean, therefore, that the BJP responses in these two cases were hypocrital? I do not believe so. In 1983 I was personally impressed by the BJP leaders' sincerity and by his defense of the faith and sentiment of the villagers, though I also thought the villagers were in fact thieves. In 1992 I believe Kalyan Singh dissembled in creating the conditions that made possible the destruction of the mosque, but I believe he expressed his true feelings and that they are consistent with those expressed in 1983. What is troubling about the feelings of such BJP leaders and the way they act upon them is their partiality to their own community and their disregard for the feelings of other communities.

The link between these two events, therefore, goes beyond feelings to identity, beyond faith to ideology. By raising the issue of faith and sentiment in village Pachpera and confining his identification with the faith and sentiment of the people to those of his own community, the BJP leader also was engaged in a process of enlarging the meaning of the theft of an idol in what I believe was a battle among thieves over a desecrated object of monetary value. From a battle among thieves, the event became transformed in his mind to a defense of the faith and sentiment of Hindus. The BJP leader was a member of the RSS and had been immersed since his youth in the ideology of Hindu nationalism. That ideology raises the faith of the Hindus of India into a coherent whole and gives it a political meaning, transforming Hindus from a heterogeneous population of believers in a multiplicity of idols, some of them not even their "own," into a political body united by a few common beliefs, such as their alleged common faith in the godship of Ram and his birth in Ayodhya. In this way, the faith of the Hindus of India has become simplified, politicized, mobilized, and rendered transcendant, the ultimate value standing above the faiths of others and the laws of the land. This is a process of communalization of faith and politics, which is the decisive link between Theft of an Idol and the destruction of the mosque at Ayodhya.

AMBIGUITY AND THE ABSENCE
OF A CENTER AND OF A "TRUTH"

One of the most remarkable features of all the cases presented in this volume is the absence of a center or the existence, as it were, of a hole in the middle, as in the ending of *Foucault's Pendulum*.[1] It must be stressed once again that none of the cases discussed were chosen for their mysterious and ambiguous character. Indeed, I did not choose them. They happened to have

[1] Belbo, the hero and creator of a Plan wholly without substance or reality, becomes enmeshed in its design and ends hanged in midair, in nothingness, at the very center of the universe marked by Foucault's pendulum, from which he extends, merged with the Absolute. The narrator, witness to the bizarre and fateful events with which the story concludes, seeks to sort out "the incontestable facts," which he does with some difficulty and without real certainty. As in our stories from life, there are incontestable deaths and absences in Eco's story, and we search for a Plan whose existence will be revealed if only we can find enough "incontestable facts," which somehow elude us. Like and unlike the narrator, we can find no peace in the absence of a "real" Plan and a real Center, though "the certainty that there is nothing to understand" should provide "peace"; Umberto Eco, *Foucault's Pendulum*, trans. William Weaver (San Diego: Harcourt Brace Jovanovich, 1989), citations from pp. 617 and 640–41.

occurred in districts that I have visited repeatedly for the past thirty-four years. I was looking for incidents of violence and of police–public confrontations and Hindu–Muslim violence in particular, but I gave no other specifications to the informants who guided me to them or to the press that publicized them. Even the Narayanpur incident, which I knew to have occurred in one of "my" districts, was not consciously selected in the research design for this project. Strange as it may seem to those who know the diversity and extent of the north Indian plains, I just happened by the village of Narainpur in my tour of this district in October 1982, where I noticed some particularly fine-looking sheafs of paddy tied in bundles and lying in the fields. Having done some previous research on the politics of agriculture and having learned something about rice cultivation in the process, I stopped the jeep to inquire about the paddy. When I asked the name of the village, I was told it was Narayanpur whereupon, after completing my questions about the paddy, I asked about the famous incident that had occurred there two years before. Thus began, rather fortuitously, my decision to pursue further the "facts" about an already well-covered case.

But the "facts" about Narayanpur, the existence of a central core of truth, proved as elusive as in all the other cases, though in each case I confess to having indulged the compulsion to reach a decision in my mind. It is certainly known about Narayanpur that a bus accident occurred, that an old woman was killed, that an altercation between the villagers and the police occurred, and that the police ultimately descended upon the village and inflicted serious harm upon the villagers. There are, however, two unsolved mysteries here. The first concerns how the police could have dared under the political circumstances of the time to engage in the atrocities upon the villagers of which they were accused. I have given my own explanation in the text, namely, the desire for revenge, but this does not explain how such a desire could have been indulged with impunity. It does not explain how such a common incident as a traffic accident leading to a death became transformed into a major police assault on a village and its occupation as in warfare. But the second mystery, introduced by the prime minister's son and ultimately the prime minister, Mrs. Gandhi, concerns the extent of the atrocities. Was every man beaten and every woman raped? There is no doubt in my mind that men were beaten, but I have no idea whether any woman was raped. Nor do I believe that the authors of the report of the inquiry commission, which was never made public and which denies that any woman was raped, knew any better. A decision was made, however, by its authors, a truth was revealed, namely, that the police had not acted improperly and that the stories concerning atrocities had been grossly exaggerated. I do not believe this truth, nor do I believe its opposite.

Insofar as Kurman Purwa is concerned, we also know some basic facts, namely, that an altercation occurred between two groups of villagers in which the police ultimately intervened on the side of one group against the other. But we do not know what was at the center of this quarrel and why the police sided with one group, raided Kurman Purwa, and beat up its inhabitants, except again because they became angry and vengeful. But over what?

What is common to both cases, indeed, is the way the accounts about them, whether they are publicized or not, fail to reveal a central core of truth. Though our own investigations have not revealed a central core in each case, we have learned enough to note that there are hidden truths. The truths that are hidden in both these cases concern the everyday character of these events and the nature of the intimate connections among police, politicians, and criminals. A further hidden truth concerns the interest of those who proclaim their sympathy with the alleged victims of atrocities and their condemnation of those who perpetrate them or allow them to happen. That interest is simply and plainly, though it is hard for many to accept and believe, that nothing be done to disturb the positions of all who gain from the perpetuation of such incidents. It is sufficient that talk about them be allowed, that the press be allowed to publicize them when they choose to do so for professional reasons or when they are acting in the interests of particular political parties, that the politicians be allowed to publicize them or hide them, that inquiry commissions be appointed to report on them, that their reports then be made public or not be made public depending upon whether their findings will benefit the ruling party at the time, and so forth, all participating in a game whose ultimate end is obfuscation.

In two of our cases, the center is blatantly missing. In Theft of an Idol, the centerpiece is gone—or perhaps it is sitting still in the *thana*, though I very much doubt it. Nor is there any way of finding out. I have constructed my own account of what happened to the idol, which would, I hope, satisfy inveterate readers of mystery and detective stories. I believe there was, in fact, a double theft: the original theft by the villagers of the idol from the Jain temple and the second theft, which forms the subject of my text, of the idol from the village in a conspiracy among several of the persons who discovered the first theft when the idol was "found." But the idol is gone and the truth cannot be known.

Rape at Daphnala is by far the most mysterious of the incidents described. Here we do not know for sure if there was a rape or even if there was a girl. If there was a girl, was she a "real girl" or a transvestite? If she was a "real girl," was she a prostitute who ran from her pimp, or was she taken by four men against her will? Is she dead or alive? How could she have disappeared completely? Were the arrested men, the "toughs" beaten by the police, really the culprits if there was a criminal act? There are no sure answers to any of these questions.

If this incident is the most mysterious, it is also the most laughable. An old man, a pimp and a trickster, made fools of everyone involved, of all those who claim to know the truths in the countryside, from the District Magistrate down to the local constables, of the sincere old Gandhian who fell for the tears of a pimp, of the rabble-rousing BJP man, who had found an issue in this out-of-the-way town to rouse the sensibilities of any decent Hindu. But some of those who were made fools of had the last laughs, not against the old pimp, but against the crowd that gathered, whose heads were beaten by the police, and the rabble-rousers who were made to sit in jail for weeks as common prisoners without the usual courtesies and decent food and treatment normally provided to high-caste political prisoners.

Yet, with all the mystery, the trickery, and the absence of a central core of truth to these two incidents, we approach with them to the center of the storm of Hindu–Muslim communalism that has been raging off and on for the past century. Can there be any doubt that an incident of the type discussed in Theft of an Idol would have set off a conflagration had it involved Hindus and Muslims at some site sacred to one or both religions? In 1963, at the great Hazratbal Mosque in Srinagar, Kashmir, a hair of the prophet Mohammad was stolen from the reliquary. When news of the theft spread, riots occurred in Srinagar and other parts of India, in which many people lost their lives. Unlike the idol in our story, however, the prophet's hair was found and certified to be authentic by the keepers of the reliquary, though, of course, nonbelievers will have their doubts whether a virtuous lie was told by its finders and authenticators to prevent further rioting. Is it not noteworthy that a single hair, more minute than the proverbial needle, easily concealed in an envelope, could be found in the Indian haystack, but an idol at least two feet high and a young girl could not be found? The truth, the missing center, it seems, can be discovered when the authorities wish it or at least the missing center can be authenticated by known truth-tellers.

There is also little doubt that a rape or an alleged kidnapping by or an elopement of a Hindu girl with a Muslim boy or man or men is a common precipitant of communal tension in cities and towns in north India where Hindus and Muslims live side by side. In the countryside, the guilty persons, if found, will be killed, even beheaded in view of the entire village and the members of their family. In town and city, the Hindu girl is likely to be killed by members of her own family. In the meantime, as in Daphnala, the police may be faced with spreading rumors, the gathering of crowds, violent incidents, and the approach of a communal riot that will tax their resources to prevent. Local Hindu leaders will come forth, ostensibly to preserve the peace, demanding that the police find the rapists or kidnappers, while instigating the crowds through fiery speeches to demand, of course, justice! It matters not to them that there is no girl, that there was no rape, and that a kidnapping was probably a willing elopement.

But, you will say, "surely there was a reality, a center, and a truth to the great Kanpur riot of 1992. The mosque at Ayodhya was destroyed, the Muslims of Kanpur, like Muslims in Bombay and elsewhere in India, even in other countries of South Asia, reacted in rage and came on the streets, and known persons such as you have yourself identified, in the person of Kala Bachcha, were at the very center of the arson, destruction, and murders perpetrated there. You met him yourself and have formed a judgment." All this is correct, but the truth of Kala Bachcha has still not been told, has not been authenticated by known truth-tellers in Kanpur, by a court, by the District Magistrate, or by an inquiry commission. Moreover, I have told in my account only a small part of the story of Kanpur, which contains many more mysteries that I know of and many of which I know nothing. Furthermore, Kala Bachcha is dead. The center of my story has been removed. No one can now go and check my story and my judgment by talking to the man himself.

Further, the very center of my story is contested terrain. How can I truly say that Kala Bachcha was not a hero, that he did not break his legs, that he was not lying in plaster instead of roaming the city with his gangs, burning, destroying, and killing? Those who claim the opposite are political opponents of his party, the BJP. They have an interest in falsifying their and his claims. The District Magistrate and the local police do acknowledge that Kala Bachcha was a criminal, but none of them have claimed personal knowledge concerning his activities during the riots. Moreover, they acknowledge that he had established some sort of relief camps, that there were even a few Muslims under his care. Persons who say they are sure that Kala Bachcha roamed the streets leading gangs in destruction, looting, and murder disagree on whether he went on motorcycle or by car. None of this shakes my personal belief that Kala Bachcha was not in plaster, that he did not jump from a burning building to save a child or from a Muslim military officer seeking him out, that he was roaming about during the riots. The inconsistencies in the accounts given by those who sought to praise him are sufficient in my mind to condemn him and to condemn also his supporters and relations as liars. But I have no proof.

What we have, therefore, are beliefs, more or less justified, more or less fixed, subject to testing through logic and the logic of others who may detect flaws in our reasoning, on the one hand. On the other hand, more abstract, but more certainly, we have representations. We can chart the interpretations, the contextualizations, the discourses of, by, and about violence and communalism in India and the interests served by different representations of them, but we cannot certainly find the truth of events. It is a curious thing to have reached such a point, that the lies, the distortions, and the approximations to some truth have a greater reality—a verity that can be documented precisely—than the events themselves. It appears that our guide through such events as those described in this volume can only be Charles

Saunders Pierce, but not the methods of contemporary social science, many of whose practitioners continue to believe that there are certain truths to be found in a multiplicity of discrete events if only we can quantify and categorize precisely our cases. Nor can we take comfort that, if we are persistent enough, apply the appropriate methods of observation, testing, and reasoning, we will find our "way among the facts" to the the truth of an event, to that which "really is."[2] On the contrary, in describing unique events, we can arrive at most to a point where belief sets in, where our inquiry, having gone round repeatedly in circles, comes to a resting point where we say, "I find no other logical explanation for this event. I challenge you to find a better one and to provide evidence for it." At the same time, our resting point cannot be separate from our presumptions, from the discourse which controls our own thinking, which selects the inquiry, the object to be investigated, and constrains the findings as well.

But why bother to describe unique events such as those discussed in this volume? Would it not be better to confine ourselves to the search for limited generalizations based upon comparative studies of the largest number of cases, selected with suitable controls to limit variation? Does not the method used in this volume provide only anecdotal material of no scientific value? On the contrary, I believe that the method used here provides a basis for generalizations that would otherwise be hard to come by and reveals linkages that would not be found by comparative statistical methods or even by controlled case studies. I hope to point them out in the remainder of this conclusion.

CONTEXTUALIZATION AND REPRESENTATION

We can learn much even with our imperfect knowledge of events from the very representations of them and the contexts in which they are placed. For every contextualization and representation of an event or set of events serves the interests of some individuals, groups, and forces in society. Sometimes, the consistencies in accounts given by particular persons or groups may even cast light back on the event itself, especially if they appear to contradict particular interests.[3]

Consider once again the discourse of faith and sentiment and the interests served by those who proclaim its reality as the predominant source of motivation and explanation for the actions of the ordinary people of rural India.

[2] Moritz Schlick, "The Foundation of Knowledge," in A. J. Ayer, ed., *Logical Positivism* (Glencoe, Ill.: The Free Press, 1959), p. 226.

[3] For example, in Theft of an Idol, the consistency in the accounts of those who claimed the idol was of no value led me to believe the idol was in fact *ashtadhatu* and that most of those who said the opposite were in collusion.

While the acceptance of this line could have other political implications, in the current Indian political context it benefits the villagers in particular ways, but only superficially, while it benefits more substantially those political forces seeking to supplant the until recently dominant state-centered ideologies of rationalism and secularism. It benefits the villagers by portraying them as innocents, even childlike, unsullied by the baser motives that predominate in an economistic world, cherishers of idols, and, in one contemporary argument, tolerant of the faith and sentiments of other.[4] It disregards many anthropological accounts of villagers in India and all over the world as clever, distrustful of outsiders, prone to violence, oppressors of those beneath them in status, and manipulative. It provides a basis for them and for those who speak in their name to see them as victims of outside forces who seek to exploit them and to take their resources for their own purposes: economic development agencies that seek to have them change their agricultural practices to serve the needs of expanding urban populations, corrupt agents of the state who seek bribes from them for services that the state is supposed to provide free or at a fixed rate, and police who find a pretext in any criminal incident in a village to make money out of it by harassing, intimidating, or even beating and killing them.

In the three village cases discussed in this volume, we have seen how acceptance of the discourse of faith and sentiment may work to the advantage of the villagers. In Narayanpur, known locally for the rather tough character of some of its inhabitants, the innocence of the villagers was presumed from the moment reports of their harassment by the police reached the press until Mrs. Gandhi's arrival on the scene to comfort them. Similarly, in Kurman Purwa, but with much less success, interested politicians rushed to the scene on the presumption that innocent villagers had once again been victimized by a marauding police force. In village Pachpera, the evident efforts of the villagers to melt down a valuable idol that never belonged to them and to hold on to it and to its potential for profit to them by building a roadside temple were discounted and justified on the grounds of their belief in the idol's sanctity and its discovery as an act of God.

Yet ultimately, in all three cases, the villagers lost out. Their presumed faith and sentiments were disregarded by the local police, who beat them, or were exploited by politicians with grander purposes. Keeping in mind the general argument I have made above that such practices as these persist because all are implicated in them and their persistence is useful to all—police, criminals, and politicians alike, and the villagers themselves when they are not being beaten—then the evidence from these three cases, though

[4] See esp. Ashish Nandy, "The Politics of Secularism and the Recovery of Religious Tolerance," in Veena Das, ed., *Mirrors of Violence: Communities, Riots and Survivors in South Asia* (Delhi: Oxford University Press, 1990), pp. 69–93.

limited in number, suggests that there is little authentic belief on anyone's part, least of all the villagers, in the purity of their faith and the sanctity of their sentiments.

At the same time, I have stated my own view that Kalyan Singh sincerely believes what he says when he argues from within the discourse of faith and sentiment. Within the movement of which he is a part, consisting of the RSS, the BJP, and the VHP, who proclaim themselves the ultimate guardians of the faith of the Hindus and the sentiments of the majority population trampled upon by a secular state that has displayed its contempt for them, there are others like Kalyan Singh, still others who are deliberately and openly manipulative of those sentiments, and many more who do not separate in their own minds Hindu religious faith and militant Hindu political practice. On the one extreme is the leader of the BJP, Lal Krishna Advani, and his closest advisers who, before throwing themselves fully into the Ayodhya movement, openly talked about their political purposes as "playing the Hindu card" for electoral advantage. Of course, an easy response to the criticism that such tactics imply mere manipulation would be that the ultimate political victory of the BJP will insure the protection of true Hindu beliefs.

At the other extreme are those who sincerely and genuinely believe that the Ayodhya movement was sanctified by god and that the temple was destroyed not by a band of fanatics but by Hanuman himself, the monkey god and the messenger of Ram. Most RSS-men, however, are somewhere in the middle, believing in the faith and sentiments of the people, but also believing that Hindu faith needs to be simplified, universalized so as to be common for all Hindus, protected by the Indian state, and harnessed by a political movement that will capture the state on behalf of a consolidated Hindu-majority population. At this point, however, it is obvious that we are very far from respect for the variety of beliefs and practices of ordinary Hindus in the countryside, many of whom actually believe in the multiple ways in which divinities and demons manifest themselves in a world that remains enchanted.

Consider next the interrelated discourses of criminality, law and order, and police brutality. Statements made under these headings are the self-justifying language of the state and the wielders of its powers. There are no crimes outside the state—though there are commandments not to violate the laws of god—nor any police either. Statements made within this discourse which, we have seen, blame either criminalized elements among the people, the politicians, or the police for riotous and violent events, all accept the overriding authority, legitimacy, and neutrality of the state without which such events either could not occur or would constitute different kinds of acts. They are statements that elevate and exalt the state, justifying the need for its order at the very moment when it is most evidently absent. Criminals stole an idol. The state must retrieve it and return it to its rightful owners. Under the orders of the court, the state's enunciator, the police do so, but they then beat the villagers and quite possibly hand the idol over to be sold in exchange for payment by its former owners and protectors to be sold in a criminalized marketplace. Further statements are then made that the police have misbehaved, engaged in unnecessary brutality, gone beyond the norms of rightful state action. All who speak and act are either agents of the state or believers in its ultimate justice or they believe that there is no other source of justice in this world.

Consider further the discourses of caste and community. Ever since the arrival of the Portuguese on Indian soil in the sixteenth century, but much more so with the establishment of British rule and its consolidation at the end of the nineteenth, the favorite category for the categorization and placement of all the diverse people of India has been caste. The use of this category, however, has by no means been confined to foreign rulers, census takers, and scholars. Though the authorities of independent India have stopped publishing census figures by caste—except for Scheduled Castes and occasionally for other castes classified as disadvantaged—caste remains the common coin of political discourse in India. Its ramifications go far beyond politics, however, and it is by no means a mere social construction, for it constitutes still the most important basis for determining kinship, eligible marriage partners, one's status in society, and, for most people, also one's life chances.

Its continuing importance and reality in matters of kinship and marriage, however, does not establish either its exclusivity or even its primacy as a motivation for political action, contestation, and violent behavior. Yet there is not much doubt in the minds of most analysts of Indian politics that caste is the single most powerful predictor of such fundamental features of Indian political life as voting behavior, distribution of portfolios in government and of patronage to citizens, and probably also of preferments in appointments to a great range of administrative posts. Since the nineteenth century also in some parts of India and increasingly in the post-Independence period in most of the country, caste has also been deliberately recognized by state governments and recently by the central government as well as a legitimate category for redistributing educational, social, and economic advantages through the Indian equivalent of affirmative action policies.

But caste is a far more diverse and malleable category—or, rather, set of categories—than is commonly thought. Its uses vary according to the arena of contestation and the prizes available for distribution. The range of terms and the size of the categories in question extend from *jati* (caste as extended kinship), to caste category (caste as a generic term for widely distributed groups with similar traditional occupations and local statuses), to *varna* (caste as one of four social orders in reference to which all the multiplicity of groups in Hindu society may be placed, ranked, and categorized according to their way of life). It includes also new definitions of caste groupings: Scheduled Castes, the modern legal term for "untouchables" or low castes generally, listed on schedules entitling them to privileges designed to offer them certain opportunities as recompense for their disadvantages in life; backward castes, those of middle status, mostly rural, who have been behind the upper, elite castes in social and educational advantages; and a variety of other terms related to these two, including Harijans ("children of god"), Mahatma Gandhi's preferred term for "untouchables," and Dalit ("oppressed"), the new term for the Scheduled Castes, the preferred term nowadays used by militant groups from among them and by upper-caste and class advocates of their interests.

We have seen other uses of caste in two of the village cases discussed in this volume. In village Pachpera, one interpretation of the violent finale related it to caste-based political-electoral conflict between one locally dominant, but middle-status or "backward" caste of Lodhas, pitted against another locally dominant caste of Brahmans for political preeminence and control over an important institution of local government. In Narayanpur, extralocal forces sought to place the police attack on the villagers there as a brutal assault on mostly low-caste and backward-caste persons, as well as Muslims.

The caste-based political account pertaining to the Pachpera incident is, I believe, a valid perspective on an aspect of it. It is also a valid perspective on the organization of political-electoral conflict in north India generally. It is deficient, however, as an explanation for the attack on the villagers, as I have shown in my account of it. It is important to stress this deficiency if only to demonstrate that there are other significant bases of local contestation in the countryside than caste. Although caste is the predominant form for structuring local political-electoral contests in the north Indian countryside, this is partly because it naturally conforms to the political structures in which it operates, not because villagers cannot relate to each other in other ways and form alliances when necessary that cross caste lines or have nothing at all to do with caste. At the level of a *pramukh* election, covering an area of approximately one hundred villages, in which the social structure of the component villages is distributed in such a way that a small number of landed castes dominate a large number of the villages, it is natural that the electoral contests will be structured accordingly. Moreover, it is not at all uncommon for intercaste violence to break out in one village or another during such electoral contests. That does not mean that caste war prevails in the countryside.

Whose interests, then, are served by framing a violent conflict such as that which occurred in village Pachpera in terms of caste? The villagers themselves claimed to see the violence against them as a conspiracy among a Muslim Congress politician, a Brahman policeman, and, by extension, the Brahman-dominated village heads who wanted to prevent Lodha and backward-caste control over the local block development council and elect their own Brahman candidate. Police Inspector Gauri saw himself as a victimized policeman caught in a struggle between political "giants." How curious it is to see the principal antagonists in a violent conflict, the victims and the accused behind-the-scenes perpetrator of the attack upon them, converging in an explanation that places them both in the category of victims of broader, objective social forces. How convenient it is also to have such contexts at hand to displace blame from oneself.

That caste is not everything is also illustrated by the forced effort by Mrs. Gandhi and the Congress to fit the violence at Narayanpur into it. Here the attempt was made to transform a violent conflict between villagers and police into a case of atrocities on so-called weaker sections of society in order to fit it within the prevailing framework of political rhetoric between the opposed forces contesting for power at the Center of the Indian political system. If caste were everything and victimization of the lower castes by the dominant landed castes the prevalent form of oppression of the weaker sections in the countryside—and, given the substantial number of documented cases of such atrocities in north Indian villages—why could Mrs. Gandhi not have found a more perfect case?

There are two answers to this question. The first is that most other cases would display similar ambiguities. The second, of course, is that the timing, the locale, and the independent discovery of the incident by the local press and further commentary upon it in the UP Legislative Assembly were the decisive factors in its selection for Mrs. Gandhi's political purposes. Mistress of demagoguery that she was, Mrs. Gandhi turned the ambiguities in Narayanpur to her advantage. The village was inhabited mostly by Scheduled Castes and Muslims, so the incident could be portrayed as an assault upon both these "weaker sections." But then an even broader appeal could be made by presenting the outlandish accusation that all the women of the village had been raped, bringing into her potential political fold the majority of the population as victims of the police under a government dominated by her opponents.

But let us not forget the origin of this incident: A woman was crushed by a bus, leaving her grandchildren as destitute orphans. In a place where the villagers know that justice would not be done unless they demanded instant relief, they suffered instead blows, broken legs, and extreme humiliation, which had little or nothing at all to do with their caste or community. They received little compensation in return despite the intervention of the leader of the land and the police responsible suffered no substantial consequences. Mrs. Gandhi's opponents, however, were replaced in the state government and defeated in the ensuing elections. No further attention was given to the issue of police reform mentioned by Mrs. Gandhi, a commission of inquiry was appointed that completely discounted the charges made by her and her son at the time, and no disruption whatsoever was caused to the routine relations of violence between villagers and the police.

CIVIL SOCIETY, THE STATE, LAW AND ORDER, AND THE POLICE

The role of the police in the three village cases discussed in this volume, their ability to act with impunity in the face of the charges made against them, the support provided to them by state agencies including senior administrative officers who shield them and inquiry commissions that absolve them from guilt, raises other questions beyond the uses of the discourse of criminality. We come face to face here with Hobbes' argument concerning the relationship among society, safety, and the state. As is well known, the sovereign, that is, the state justifies its existence by rescuing the people from the war of all against all that is the state of nature, guaranteeing as a condition for the loyalty of the people their safety in society. Yet David Bayley and this author, writing independently of each other at the time, wrote in 1983 of the prevailing, "Hobbesian" state of war in rural India.[5] Were we both perhaps engaging in a bit of rhetorical excess in so characterizing a state and society that proclaims itself and has been acknowledged by many independent observers to be "the largest democracy in the world," where competitive elections have been held in a nearly unbroken stream since Independence, where voting turnout is usually higher than in the United States, and where numerous other forms of mass participation are regular occurrences?

If one's image of the war of all against all is of constant bloody warfare, of barricaded huts, and of a complete absence of order in which no man can be trusted and all are potential murderers, then this is not the case in rural north India. If, however, the image suggests instead settled life in which villages maintain their own order, but are distrustful of all outsiders, where marauding bands of robbers may descend upon the villages in the night, and where the villagers must provide for their own security, then we are not in fact far from this situation, whatever it may be called, in rural north India. But, there is still more to the state of "civil society" in north India.

Villagers in north India do not discern a society based on abstract law and prevailing order. Nor is this because they are primitives unused to the order of the state and its courts. Rural Indians are among the most litigious people in the world. They know how to use the courts or to find people who can

[5] See David H. Bayley, "The Police and Political Order in India," *Asian Survey* 23, no. 4 (April 1983): 484–96; and Paul R. Brass, "National Power and Local Politics in India: A Twenty-Year Perspective," *Modern Asian Studies* 17, no. 1 (February 1984): 89–118.

make the courts useful to them. Moreover, the courts are used rather more imaginatively in north India than in many other parts of the world, both to seek "justice" in some cause in which one feels it has been denied and to harass one's rivals and opponents. The police for their part do the same: They are notorious for instituting false cases against persons both in the countryside and in the city and they, too, make use of their own power and the power of the courts to harass and intimidate, primarily to earn money for themselves, but also to protect themselves and seek further revenge against their victims. In this respect, as in so many others, we do not have a simple case only of the agents of an unjust state misusing their powers against innocent persons, but a social system in which all are engaged in such actions. To say this should not imply that there are no victims, that the villagers beaten by the police are as guilty as the police who beat them. It is only to note that remedies cannot be provided simply by administrative solutions, by training the police to be better, not worse, than civilians. Ways rather must be found to alter prevalent practices in society as a whole, for which outsiders cannot provide solutions.

We come still closer to the "Hobbesian" world when we consider the perceptions by the villagers of the police as marauders, equivalent to *dacoit*s, not their protectors, but rather an additional, more powerful, and more dangerous band of robbers than those for whom robbery is a vocation. In this perspective, the reality in the countryside is warfare and the villages are armed camps. There is terror in the countryside and uncertainty about one's personal safety. Here there is a bit of exaggeration, for the dangers to the peaceful lives of Indian villagers are probably no greater than those that face urban residents in north American cities today.

Yet, if we lower our standards for the state of war somewhat or raise our standards for establishing the existence of "civil society" and "law and order," then the state of war of all against all again appears somewhat less far-fetched. At the center of this war are the police, the agents of the state, who everybody acknowledges must be brought under control for they do indeed contain a large force of dishonest, intimidating, terrorizing, and marauding elements. However, hardly anyone demands that this force be transformed into a modern, professional corps. Instead, all seek to bring the police under their own control: to oversee their recruitment, their posting, and their behavior, to insure that they act on one's behalf and not on behalf of one's enemies. Nor is it only the politicians who try to control the police. In rural Aligarh, in the area around village Pachpera, the police were perceived to be partial to, in effect under the control of the landed Brahman castes and their political elites. The Lodhas and their political leaders sought to change that situation, to defeat their political and economic rivals and, thereby, bring the police under *their* control. The idea that the police might be trained to treat

Lodhas and Brahmans impartially probably has never occurred to most people in the area.

Although, therefore, it may be exaggerating things to say that there is no civil society, no law and order, that there is instead a state of lawlessness in the countryside, we also do not have its opposite. Rather, we have a network of power relations among police, criminals, and politicians in which the use of force and violence is, if not routine, at least not something unexpected or exceptional. In this context, therefore, it is not that there is either law and order or there is not law and order. Rather, the very term is a mask that hides the operations of civil society, the authentic relations between police and people. So is the term "criminality." These, as I have noted above, are in effect word-weapons taken from a discourse without practices consistent with it. All sides among the politicians are using the police against each other, while accusing the other side of doing that very thing, as if it were something exceptional. Everybody accuses everybody else of corruption, which leads one to the supposition that all, therefore, are guilty of it.

When an event occurs in the countryside, such as the theft of an idol, neither of the two standard descriptions of police behavior is correct. The police are neither acting simply as agents of the state by implementing the orders of the court nor are they simply misbehaving in some kind of aberrant way. They are doing what they normally do, entering into one side or another of a local conflict. Moreover, the struggle is not simply for control of an idol, but for control over the police. He who controls the police controls the idol.

The discourse of police misbehavior and brutality shields the not-so-innocent villagers from acknowledgment of their own misbehavior. Yet, in Narayanpur, the incident that precipitated the police atrocities was not village thievery. How does this incident fit into the general argument being made here? Despite the difference between the two instances, they can in fact be fit into the same context. The Narayanpur villagers perceived rightly that they would not receive justice from the bus owner, the police, or the judiciary. They required instant justice because they knew that, once the driver was gone, so also were their hopes of relief unless they took further action of their own, which they did next time they could stop a bus owned by the same person. Had they sought the help of the law, the police, and the judiciary, they would have had to enter the network of power relations, which would mean delay, bribery, and division of the spoils among all who touched the case, with only the leavings going to the orphaned children. Similarly, what the Jains needed in village Pachpera was also instant justice, the immediate return of their idol. The delay, the resort to the courts, all provided only time for myriad interested parties to become involved, to form

alliances, to make deals, and ultimately to descend under the cover of the
night and the authority of the law of the state, another area of darkness, to
recapture the idol.

It is noteworthy also, in Rape at Daphnala, as in all the village cases, that
it was generally assumed by virtually all persons involved in or with knowledge of the incident that the police must have been in cahoots with the
*goonda*s. All believe the police took money. All point to standard police
practices. A witness and the *goonda*s are arrested; the *goonda*s are then
released and the witness detained! Persons on opposite sides of the same
dispute also assume the police have misbehaved. Mr. Nuruddin in
Daphnala, on the opposite side in the confrontation from the BJP/Arya
Samaj activists, also believes that the police acted improperly in relation to
the *goonda*s, but he thinks they registered false cases against them rather
than being in cahoots with them! It is also possible to hold both views
simultaneously, namely, that the police were initially in cahoots with the
*goonda*s but, under pressure to produce the alleged rapists after releasing the
suspects, then registered false cases against them. Notice also the routine
beating of the *goonda*s, acknowledged even by the District Magistrate. Intervention by superior officers involves not a suspension of the beatings, but
further beatings administered or supervised directly by them. No one interviewed volunteered the idea that such practices might be inappropriate.

Moreover, police actions in criminal cases such as Rape at Daphnala cannot be separated from the prevailing alignment of political forces. It is assumed that it is necessary to bring to the police station the leading politician
of the town to persuade the police of the need to do their duty. Since he was
a Muslim, his participation was also required to prevent the situation from
taking on a communal coloration. But, when the case falls apart and the
same politician discerns that his opponents will benefit from any further
pursuit of it, he withdraws his support and the police suspend their search
for the girl or the pimp. We are then told that the police in general in
Daphnala are on his side and that they have been used to implicate his rivals
in false cases. While the charge may or may not be true, the police are now
free to take revenge, as they generally do when they are assaulted or made
fools of. The BJP/Arya Samaj activists and the crowds that assemble under
their leadership are beaten and their leaders mocked and jailed.

TALK AND SILENCE

I have argued so far that much, probably most, perhaps even all the talk
about police brutality in rural north India is a mask that covers over the
network of power relations in which all are implicated, few are wholly victims. But there are victims, even innocent victims of police brutality. Moreover, the force brought to bear upon the villagers is out of proportion to their

own misbehavior. Nor, once again, is India unique in this regard. One has only to think of the ghastly incineration of eighty men, women, and children caused by the incompetent American FBI in Waco, Texas, using not sticks and antiquated guns, but tanks and other high-technology armaments, to moderate any feelings of superiority that members of an advanced industrial society might entertain in these matters.

In these circumstances, are the politicians not doing their job when they draw attention to the worst cases or to some of the cases, even if it serves their immediate political interests to do so? I have tried to show, in my comparison of the Narayanpur and Kurman Purwa incidents, that the gains of the villagers from the attention drawn to them in this way are small and that, in some respects, they not only do not gain, but are twice victimized by the attention. Moreover, even if victimized villagers receive some relief or recompense for their sufferings in particular cases, the benefit is not spread significantly beyond the particular cases selected for dramatization.

That is to say, there is arbitrariness in the selection of incidents to be publicized. Such selectivity in turn leads to misidentification of incidents as belonging to a type of victimization said to be rampant in society. Narayanpur was *not* a case of victimization of Scheduled Castes and Muslims by dominant castes and by the police, but there are many cases that do better fit that description, which fall out of the net of discovery and propaganda unless it suits the political interests of politicians at the time. Belchi, an authentic massacre of low-caste persons by dominant landowning castes, was also dramatized by Mrs. Gandhi's visit to the site, but the timing again suited the political purposes of launching her return to power.

Most important, the selection of particularly atrocious incidents of violence underplays its pervasiveness in everyday life. The exposure of such incidents makes those who discover and publicize it feel virtuous. They will think that they have at least made a contribution to the prevention of such incidents in future, but they have less interest in the day-to-day harassment, intimidation, and violence perpetrated against ordinary people without protectors, who have no defenses against the police. Moreover, the exposure hides the truth that a certain level of violence and atrocity is acceptable in police–village confrontations and in the police stations, that it becomes a matter of concern not even when a limit is transgressed, but when it can be claimed both that a limit has been transgressed and when the alleged transgression can be used to embarrass one's political opponents. Talk and silence thus reinforce each other, both contributing to the continuance of the institutions and practices that perpetuate violence and atrocities.

The perpetuation of violence and atrocities in the countryside has much to do with the absence of police accountability to the communities in which they serve. Throughout the post-Independence period in India, struggle for control of the police by competing political forces at the local level has been the predominant form of accountability. The police are accountable to their controllers—the local politicians, the senior police officers in the district and state, and the ministers in the state government. We have seen, however, that at times of intense political competition, that control may break down and the police go on rampages. Even when the police are under effective local control, that control is partial and may be used against others. Placing the police under control in this situation does not mean providing a general sense of safety, security, and reliability, but only a limited sense for that segment of the population allied to the controllers. Police control of this type is, therefore, an instrument to protect oneself and one's followers and to be denied to or used against one's rivals and their supporters. Local control, however, may be upset when the dominant politicians in the districts are at odds with the leaders, factions, and parties in power in the state government, who may then exercise their control and reverse the relations of dominance at the local level. The system, therefore, is doubly unstable; as a consequence of local rivalries and as a consequence of alliances and rivalries that run from the district to the state level.

Finally, in stage-managed affairs such as that at Narayanpur, the interests of the victims become incidental. Certainly in Narayanpur, those interests receded into the background in the hailstorm of rhetoric concerning who was responsible for the atrocities. Further, the evident misbehavior and brutality of the police also became incidental to the political conflicts between opposing political forces. Mrs. Gandhi's statements concerning the police actions were extraordinarily gentle and indulgent compared to her attacks on her political opponents, who themselves took the lead in exposing the incident to public view. She thought that the police action suggested the need to identify "flaws" in police training, a need to study the matter, but she also stressed the importance of avoiding too harsh a criticism of the police. It was necessary to keep up their morale, but, of course, they should not be allowed to get away with atrocities. The problem, therefore, was reduced to an administrative one, the police who committed the brutalities suffered the usual mild, administrative punishments of temporary suspension, and no known changes were made in police training to prevent such incidents in the future.

Nor was much mention made of the underlying social attitudes and practices that make such incidents recurring features of life in the north Indian countryside. Few noted the absence of trust between villagers and police in general. Few commented on the general assumption among the villagers that the police would want their cut from the compensation to be given to the children of the woman killed by a bus. No one remarked that what was involved here was not simply police brutality but warfare, a field of power relations in which attack and revenge occur when the rules of everyday life are broken or when the rules defy the most elementary standards of decency.

The rules are that everybody gets a cut, but there are times when the rules need to be relaxed, when it becomes indecent to prey upon those who have already suffered a great loss. Thus, what we have in the north Indian countryside are a set of formal rules and practices obeyed by few, a set of informal rules and practices followed by most, and a lack of legitimacy attached to both because the first are known to be ineffective and partial while the second set no limits to extortion.

THE DISCOURSE OF COMMUNALISM
AND THE IDEOLOGY OF THE NATION-STATE

We come at last to the discourse of communalism, which in turn is connected to its encompassing progenitor, the ideology of the modern nation-state, the predominant political doctrine of our times, the grandest human construction of modernity. It is the central argument of this book that there is a direct link between the struggle among three ideologies that have been contesting for dominance on the Indian subcontinent since the nineteenth century and the communal violence that persists in India up to the present, though its intensity, scale, and frequency ebb and flow over time. The three ideologies have been Hindu nationalism, Muslim separatism, and secularism. Supposedly antagonistic, they have shared a common goal: unity of the entire population or of one of the two largest segments of it into united wholes to contest for power at the Center. Moreover, there are no other possible ideologies available for such a task.

Consider Hindu nationalism first, whose particular manifestations proceed from two basic assumptions. First, all Hindus, irrespective of sect, language, or caste, are one, united by systems of beliefs, philosophical principles, and rituals, sharing a common history that precedes both the British and Muslim invasions. Second, as the majority population, their beliefs and history should provide the ideological base for the Indian state, which should be seen as a Hindu state.

The Muslim separatist counterpart to the Hindu nationalist ideology also contains two basic premises. The first is that all Muslims in South Asia are one nation equal to the Hindus. Second, and following from the first, power must be shared equally with the Hindus or they must have a state of their own.

The third ideology, secular nationalism, is derived in part from Western ideologies of the secular state, but it rests equally in India upon the differences between the other two. That is to say, a principal justification for the necessity of secular nationalism is that the very differences between the first two require the removal of religion and communal identity from the struggle for power in Indian politics. The state must be a neutral force above both Hindus and Muslims, preventing them from attacking each other and destroying the unity of the Indian state. Within the secular state, all citizens of India are entitled to equal rights as individuals irrespective of their religion or communal identification.

The partition of India and the assassination of Mahatma Gandhi by a person identified with militant Hindu nationalism together discredited two of the ideologies contesting for dominance in independent India and established secularism as the dominant state ideology in the country for four decades. However, its dominance has been challenged during the past decade by events, movements, and critique. The challenge of events has been principally the increasing numbers, intensity, and scale of Hindu–Muslim killings. The challenge of movements has come with the rise of Hindu nationalism and the proliferation of organizations promoting its goals, strategies, and tactics. There was also a much more feeble and now overshadowed countervailing rise of Muslim solidarity.

The critique of secularism has come from three sources: nationalist Hindus, Muslim leaders, and secular intellectuals. The nationalist Hindu argument has been that the dominant secular ideology has been a "pseudo-secularism" that has favored minorities, Muslims in particular, against Hindus. For their part, most Muslims now feel that the secular state has not protected them in fact. For their part, leading intellectuals say the secular ideology is not appropriate for India, where faith is so important in people's lives, calling instead for the recognition of the tolerant message of all the faiths of India as the underlying basis for the Indian state.[6]

The main opposing force to ascendant Hindu nationalism, however, is not the alternative state ideologies, but the rise of intercaste conflict, especially in north India simultaneously with the rise of Hindu nationalism. Taking the form of a demand for special privileges for the middle-status, backward castes, to enable them to compete effectively for social and educational advancement with the elite castes, which in turn precipitated resentment among the upper castes and some violence, a political counterforce has been created in north India in its two most populous states, UP and Bihar. Here, the secular ideology has also again come to the fore, and has been used as the intellectual base for a political coalition of backward castes with low castes and Muslims.

Caste conflicts, which have had a long history in many of the Indian states, exploded on the national scene in August 1990 as a consequence of then Prime Minister V. P. Singh's announcement concerning the establishment of reserved places for backward castes in public sector jobs under the control of the central government. This announcement itself was partly designed to undermine the rise of the BJP and its efforts to consolidate Hindus

---

[6] The two leading protagonists for this point of view in India are T. N. Madan, "Secularism in Its Place," *Journal of Asian Studies* 46, no. 4 (November 1987): 747–60; and Ashish Nandy, "The Politics of Secularism."

and to bring that party to power at the Center by appealing to the lower half of Hindu society. Even more infuriating to the BJP was the effort by the Janata Dal to appeal to the Muslim vote while dividing the Hindu vote. The response of the RSS "family" of organizations was to intensify the efforts to consolidate the Hindu vote through the mobilization around the Babari Masjid/Ram Janmabhumi issue. Initial success in the 1991 elections in UP and, to some extent, at the Center, was followed by an equally successful counterconsolidation and alliance among the backward castes, Scheduled Castes, and Muslims, which checked the rise of the BJP in UP, already stalled in the other large Indian state of Bihar by the same coalition.

The stakes in this struggle are for the entire future direction of Indian politics and control over the Indian state and its future form. A Hindu nationalist state will suppress all perceived minority threats to its integrity and strength. Although the BJP claims to favor decentralization, its emphasis on a strong Indian state is inherently centralist. The countervailing forces of mobilization of the lower half of north Indian society and the forces of caste mobilization in general logically imply as well decentralization and enhanced power for the states against the Center, for they emphasize the particular interests, needs, and claims of groups in society defined within their regional and local contexts.

Every major contest among the nationalist ideologies competing for dominance in modern Indian history during the past century has been accompanied by Hindu–Muslim riots. Even modest demands by Muslim politicians in the 1960s for recognition of their cultural, educational, and language rights within the Indian state precipitated political reactions, opposition, and violence. Hindu–Muslim violence took its first significant upswing in the post-Independence period at that time, but it varied in intensity, in focus, in precipitating incidents, and in the pretexts for them until 1990–91. At that point, a new wave of violence with a ferocity and scale not seen since partition, occurred in the aftermath of L. K. Advani's *rath yatra* to Ayodhya, repeated with even greater savagery and magnitude after December 6, 1992.

These recent riots raise old issues, but they also involve new features. Among the older issues are the interrelated questions whether the two communities are coherent and internally conscious of their separateness and whether Hindu–Muslim violence arises out of deep-seated Hindu–Muslim antagonisms, based in the distinctive history, culture, and religions of the two communities. The predominant images of Hindu–Muslim relations in India and among many observers from abroad is that there are two well-defined religious communities in India and that they are not only separate but antagonistic to each other. In reality, however, there remain considerable heterogeneity, fragmentation, and even intermingling of religious practices and observances among Hindus and Muslims in India.

One of the main purposes of the Ayodhya movement, in fact, has been to overcome that reality, to bring all the Hindus of India together on a common platform, in this case around the god Ram. It is not, however, a fact that Hindus have been seething for centuries over the alleged destruction of a Ram temple there and the construction of the Babari Masjid on its site. It is, moreover, false to say even that the mosque was built upon a Ram temple destroyed for the purpose. Most important, it is doubtful that Ram has the unifying capacity required to bring all the Hindus of India together in either a religious or political unity. The Ram Janmabhumi movement, the arousal of deep feelings on the issue, and the intensification of Hindu–Muslim antagonisms that resulted from them are all political creations, part of a design to create a new Hindu community, a new religion of Ram, and a new political religion.

What is new, though there are precedents for it in previous days of Hindu–Muslim conflict, is the deliberate inculcation among the RSS cadres who provide the shock troops for the entire "family" of its organizations, including the BJP, the VHP, the Bajrang Dal, and others of a cult of violence aimed at the intimidation of Muslims, their selective killing, and the destruction of their properties during riots. In this cult of violence, the Muslims are portrayed as the aggressors, the Hindus as defenders, the Muslims as experts in the wielding of knives and in the art of killing, the Hindus as novices who must learn the art of their enemies. Those well-skilled in the practices of violence, prepared to use them against Muslims, are portrayed as heroes.

This new Hindu–Muslim violence, however, falls short still of the type used by Nazi storm troopers in Germany during the rise of Hitler. The new violence falls on the border between riots and pogroms, retaining many of the features of the former while taking on some of the latter. These new riots are not fully orchestrated pogroms, but dramatic productions with large casts of extras, many of whom follow their own scripts. Moreover, the productions arise out of circumstances only partly created deliberately and bring in a multiplicity of interests and forces, not all or even most of them under the control of the RSS.

It is, therefore, my argument that the persistence of Hindu–Muslim conflicts in India is neither natural nor inevitable. There is, on the contrary, a paradox at the heart of the discourse of communalism, namely, that Muslim political, emotional, and economic integration in India was taking place in the post-Independence period in the face of increased Hindu hostility and communal violence directed against Muslims.[7] The culprit is not Muslim separatism, a defunct ideology in the Indian context outside of Kashmir, but the two other ideologies; both secularism and Hindu nationalism.

[7] On this point, see Paul R. Brass, *The Politics of India Since Independence*, 2nd ed. (Cambridge: Cambridge University Press, 1994), pp. 230–47 and 264.

Secularism has been an ideology of a strong centralized state that has defined itself in such a way as to place the Indian state not at a remove from religion, communalism, and Hindu–Muslim issues, but at the center of them. While proclaiming the irrelevance of religion and community to citizenship, the national leadership has consistently defined India as a country containing two large religious groups that will tear each other apart if the state is not strong enough to prevent it. Moreover, the ruling party during Nehru's time proclaimed itself the protector of the Muslims and used the threat of Hindu nationalism to Muslim well-being in order to get their votes. Ultimately, however, Nehru's descendants, Indira and Rajiv Gandhi, turned away from this strategy to garner Hindu votes, a strategy whose disastrous consequences continue to unfold not only in Hindu–Muslim violence but with the disintegration of the Indian National Congress itself, which is no longer a viable political party in north India.

For its part, Hindu nationalism has exploited Congress opportunism and turned the official secular ideology on its head. Hindu nationalists argue that India cannot be a true secular state as long as Muslims have their own separate personal laws, their own national university (Aligarh Muslim University), and a state within India, Kashmir, with a special status. This is not, moreover, a fundamentalist ideology. It is a form of secular ideology of state exaltation that says, *contra* the existing secular ideology, that India cannot define itself as a society containing two antagonistic religions, but as a society with one culture, a Hindu culture, in which all must partake if they want to be true citizens. A strong state must have a single, unified nation, they insist, and the Muslims are an obstacle to that goal until they become political Hindus.

We come here to the answer to the questions posed at the beginning of this volume, namely, why have Hindu–Muslim riots become endemic, why does Hindu–Muslim communalism persist, why does a consensus on Hindu–Muslim relations not emerge? The ultimate answer is because, as with secessionism, the issue is inseparable in the minds of the dominant upper-caste and upper-class elites of the country from the security and greatness of the Indian state. Secessionism and Hindu–Muslim conflict are seen equally as dangers to Indian unity. Therefore, there must be a strong central state to prevent either of these forces from weakening the Indian state.

The method pursued until recently was to stress the dangers while pursuing accommodationist policies in practice. The method increasingly used by the central government in the case of secessionism and proposed to be strengthened by the BJP is brutal suppression of all secessionist threats and insistence on the full integration of Muslims in India as politically Hindu Indians. Absent from both methods is a genuine ideology of secularism and individual citizenship, which insists that the business of the state has nothing to do with religion and that the peoples of India are defined not artificially and falsely as majorities and minorities, but as equal citizens of a free and democratic society.

TALK AND ACTION

But the existence of a discursive formation such as Hindu–Muslim communalism does not provide us with a satisfactory explanation for the outbreak of riots or for their level of intensity, destruction, and murder in particular times and places. Why specifically was a riot prevented or, rather, why did a riot not happen in Daphnala in 1983? And why did such a massive conflagration occur in Kanpur in December 1992? There are many ways of approaching this kind of issue. One common one, used in studies of American urban riots in the 1960s, is to select past riot sites and non-riot sites, compare them according to various demographic and ecological criteria, and then develop an hypothesis or set of hypotheses to postdict why riots occurred in some sites and not others. This type of method is now being used in the study of riots in India with some useful results already,[8] though I have reservations concerning the ultimate utility of the approach and its ability to predict the future rather than simply postdict the past. I do not wish to make a methodological critique here of this method, but rather I propose to offer an alternative approach that has emerged from my ethnographic studies. This is an approach whose generalizations derive from the dynamics of particular riot events, rather than from systematic cross-site comparisons.

The ethnographic studies presented in this volume suggest to me the primacy of two sets of factors. The first concerns whether there exists at a particular site, for whatever reasons, historical or otherwise, an "institutionalized riot system." By an institutionalized riot system, I mean a network of actors, groups, and connections involving persons from different social categories whose effect, leaving aside intentions for the moment, is to keep a town or city in a permanent state of awareness of Hindu–Muslim relationships. The actors and groups include especially activists belonging to particular political parties, cultural groups, or religious organizations, such as the BJP, the RSS, and the Arya Samaj. The connections are those between such activists and persons and groups trained in the use of weapons. The latter have especially included throughout modern Indian history criminals and other persons operating on the margins of civil society, but they may also include and increasingly do include specific formations such as the Bajrang Dal in the RSS "family" of organizations and the Shiv Sena in Maharashtra.

---

[8] See esp. Ashutosh Varshney, "The Limits of the Master Narrative: A Tale of Two Cities, Hyderabad and Lucknow," unpublished paper presented at the panel on "Communal Violence in India: Contemporary Research," at the annual meetings of the Association for Asian Studies in Washington, D.C., April 7, 1995.

At the core of the system are "riot specialists," persons who are active at all times in monitoring the daily life of the town or city in the areas in which they reside or which they frequent. These riot specialists include persons from all walks of life, scruffy young hooligans as well as college and university professors, who perform roles according to their status in life. The less respectable persons may act simply as reporters of incidents, who will alert the more respectable persons concerning some alleged event: A Hindu woman has been "kidnapped" or raped, a cow has been poisoned. Similar events may happen on the Muslim side, but the Hindu communal side is more fully developed in north Indian cities and towns and more aggressive on these matters.

Once an incident has been reported, to a public person of status such as a university professor with militant Hindu sentiments or affiliations or a BJP activist or elected representative or similarly placed person on the Muslim side, the incident will be assessed concerning its importance. It may be used simply to alert the civil and police administration to the alleged need for action to prevent a potential danger to communal peace or it may be used for purposes of political mobilization. If the incident is frivolous, an elected representative will not spoil his reputation by bringing it to the attention of the civil or police administration, but other activists may do so.

The persons who bring such matters to the attention of the authorities probably do not "intend" to foment a communal riot. They may believe the contrary, that they are truly acting to preserve the peace. The effect, however, is quite different. It is to maintain a general state of tension and alertness to Hindu–Muslim relations such that when a nonfrivolous event occurs, a rape or a killing of a Hindu by a Muslim or vice-versa in a fracas of some sort, and if that event occurs—or is staged—at a point when communal mobilization will be of political utility, then rumors and messages will circulate leading to the gathering of crowds. A delegation may proceed to police headquarters or to the office of the district magistrate. Among the most deliberately provocative acts is the formation of a procession to move through the city streets, even through the neighborhoods where communal relations are particularly tense.

At this point, a game of brinkmanship is being played, which may or may not lead to a scuffle and to a riot. The moments when incidents in Hindu–Muslim relations may be selected for dramatization in this way are especially at election times, when particular political parties—and not just the BJP—may wish to stand forth as the protector of one community against the alleged threats of the other and may seek to present their political rivals as protectors of the other community, the allegedly aggressive community. Other moments are times of general political mobilization such as occurred before partition in 1946–47 and during the recent Ram Janmabhumi movement.

Riot specialists are, therefore, specialists in the conversion of incidents in the relations between communities, in this case between Hindus and Muslims, into occasions for riots. When the time is right for the fomenting of a large-scale disturbance, then students, hooligans, low-caste persons from slums and outlying areas, criminals, and special squads of trained activists such as the members of the Bajrang Dal will be brought in. They are a reserve army, a mixture of *lumpen* elements and others. In riot-prone areas, they have most likely been used before and will be ready to come out on such occasions when they receive the word. In the most extreme cases, larger crowds may also come into the streets, drawn from many walks of life. In the midst of the apparent chaos, "heroes" such as Kala Bachcha may also emerge.

It is, therefore, my argument, which could be generalized into an acceptable social science hypothesis, that riots are most likely to occur in "riot-prone" cities and towns, which in turn are defined as cities with well-developed riot systems as I have described them. The generalization has an apparent tautological character to it, which may lead to the further question why such riot systems themselves develop, which then takes the social scientist back to the comparative method and the selection of sites for study according to strict demographic and ecological criteria. However, I think it is not tautological and that, though they do not use the terms adopted herein, district magistrates and the district police administration are fully familiar with the operations of riot systems, know where they are more and less well developed, know the principal actors and conversion specialists in each town, have their names in files, and know how to use this information to prevent riots when they appear to be imminent and to bring them under control when they start.

That brings me to my second set of factors in the explanation of riot events, namely, the actions of the local and state administrative authorities. The facts are known to all; they are available in reports handed from one district magistrate to the next, one SSP to the next. The capacities and sympathies of district administrative officers also are known. Therefore, one cannot ignore the intent or the will of the state government and the district administration to act upon what it knows to head off or control riots. Some chief ministers or political parties make it their business to say that there will be no riots under their rule. When they say so and mean it, they can usually prevent them or limit their effects. They do it by, first, letting it be known to their own political supporters that they want communal peace during their administration and second, by letting it be known throughout the state administration that all officers will be held accountable if they allow riots to develop under their watch. Third, they identify the riot-prone districts and the officers who have reputations for both firmness and impartiality and they send the latter to those districts.

The comparison between Daphnala and Kanpur illustrates my point quite well. Mr. Timothy Matthew, known for his honesty, integrity, impartiality, and firmness, an outsider to the state and its politics, neither a Hindu nor a Muslim, but a Christian from Kerala, was sent to Meerut district to replace the District Magistrate under whose watch the great Meerut riot of 1982 occurred. He succeeded in bringing the riot situation under control after his arrival and then made it clear that no riots in Meerut town or anywhere else in his district would be allowed to develop. He took a personal interest, therefore, in the situation at Daphnala, went to the site as soon as he received news of the riot potential there, suspended an officer who had not informed him immediately, and acted with firmness and ultimately harshness to make sure that no Hindu–Muslim communal riot occurred there. Of course, he was not able to prevent the police–public confrontation and rioting that took place, but he was satisfied that he achieved his main purpose, to prevent the citizens of the town and the villagers who had come to the town for the weekly bazaar from setting out to kill each other.

In Kanpur, quite in contrast, a district administration headed by a district magistrate known both for his sympathies with the BJP and for his utter ineffectiveness in riot situations (having demonstrated both his inclinations and incompetence at Ayodhya in the demonstration of 1991) was posted in Kanpur at the time of the outbreak of the December 6, 1992 riots. He failed utterly to prevent the spread of the riots, in which party members of the BJP were active. He even made a pathetic appeal in the newspapers for the BJP MLA from the constituency in which the killings of Muslims occurred to come back to the city to help bring the situation under control. His incompetence and ineffectiveness having been again demonstrated and his BJP sympathies being well known to all, the state administration that replaced the BJP government after December 6 sent a man known, like Timothy Matthew, to be both impartial and effective in such situations, to stop the rioting. Mr. Kapil Deo brought the riot under control shortly after his arrival— though some argue it died a natural death. Kanpur now being clearly on the list of riot-prone cities and towns in UP, when the SP government of Mulayam Singh Yadav came to power, defeating the BJP in the November 1993 elections, he kept Mr. Kapil Deo in Kanpur as commissioner of the entire division. When Kala Bachcha was killed in February 1994, Mr. Kapil Deo and the entire civil and police administration of the city acted decisively to contain the rioting that followed upon the murder.

In none of these cases can we say with absolute assurance that the posting of a particular officer was decisive. What we can say with assurance is that the state government and the district administration have the knowledge and the power to contain and control riots when they develop and probably to prevent them before they happen. The Indian state and most of its state governments are not "weak," lacking the authority or the power to act decisively when they choose to do so. When riots start, it is often because of intense political competition at either or both the district and state levels, that is, because at least one strong party or other political force is willing to pursue the game of brinkmanship. When the authorities do not act decisively to contain and control riots, it is not because they do not have the means to do so, but because, for political reasons, they choose not to do so.

It will be said that the Indian state may not be a "weak" state, but its police forces in a province such as UP are thoroughly communalized, partial, hostile to Muslims. I believe this to be true, but then the recruitment of such officers is controlled by the state government and the district administrations. The government of UP at the time of partition eliminated most Muslims from the state police forces, reducing their numbers from approximately half to less than 5 percent. It is no accident, moreover, that upper castes have dominated state and district politics and the civil and police administration in this state since Independence. That situation has now been transformed in the state of Bihar and is in the process of transformation in UP, where backward castes, lower castes, and Muslims are being recruited into these services in much greater numbers than ever before. When the victims themselves are put in power, as they have been in Bihar, where the chief minister, Laloo Prasad, does not allow communal riots in his state, riots may not disappear, but they become far more difficult to perpetrate. It is, however, partly the case, as some have charged, that one form of violence is then replaced by another, communal riots by caste wars.[9] Another context is provided for the channeling of the conflicts and violence endemic in a society whose social and economic practices favor hierarchy, gross inequalities, privilege, favoritism, and corruption. Violence can hardly be eliminated now or in the foreseeable future in such a society, but its forms and its targets may be changed and its scale may be reduced through political and policy changes, changes in the discourses of violence, and changes in leadership, institutions and structures.

---

[9] Ashghar Ali Engineer has remarked "that caste and communal conflict are the two sides of the same coin in the assertion of political power" in UP and in Kanpur specifically and, further, that the outburst of communal violence in Kanpur is certainly the result of emergence of new political forces led by the lower castes on UP's political horizon"; see his "Communal Violence in Kanpur," *Economic and Political Weekly*, 19, no. 9 (February 26, 1994): 473.

INDEX

The History of Everyday Life: Reconstructing Historical Experiences and Ways of Life *edited by Alf Lüdtke*

The Savage Freud and Other Essays on Possible and Retrievable Selves *by Ashis Nandy*

Children and the Politics of Culture *edited by Sharon Stephens*

Intimacy and Exclusion: Religious Politics in Pre-Revolutionary Baden *by Dagmar Herzog*

What Was Socialism, and What Comes Next? *by Katherine Verdery*

Citizen and Subject: Contemporary Africa and the Legacy of Late Colonialism *by Mahmood Mamdani*

Colonialism and Its Forms of Knowledge: The British in India *by Bernard S. Cohn*

Charred Lullabies: Chapters in an Anthropology of Violence *by E. Valentine Daniel*

Theft of an Idol: Text and Context in the Representation of Collective Violence *by Paul R. Brass*

About the Author

PAUL R. BRASS is Professor of Political Science and International Studies at the University of Washington. He is the author of many books, most recently *Riots and Pogroms*; *Ethnicity and Nationalism: Theory and Comparison*; and *The Politics of India since Independence* (2d edition), a volume of the *New Cambridge History of India*.